Supervision
A Redefinition

EIGHTH EDITION

Supervision

A REDEFINITION

Thomas J. Sergiovanni
Trinity University

Robert J. Starratt
Boston College

Boston   Burr Ridge, IL   Dubuque, IA   Madison, WI   New York
San Francisco   St. Louis   Bangkok   Bogotá   Caracas   Kuala Lumpur
Lisbon   London   Madrid   Mexico City   Milan   Montreal   New Delhi
Santiago   Seoul   Singapore   Sydney   Taipei   Toronto

Higher Education

SUPERVISION: A REDEFINITION
Published by McGraw-Hill, a business unit of The McGraw-Hill Companies, Inc., 1221 Avenue of the
Americas, New York, NY, 10020. Copyright © 2007, 2002, 1998, 1993, 1988, 1983, 1979, 1971 by
The McGraw-Hill Companies, Inc. All rights reserved. No part of this publication may be reproduced
or distributed in any form or by any means, or stored in a database or retrieval system, without the
prior written consent of The McGraw-Hill Companies, Inc., including, but not limited to, in any
network or other electronic storage or transmission, or broadcast for distance learning.
Some ancillaries, including electronic and print components, may not be available to customers
outside the United States.

This book is printed on acid-free paper.

1 2 3 4 5 6 7 8 9 0 DOC/DOC 0 9 8 7 6

ISBN-13: 978-0-07-313126-9
ISBN-10:   0-07-313126-1

Vice President and Editor-in-Chief:
   Emily Barrosse
Publisher: *Beth Mejia*
Executive Editor: *David Patterson*
Editorial Coordinator: *Emily Pecora*
Executive Marketing Manager: *Pamela S. Cooper*
Project Manager: *Catherine R. Iammartino*
Art Director: *Jeanne Schreiber*
Associate Designer: *Marianna Kinigakis*
Art Editor: *Emma C. Ghiselli*

Senior Photo Research Coordinator:
   Alexandra Ambrose
Cover Credit: © *Jacobs Stock Photography/*
   Getty Images
Production Supervisor: *Janean A. Utley*
Composition: *Interactive*
   Composition Corporation
Printing: *45# New Era Matte,*
   R.R. Donnelley & Sons

Library of Congress Control Number: 2006922895

The Internet addresses listed in the text were accurate at the time of publication. The inclusion of
a Web site does not indicate an endorsement by the authors or McGraw-Hill, and McGraw-Hill
does not guarantee the accuracy of the information presented at these sites.

www.mhhe.com

About the Authors

THOMAS J. SERGIOVANNI is Lillian Radford Professor of Education at Trinity University. He received his master's degree from Teachers College, Columbia University, and his EdD in educational administration from the University of Rochester. An active teacher, writer, and editor, he brings to the text his extensive experience teaching and writing about educational administration and supervision. His recent books include *Moral Leadership, Building Community in Schools, Leadership for the Schoolhouse. The Lifeworld of Leadership, Strengthening the Heartbeat: Leading and Learning Together in Schools, and The Principalship: A Reflective Practice Perspective*, fifth edition.

ROBERT J. STARRATT is Professor of Educational Administration at the Lynch School of Education at Boston College. He received a master's degree in philosophy from Boston College, a master's degree in education from Harvard University, and a doctor of education degree in educational administration from the University of Illinois. He has served as chair of the educational administration programs at Boston College and at Fordham University, and has lectured extensively both nationally and internationally on various aspects of educational leadership. He has also written extensively about various aspects of educational leadership. His recent books include *Ethical Leadership, Centering Educational Administration, The Drama of Leadership, Building an Ethical School, and Leaders with Vision*.

Contents

14   Supervision and Summative Evaluations   296

PART FOUR

Providing Leadership   313

15   Motivation, Satisfaction, and the Teachers' Workplace   315

Preface

Completing a book used to have a certain finality to it. One could place it in a prominent part of one's library and get on with other projects. If an author wished to change a position taken in that book in a subsequent publication, it was an easy matter of a footnote reference. This book, however, has refused to be finished.

Despite numerous changes as the book evolved over the first four editions, the underlying theory had remained the same. That was not the case with the fifth, sixth, and seventh editions and is not the case with this edition. Expectations and assumptions about schools have changed so significantly that schooling is now being redefined. This redefining includes new understandings about school structures, time frames, standards, accountability, professionalism, teaching and learning, teacher development, leadership, and sources of authority for what is done. In such a dramatically altered context, supervision itself has to be redefined. We need not only do new ways to do old things but also a change in the theory itself that underlies supervisory thought and practice.

THE EVOLVING NATURE OF SUPERVISION

In editions one and two, published in the 1970s, we characterized school supervision as being largely ritualistic. Supervisors continued to be hired and university courses continued to be offered in the subject, but much of what took place under the name of supervision seemed not to matter very much. A good deal of the supervisor's time was spent on administrative matters. Teacher-evaluation systems tended to be perfunctory. Overall, a certain complacency characterized the role and function of supervision.

The third edition, published in 1984, noted that a mild renaissance of interest in supervision and supervisory activities was in the making. At the national level, the Association for Supervision and Curriculum Development had begun to place stronger emphasis on supervision. The literature in the field was expanding and improving in quality. For classroom supervision, clinical strategies and artistic strategies began to emerge and to compete successfully with more traditional checklist approaches to teacher evaluation. At least this was the case in the literature and at academic conferences, if not in actual practice. Publications focusing on problems and issues in supervision increased in popularity, becoming among the most popular offered by the Association for Supervision and Curriculum Development. Supervisory topics were appearing more frequently on the programs of this organization's national and regional conferences. The founding of the Conference of Professors of Instructional Supervision in 1976 was evidence that scholars studying problems of supervision were increasing in numbers, interested in identifying themselves and in establishing better communication networks and developing more systematic approaches to research and development.

As the fourth edition of this book appeared in 1988, supervision was becoming the "in thing" in American schooling. What previously was a mild renaissance had turned into a revolution. Supervision began to rank high on the agendas of both state policy makers and local school administrators. Many states, for example, began to mandate increases in supervision and evaluation of teachers. These mandates ranged from required "training" in the techniques of supervision and evaluation for principals and supervisors to the provision of comprehensive and standardized state systems of supervision and evaluation. Many of these systems were based on a body of research associated with the teaching-effectiveness and school-effectiveness movements. This research noted that "effective schools" were characterized by principals and other supervisors who exercised strong instructional leadership. It noted further that one best way to teach could be identified, provided for, and evaluated.

Instructional leadership became the hot topic in thousands of seminars and workshops provided for administrators and supervisors by states, professional associations, local school districts, and individual entrepreneurs. Some states even went so far as to mandate that all principals and supervisors go through state-approved and state-sponsored instructional leadership training programs as a condition of their continued employment and as part of a licensing system to certify them as teacher evaluators.

The academic side of the professional educational community experienced a similar flurry of interest in supervision. In 1985 the Association for Supervision and Curriculum Development established the *Journal of Curriculum and Supervision.* Scholarly articles on supervision and evaluation began to appear more frequently in such established publications as *Curriculum Inquiry* and *Educational Evaluation and Policy Analysis.* The *Journal of Personnel Evaluation in Education* was established in 1986. The prestigious American Educational Research Association established a special-interest group in instructional supervision in 1983. This marked the beginning of a concentrated and continuous appearance of sessions devoted to supervision at the annual meeting of this association.

With the appearance of the fifth edition of this book in 1993, the emphasis in supervision had shifted from evaluating teachers to promoting teacher development and building professional community among teachers. Further, the characterization of principals and other supervisors as instructional leaders had given way to supervisors as developers and leaders of leaders. Supervision remains an important role that principals and other designated supervisors must emphasize. But supervision is also a function.

Responsibility for this function is stretched over many roles—a theme this book discusses on several occasions. In these new configurations, teachers assume more of the responsibility for providing instructional leadership.

The publication of the sixth edition in 1998 found supervision to be at a critical point in its evolution. We were in the midst of a powerful standards movement that fostered a new age of thinking about accountability aimed not just at students and what they learn but at teachers and how they teach. It became clear that, whatever else was done to improve schools, little would be accomplished without improving teaching. Teacher quality became the mantra as reformers pushed hard to make changes. States were setting higher standards for preparing teachers. Both the National Board for Professional Teaching Standards and the National Council for the Accreditation of Teacher Education became influential forces for changes that would strengthen the teaching profession. The Teacher Education Council, incorporated in 1997, provided still another service for reform. School districts became much more serious about using teacher evaluation as a lever for school improvement. Professional development was moving to center stage, having been reinvented from a series of isolated and disconnected events removed from the classroom to a seamless commitment to continual improvement situated in the classroom. During the last decade, the National Staff Development Council (NSDC) became a key player in developing and improving supervision. Dennis Sparks, the council's executive director, believes that capacity building, especially teacher learning, will help supervision become a more powerful lever for change.

As the seventh edition appeared, it was clear that supervision continued to emerge as a key role and function in the operation of schools. Still at issue, however, is the form and substance of this new emergence and interest, how its influence will be felt by teachers, and what its effects will be on teaching and learning over the long haul. Will this "new supervision," for example, provide support for teachers and enhance their roles as key professional decision makers in the practice of teaching and learning? Or will this new supervision result in increased regulation and control of teachers and teaching? If the latter, what are the consequences of supervision for teacher professionalism and for teaching and learning? Will attempts to share traditional supervisory roles, functions, and responsibilities with teachers; to advance teacher leadership; and to promote collegial patterns of supervision that emphasize reflective conversation and shared inquiry result in broad teacher empowerment that leads to professional community? Or will attempts to share traditional roles, supervisory functions, and responsibilities with teachers lead to the development of a new hierarchy that benefits some teachers but not most? The increased importance attributed to supervision then and now is attractive. But whether this new emphasis will develop into promises fulfilled or promises broken will depend, we believe, on the form that supervision takes in the next few years. Much will depend on how the standards movement plays itself out over the next several years. Will this movement be a transformative force for creating a new profession of teaching and supervision? Or will this movement become still another managerial intrusion with opposite effects?

During the last decade, a new player in the standards movement has emerged. This player is the field of supervision itself. Recently, supervision scholars have gathered to tackle such questions as these: Should there be standards for the development and practice of supervision? If so, what should these standards be? As we examine this book together, let us be mindful that the further development of supervision and the nature of its practice will be dramatically affected should standards materialize.

Chapter 10 of this book, "Using Standards in Supervision," squarely broaches these questions. The work of Steve Gordon and his colleagues is of particular interest. They have prepared a book that debates the issue and proposes standards for consideration by the supervision community.

Since their work is now in progress, we are not able to include its details in the eighth edition of *Supervision: A Redefinition.* We can be mindful of developments, nonetheless, by monitoring Steve Gordon's Web site and the Web site of the Center for School Improvement he directs at Texas State University. These are the questions that provide the context for the eighth edition of this book. Clearly, the press for accountability affects everything that today's supervisors do.

SUPERVISION RESPONDING TO THE ACCOUNTABILITY AGENDA

The accountability agenda for school renewal reflects one aspect of a much larger collection of influences that are causing a ferment of concern about the shortcomings of schooling in its present state. What follows is a brief overview of some of these influences. In subsequent chapters, we will touch on many of these influences in greater detail.

POLITICAL INFLUENCES   Federal, state, and local authorities call for school restructuring in view of international test data that they believe indicate American youth lag behind the youth of other countries on various measures of school achievement.

ECONOMIC INFLUENCES   Business executives and government officials maintain that American youth are unprepared for the technological demands of the 21st-century workplace. Continued advances in economic productivity require investment in high-quality education, especially in developing workplace skills.

COGNITIVE SCIENCE RESEARCH   This relatively new field has brought new understanding of how "experts" think and work in a variety of fields, which suggests how schools might prepare novice-experts. Cognitive science also has expanded our understanding of how the mind processes information, leading to suggestions on strengthening inquiry and reasoning skills and large frameworks (mental models, knowledge representations) for making and interpreting meaning. Research on multiple intelligences, especially in young children, has led to experimental learning settings that support the fuller development of these various intelligences, thus providing clues for an enriched curriculum that is more responsive to the diversity of talent children bring to their early classrooms.

CONSTRUCTIVIST LEARNING THEORY AND RESEARCH   This relatively new branch of psychology has shed light on how students actively produce knowledge and understanding, which suggests new approaches to designing learning tasks and activities. Constructivist research also has helped illuminate how background variables influence the way students process learning tasks and relate school learning to prior experiences.

PHILOSOPHY AND SOCIOLOGY   There is widespread acceptance that knowledge is a social, cultural, and political construct. There has been a shift from "What we know is real" to "What is real is what we know." Instead of denying the existence of objective reality, this view accepts knowledge as partial and tentative, open to correction and modification, but in its present form simultaneously revealing and distorting reality. Knowledge is seen as both a product and a medium of socialization and power.

RESEARCH IN ACADEMIC DISCIPLINES   Studies have more clearly identified methods of inquiry and strong inclusive frameworks that define the disciplines, thus suggesting new approaches to developing students as novice-experts in individual academic disciplines.

CURRICULUM THEORY AND RESEARCH   Such research has developed a new understanding of cultural, gender, and class bias in teaching materials and in curriculum tracking. This has led to various attempts to construct a curriculum that is more sensitive to gender, cultural, and language differences among students.

LEGAL POLITICS OF PLURALISM AND INCLUSION   Parents and other student advocates have forced new policies governing the treatment of special education, bilingual, and minority culture children, which in turn challenge traditional school structures and environments.

RESEARCH ON STUDENT ASSESSMENT   Research has introduced the notions of performance and authentic assessments, which in turn suggest a new understanding of learning. Following the dictum that what gets tested and how it gets tested directly influence (if not control) what gets taught and how, these new assessments substantially refocus the classroom on the active production and performance of student work.

RESEARCH ON PROFESSIONAL PRACTICE   Professional-practice research has focused on how teachers respond intuitively to developments in the classroom, interpreting verbal and nonverbal signals from students, altering the lesson plan when it is not working, going off into unplanned tangents when the needs of the moment seem to dictate it, bringing their biases and stereotypes into play in what and how they teach, and so on. Studies contrasting expert with novice teachers reveal what teachers have to know and how they bring this knowledge to bear on their teaching strategies. These studies have also revealed how teachers can engage in action research to improve their understanding of and response to the students in their classes. It has also documented how teachers working together can recreate the curriculum and the learning environment of the school, when they are given the autonomy to do so. The implications of this research are that teachers have enormous reservoirs of knowledge and experience that enable them to solve many of the problems within the restructuring agenda, when they are given the proper autonomy and support.

RESEARCH ON SECOND-ORDER CHANGE   This research has provided new understanding about the dynamics of second-order change (deep, substantial, total institutional change—the kind of change demanded by the restructuring agenda), especially about the need to "re-culture" the institution as the restructuring is being attempted (changing assumptions, beliefs, and values as the community attempts to change structures and environments), as well as about the need for participation, ownership, and ongoing professional development.

MORAL QUESTIONS

Supervision often is defined by criteria extrinsic to the moral qualities of teaching and learning. For us, supervision takes its moral character from its close involvement with the intrinsic moral qualities of teaching and learning. That is to say, teaching by its very nature assumes a caring for the one taught and a respect for the integrity of what is being taught and its connection to the past, present, and future life of the community. Not to care for the person being taught, or to distort the meaning of what is being taught, violates the very idea of teaching. Supervision is an activity that involves another in supporting and furthering that caring for the learner and respect for the significance of what is taught. The moral authority of the supervisor is joined with the moral authority of the teacher.

Though we continue to emphasize the skills and practical applications of such traditional supervisory processes as in-class supervision, enhancing reflection about teaching and learning, teacher evaluation, and staff development, these activities are recontextualized and substantially altered. In schools as learning communities, these activities imply deeper, professional, and moral concerns at work. In a new supervision, responsibility for these functions is no longer the exclusive domain of principals, supervisors, and others positioned within the school hierarchy. Instead, they embrace a common set of concepts and skills that are shared by everyone involved in the process of improving schooling. The supervisor's role remains important but is understood differently. She or he emerges as an advocate, developer, and linking pin in relationship to the teacher's efforts to improve the process of teaching and learning.

Finally, supervision is seen not as a separate function removed from the dynamics of institutional reinvention that is going on in schools, but as a necessary element of such dynamics. Those exercising supervisory responsibilities are in a unique position to nurture, develop, and articulate the community's vision of what a learning community can and should be.

In our view, supervision, properly redefined, can be the linchpin for deep school improvement efforts aimed at improving teacher quality, making schools more thoughtful and caring places for students, and increasing levels of authentic and rigorous student learning. First published in 1971, this edition continues a 36-year tradition of continually redefining the field of supervision in response to changing school contexts, policies, and realities. Several new themes are added or expanded in this edition. These themesdeal with issues of classroom supervision, promising practices, the use of teaching standards in supervision and evaluation, and building a culture of continuous improvement. These practical applications are supported by a conception of supervision as moral agency that has been a part of this book's tradition. This is a challenging book that asks a great deal from readers and in return provides them with a solid foundation for dealing with the complex problems now facing the practice of supervision in our schools.

Thomas J. Sergiovanni
Robert J. Starratt

ACKNOWLEDGMENTS

The authors gratefully acknowledge the contributions of the following reviewers who commented on the manuscript at various stages during the development of the eighth edition.

Diane C. Bechtold, Pennsylvania State University
Melanie Biermann, Frostburg State University
Dennis C. Buss, Rider University
Robin R. Dexter, University of Wyoming
Sandra L. Gupton, University of North Florida
Patricia Hoehner, University of Nebraska–Kearney
Leslie Jones-Hamilton, Nicholls State University
Charles Kline, Purdue University
Joslen Letscher, University of Detroit–Mercy
Oneida Martin, Tennessee Tech University
Patricia Rea, George Washington University
Doug Thomas, Central Missouri State University
John R. Tollett, Northwestern State University of Louisiana
Sean S. Warner, Norfolk State University

Supervision
A Redefinition

PART ONE

Perspectives for Supervision

CHAPTER 1

A Framework for Supervision

INTRODUCTION

The purpose of supervision is to help schools contribute more effectively to student achievement. With this purpose in mind, we provide a framework in this chapter to help in understanding how schools contribute effectively to this goal. The framework shows how instructional capacity, instructional quality, and student engagement can become three powerful pathways to academic success for all students. How the pathways are understood and traveled depends on one's theory of supervision. To illustrate this point, we provide a scenario that shows how four supervisors, each representing a different theory, size up a school-improvement problem and offer solutions. The theories, labeled A, B, C, and D, are discussed, and examples of how they work in the real world of supervision are presented.

SOME BACKGROUND

For the past several decades, the federal and state governments of the United States and many industrialized nations around the world have focused significant attention on school improvement. Eager to remain competitive in the global marketplace, these governments are calling on schools to produce a workforce that can adapt to the rapidly changing technologies of production, the accelerated rate of technological invention, and the application of sophisticated technology to almost all forms of work, from banking to wine growing, from auto mechanics to nursing, from teaching to professional athletics. Governments have passed legislation and policy initiatives demanding improved academic achievement by all students, achievement within more rigorous and complex curriculum guidelines, achievement that is measurable and meets increased standards of learning on state-mandated tests. These policy initiatives often include standards of effective teaching by which teachers will be evaluated, state-imposed tests of literacy and content knowledge for teaching licensure, and requirements for continuing education for the periodic renewal of the license to teach. Besides these initiatives, some states and large city school systems are holding teachers and administrators accountable for the poor academic achievement of their students—accountable to the extent that teachers and administrators can be removed from consistently underperforming schools. Many of these ideas are at the center of the reforms mandated by the federal government's No Child Left Behind (NCLB) initiative.

Under the relentless pressure of these policy initiatives, teachers and supervisors have had to reconsider and reconstruct the activity of teaching and reconstruct the process of supervision. From the teacher's perspective, teaching has to be far more responsive to the variety of students' talents, readiness to learn, interests, and cultural and linguistic backgrounds. The notion that there is one teaching strategy that works for all children, if it was ever genuinely embraced, can no longer be defended. The attitude of the policy community is that if the students are not learning, it is the teacher's fault. No longer can teachers blame the students, the students' parents, or the ineffective teaching of prior teachers. The failure of students to learn in any given classroom is considered the failure of the teacher to find a way to enable the students to learn.

Teachers face an additional challenge. Not only is there pressure on teachers to ensure that all children reach acceptable levels of achievement, but achievement levels themselves are being raised. Metacognitive learning is being introduced into the early grades. That is, students are expected to reflect on how they are learning and to be more aware of learning-attack strategies. This calls for higher levels of-reasoning previously thought by many to be beyond the cognitive developmental levels of younger students. Teaching for simple recall of facts, for memorized answers is no longer sufficient. Students have to explain relationships between pieces of information, and that requires a higher level of learning. In turn, those demands for student learning place new demands on teachers to develop a repertory of teaching strategies and lesson-design features that call for that higher-level learning.

Supervisors are likewise challenged by the new policy emphasis on school renewal. They are obliged to concentrate on what students are learning in relationship to what curriculum standards and state tests indicate they are supposed to be learning. Rather than looking for teaching strategies that the school systems consider effective classroom by classroom, supervisors have to look for observable evidence that students are learning as a result of the various stimuli presented by all their teachers. Supervisors are challenged to sit down, not simply with individual teacher after individual teacher to discuss specific teaching skills, but more so with groups of teachers to discuss which students are learning at the required levels and which are not and to develop and design new ways to foster the required learning. Sometimes the learning difficulties are caused by bilingual challenges faced by students, sometimes by difficulties faced by special-needs children, and sometimes by stresses within the home environment. The job of the supervisor is to help teachers pinpoint the source of the developing difficulty, bring in additional resource people when called for to work with the teachers, and monitor the gradual improvement in the students' learning. But teachers, too, have supervisory responsibilities. No matter how capable are designated supervisors, as long as supervision is viewed as doing something *to* teachers and *for* teachers but not *with* teachers, its potential to improve schools will not be fully realized. Further, unless teachers become sufficiently self-managing by accepting more responsibility for their own learning and development, the capacity of the school to provide needed help will be severely taxed.

BOTH ROLE AND FUNCTION

In today's reform climate, supervision is best understood as both a role and a function. When, for example, principals, department chairs, central office subject-matter specialists, and other formally designated supervisors visit classrooms to help teachers improve their practice, they are exercising their formal supervisory roles. They do this by engaging in such functions as observing teaching and providing helpful comments, helping teachers to reflect on their practice, teaching a demonstration lesson, suggesting items teachers might include in their portfolios, disaggregating test score data, and conducting formal evaluations of teaching as required by district or state policy.

But others, too, engage in supervisory functions, even though they are not formal supervisors. Teachers, for example, engage in supervisory functions when they visit each other's classes to learn and to provide help, to critique each other's planning, to examine together samples of student work, to pour over the most recent test scores together, to puzzle together over whether assignments they are giving students are appropriate or whether student performance levels meet important standards, to share portfolios and to engage in other activities that increase their learning, the learning of their colleagues, and the quality of teaching and learning that students receive.

The supervisory functions are so important in helping schools contribute effectively to rigorous and authentic learning that they cannot be rationed to just those who have formal supervisory responsibilities. Principals and other formal supervisors, therefore, have two broad responsibilities:

- to provide the most effective supervision they can for teachers; and
- to provide the conditions, help, and support teachers need to engage in the supervisory functions for themselves as part of their daily routine.

By fulfilling these responsibilities, supervisors can build a culture of supervision in the school that includes a commitment to continuous learning. Within this culture teachers become members of communities of practice. Communities of practice are formed as teachers come together in a common effort to help each other teach and learn, to care for each other, and to work together in advancing student academic achievement. The ties that bind teachers and their work together within such communities are such that teachers think of themselves as being less involved in a collection of individual practices and more involved in a single, shared practice of teaching.

LEADING AND LEARNING TOGETHER

Little is likely to happen unless principals and other formal supervisors focus their leadership on learning. Building the capacity of teachers, then giving them the discretion they need to practice effectively, and finally, holding them accountable for helping students be effective learners in a caring environment are the benchmark indicators of leadership for learning. But bringing together leadership and learning does not work well in promoting effective teaching and learning for students when the focus is only on meeting the learning needs and interests of teachers one at a time. This one-at-a-time approach is a great way to help teachers get smarter. But smart teachers and smart schools are not the same. A school gets smarter when what teachers learn and what teachers do are aligned with the school's purposes. A school gets smarter when the school itself is the prime beneficiary of learning.

Richard Elmore reminds us that learning for teachers can be a private good or a public good.[1] When learning is a private good, teachers benefit as individuals. This is the most common pattern of teacher learning. When learning is a public good, teachers benefit and the school benefits too. Teachers, for example, may learn a lot more about literacy and numeracy strategies, but only when this individual capacity becomes part of the school's collective capacity does what is learned help us achieve our student learning goals. Only then do schools become smarter too.

The greatest asset a school has is its collective IQ. Supervisors have to figure out how to harness this intelligence, how to develop it, and how to use it effectively. This is more likely to happen when teachers are connected around common purposes and themes and when they are connected to each other in a shared practice. When this happens, they are likely to feel a sense of responsibility for each other and to feel a moral obligation to work together to help achieve the school's purposes. Learning that counts the most in a school is learning that supports the public good.

But what about accountability? In this age of standards, high-stakes testing, and results, shouldn't we be talking about holding teachers accountable? How can we hold teachers accountable without getting involved in evaluating teachers? Where does teacher evaluation fit into the supervisory picture? In today's climate of reform, supervision must retain an important stake in accountability. If supervision is divorced from accountability, neither supervision nor accountability will get the support it needs to be effective.

Teachers need to be involved in supervision to overcome the isolation they experience. And teachers need to be involved in supervision to become continuous learners. When they are working together and learning together, teaching improves. Better teaching means improved student learning. When students are not learning well, and when teachers are not teaching well, the problem may be the quality of supervision the school provides. In a sense, those of us who are supervisors need to be held accountable for providing systems of supervision that make sense to teachers, that teachers will want to be a part of, and that will help teachers be more effective in the classroom.

[1]Richard F. Elmore, *Bridging the Gap Between Standards and Achievement: The Imperative for Professional Development in Education*, Washington, DC: Albert Shanker Institute, 2002.

But this stake in accountability must represent less a supervisory event and more a supervisory norm—a strong value that permeates the culture of the school. As this norm takes hold, supervisors will be able to engage in a number of roles. Among them are colleague, teacher developer, keeper of the vision, and designer of learning opportunities. They will be able to maintain, as well, a healthy concern for quality control as they strive to push the learning curves of teachers and schools to the limit and as they function as stewards on behalf of parents and students.

A FRAMEWORK FOR SUPERVISION

Earlier it was noted that, *the purpose of supervision is to help increase the opportunity and the capacity of schools to contribute more effectively to students' academic success.* With this purpose in mind, we set the scene for supervision by providing a framework for understanding how schools contribute to academic success and for understanding the critical role that supervision can play in this process. This framework is responsive to today's policy context of school renewal that requires the integration of bureaucratic aspects of supervision (for example, the legislated mapping of teaching to test results) and human resources aspects of supervision that seek to invest in teacher learning and other capacity-building strategies. One way to conceptualize this integration is to consider Newmann's[2] work on pathways to learning. This work is summarized in the model that appears as Figure 1–1. Note that in the center of the figure, instructional capacity, instructional quality, and student engagement are listed as the three pathways that supervisors travel in helping schools become more successful. Social supports and structural supports are listed in the figure on both sides of the supervisory pathways as important dimensions of leadership that support their development and effectiveness. The pathways are detailed below:[3]

1. *Instructional capacity* is defined as features of the school's organizational characteristics that support teaching and learning. Among them are teachers' knowledge of the subjects they teach, skill in teaching and classroom management, dispositions that promote achievement (i.e., high expectations, sensitivity to individual differences, commitment to caring), access to a high-quality curriculum, teaching materials, technology, adequate physical space, and access to a strong professional community that supports high-quality teaching and learning and is committed to teachers' thinking, planning, and working together in ways that enhance their abilities and performance as teachers.

---

[2]Fred M. Newmann, "How Secondary Schools Contribute to Academic Success," in Kathryn Borman and Barbara Schneider (eds.), *The Adolescent Years: Social Influences and Educational Challenges,* Ninety-Seventh Yearbook of the National Society for the Study of Education, Part I. Chicago: University of Chicago Press, 1998, pp. 88–108. Though Newmann focuses on secondary schools, he does not believe that major differences exist in the factors that contribute to student achievement in secondary schools as compared with elementary schools. In his words, ". . . the research has not revealed major differences within the two levels of schooling that affect students' academic success."

[3]Ibid., p. 89.

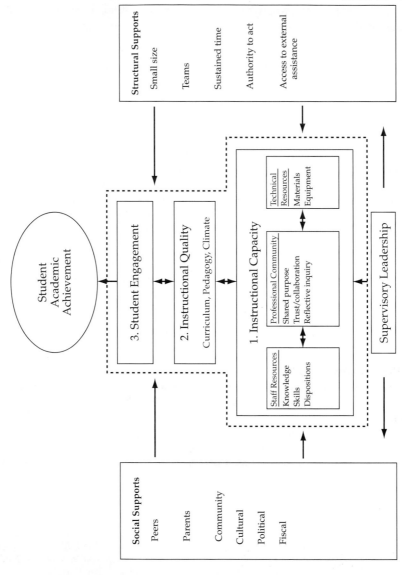

FIGURE 1–1. Instructional Capacity, Instructional Quality, and Student Engagement: Pathways to Academic Achievement.

2. *Instructional quality* is defined as curriculum content grounded in the academic and professional disciplines that demands in-depth understanding and application; teaching addressed to the mastery of basic information and skills as well as deep understanding and complex thinking; and a climate for learning characterized by high expectations, an orderly environment, and a commitment to caring and cooperation.

3. *Student engagement* is defined as students' commitment to and participation in learning.

When a school's instructional capacity improves, teachers have access to a high-quality curriculum, teaching improves, and teachers help one another, leading to improvements in instructional quality. Instructional quality, in turn, is a major contributor to promoting higher levels of student engagement, the gateway to improved learning.

In effect, the pathways ask three questions: What will we learn together and how will we work together? How are we providing quality teaching and learning in a caring environment? Are we being successful in helping students be connected to each other, their work, and their responsibilities?

Newmann is quick to point out that helping schools become more effective contributors to student learning requires more than traveling the supervisory pathways. In discussing student engagement, for example, he notes that "Student engagement results both from the quality of the instructional setting and from the level of social support from peers, parents, and the community beyond the school."[4] Added to the social supports are structural supports such as small school size, decentralized school management, and encouraging teachers to work in more cooperative and collegial ways. Both social and structural supports are important leadership concerns that, if properly handled, can make it easier to travel the supervisory pathways.

It is a lot easier to separate the pathways from their supports in a book. On the job, supervisors have to worry about both the general leadership that is required in a school and the kind and quality of supervisory leadership they must provide. In sum:

- Supervisory leadership focuses on improving a school's instructional capacity and instructional quality and on strengthening student academic engagement.
- General school leadership focuses on improving the amount and kind of social support and structural support that the school can make available to teachers and students.

What does supervisory leadership look like? How does it work in practice? Not everyone agrees. Supervisory leadership is contested with different views competing for attention. Following Newmann, we believe that the heart of supervisory leadership is designing opportunities for teachers to continuously expand their capacity to learn, to care, to help each other, and to teach more effectively. We view schools as learning communities where students, teachers, and supervisors alike are learners and teachers depending upon the circumstances. Learning for one group inevitably

---

[4]Ibid., p. 91.

leads to learning for all.[5] And we believe that building the school's instructional capacity is an important means to improve student academic achievement.

What are your views? What are the practices of supervision you observe every day in your school? What are the assumptions behind these practices? What views have dominated the way supervision has evolved over the last century? We examine these questions in the next section.

IMAGES OF SUPERVISION SCENARIO

Let us journey into the world of supervision by involving ourselves in Metro City's school improvement efforts. Place yourself in the role of school supervisor in Metro City. A year ago another school in Metro City was selected by the superintendent and central office staff to become a model school. This school was to incorporate a new educational system featuring explicit goals and teaching objectives across grade levels and a highly structured and tightly paced curriculum linked to the objectives. The curriculum included new textbooks and workbooks for all the major subject areas as well as carefully thought-out assignments and activities designed to provide students with needed practice. Daily and weekly lesson plans were provided to make things easier for teachers and to ensure that students received the same instruction and assignments. Criterion-referenced weekly, six-week, and semester tests were included in the package. The system provided as well for test scores to be evaluated by grade level and by each class within the grade level every six weeks to monitor student progress. Teachers were formed into quality-control committees, or quality circles, to discuss the scores and in instances of low scores to come up with ways the system might be better implemented. The administration was particularly proud of this quality-circle concept, for it wanted teacher participation.

The Metro City administration felt that if teachers became familiar with the system and if they followed directions and protocols faithfully, they would teach successfully. An incentive system was also introduced. Teachers were trained in the methods of teaching that the district felt were necessary to deliver the new curriculum effectively and efficiently. Observation checklists containing desired teacher behaviors were used to evaluate teacher performance. Teachers scoring the highest received cash bonuses.

To help things along, the principal received extensive training in the new curriculum and in staff supervision and evaluation. Further, a supervisor who had a thorough understanding of the new curriculum, the testing procedures, the daily and weekly lesson plans, the needed teaching to make things work, and the evaluation system was assigned to the school. Both principal and supervisor provided instructional leadership by monitoring teaching carefully to ensure compliance with the new system and by providing help to teachers who were having difficulty in complying.

Prior to the beginning of the school year, teachers were provided with a carefully planned and implemented weeklong training program, receiving a week's

[5]See for example, Tony Townsend, Paul Clarke, and Mel Ainscow (eds.), *Third Millennium Schools: A World of Differences in Effectiveness and Improvement,* Rotterdam: Swets & Zeitlinger, 1999.

salary for their participation. Schools ran on a half-day schedule for the first week, thus allowing additional training and debugging. The training seemed to be successful, for by the end of September teachers appeared to develop an acceptable level of understanding and competence in using the system. The central office had high hopes for the success of this new initiative and saw it as a model for export to other schools in the district.

Before the introduction of the new educational system, the teachers and principal of this school enjoyed a reputation for being a closely knit faculty with high morale. This situation began to change shortly after the new system was introduced. Teachers began to complain. They did not like the new curriculum, feeling that frequently it did not fit what they thought was important to teach. They complained of pressure from the tests. They found themselves teaching lessons and adopting teaching strategies that they did not like.

The teachers were particularly disturbed that each day, the tests and their content became more and more the curriculum. They expressed displeasure, too, with the overall climate in the school, describing it as increasingly impersonal with respect to students and competitive with respect to colleagues. Discontent among teachers grew as the semester continued. Things really began to sour when it became apparent that student performance did not measure up to the high expectations of the administration. The administration was puzzled as to why such a well-thought-out and carefully implemented educational system was not working in this school. Shortly after the spring break, the principal became disillusioned enough to request a transfer. The supervisor was equally discouraged.

With the departure of the principal imminent, the superintendent asked you and three other supervisors to review matters at the school in an effort to determine the source of the supervision problems and to arrive at a solution to these problems. Each of the supervisors was asked to work independently to develop solutions and to bring ideas to the meeting that is to take place shortly. How will you respond to the superintendent's request? Take a few minutes to develop an outline or framework that summarizes your views.

Below are descriptions of how the four supervisors sized up the problems at this school and the solutions that they proposed. Each of the supervisors was working from an image or an implicit theory of how the world of schooling, and perhaps even the world itself, works. Which of the four descriptions best matches your own view of the situation and your opinion as to how the situation might be remedied?[6]

Supervisor A

You feel that the present problems in the redesigned school are obviously attributable to the people who work there. If the teachers have not yet adapted to the new curriculum and its procedures, they probably are incapable of functioning in a school

---

[6]The role perspectives for supervisors A, B, C, and D are adapted for use in a school context from Leonard D. Goodstein and J. William Pfeiffer (eds.), *The 1985 Annual: Developing Human Resources,* San Diego: University Associates, 1985, pp. 49–52. Reprinted with permission of John Wiley & Sons, Inc.

committed to school improvement. It is also possible that the principal and the new supervisor are not the experts they were assumed to be and are therefore to blame for inadequate monitoring of the system and for their inability to provide the teachers with the proper help and supervision needed so that they might use the system better.

If you had had your way from the beginning, you would have staffed the school with new teachers. A systemwide search would have been conducted to find the kinds of teachers who would best fit such a system: those who would carefully follow the pattern of teaching and working that the system requires. In the introduction of the new system at the school, you believe that too much emphasis was placed on helping existing teachers to develop a conceptual understanding of the new procedures. This resulted in too many questions, too much confusion, doubts, and other problems. All teachers needed to know was how they fit into the system, what their jobs were, and what outcomes were expected. Clearer directions and expectations combined with better training and close monitoring would have provided the needed controls to make the system work.

You believe that the curriculum, the lesson plans, the materials, the tests, the teaching design, and the evaluation system introduced into the school are the best available. Although you know that it is possible for snafus to occur and that no educational system can be designed perfectly, you attribute the failure in this case to the unwillingness and inability of the teachers to do what they were supposed to do. Therefore, during the upcoming meeting you plan to make it clear that the problem is not the new educational system but the teachers who are using it. The answer is not to change the system but to train teachers better and to more closely monitor the teachers or to find teachers who are willing to use the system in the way it is intended.

Supervisor B

You are convinced that the source of the problems at the redesigned school is the lack of emphasis on human relations. Throughout the year the teachers and other employees have been complaining. As you suspected from the outset, the teachers were not consulted about the type of curriculum or the procedures that should be used, just as they were excluded from the decision-making process that led to the development of this model of the school of the future. You believe that teachers want to feel that they have a say in the matters that influence them. They want to be remembered and noticed, to be considered important. The formula for success is simple and straightforward. When these conditions do not exist, morale sinks. When teachers are satisfied and morale is high, on the other hand, they are more cooperative and more willing to comply, and their performance improves.

The teachers state that the new curriculum and teaching procedures are too cumbersome and rigid and thus make it impossible for them to work comfortably. As you have always said, when the school fulfills its responsibility to teachers' needs, everything else falls into place and school goals are met automatically. Making sure that teachers are happy is key. Under the new system, teachers have to cope not only with a reduction in the amount of teamwork that previously had promoted morale and satisfaction but also with new supervisors who were hired or trained because of their technical skills instead of their human skills.

During the upcoming meeting you plan to discuss top management's error in judgment. You intend to point out that teachers must be noted and appreciated, that the evaluation system is competitive and thus disruptive to group harmony, and that providing a little attention and lots of cheerleading can go a long way toward making things work. Fix the human relationship problems, and teachers will gladly cooperate with the administration in implementing the new system.

Supervisor C

In your opinion, the problems in the redesigned school are attributable to one source: a failure to provide teachers with opportunities to fulfill their individual needs for autonomy and their natural desire to do competent work. You form this opinion on the basis of what you have learned about teachers in general as well as those at this troubled school. The teachers in this school, like those in your own school, are mature adults who, under the right motivating conditions, want to do their best for the school; they want to enjoy their work and are capable of supervising themselves. Indeed, their performance record and their level of job satisfaction before the redesigning process prove that to be the case. The formula for success is simple and straightforward: Give people responsibility and authority to make decisions about how they are to work, and they respond with increased motivation. Provide them with opportunities to be successful in accomplishing their goals, and their performance improves. The best strategy is to provide the overall framework and let teachers figure out how to implement it. With the right climate, teachers respond to general expectations, need broad goals, and want to be held accountable if trusted and given the discretion to make the implementing decisions that make sense to them. In this school not enough attention was given to creating that climate.

In its plans to redesign the school, top administration overlooked these facts and chose to treat employees like children. A new supervisor was brought in to monitor the work of teachers, and a new educational system was programmed to keep track of their comings and goings. The teachers were expected to meet new organizational goals for increased student performance while their needs for achievement, autonomy, self-direction, and a sense of fulfillment were ignored. Under the circumstances, a drop in performance was inevitable. You feel strongly that the present school attitude toward teachers is counterproductive, and you plan to make your feelings known during the upcoming meeting. The instructional system in the redesigned school cannot be salvaged in its present form. The overall goals and purposes may be OK and it may be appropriate to provide teachers with general frameworks and directions, but at the operational level a new system needs to be developed with teachers as full shareholders and decision makers in its design and implementation.

Supervisor D

You believe that the changes introduced were not realistic. They did not reflect the way schools actually work or how teachers think and behave. The curriculum and instructional system and the teaching and evaluation design that were introduced featured discrete goals, structured tasks, easily measured outcomes, sure operating procedures, clear lines of authority, and a single best way to organize, teach, and evaluate. The problem, as you see it, is that these characteristics are suitable for teaching and learning environments that are stable and predictable and for instances in which student and teacher needs and styles are uniform. But schools have multiple and competing goals, unstructured tasks, competing solutions, difficult-to-measure outcomes, unsure operating procedures, and unclear and competing lines of authority. Further, teachers and students have diverse needs and styles. You hope to explain that these are characteristics of dynamic environments. What works in the first instance may not work in the second.

You remember reading somewhere that schools are "managerially loose and culturally tight," and you intend to build your arguments around this idea. What counts for teachers is not so much the management system that is provided but what they believe, the values they share, and the assumptions they hold. When values are held collectively, they become defining characteristics of the school's culture. Changing schools, as you see it, means changing school cultures.

You plan to recommend that the present system be put on hold. You will also recommend that the faculty and administration spend the next year coming to grips with the values they share about teaching and learning, what schools are for, how best to evaluate, and how they might best work together. They should then conduct a needs assessment that identifies the norms and values that are now in place in the school as evidenced by what is now going on, and come to grips with what needs changing. This sort of reflection, you believe, will enable them to create a new culture for their school—one with different and more effective norms. You intend to point out that in this renormed school, less emphasis will need to be given to prescribing what needs to be done and to providing direct supervision. Shared values and purposes, a common perspective on what needs to be done to improve the school and a shared commitment to change, in your view, should function as substitutes for direct supervision and should help teachers to become self-managing.

Each recommendation of the four supervisors represents a different, albeit exaggerated, image or theory of what supervision is, how schools work, and what is important to teachers. Make your selection by ranking the four in a way that reflects your view of supervision. Does a clear favorite emerge? You probably feel more comfortable by combining some of the views. What combined image would you propose? By deciding, you are revealing your own personal theory. The theories of each of the supervisors are described below.

SCIENTIFIC MANAGEMENT, HUMAN RELATIONS, AND NEOSCIENTIFIC MANAGEMENT SUPERVISION

Many of the supervisory practices found in schools today are based on one theory or a combination of two theories of supervision: traditional scientific management and human relations. These theories are reflected in the images of supervision portrayed by supervisors A and B, respectively. In our view, neither theory of supervision is adequate to provide a model for school supervision. In later sections we propose human resources and normative supervision, the view of supervisors C and D, respectively, as approaches that are more sound from a scientific point of view and more accurate in their fit to the realities of practice.

Scientific management supervision, image A, emerged from the thinking and work of Frederick Taylor and his followers during the early 1900s. Many of the ideas that shaped this theory stem from his experience and research on supervision in America's steel industries. For example, Taylor analyzed the loading of pig iron onto railroad cars at a Bethlehem, Pennsylvania, steel plant. Noting certain inefficiencies, he devised techniques for increasing the workers' productivity. His techniques were "scientific" in the sense that they were based on careful observation and task analysis. Taylor determined, for example, that the equipment the workers were using was inadequate to the task. He substituted standardized shovels and other standardized work equipment designed specifically for the tasks to be done. Once the best way of doing something was established, he instructed workers to do exactly as they were told and only as they were told. By closely adhering to his methods and by using the equipment he provided, the workers were able to increase their average loading per day from 12 to 47 tons. Taylor felt that the secret to scientific management was a compliant worker who did not think too much but instead followed directions exactly.[7] The directions, of course, were to be based on "scientifically validated" methods of doing the job. The scientific management recipe is as follows:

- Identify the best way.
- Develop a work system based on this "research."
- Communicate expectations to workers.
- Train workers in the system.
- Monitor and evaluate to ensure compliance.

Scientific management ideas carry over to school supervision when teachers are viewed as implementers of highly refined curriculum and teaching systems and where close supervision is practiced to ensure that they are teaching the way they are supposed to and that they are carefully following approved guidelines and teaching protocols. Control, accountability, and efficiency are emphasized in scientific management within an atmosphere of clear-cut manager-subordinate relationships. Though vestiges of this brand of supervision can still be found in schools, by and large, traditional scientific management is not currently in favor. Its basic premises and precepts, however, are still thought to be attractive by many policy makers, administrators, and supervisors. The ideas have not changed, as will be discussed later, but strategies for implementing these ideas have.

Human relations supervision, image B, emerged during the 1930s. The work of Elton Mayo, a social philosopher and professor of business administration at Harvard University, is considered important in the development of human relations supervision. Mayo believed that the productivity of workers could be increased by

---

[7]See, for example, Frederick Taylor, *The Principles of Scientific Management,* New York: Harper & Row, 1911. Reprinted by Harper & Row in 1945. See also Raymond Callahan, *Education and the Cult of Efficiency,* Chicago: University of Chicago Press, 1962.

meeting their social needs at work, providing them with opportunities to interact with each other, treating them decently, and involving them in the decision-making process. His classic research study at the Western Electric Hawthorne plant during the 1920s gave testimony to those ideas.[8] Ultimately, human relations supervision was a successful challenger to traditional scientific management. When it was applied to schooling, teachers were viewed as whole persons in their own right rather than as packages of needed energy, skills, and aptitudes to be used by administrators and supervisors. Supervisors needed to work to create a feeling of satisfaction among teachers by showing interest in them as people. It was assumed that a satisfied staff would work harder and would be easier to work with, to lead, and to control. Participation was considered an important supervisory method, and its objective was to make teachers *feel* that they were useful and important to the school. "Personal feelings" and "comfortable relationships" were the watchwords of human relations.

Human relations supervision is still widely advocated and practiced. Human relations promised much but delivered little. Its problems rested partly with misunderstandings as to how this approach should work and partly with faulty theoretical notions inherent in the approach itself. The movement actually resulted in widespread neglect of teachers. Participatory supervision became permissive supervision, which in practice was laissez-faire supervision. Furthermore, the focus of human relations supervision was, and still is, an emphasis on "winning friends" in an attempt to influence people. To many, winning friends was a slick tactic that made the movement seem manipulative and inauthentic, even dishonest. Though this approach developed a considerable following during the 1930s through 1950s, it became clear that increases in school productivity would not be achieved merely by assuring the happiness of teachers.

School reforms that began in the early 1980s and continue today suggest a new, renewed interest in scientific management thinking, though its shape and form in practice have changed considerably from the more traditional form. This *neoscientific* management is in large part a reaction against human relations supervision with its neglect of the teacher in the classroom and its lack of attention to accountability. Neoscientific management shares with traditional management an interest in control, accountability, and efficiency, but the means by which it achieves these ends is far more impersonal. For example, there is a renewed interest in closely monitoring what it is that teachers do, the subject matter they cover, and the teaching methods that they use. But checking daily lesson plans and visiting classes daily to *inspect* teaching often breeds resentment and results in tension between teachers and supervisors. A more impersonal way to control what it is that teachers do is to introduce standardized criterion-referenced testing and to make public the scores by class and school. Since it is accepted that what gets measured gets taught, tests serve as an impersonal method of controlling the teacher's work.

---

[8]See, for example, Elton Mayo, *The Human Problems of an Industrial Civilization,* New York: Macmillan, 1933; and F. J. Roethlisberger and W. J. Dickson, *Management and the Worker,* Cambridge MA: Harvard University Press, 1949.

Human relations supervision and the two versions of scientific management share a lack of faith and trust in the individual teacher's ability and willingness to display as much interest in the welfare of the school and its programs as that presumed by administrators, supervisors, state and federal policy makers, and the general public. Within traditional scientific management, teachers are heavily supervised in a face-to-face setting in an effort to ensure that good teaching will take place. In human relations supervision, teachers are provided with conditions that enhance their morale and are involved in efforts to increase their job satisfaction so that they might be more pliable in the hands of management, thus ensuring that good teaching will take place. In neoscientific management, impersonal, technical, and rational control mechanisms substitute for face-to-face close supervision. Here it is assumed that if visible standards of performance, objectives, or competencies can be identified, the work of teachers can be controlled by holding them accountable to these standards, thus ensuring better teaching.

Sometimes neoscientific management and human relations are combined into one theory of action. For example, the work of teachers may be programmed by an impersonal system of regulation and control, but day-to-day supervision might emphasize pleasant and cordial relationships, building teachers up (telling them, for example, how important they are), encouraging positive attitudes, and rewarding teachers who conform.

HUMAN RESOURCES SUPERVISION

In 1967 the Association for Supervision and Curriculum Development's Commission on Supervision Theory concluded its four-year study with a report entitled *Supervision: Perspectives and Propositions.*[9] In this report, William Lucio discussed scientific management and human relations views of supervision and spoke of a third view—that of the revisionists—which sought to combine emphasis on both tasks and human concerns into a new theory. Standard-bearers of the revisionists were Douglas McGregor, Warren Bennis, Chris Argyris, and Rensis Likert.[10]

Beginning with the second edition of this book, we have referred to the concepts and practices associated with this new theory as *human resources supervision.*[11] This is the theory of supervision that supervisor C relies upon. The distinction between human resources and human relations is critical, for human resources is more than just another variety of human relations. Human resources represents a

[9]William Lucio (ed.), *Supervision: Perspectives and Propositions,* Washington, DC: Association for Supervision and Curriculum Development, 1967.

[10]Douglas McGregor, *The Human Side of Enterprise,* New York: McGraw-Hill, 1960; Warren Bennis, "Revisionist Theory of Leadership," *Harvard Business Review,* vol. 39, no. 2 (1961), pp. 26–38; Chris Argyris, *Personality and Organization,* New York: Harper & Row, 1957; and Rensis Likert, *New Patterns of Management,* New York: McGraw-Hill, 1961.

[11]This distinction was first made by Raymond Miles, "Human Relations or Human Resources?" *Harvard Business Review,* vol. 43, no. 4 (1965), pp. 148–163; and by Mason Haire, Edwin Ghiselli, and Lyman Porter, *Managerial Thinking: An International Study,* New York: Wiley, 1966.

higher regard for human need, potential, and satisfaction. Argyris captured the new emphasis succinctly, as follows:

> We're interested in developing neither an overpowering manipulative organization nor organizations that will "keep people happy." Happiness, morale, and satisfaction are not going to be highly relevant guides in our discussion. Individual competence, commitment, self-responsibility, fully functioning individuals, and active, viable, vital organizations will be the kinds of criteria that we will keep foremost in our minds.[12]

Leadership within this new kind of supervision was to be neither directive nor patronizing, but instead, supportive.

> The leader and other processes of the organization must be such as to ensure a maximum probability that in all interactions and in all relationships within the organization, each member, in light of his background, values, desires, and expectations, will view the experience as supportive and one which builds and maintains his sense of personal worth and importance.[13]

Douglas McGregor, pointing out that every managerial act rests on a theory, provided a new theory more conducive to human resources management. Theory Y, as he called it, was based on optimistic assumptions about the nature of humankind and provided a more powerful basis for motivating workers than the older Theory X.

> Theory X leads naturally to an emphasis on the tactics of control—to procedures and techniques for telling people what to do, for determining whether they are doing it, and for administering rewards and punishments. Since an underlying assumption is that people must be made to do what is necessary for the success of the enterprise, attention is naturally directed to the techniques of direction and control. Theory Y, on the other hand, leads to a preoccupation with the *nature of relationships*, with the creation of an environment which will encourage commitment to organizational objectives and which will provide opportunities for the maximum exercise of initiative, ingenuity, and self-direction in achieving them.[14]

The assumptions about people associated with Theory X are as follows:

1. Average people are by nature indolent—they work as little as possible.
2. They lack ambition, dislike responsibility, prefer to be led.
3. They are inherently self-centered, indifferent to organizational needs.
4. They are by nature resistant to change.
5. They are gullible, not very bright, ready dupes of the charlatan and demagogue.[15]

One can find many instances in schools when the assumptions of Theory X do indeed seem to be true. Teachers, for example, seem to work only minimally and

---

[12]Chris Argyris, *Integrating the Individual and the Organization,* New York: Wiley, 1964, p. 4.

[13]Likert, op. cit., p. 103.

[14]McGregor, op. cit., p. 132.

[15]These assumptions are quoted from McGregor's essay "The Human Side of Enterprise," which appears in Warren G. Bennis and Edgar H. Schein (eds.), *Leadership and Motivation: Essays of Douglas McGregor,* Cambridge, MA: MIT Press, 1966. The essay first appeared in *Adventure in Thought and Action,* Proceedings of the Fifth Anniversary Convocation of the School of Industrial Management, MIT, April 9, 1957.

then only under close supervision. Few instances of teacher initiative can be found. Instead, teachers seem to be defensive and preoccupied with maintaining the status quo. McGregor argued that when such conditions exist, the problem may be less with workers and more with the expectations that their administrators and supervisors have of them. Sensing negative assumptions and expectations, teachers are likely to respond in a negative way. This is an example of the self-fulfilling prophecy. Fundamental to Theory X is a philosophy of direction and control. This philosophy is administered in a variety of forms and rests upon a theory of motivation that is inadequate for most adults, particularly professional adults.

The assumptions about people associated with Theory Y, on the other hand, are as follows:

1. Management is responsible for organizing the elements of productive enterprise—money, materials, equipment, people—in the interest of economic (educational) ends.
2. People are *not* by nature passive or resistant to organizational needs. They have become so as a result of experience in organizations.
3. The motivation, the potential for development, the capacity for assuming responsibility, the readiness to direct behaviors toward organizational goals are all present in people; management does not put them there. It is a responsibility of management to make it possible for people to recognize and develop these human characteristics for themselves.
4. The essential task of management is to arrange organizational conditions and methods of operation so that people can achieve their own goals *best* by directing *their* own efforts toward organizational objectives.[16]

Basic to Theory Y is building identification of and commitment to worthwhile objectives in the work context and building mutual trust and respect. Success in work is assumed to be dependent on whether authentic relationships and the exchange of valid information are present.

Advocates maintain that school conditions created by human resources management result in a better life for teachers and more productive schooling. Satisfaction and achievement are linked in a new and more expansive way. Instead of focusing on creating happy teachers as a means to gain productive cooperation, the new supervision emphasis is on creating the conditions of successful work as a means of increasing one's satisfaction and self-esteem. As Frederick Herzberg described the new emphasis:

> To feel that one has grown depends on achievement of tasks that have meaning to the individual, and since the hygiene [satisfaction] factors do not relate to the task, they are powerless to give such meaning to the individual. Growth is dependent on some achievements but achievement requires a task. The motivators are task factors and thus are necessary for growth; they provide the psychological stimulation by which the individual can be activated toward his self-realization needs.[17]

[16]McGregor in Bennis and Schein, op. cit., p. 15.
[17]Frederick Herzberg, *Work and the Nature of Man,* New York: World, 1966, p. 78.

HUMAN RELATIONS AND HUMAN RESOURCES SUPERVISION COMPARED

Neoscientific management and scientific management are really the same theory, though each has a slightly different look in practice. Human relations and human resources supervision, however, are two different theories. For example, although both are concerned with teacher satisfaction, human relations views satisfaction as a means to a smoother and more effective school. It is believed that satisfied workers are happier workers and thus easier to work with, more cooperative, and more likely to be compliant. Supervisors find it easier to get what they want from teachers when human relationships are tended to. Consider, for example, the practice of shared decision making. In human relations supervision, this technique is used because it is believed it will lead to increased teacher satisfaction. This relationship is depicted as follows:

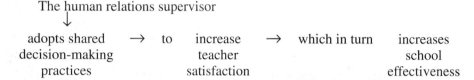

The human relations supervisor

adopts shared → to increase → which in turn increases
decision-making   teacher   school
practices   satisfaction   effectiveness

The rationale behind this strategy is that teachers want to *feel* important and involved. This feeling in turn promotes in teachers a better attitude toward the school, and therefore they become easier to manage and more effective in their work.

Within human resources supervision, by contrast, satisfaction is viewed as a desirable *end* toward which teachers work. Satisfaction, according to this view, results from successful accomplishment of important and meaningful work, and this accomplishment is the key component to building school success. The human resources supervisor, therefore, adopts shared decision-making practices because of their potential to increase school success. The supervisor assumes that better decisions will be made, that teacher ownership and commitment to these decisions will be increased, and that the likelihood of success at work will increase. These relationships are depicted as follows:

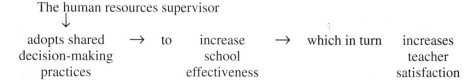

The human resources supervisor

adopts shared → to increase → which in turn increases
decision-making   school   teacher
practices   effectiveness   satisfaction

Human relations supervision is much more closely aligned with the assumptions of Theory X than with those of Theory Y, even though when experienced, human relations supervision results in a softer form of control.

REVISITING THE SUPERVISORS

Let us now revisit supervisors A, B, C, and D.

Scientific management and neoscientific management constitute the theories that govern the thinking and practice of supervisor A. This supervisor supports a highly structured and finely tuned teaching and learning system characterized by close connections among objectives, curriculum, teaching methods, and testing. Supervisor A believes that if teachers do what they are supposed to, the system will produce the results that are intended.

Human relations constitutes the theory to which supervisor B gives allegiance. Supervisor B is concerned with the teaching system's insensitivity to teachers' needs. Further, teachers were not consulted about the system to be implemented and thus feel left out. The answer to this supervisor is to back off and try again, this time getting teachers involved and making compromises in the proposed changes that get in the way of teachers' social interaction and other needs. With the right human relations strategy, supervisor B believes, any school-improvement initiative will be successful. It is just a matter of how effectively you work with people.

Supervisor C comes closest to operating from within the human resources perspective. This supervisor believes that successful teaching and school improvement occur when teacher motivation and commitment are high. Being in charge of one's work life and being held accountable to shared values and broad goals contribute to motivation and commitment. Authentic participation in decision making and providing responsibility are viewed as key supervisory strategies by supervisor C.

Supervisor D's analysis of the problems in Metro City represents a fairly new image of supervision. Supervisor D relies much less on direct supervision, whatever its form. No matter how enlightened such supervision might be, supervisor D reasons, it still depends largely upon some external force to make things happen. Even in the case of human resources supervision, at the base is an exchange of higher-level need fulfillment for some sort of work compliance. Instead, supervisor D seeks to build substitutes for supervision into the everyday life of the school. Prime among these substitutes are norms, obligations, relational trust, culture, and other forms of community characteristics. The more deeply held are these substitutes, the more likely are people to be internally motivated.

It is hard to put a label on supervisor D's theory of supervision. Providing substitutes, for example, suggests that supervision as it is now being practiced should be replaced by something else. Supervisor D highlights shared values. Shared values can take many forms. Sometimes they are expressed as professional norms or community norms or the felt need for teachers to care about each other and to help each other. As schools are restructured as true learning communities, shared norms and ideas become the source of authority for what supervisors, teachers, and students do. These sources of authority replace bureaucratic and interpersonal authority by speaking to community members in a moral voice and calling them to do the right thing. These and other substitutes for supervision will be discussed in the next and subsequent chapters of this book.

This "normative" supervision that characterizes supervisor D's views is based on several premises that are at odds with more traditional approaches to supervision.

- One premise is that while self-interest may be an important source of motivation for teachers, most are both capable of sacrificing self-interest and willing to do so for more altruistic reasons if conditions are right.
- Another premise is that preference, values, emotions, and beliefs are equally if not more powerful teacher motivators than are logic, reasoning, and scientific evidence.
- A third premise is that teachers and others do not make decisions simply as isolated individuals. Instead, what they think, believe, and ultimately do is shaped by their memberships in groups and their connections with other people. They are more responsive to norms than they are to either rules or needs—a condition that seems to apply to students as well.[18]

It is important to conclude this discussion of images of supervision with the warning given as we began. Each of the supervisory models sketched above provides an oversimplification, and probably none is exclusively adequate. Successful supervision is shaped by the circumstances and situations that the supervisor faces, and at different times, different models may be appropriate. Still, it matters greatly which of the general theories of supervision or which combination one accepts as her or his *overarching framework*. The images of supervision twist and turn with new policy developments in teaching and learning.

SUMMARY

In Chapter 1 we have provided a framework for understanding and practicing supervision. This framework includes three leadership pathways that supervisors must travel as they seek to improve academic achievement in their schools: promoting instructional capacity; providing instructional quality; and ensuring student engagement. As capacity, quality, and engagement improve, so does student achievement.

We have discussed three major themes: viewing supervision as both a role and a function, recognizing the importance of linking leading and learning as a strategy for change, and examining four theories of supervision (scientific management, human relations, human resources, and normative, or cultural). The theories are modeled by supervisors A, B, C, and D, using the Metro City images of supervision scenario. The recommended theories are embodied by supervisors C and D.

SOME REFLECTIONS

1. Which of the four theories of supervision, A, B, C, or D, best describes how supervision actually takes place in your school or school district? What do you do if you subscribe to the practices of theories C and D but are required to use the practices of theories A and B?

---

[18]See, for example, Thomas J. Sergiovanni, *Moral Leadership: Getting to the Heart of School Improvement,* San Francisco: Jossey-Bass, 1992; Thomas J. Sergiovanni, *Strengthening the Heartbeat: Leading and Learning Together in Schools,* San Francisco: Jossey-Bass, 2005; and Robert J. Starratt, *Ethical Leadership,* San Francisco: Jossey-Bass, 2004.

2. Give examples of scientific management theory and practice in today's leadership and supervision.

3. Consider Richard Elmore's distinction between teacher learning as a private good and as a public good. The teacher is the prime beneficiary of the former, and the school is the prime beneficiary of the latter. Joining Elmore, we pointed out that smart teachers do not necessarily lead to smart schools. Schools get smarter when what teachers know is aggregated and when this aggregated knowledge is linked to school purposes. What is your position? Explain your position to a colleague. How do you think teachers are likely to respond to these distinctions?

4. Explain what it means to say that supervision is first and foremost a function that is distributed across many roles.

5. Supervisor D advocates a normative theory of supervision. At the center of this theory are three main assumptions about human nature: Most teachers are both capable of sacrificing their self-interests and willing to do so on behalf of the common good; preferences, values, emotions, and beliefs are powerful motivators of human behavior; and what teachers think and believe is shaped by their membership in groups and connections with other people. To what extent do these assumptions reflect teachers you know? Use a scale of 1 to 10 to rate the extent to which you believe the assumptions to be true, with 10 being "very true" and 1 being "not true." Be prepared to defend your ratings.

CHAPTER 2

Sources of Authority for Supervisory Leadership

INTRODUCTION

Why should teachers cooperate with their principals? Why should students comply with the requests of their teachers? The question of authority is important. What are the sources of authority that designated and informal supervisors can use to get people to do things differently? If teachers, for example, do not view the sources of authority used with them as being legitimate, it is unlikely they will change what they are doing in any meaningful way. This chapter sorts out the authority question, pointing out that supervisors can choose from bureaucratic, personal, professional, and moral authority. There is a place for all four, but it makes a difference which sources are at the center of practice and which sources are at the periphery.

In this chapter professional authority and moral authority are recommended. The strengths of professional authority and the strengths of moral authority are in their ability to connect people morally to the school and its purposes. It is difficult to understand moral authority without understanding how idea-based leadership works. In idea-based leadership, people gather around ideas, share them, and publicly commit to them. The public commitment makes them morally obliged to embody these ideas in their practice. The purpose of this chapter is to show how idea-based leadership works—how idea-based leadership helps promote student achievement and helps improve the school.

SOME BACKGROUND

The four supervisors described in Chapter 1 want to improve Metro City's schools. Supervisors A and B choose slightly different paths but *follow a similar route* to achieve this goal. This is also the case for supervisors C and D. Thus each of the pairs of supervisors represents two different conceptions of supervision, and each of the two different conceptions of supervision leads to different consequences in the school.

Let us refer to these broad conceptions as *Supervision I* and *Supervision II*. Supervision I represents a supervision that is bureaucratic in nature and that reflects a dim view of the motives and capabilities of teachers. For these reasons the supervision needed in Supervision I is management-oriented and is intended to be sure that teachers are doing what they are supposed to in the way that the supervisors require. Some supervisors of this type rely heavily on their personality and other human relations tools to get compliance. Teachers might be involved, for example, not because their contributions are valued but because they will feel better as a result. When teachers are satisfied in this way, it is argued, they are easier to supervise. Supervision II, by contrast, represents an emerging pattern that can change not only the way supervision is understood and practiced but also our understanding of how to effect change, what really counts when it comes to motivating teachers, what leadership is, how to be helpful to teachers in the classroom, staff development means, what and how to help teacher evaluation become more useful. While Supervision I and Supervision II both search for ways to help schools improve their capacity to promote academic achievement, they lead to different practices.

At the end of this chapter, the assumptions and principles underlying Supervision I and Supervision II are compared. To set the stage for this chapter, we begin by examining the sources of authority that may be used for getting teachers to respond positively to supervision. Different sources lead to different consequences. Each of the four supervisors in Chapter 1 relies on a different source of authority. "Authority" refers to power that is used to influence how teachers think and what teachers do about teaching and learning. The success or failure of any supervisory strategy rests on the match that exists between the source of authority that the supervisor relies upon and the specifics that define the situation at hand.

THE SOURCES OF AUTHORITY[1]

Supervisory policies and practices can be based on one source or a combination of four broad sources of authority:

- *Bureaucratic,* in the form of mandates, rules, regulations, job descriptions, and expectations. When supervisory policies and practices are based on bureaucratic authority, teachers are expected to respond appropriately or face the consequences.
- *Personal,* in the form of leadership style, motivational know-how, and human relations skills. When supervisory policies and practices are based on personal authority, teachers are expected to respond to the supervisor's personality, to the pleasant environment provided, and to incentives for positive behavior.
- *Professional,* in the form of experience, knowledge of the craft of teaching, research knowledge, and personal expertise. When supervisory policies and

---

[1]The discussion in this chapter of sources of authority for supervision is based on Thomas J. Sergiovanni, "Moral Authority and the Regeneration of Supervision," in Carl Glickman (ed.), *Supervision in Transition,* Alexandria, VA: Association for Supervision and Curriculum Development, 1992; and "The Sources of Authority for Leadership," in Thomas J. Sergiovanni, *The Moral Dimensions in Leadership,* San Francisco: Jossey-Bass, 1992, chap. 3.

practices are based on professional authority, teachers are expected to respond to common socialization, accepted tenets of practice, and internalized expertise. When professional authority is used, research is not assumed to tell teachers what to do, but to *inform* the decisions that they make about their practice.

- *Moral,* in the form of obligations and duties derived from widely shared values, ideas, and ideals. When supervisory policies and practices are based on moral authority, teachers are expected to respond to obligations and shared commitments and to the interdependence that comes from these shared commitments.

Each of the four sources of authority has a place and should be used by supervisors. But some of the sources should be more dominant than others. Authority underlying Supervision I, for example, is a combination of bureaucratic and personal authority. Supervision II is based primarily on professional and moral authority.

Supervisor A relies heavily on bureaucratic authority in implementing the instructional system in Metro City. The system itself, for example, is based on the school effectiveness and teaching effectiveness research in vogue during the 1970s and 1980s. Supervisor A appeals to the type of authority advocated in this research: "Research says that these are the indicators of effective teaching"; "Research says that tightly aligned curriculum and teaching to objectives and then testing for mastery produces better results"; and so on. Further, the teaching, supervisory, and testing processes to be followed are specified as rule-bound standard operating procedures. A system of monitoring is provided to check compliance, and penalties are levied for noncompliance. In the ideal, supervisor A reasons, the school should recruit teachers who are willing to go along with the desired instructional system at the outset. The reason is that bureaucratic sources of authority exist *independent* of people and of situations. What is unique about a particular classroom or what hunches the teacher has about what is going on or should be going on are not considered to be very important.

Supervisor B, on the other hand, recommends relying on certain kinds of knowledge about human behavior in developing personal authority, which is expressed as human relations leadership. The instructional system itself is not questioned, and the weight of bureaucratic authority is accepted but not emphasized. Bureaucratic sources of authority may motivate supervisors, but not teachers. Supervisor B might say: "Yes, research says so-and-so, but if you want teachers to follow the research, don't preach it, just treat them right"; "Procedures have to be followed, but in seeking compliance, emphasize positive rewards rather than negative penalties"; or "Remember to involve teachers because they like to be involved and as a result are more likely to cooperate with you." Whether the research in question fits a particular teacher's personality or teaching situation and whether the research being used allows teachers to have the discretion they need to make good and responsive decisions about their teaching are less important. Supervisor B sees rewards as better than reason and seeks to involve teachers in decision making because they will be more satisfied and as a result, less troublesome to supervise.

Supervisor C too relies on a form of personal authority but one that is different from that used by supervisor B. Bureaucratic sources of authority are not ignored, but they count less. Further, they are understood differently by supervisor C than by supervisor B. For example, supervisor C believes that it is OK to have a general sense of what is to be accomplished. Teachers are then involved in fleshing out this general sense into a more specific design. Bureaucratic rules in this case take the form of broad policies that guide the decision-making process. *Research, too, plays a role, but is viewed less as a script to be followed and more as a series of revelations that can inform the shared decision-making process.* Supervisor C relies heavily on developing the right interpersonal climate and on meeting teachers' needs for achievement, esteem, recognition, and autonomy.

Supervisor D views sources of bureaucratic authority in a fashion similar to that of supervisor C. Personal authority also has its place. But what matters most are shared values and beliefs that become norms governing behavior. These norms are connected to the teacher's sense of professionalism, knowledge of the craft of teaching, and membership in the school as a learning community. Norms represent a form of moral authority. Professional authority and moral authority are the two sources relied upon most by supervisor D.

In the sections that follow, we take a closer look at each of the four sources of authority, examining the assumptions underlying each one when it is used as the prime source, the supervision strategies suggested by each, and the impact each one has on the work of teachers and on the teaching and learning process.

BUREAUCRATIC AUTHORITY

As suggested above, bureaucratic authority relies heavily on hierarchy, rules and regulations, mandates, and clearly communicated role expectations as a way to provide teachers with a script to follow. Teachers, in turn, are expected to comply with this script or face consequences. There may be a place for this source of authority even in the most progressive of schools, but when this source of authority is *prime,* the following assumptions are made:

Teachers are subordinates in a hierarchically arranged system.

Supervisors are trustworthy, but you can't trust subordinates very much.

The goals and interests of teachers and those of supervisors are not the same; thus, supervisors must be watchful.

Hierarchy equals expertise; thus, supervisors know more about everything than do ordinary teachers.

External accountability works best.

With these assumptions in place, it becomes important for supervisors to provide teachers with prescriptions for what, when, and how to teach, and for governing other aspects of their school lives. These are provided in the form of expectations. Supervisors then practice a policy of "expect and inspect" to ensure compliance with these prescriptions. Heavy reliance is placed on predetermined standards to which teachers must measure up whether or not the standards fit the teaching and learning situation. Since teachers often will not know how to do what needs to be done, it is important for supervisors to identify their needs and then to "in-service" them in some way. Directly supervising and closely monitoring the work of teachers is key to ensuring continued compliance with prescriptions and expectations. To the extent possible, it is also a good idea to figure out how to motivate teachers and encourage them to change in ways that conform with the system.

The consequences of relying primarily on bureaucratic authority in supervision have been carefully documented in the literature. Without proper monitoring, teachers wind up being loosely connected to bureaucratic systems, complying only when they have to.[2] When monitoring is effective in enforcing compliance, teachers too often respond as technicians who execute predetermined scripts and whose performance is narrowed. They become, to use the jargon, "deskilled."[3] When teachers are not able to use their talents fully and are caught in the grind of routine, they become separated from their work, viewing teaching as a job rather than a vocation, and treating students as cases rather than persons.

Readers probably will have little difficulty accepting the assertion that supervision based primarily on bureaucratic authority is not a good idea. The validity of most of the assumptions underlying this source of authority may be appropriate for some teachers but are suspect for most. Few, for example, believe that teachers as a group are not trustworthy and do not share the same goals and interests about schooling as do their supervisors. Even fewer would accept the idea that hierarchy equals expertise. Less contested, perhaps, would be the assumptions that teachers are subordinates in a hierarchically arranged system and that external monitoring works best. Supervision today, for example, relies heavily on predetermined standards. Because of this reliance, supervisors spend a good deal of time trying to figure out strategies for motivating teachers and encouraging them to change. Supervision becomes a direct, intense, and often exhausting activity as a result.

PERSONAL AUTHORITY

Personal authority is based on the supervisor's ability to use motivational techniques and to practice other interpersonal skills. It is assumed that because of this style of leadership, teachers will want to comply with the supervisor's wishes. When human relations skills become the prime source of authority, the following assumptions are made:

> The goals and interests of teachers and supervisors are not the same. As a result, each must barter with the other so that both get what they want by giving something that the other party wants.

[2]See, for example, Karl Weick, "Educational Organizations as Loosely Coupled Systems," *Administrative Science Quarterly,* vol. 21, no. 2 (1976), pp. 1–19; and Thomas J. Sergiovanni, "Biting the Bullet: Rescinding the Texas Teacher Appraisal System," *Teachers Education and Practice,* vol. 6, no. 2 (Fall/Winter 1990–1991), pp. 89–93 and *Leadership: What's in It for Schools?* London: Falmer Press, 2001.

[3]See, for example, Arthur E. Wise, *Legislated Learning: The Bureaucratization of the American Classroom,* Berkeley: University of California Press, 1979; Susan Rosenholtz, *Teachers' Workplace: The Social Organization of Schools,* New York: Longman, 1989; Linda McNeil, *Contradictions of Control: School Structure and School Knowledge,* New York: Routledge & Kegan Paul, 1986; and Thomas J. Sergiovanni, *Strengthening the Heartbeat: Leading and Learning Together in Schools,* San Francisco: Jossey-Bass, 2005.

Teachers have needs; if these needs are met, the work gets done as required in exchange.

Congenial relationships and harmonious interpersonal climates make teachers content, easier to work with, and more apt to cooperate.

Supervisors must be experts at reading the needs of teachers and handling people in order to barter successfully for increased compliance and performance.

These assumptions lead to a supervisory practice that relies heavily on "what gets rewarded gets done." Emphasis is also given to developing a school climate characterized by a high degree of congeniality among teachers and between teachers and supervisors. Often personal authority is used in combination with bureaucratic authority. When this is the case, very few of the things that the supervisor wants from teachers are negotiable. The strategy is to obtain compliance by trading psychological payoffs of one sort or another.

Personal authority is also important to the practice of human resources supervision. In this case, however, as suggested in Chapter 1, it takes a slightly different twist. The emphasis is less on meeting teachers' social needs and more on providing the *conditions of work* that allow people to meet needs for achievement, challenge, responsibility, autonomy, and esteem—the presumed reasons for finding deep fulfillment in one's job.

The typical reaction of teachers to personal authority, particularly when connected to human relations supervision, is to respond as required when rewards are available but not otherwise. Teachers become involved in their work for calculated reasons, and their performance becomes increasingly narrowed. When the emphasis is on psychological fulfillment that comes from the work itself (emphasizing challenging work, for example) rather than the supervisor's skilled interpersonal behavior, teachers become more intrinsically motivated and thus less susceptible to calculated involvement and narrowing of performance. But in today's supervision, this emphasis remains the exception rather than the rule.

Suggesting that using personal authority and the psychological theories that inform this authority as the basis for supervisory practice may be overdone and may have negative consequences for teachers and students is likely to raise a few eyebrows. Most supervisors, for example, tend to consider knowledge and skill about how to motivate teachers, how to apply the correct leadership style, how to boost morale, and how to engineer the right interpersonal climate as representing the heart of their work. It is for many supervisors the "core technology" of their profession.

We do not challenge the importance of supervision based on personal authority that emphasizes interpersonal themes. Indeed, we argued for its importance in earlier editions. We do question, however, whether this approach to supervision should continue to enjoy the prominence that it does. We believe there is ample evidence for the position that personal and bureaucratic sources of authority should do no more than provide support for a supervisory practice that relies on professional and moral authority. The reasons, we argue here and elsewhere in this book, are that psychologically based leadership and supervision cannot tap the full range and

Examining the effectiveness of various sources of authority raises nagging questions about the overuse of personal authority, for example, why should teachers follow the lead of their supervisors?

> Is it because supervisors know how to manipulate effectively?
>
> Is it because supervisors can meet the psychological needs of teachers?
>
> Is it because supervisors are charming and fun to be with?

or

> Is it because supervisors have something to say that makes sense?
>
> Is it because supervisors have thoughts that point teachers in a direction that captures their imagination?
>
> Is it because supervisors speak from a set of ideas, values, and conceptions that they believe are good for teachers, for students, and for the school?

These questions raise yet another question: Do supervisors want to base their practice on glibness or on substance? Choosing glibness not only raises moral questions but also encourages a vacuous form of leadership and supervisory practice. It can lead to what Abraham Zaleznik refers to as the "managerial mystique," the substitution of process for substance.[*]

[*]Abraham Zaleznik, *The Managerial Mystique: Restoring Leadership in Business,* New York: Harper & Row, 1989.

Exhibit 2–1. The Overuse of Personal Authority in Supervision.

depth of human capacity and will. This source of authority cannot elicit the kind of motivated and spirited response from teachers that will allow schools to work well. We hope to build a case for this assertion in Chapters 4 and 6, where we examine what is important to teachers at work. See Exhibit 2–1 for a summary of overuses of personal authority.

Another reason for our concern with the overuse of personal authority is that there are practically and morally better reasons for teachers and others to be involved in the work of the school than those related to matters of the leader's personality and interpersonal skills. Haller and Strike, for example, believe that building one's expertise around interpersonal themes raises important ethical questions. In their words:

> We find this an inadequate view of the administrative role . . . its first deficiency is that it makes administrative success depend on characteristics that tend to be both intangible and unalterable. One person's dynamic leader is another's tyrant. What one person sees as a democratic style, another will see as the generation of time-wasting committee work. . . . Our basic concern with this view . . . is that it makes the administrative role one of form, not content. Being a successful administrator depends not on the adequacy of one's view, not on the educational policies that one adopts and how reasonable

they are, and not on how successful one is in communicating those reasons to others. Success depends on personality and style, or on carefully chosen ways of inducing others to contribute to the organization. It is not what one wants to do and why that is important; it is who one is and how one does things that counts. We find such a view offensive. It is incompatible with the values of autonomy, reason and democracy, which we see among the central commitments of our society and educational system. Of course educational administrators must be leaders, but let them lead by reason and persuasion, not by forces of personality.[4]

Carl Glickman raises still other doubts about the desirability of basing supervisory practice on psychological authority. He believes that such leadership creates dependency among followers.[5]

PROFESSIONAL AUTHORITY

Professional authority presumes that the expertise of teachers counts, and if this expertise is fully developed, counts the most. Teachers, as is the case with other professionals, are *superordinate* to the knowledge base that supports their practice. Professionals view knowledge as something that informs but does not prescribe practice.[6] What counts as well is the ability of teachers to make judgments based on the specifics of the situations they face. They must decide what is appropriate. They must decide what is right and good. They must, in sum, create professional knowledge in use as they practice. For this reason, teaching cannot be successfully standardized.[7] Teachers, like other professionals, cannot be effective when following scripts. Instead, they need to *create knowledge in use* as they practice, becoming skilled surfers who ride the wave of teaching as it uncurls.[8] This ability requires a high level of reflection, understanding, and skill.

   Professional authority is based on the informed knowledge of the craft of teaching and on the personal expertise of teachers. Teachers respond in part to this expertise and in part to internalized professional values, to accepted tenets of practice that define what it means to be a teacher.

---

[4]Emil J. Haller and Kenneth A. Strike, *An Introduction to Educational Administration: Social, Legal and Ethical Perspectives,* New York: Longman, 1986, p. 326.

[5]Carl D. Glickman, "Right Question, Wrong Extrapolation: A Response to Duffey's 'Supervising for Results,'" *Journal of Curriculum and Supervision,* vol. 6, no. 1 (Fall 1990), pp. 39–40.

[6]Thomas J. Sergiovanni, "The Metaphorical Use of Theories and Models in Supervision: Building a Science," *Journal of Curriculum and Supervision*, vol. 2, no. 3 (1987), pp. 221–232.

[7]See, for example, Linda Darling Hammond, Arthur E. Wise, and S. R. Pease, "Teacher Evaluations in an Organizational Context: A Review of Literature," *Review of Educational Research*, vol. 53, no. 3 (1983), pp. 285–328; Sergiovanni, "The Metaphorical Use of Theories and Models," op. cit.; Lee S. Shulman, "A Union of Insufficiencies: Strategies for Teacher Assessment in a Period of Educational Reform," *Educational Leadership,* vol. 16, no. 3 (1988), pp. 36–41; and Michael Huberman, "The Social Context of Instruction in Schools," Paper presented at American Educational Research Association Annual Meeting, Boston, April 1990.

[8]Thomas J. Sergiovanni, "Will We Ever Have a TRUE Profession?" *Educational Leadership*, vol. 44, no. 8 (1987), pp. 44–51.

When professional authority becomes the primary source for supervisory practice, the following assumptions are made:

Teaching and learning contexts are different; thus, no one best way to practice exists.

"Scientific knowledge" and "professional knowledge" are also different; professional knowledge is created as teachers practice.

The purpose of scientific knowledge is to inform, not prescribe, the practice of teachers and supervisors.

Professional authority is not external but is exercised within the teaching context and from within the teacher.

Authority in context comes from the teacher's training and experience.

Authority from within comes from the teacher's professional socialization and internalized knowledge and values.

Supervisory practice that is based primarily on professional authority seeks to promote a dialogue among teachers that makes explicit professional values and accepted tenets of practice. These are then translated into professional practice standards. With standards acknowledged, teachers are then provided with as much discretion as they want and need. When professional authority is fully developed, teachers will hold each other accountable in meeting these practice standards with accountability internalized. The job of the supervisor is to provide assistance, support, and professional development opportunities. Teachers respond to professional norms, and their performance becomes more expansive.

Though it is common to refer to teaching as a profession, not much attention has been given to the nature of professional authority. When the idea does receive attention, the emphasis is on the expertise of teachers. Building teacher expertise is a long-term proposition. In the meantime much can be done to advance another aspect of professionalism—*professional virtue*. Professional virtue speaks to the norms that define what it means to be a professional. Once established, professional norms take on moral attributes. When professional norms are combined with norms derived from shared community values, moral authority can become a prime basis for supervisory practice.

MORAL AUTHORITY

Moral authority is derived from the obligations and duties that teachers feel as a result of their connection to widely shared community values, assumptions, ideas, research frameworks, and ideals. When moral authority is in place, teachers respond to shared commitments and felt interdependence by creating communities of practice. And schools too take on the characteristics of communities.

Communities are defined by their center of shared values, beliefs, and commitments. In communities, what is considered right and good is as important as what works and what is effective; teachers are motivated as much by emotion and belief as they are by self-interest; collegiality is understood as a form of professional virtue.

In communities, supervisors direct their efforts toward identifying and making explicit shared values and beliefs. These values and beliefs are then transformed into informal norms that govern behavior. With these in place, it becomes possible to promote collegiality as something that is felt internally and that derives from morally driven interdependence. Supervisors can rely less on external controls and more on the ability of teachers as community members to respond to felt duties and obligations. The school community's informal norm system is used to enforce professional and community values. Norms and values, whether derived from professional authority or moral authority, become substitutes for direct supervision as teachers become increasingly self-managing. The four sources of authority for supervision with consequences for practice are summarized in Table 2–1.

LEADING WITH IDEAS

Moral authority is the key to practicing leading with ideas. Once we have made a public commitment to a set of ideas, we are obliged to embody these ideas in our practice. We do not comply simply because of bureaucratic reasons or simply because of the "charm quotients" of our leaders. We comply, instead, because of the commitments we have made. Commitments are in many respects like promises, and promises made should be promises kept. Obligations are important as schools begin to evolve into communities of responsibility.

The effective use of moral authority assumes that the members of a school community have struggled together to decide on the ideas. And the effective use of moral authority assumes that there is sufficient discretion in implementation policies and designs to allow for teachers to make responsive decisions. Without enough discretion teachers will not be able to teach effectively. There is, in other words, a kind of instructional coherence that is general enough to avoid scripting but specific enough to provide direction.

Leading with ideas is particularly important when dealing with accountability. An effective evaluation strategy is a layered one that begins in the classroom and ends at the school district office. Accountability talk (the engagement of learning through talk) is a good example. Teachers create norms of accountability talk in the classroom by modeling, questioning, and leading conversations that help students sharpen their thinking as they address key concepts in their learning standards. An effective accountability talk strategy succeeds when teachers become accountable to their learning community, to the knowledge base for which they are responsible, and for cultivating rigorous thinking. Teachers create norms of accountability when they function as communities of practice that help each other, share student work, plan lessons together, and share the results. Further, they are committed to the idea that what they know and what they learn must be shared with others if it is to serve the common good. But leading with ideas must reach beyond individual students, beyond individual classrooms, beyond individual communities of practice to the school and to the school district as a whole.

TABLE 2–1. The Sources of Authority for Supervisory Policy and Practice

Source	Assumptions When Use of This Source Is Prime	Supervisory Strategy
Bureaucratic authority Hierarchy Rules and regulations Mandates	Teachers are subordinates in a hierarchically arranged system.	"Expect and inspect" is the overarching rule.
Teachers are expected to comply or face consequences.	Supervisors are trustworthy, but you cannot trust teachers very much.	Rely exclusively on predetermined standards to which teachers must measure up.
	Goals and interests of teachers and supervisors are not the same; thus, supervisors must be watchful.	Identify teachers' needs and "in-service" them.
	Hierarchy equals expertise; thus, supervisors know more than teachers.	Directly supervise and closely monitor the work of teachers to ensure compliance.
	External accountability works best.	Figure out how to motivate teachers and get them to change.
Personal authority Motivation technology Interpersonal skills Human relations leadership	The goals and interests of teachers and supervisors are not the same but can be bartered so that all get what they want.	Develop a school climate characterized by congeniality among teachers and between teachers and supervisors.
Teachers will want to comply because of the congenial climate provided and to reap rewards offered in exchange.	Teachers have needs; if those needs are met, the work gets done as required in exchange.	"Expect and reward."
	Congenial relationships and harmonious interpersonal climates make teachers content, easier to work with, and more apt to cooperate.	"What gets rewarded gets done."
	Supervisors must be expert at reading needs and handling people in order to successfully barter for increased compliance and performance.	Use personal authority in combination with bureaucratic authority.
Professional authority Craft knowledge and research findings.	No one best way to practice exists.	Promote a dialogue among teachers that makes explicit professional values and accepted tenets of practice.

TABLE 2–1. (*continued*)

Source	Assumptions When Use of This Source Is Prime	Supervisory Strategy
Teachers respond on basis of common socialization, professional values, accepted tenets of practice, and internalized expertness.	"Scientific" knowledge and "professional" knowledge are different; professional is created in use as teachers practice.	Translate above into professional practice standards.
	The purpose of scientific knowledge is to inform, not prescribe, practice.	Provide teachers with as much discretion as they want and need.
	Authority cannot be exclusively external but comes as well from the context itself and from within the teacher.	Require teachers to hold each other accountable in meeting practice standards.
	Authority from context comes from training and experience.	Make available assistance, support, and professional development opportunities.
	Authority from within comes from socialization and internalized values.	
Moral authority Obligations and duties are derived from widely shared community values, ideas, and ideals.	Schools are professional learning communities.	Identify and make explicit the values and beliefs that define the center of the school as community.
Teachers respond to shared commitments and felt interdependence.	Communities are defined by their center of shared values, beliefs, and commitments.	Translate the above into informal norms that govern behavior.
	In communities:	
	What is considered right and good is as important as what works and what is effective.	Promote collegiality and the development of communities of practice as internally felt and morally driven interdependence.
	People are motivated as much by emotion and beliefs as by self-interest.	Rely on ability of community members to respond to duties and obligations.
	Collegiality is a professional virtue.	Rely on the community's informal norm system to enforce professional and community values.

Source: Thomas J. Sergiovanni, "Moral Authority and the Regeneration of Supervision," in Carl Glickman (ed.), *Supervision in Transition,* 1992 ASCD Yearbook, Alexandria, VA: Association for Supervision and Curriculum Development, 1992, pp. 203–214. © Thomas J. Sergiovanni. See also Sergiovanni, *Moral Leadership: Getting to the Heart of School Improvement.* San Francisco: Jossey-Bass, 1992; and Thomas J. Sergiovanni, *Strengthening the Heartbeat: Leading and Learning Together in Schools,* San Francisco: Jossey-Bass, 2005.

ACCOUNTABILITY WRIT LARGE

In the past it was enough to focus supervision on individual teachers. Supervisors visited teachers to observe teaching. These observations often led to a series of conferences with the supervisor, to the development of individual improvement plans, and to other forms of help.

During the last decade, the province of supervision has been expanded to include groups of teachers that ideally function as small communities of practice. Increasingly, these communities are committed to teachers helping each other learn more about their practice and for teachers to join in a shared practice. More and more the action is shifting away from teachers one at a time to grade levels, departments, teams, and other groupings of teachers. In these settings teachers come to share lesson plans, involve themselves in peer coaching and group clinical supervision, study lessons together, develop common assessments, and use other ways and means to work together with colleagues. These arrangements change the landscape of supervision from supervisors working one-on-one with teachers to teachers working together with the help of both designated and informal supervisors. Common lesson plan files have cropped up in schools here and there. Some schools rarely meet as a whole faculty, preferring to have meeting time that allows departments, grade levels, and other groupings to meet instead. In other places teachers take turns visiting each other's classes and hosting reflective practice conversations.

The province of supervision is changing again as central offices become more involved in instructional leadership. There is no doubt that the individual emphasis and the group emphasis in supervision will remain important. But, as quality supervision continues to join with teacher learning as key levers for improving schools, the emphasis will broaden to include whole school and whole school district change. It is not that individual and group supervision have failed. It is just that instructional coherence across the district is difficult to achieve without an emphasis on the school itself and on the school district itself. And without instructional coherence, school improvement efforts will be less effective.

INSTRUCTIONAL COHERENCE

Newmann, Smith, Allensworth, and Bryk define instructional coherence as "a set of interrelated programs for students and staff that are guided by a common framework for curriculum, instruction, assessment, and learning climate and that are pursued over a sustained period."[9] These researchers found "a strong positive relationship between improving coherence and improving student achievement."[10]

---

[9]Fred M. Newmann, BetsAnn Smith, Elaine Allensworth, and Anthony S. Bryk, "Instructional Program Coherence: What It Is and Why It Should Guide School Improvement Policy," *Educational Evaluation and Policy Analysis,* vol. 23, no. 4 (2001), p. 297.
[10]Ibid., p.305.

There is a thin line between instructional coherence and the kind of excessive standardization that leads to hyper-rationality. The idea is not to reduce the discretion that teachers have but to provide a framework for their decision making that increases their efficacy—the effect they are having on improved student achievement. Instructional coherence should enhance, not undermine, the work of teachers. Newmann, Smith, Allensworth, and Bryk explain:

> It is important to place strong instructional program coherence in perspective and to understand it not as the overriding task of school improvement or as a substitute for key supports for teaching and learning, but as a strategy for maximizing those supports. Strong instructional program coherence could, for instance, undermine the development of teachers' professional community if it insisted on such regimented instruction that teachers had no opportunity to exercise expertise or raise questions about selected methods or programs. . . . Similarly, teachers' professional development opportunities might be made so uniform as to prevent individuals from learning skills unique to their teaching situation or background. The pursuit of greater program coherence must respond to appropriate forms of differentiation and be receptive to new or altered programming for staff and for students when clearly necessary. . . .
>
> A school could become highly coherent (and could even increase student scores on standardized tests) by instituting instructional frameworks that are narrowly focused on the most rudimentary academic tasks. . . . Thus the ultimate value of strong program coherence will always depend on the perceived educational legitimacy of what students learn and how they learn it.[11]

Balance is required between the need for discretion on the one hand and the need for direction on the other. Instructional coherence works best when teachers are able to teach to their strengths. "But teaching whatever they please, whenever they please is not the answer to the problem. Think of coherence as a compass that carefully and deliberately points the way while allowing travelers enough discretion so that they may choose one path over another providing that instructional coherence is not endangered."[12]

ESSPAR: IDEAS IN ACTION

Increasingly, schools are adopting theories of action, usually in the form of assumptions presumed to be true, to back up their leadership. Sometimes these assumptions are based on convictions. But many are research-based. One well-known research-based theory of action is the Principles of Learning developed by the Institute for Learning at the University of Pittsburgh.[13] When linked to standards, the Principles of Learning not only inform what will be taught, they also govern how teachers will teach and how they will be assessed. Yet there are no scripts.

---

[11]Ibid., p. 313. See also Sergiovanni, *Strengthening the Heartbeat,* op. cit., p. 157.
[12]Ibid.
[13]"Principles of Learning," Learning Research and Development Center at the University of Pittsburgh. These principles can be accessed at www.instituteforlearning.org/develop.html.

Plenty of room exists for teachers to use their own creativity and to rely on teaching methods that they understand and enjoy.

A particularly useful framework of ideas that includes tools for assessing and improving schools has been developed by the Panasonic Foundation. Called Essential School System Purpose and Responsibilities (ESSPAR), this research-based framework presents a set of ideas that can be used as a source of authority for assessing where a school is on the road to school improvement, where it would like to be, and what it needs to do to improve. In the foundation's words:

> ESSPAR is a tool for assessing school district progress in achieving high-quality education for all students—what the Panasonic Foundation calls "ALL MEANS ALL." The tool is based on what the Panasonic Foundation takes to be the fundamental purpose of school systems[14] and the eight system responsibilities that are essential to fulfilling that purpose. Implicit in this purpose is the Foundation's firm belief that every child can and will learn at high levels if provided high-quality instruction.[15]

Further, "ESSPAR is designed for use by schools, system leaders, and a district's external partners, to engage in deep introspection, dialogue, and assessment/ self-assessment about systemic reform. The investigative questions under each responsibility will help in continuously examining the gaps between a system's goals and its current reality. The findings should guide the system's improvement efforts."[16]

ESSPAR, which appears in Appendix 2–1, assumes that the purpose of school systems is the education of all students to high levels through high-quality instruction. To successfully meet this purpose, school systems must fulfill eight responsibilities:

1. Clarify and promote the core value that all students can and will learn at high levels.
2. Ensure a culture and climate of care, commitment, collaboration, and continuous improvement.
3. Establish high learning standards and promote standards-based teaching and learning so that all students can learn at high levels.
4. Establish clear and specific performance expectations for all system personnel to support all students meeting the standards.
5. Ensure that all system personnel have the capacity to meet the performance expectations.
6. Allocate fiscal and material resources to support the system's essential purpose and core value.

---

[14]The foundation includes school boards, administrators, teachers, other employees, and unions and associations in its definition of "school system."

[15]The source of all references to ESSPAR in Chapter 2 itself is Panasonic Foundation Discussion Draft 6/25/04, "Essential School System Purpose and Responsibilities (ESSPAR)," p. 1. ESSPAR itself appears in Appendix 2–1: Essential School System Purpose and Responsibilities (ESSPAR) Investigative Questions for Assessing Progress. The source for this material is Essential School System Purpose and Responsibilities (ESSPAR): A Tool for Assessing School System Progress Toward ALL MEANS ALL, Panasonic Foundation Inc., Two Panasonic Way, 7B-0, Secaucus, New Jersey 07094.

[16]Panasonic Foundation Discussion Draft 6/25/04, p. 1.

7. Implement a shared-accountability system that holds students, schools, central office staff, and the system itself accountable for all students meeting high standards.
8. Engage in advocacy, coalitions, and other significant relationships at the school, local, state, and national levels so that the system can achieve its essential purpose and core value.

Carefully review the ESSPAR tool for assessing progress that appears in Appendix 2–1, noting that for each of the eight responsibility areas a bank of investigative questions is provided. Assume that you agree with the ESSPAR approach and you consider the investigative questions useful. Working alone or with a partner, use the assessment protocols to gauge how well the school you choose is doing on the road to school improvement. Use the following directions:

1. For each "how well" question, rate how well the school is progressing using a scale of 1 to 10, with 1 being "not very well at all" and 10 being "very well."[17]
2. For each "how" question, give an example of what the school you are studying is actually doing in this area.
3. Record your responses on the ESSPAR Assessment Tool form that appears in Appendix 2–2.

DISTRIBUTED ACCOUNTABILITY

Frameworks like ESSPAR distribute accountability across various levels of a school district. They create a climate of responsibility that stretches from an individual teacher in his or her classroom in a given school all the way to the central office. At the heart of this climate of accountability is the cultivation of a collective responsibility for the success of the school. Accountability and continuous learning go hand in hand. Accountability helps define what the purposes of learning are, and this is necessary to help those purposes be realized.

In Chapter 1 we mentioned that the greatest asset a school has is its collective IQ. An important challenge for supervision is to aggregate what teachers know, thus enlarging school intelligence and increasing the school's capacity to improve. Those with formal responsibility for supervision as well as those with informal responsibility for supervision are in a good position to help schools get smarter. They can do this by creating communities of practice. Such communities have a shared sense of purpose, engage regularly in accountability talk, and give teachers the discretion that they need to make responsive decisions and to take responsive action. When you think of communities of practice, think of a network of knowledge clusters all across the school. Without these clusters, more limited knowledge monopolies are likely to emerge—monopolies that fence in what they know rather than share it.

---

[17]Our purpose is not to measure anything but to respond to ESSPAR's investigative questions in a way that encourages reflection and conversation among peers. We believe that using the 10-point scale is helpful for this purpose.

The ESSPAR approach to school improvement assumes that the essential purposes, enabling purposes, and responsibilities that people are obligated to embody in their practice can become powerful sources of authority for leadership and school improvement. These sources of authority continue to strengthen as

all system employees have a shared understanding of the school system's essential purpose.

all system employees have a shared understanding of the district's focus on high-quality instruction and of their role in supporting it.

system leaders promote and demonstrate active support for high-quality instruction and learning for all students.

system leaders maintain a single-minded focus on teaching and learning, and enable schools to do so by minimizing diversions and noninstructional burdens on schools.

the system establishes and communicates a shared vision of its future that reflects its essential purpose.

this shared vision drives the system's strategic direction and day-to-day decisions.

Exhibit 2–2. Ideas as Sources of Authority for Supervision.

Source: Summarized from "School System Purpose" in Essential School System Purpose and Responsibilities (ESSPAR): A Tool for Assessing School System Progress Toward ALL MEANS ALL, Panasonic Foundation Inc., Two Panasonic Way, 7B-0 Secaucus, New Jersey 07094.

The success of the Principles of Learning, the ESSPAR framework for school improvement, and other similar ideas depends on a decentralized commitment to a basic principle of empowerment—teachers and others are encouraged to do what they think is right provided that what they do embodies the values and purposes that are shared, serves the common good, and strengthens the character of teaching and learning. For ESSPAR, that means it is OK to take an action as long as it embodies ESSPAR's core values, reflects ESSPAR's purposes, and supports the responsibilities that are believed to be necessary for purposes to be realized. This empowerment rule, which applies to everyone, is illustrated in Exhibit 2–2.

TRUST FIRST

With purposes, values, and frameworks in place, trust may be more important than agreement in building coherence for the long run. If we trust each other, we need not agree on everything for us to work together effectively. If we do not trust each other, it is very likely that if we do not agree, we will not be able to work together.[18] The more teachers, administrators, central office staff, and school-based administrators

[18]Anthony Bryk and Barbara Schneider, *Trust in School: A Core Resource for Improvement*, New York: Russell Sage Foundation, 2002.

trust each other, the more collegial they are likely to be. Together, trust and collegiality immunize schools from the negative effects of disengagement and lack of commitment to what the school or school district is about and is trying to accomplish. With trust and collegiality in place, all that is required is that core assumptions, values, and basic implementing frameworks exit and are used. Under these conditions the best coherence strategy seems to be the following: Start with building trust and use this quality to craft action theories and strategies.

The ESSPAR assessment protocols help schools and school districts build the necessary coherence by providing a compelling statement of purpose and then describing the eight responsibilities that must be embodies in the behavior of everyone in the school and school district. This is the kind of coherence that can strengthen moral authority as the basis for what people do.

SUPERVISION II

Community and professional norms as expressions of moral authority play major roles in Supervision II, the recommended alternative to today's supervisory practice. Chapter 4, "Supervision as Moral Action," and Chapter 8, "Developing Teacher Leadership," extend this theme by examining how moral authority is expressed in day-to-day supervisory practice.

In this section, some of the basic assumptions and underlying principles that differentiate Supervision I from Supervision II are provided. We could have chosen to speak of traditional supervision versus new supervision, principal-centered supervision versus teacher-centered supervision, bureaucratic supervision versus professional supervision, controlling supervision versus capacity building supervision, or some other more descriptive language to contrast the two theories. All these contrasts are helpful and apply. Still, we chose "Supervision I" and "Supervision II" because they are more neutral titles. We thought that with neutral titles, the two theories of supervision would be able to accommodate some disagreements while still letting people buy in to the overall theoretical framework. Supervision II combines Theory Y from human resources supervision with the belief that people are morally responsive and are able to sacrifice self-interests for the right reasons. Supervision I, by contrast, relies heavily on the assumptions of Theory X as described earlier.

In Supervision I, a great deal of emphasis is given to understanding, researching, and improving supervisory *behavior*. Supervision II, by contrast, emphasizes *action*. Behavior is very different from action. Behavior is what we do on the surface. Action implies intentionality and free choice.

Because of this difference between behavior and action, Supervision II focuses more on interpretation. There is concern not only for the way things look but also for what things mean. The metaphors "phonetics" and "semantics" can help explain this distinction.[19] Tending to supervisory and teaching behaviors as they appear on the surface is an example of the phonetic view. It does not matter so much whether

---

[19]Sergiovanni, "Will We Ever Have a TRUE Profession?"

the supervisor is involved in leading, coaching, managing, evaluating, administering, or teaching. If the emphasis in these activities is on "the looks and sounds" of behavior, on the form or shape that this behavior takes as opposed to what the behavior means to teachers and students, the view is phonetic.

Identical behaviors can have different meanings as contexts change and as different people are involved. For example, a supervisor may walk through the classrooms of several teachers on a regular basis, making it a practice to comment to teachers about what is happening and to share her or his impressions. For supervisor A, teachers may consider this behavior inspectorial or controlling and view this supervisor as one who is closely monitoring what they do. For supervisor C, this same behavior may be considered symbolic of the interest and support that the supervisor provides to teachers. In this case, supervisory behavior is interpreted as being caring and helpful. At one level, the phonetic, the behavior is the same for both supervisors. At another level, the semantic, the behavior carries different meanings. When concerned with different interpretations and meanings, one is tending to the semantic aspects of supervision.

Motivation in Supervision I focuses primarily on "what gets rewarded gets done." Motivation in Supervision II is based on "what is rewarding gets done" and "what is believed to be right and good gets done." These latter emphases, as will be discussed in Chapter 15, not only reflect more completely what is important to teachers at work but also result in less emphasis on direct control-oriented supervision. When motivated by intrinsically satisfying and meaningful action, teachers become self-managing.

In Supervision I, it is assumed that supervisors and teachers make "rational" decisions on the basis of self-interest and as isolated individuals. Supervision II recognizes the importance of emotions and values in making decisions and the capacity for humans consistently to sacrifice self-interest as a result. Further, Supervision II recognizes that our connections to other people to a great extent determine what we think, what we believe, and the decisions that we make. These two themes will be explored further in Chapters 3, 5, and 15.

Supervision I takes place in the context of hierarchically differentiated roles. "Supervision" and "designated supervisor" go together. Supervision is something that supervisors do to teachers. A teacher studies to become a supervisor, becomes licensed, and thus is allowed to practice supervision. Supervision, in other words, is a formal and institutionalized process linked to the school's organizational structure.

Supervision II views supervision as both a role and function. Supervision, in other words, is not necessarily shaped by organizational structure and is not necessarily legitimized by credentials. Instead, it is a set of ideals and skills that can be translated into processes that can help teachers and help schools function more effectively. Supervision is something that not only principals and hierarchically designated supervisors do but teachers and others do as well. Thus, such ideas as collegial supervision, mentoring supervision, cooperative supervision, and informal supervision are important in Supervision II. In a sense, these processes are often in place in schools anyway. Teachers respect each other's craft knowledge and typically depend on each other for help. One of the purposes of Supervision II,

therefore, is to deinstitutionalize institutional supervision and to formalize the informal supervision among teachers that now takes place in many schools.

WHAT ABOUT CONTROL?

It is difficult to talk about the sources of authority for supervision without also talking about control. For example, supervision is a process designed to help teachers
and supervisors learn more about their practice, to be better able to use their knowledge and skills to serve parents and schools, and to make the school a more effective learning community. For these goals to be realized, a degree of control over
events is necessary, and in this sense supervision is about control. But it makes a
difference how control is expressed in schools. The wrong kind of control can cause
problems and lead to negative consequences despite the best of intentions.

Control is understood differently in Supervisions I and II. For example, the
management theorist Henry Mintzberg proposed that the work of others can be controlled by

- providing direct and close supervision of what people are doing;
- standardizing the work that needs to be done, then fitting people into the work
  system so that they are forced to follow the approved script;
- standardizing outputs and then evaluating to be sure that output specifications
  have been met;
- socializing people through the use of norms of one sort or another; and
- arranging work circumstances and norms in a way that people feel a need to be
  interdependent.[20]

When referring to socializing people, Mintzberg had in mind professional norms.
The norms that come from common purposes and shared values provide still another control strategy that can be added to Mintzberg's list.[21]

In Chapter 1, supervisor A relied heavily on providing direct supervision, standardizing the work, and standardizing outputs as the preferred ways to control what
teachers were doing and how. By contrast, supervisor D recommended relying on the
process of socialization, building interdependencies, and developing purposes and
shared values. Which of the two views makes the most sense? In part, the answer to
this question depends upon the degree of complexity of the work to be supervised.

Fostering professional socialization, developing purposes and shared values,
and building natural interdependencies among teachers are unique in that they are
able to provide a kind of normative power that encourages people to meet their
commitments. Once in place, the three become substitutes for traditional supervision, since teachers tend to respond from within, becoming self-managing. Since
these strategies do not require direct supervision or the scripting of work, they are

---

[20]Henry Mintzberg, *The Structure of Organizations,* New York: Wiley, 1979.
[21]Karl Weick, "Educational Organizations as Loosely Coupled Systems" *Administrative Science Quarterly*
vol. 21, no. 1, pp. 1–19; and Thomas J. Peters and Robert H. Waterman, *In Search of Excellence,* New York:
Harper & Row, 1982.

better matched to the complex behaviors that are required for teaching and learning to take place successfully. These are the strategies that provide the framework for control in Supervision II.

Differences between Supervision I and Supervision II can be summarized as follows:

Supervision I emphasizes:	*Supervision II emphasizes:*
Theory X assumptions	Theory Y assumptions
teaching and learning as behavior	teaching and learning as action
phonetics only	phonetics and semantics
extrinsic motivation	intrinsic and moral motivation
self-interest	the common good
supervisory roles	supervisory functions
supervisory structures	culture of supervision
managing	self-managing

THE IMPORTANCE OF CAPACITY BUILDING

From the discussion so far, it appears that Supervision II is the preferred method and no room exists for practices associated with Supervision I. Similarly, bureaucratic and personal authority should be abandoned for leadership and supervision based on professional and moral authority. But the reality is that ideas from both views of supervision have a place in a unified and contextually oriented practice. Most teachers have a natural inclination to respond to Supervision II. As this approach comes to dominate supervisory practice, schools will very likely be better places for teachers and students. But some teachers will not be ready to respond. Others may want to respond but lack the necessary knowledge and skill to function in this new environment. Furthermore, in many places the existing culture of teaching does not encourage the practices associated with Supervision II. What should supervisors do?

We believe the answer is to start where teachers are now and to begin the struggle to change the existing norms in schools so that Supervision II becomes acceptable. Of particular importance in this struggle will be the emphasis supervisors give to capacity building. Take teacher leadership, for example. Before we can expect teachers to accept fuller responsibility for providing leadership, they must be encouraged to do so and they must know how to provide this leadership. Both of these goals are best achieved when teachers are members of a support network that strives to become a community of leaders. For teachers to be developers and supervisors of classroom learning communities, they must be part of a learning community themselves. Capacity building and changing school norms are what Michael Fullan describes as "reculturing."[22] Whatever is the focus of supervisory work, if Supervision II is to be the framework for embodying that focus, then reculturing will be at the heart of supervisory work.

[22]Michael Fullan, *Change Forces: The Sequel,* London: Falmer Press, 1999.

SUMMARY

In this chapter we have examined the sources of authority that supervisors can use to bring about improvements in their schools. We have identified four sources: bureaucratic authority, personal authority, professional authority, and moral authority. The strengths of each of the four are discussed, as are their underlying assumptions. Professional authority and moral authority are recommended because of their ability to connect people morally to each other, to their work, and to their responsibilities. Particular attention is given to the use of idea-based leadership. Examples discussed are the Principles of Learning framework developed at the University of Pittsburgh by Lauren Resnick and her colleagues[23] and Essential School System Purpose and Responsibilities (ESSPAR), developed by the Panasonic Foundation. ESSPAR is a tool for assessing a school's progress or a school system's progress toward reaching its school-improvement objectives. Readers are then invited to use the ESSPAR tool to assess a school with which they are familiar. The chapter ends with a comparison of Supervision I and Supervision II, pointing out that Supervision II is the preferred theory because of its ability to build the capacities of teachers and schools.

SOME REFLECTIONS

1. The Principle of Empowerment says that teachers and others are encouraged to do what they think is right, provided that what they do embodies the values and purposes that are shared, serves the common good, strengthens the character of teaching and learning, and supports our culture. How would teachers feel about trading this kind of loyalty and fidelity to purposes and norms in exchange for discretion? Try asking some teachers that you know.
2. Carefully review the ESSPAR Investigative Questions for Assessing Progress, which appear as Appendix 2–1. Then, joining with a colleague or two, use the questions to assess your school. Where are you now in meeting each of the eight responsibilities? Recognizing that Rome was not built in a day, develop a strategy and a plan of action designed to improve your school's efforts. Remember that in the end, changes in thinking and in behavior involve changes in a school's culture. Share your work with others.
3. Yes, instructional coherence is important, but what safeguards are necessary to ensure that coherence does not become a script that everyone must follow?

Appendix 2–1
Essential School System Purpose and Responsibilities (ESSPAR) Investigative Questions for Assessing Progress

School System Purpose

The essential purpose of school systems is the education of all students to high levels through high-quality instruction—All Means All—so that they may use their minds well and become productive, responsible citizens.

---

[23]"Principles of Learning," Learning Research and Development Center at the University of Pittsburgh. See www.instituteforlearning.org.

School System Responsibilities

Based on the essential purpose, the essential responsibilities of school systems are as follows:

Responsibility 1: Core Value

To clarify and promote the core value that all students can and will learn at high levels

   1a. Does the system have an explicit statement of this value? Do principals, teachers, and central office personnel articulate this value in the same way? How? How well?

   1b. Do system employees at all levels demonstrate the belief that all students can and will learn at high levels? How? How well?

   1c. Do the system's policies, structure, and practices express, reflect, and embody this value? How? How well?

   1d. Does this value drive decision making? How? How well?

   1e. Is this value sustained over time and through changes in leadership? How? How well?

Responsibility 2: Culture and Climate

To ensure a culture and climate of care, commitment, collaboration, and continuous improvement

   2.a Do system leaders promote a genuine concern for and commitment to the success of all students? How? How well?

   2.b Do system leaders promote a climate of trust, respect, honesty, and openness at all levels and among all stakeholder groups? How? How well?

   2.c. Do system leaders promote a culture of risk taking to find solutions and support learning from both success and failure? How? How well?

   2.d Do system leaders promote active, two-way communication among stakeholders? How? How well?

   2.e Are decision-making processes clear, transparent, adhered to, and effectively communicated? How? How well?

   2.f Do system leaders take special care to hear from students and those closest to the students—i.e., parents and school staff? How? How well?

   2.g Do system leaders create a culture of continuous improvement to ensure that the quality of learning improves for every student? How? How well?

Responsibility 3: Standards-Based Teaching and Learning

To establish high learning standards and define the instructional practices and structures that will result in all students learning at high levels

   3.a Has the system established explicit content and performance standards and curriculum frameworks that define high-quality student learning in all the content areas? Are they aligned with each other? How? How well?

   3.b Do the learning standards guide the work of students, teachers, principals, and central office personnel? How? How well?

   3.c Are standards regularly communicated to parents, students, and other stakeholders? How? How well?

   3.d Has the system clearly defined, described, and communicated—especially to instructional staff—the quality of instructional practice necessary for students to achieve standards? How? How well?

Responsibility 4: Performance Expectations for Staff

To establish clear and explicit performance expectations for all system personnel to support—directly or indirectly—all students meeting high standards

4.a Does the system have explicit performance expectations for all personnel in the district? How? How well?

4.b Do the performance expectations at all levels for all personnel—instructional and non-instructional—express explicitly and clearly how each role/position/function supports student learning? How? How well?

4.c Do the performance expectations include the responsibility to engage in continuous improvement by regularly examining practice in light of results? How? How well?

Responsibility 5: Professional Learning and Human Resources

To ensure that all system personnel have the capacity to meet the performance expectations

5.a Are principals, teachers, instructional coaches, and noninstructional staff recruited, inducted, and assigned to meet each school's unique instructional needs? How? How well?

5.b Does the system recruit, induct, and assign all other personnel so that the "right" people are in the right positions? How? How well?

5.c Does the system provide high quality instructional leaders for all classrooms in all schools? How? How well?

5.d Does the system provide effective leadership at all levels in support of high-quality instruction? How? How well?

5.e Does the system's professional development plan continuously build the capacity of all personnel to meet their performance expectations? How? How well?

5.f Is professional development based on analyses of data revealing unique student needs in particular settings and at particular levels? How? How well?

5.g Does the system provide professional development for its personnel at all levels to use data appropriately? How? How well?

5.h Are professional development activities evaluated in terms of their impact on teaching and learning outcomes? How? How well?

Responsibility 6: Fiscal and Material Resources

To ensure that the allocation of fiscal and material resources supports the system's essential purpose, especially at the school level

6.a Are the system's fiscal and material resources allocated and aligned to support the system's essential purpose? How? How well?

6.b Are the system's fiscal and material resources allocated to schools equitably (not necessarily equally) on the basis of individual school needs, so that all schools can serve all students well? How? How well?

Responsibility 7: Accountability

To implement a shared-accountability system that holds students, schools, central office staff, and the system itself accountable for all students meeting high standards

7.a Does the system hold students, schools, central office staff, and the system itself accountable for the achievement of learning standards by all students? How? How well?

7.b Does the system hold itself accountable for providing timely and effective support and assistance for all schools, but especially for schools where students are not meeting standards? How? How well?

7.c Does the system hold all personnel and itself accountable for meeting performance expectations? How? How well?

7.d Are multiple forms of assessment that are aligned with learning standards, as well as other indicator, used to measure student achievement and school progress—both in the short term and over time? How? How well?

7.e Does the system provide accurate, timely, appropriately disaggregated, and user-friendly data to schools? How? How well?

7.f Is instructional, organizational, and policy decision making at all levels driven by data? How? How well?

7.g Is student progress in meeting standards regularly and effectively communicated to students, parents, and the community? How? How well?

Responsibility 8: Advocacy and Engagement

To engage in advocacy, coalitions, and other significant relationships at the school, local, state, and national levels so that the system can achieve its essential purpose and core value

8.a Does the system give voice to and advocate for students and families, especially those who traditionally have been underserved? How? How well?

8.b Does the system support schools in developing partnerships with families and the community in order to achieve the essential purpose and core value? How? How well?

8.c Do system and school leaders mobilize and sustain broad internal and community support for the core value? How? How well?

8.d Do system leaders advocate at the local, state, and national levels for policies, practices, and resources needed to achieve the system's essential purpose and core value? How? How well?

Source: Essential School System Purpose and Responsibilities (ESSPAR): A Tool for Assessing School System Progress Toward ALL MEANS ALL, Panasonic Foundation Inc., Two Panasonic Way, 7B-0, Secaucus, New Jersey 07094. Used with permission. Please note that the tool for recording ESSPAR Assessment responses appears as Appendix 2–2.

Appendix 2–2
ESSPAR Assessment Tool

1. *Core Value*

1.a How well

   Not very well   1   2   3   4   5   6   7   8   9   10   Very well

   How _____

1.b How well

        Not   1   2   3   4   5   6   7   8   9   10   Very

How _____

_____

1.c How well

        Not   1   2   3   4   5   6   7   8   9   10   Very

How _____

_____

1.d How well

        Not   1   2   3   4   5   6   7   8   9   10   Very

How _____

_____

1.e How well

        Not   1   2   3   4   5   6   7   8   9   10   Very

How _____

_____

2.   *Culture and Climate*

2.a How well

        Not   1   2   3   4   5   6   7   8   9   10   Very

How _____

_____

2.b How well

        Not   1   2   3   4   5   6   7   8   9   10   Very

How _____

_____

2.c How well

        Not   1   2   3   4   5   6   7   8   9   10   Very

How _____

_____

2.d How well

        Not   1   2   3   4   5   6   7   8   9   10   Very

How _____

_____

2.e How well

        Not   1   2   3   4   5   6   7   8   9   10   Very

How _____

_____

2.f How well

        Not   1   2   3   4   5   6   7   8   9   10   Very

How _____

_____

2.g How well

        Not   1   2   3   4   5   6   7   8   9   10   Very

How _____

_____

3. *Standards-Based Teaching and Learning*

3.a How well

        Not   1   2   3   4   5   6   7   8   9   10   Very

How _____

_____

3.b How well

        Not   1   2   3   4   5   6   7   8   9   10   Very

How _____

_____

3.c How well

        Not   1   2   3   4   5   6   7   8   9   10   Very

How _____

_____

3.d How well

        Not   1   2   3   4   5   6   7   8   9   10   Very

How _____

_____

4. *Performance Expectations for Staff*

4.a How well

        Not   1   2   3   4   5   6   7   8   9   10   Very

How _____

_____

4.b   How well

Not   1   2   3   4   5   6   7   8   9   10   Very

How _____

_____

4.c   How well

Not   1   2   3   4   5   6   7   8   9   10   Very

How _____

_____

5.   *Professional Learning and Human Resources*

5.a   How well

Not   1   2   3   4   5   6   7   8   9   10   Very

How _____

_____

5.b   How well

Not   1   2   3   4   5   6   7   8   9   10   Very

How _____

_____

5.c   How well

Not   1   2   3   4   5   6   7   8   9   10   Very

How _____

_____

5.d   How well

Not   1   2   3   4   5   6   7   8   9   10   Very

How _____

_____

5.e   How well

Not   1   2   3   4   5   6   7   8   9   10   Very

How _____

_____

5.f   How well

Not   1   2   3   4   5   6   7   8   9   10   Very

How _____

_____

5.g How well

        Not   1   2   3   4   5   6   7   8   9   10   Very

How _____

_____

5.h How well

        Not   1   2   3   4   5   6   7   8   9   10   Very

How _____

_____

6.   *Fiscal and Material Resources*

6.a How well

        Not   1   2   3   4   5   6   7   8   9   10   Very

How _____

_____

6.b How well

        Not   1   2   3   4   5   6   7   8   9   10   Very

How _____

_____

7   *Accountability*

7.a How well

        Not   1   2   3   4   5   6   7   8   9   10   Very

How _____

_____

7.b How well

        Not   1   2   3   4   5   6   7   8   9   10   Very

How _____

_____

7.c How well

        Not   1   2   3   4   5   6   7   8   9   10   Very

How _____

_____

7.d How well

        Not   1   2   3   4   5   6   7   8   9   10   Very

How _____

_____

7.e How well

        Not   1   2   3   4   5   6   7   8   9   10   Very

     How _____

     _____

7.f How well

        Not   1   2   3   4   5   6   7   8   9   10   Very

     How _____

     _____

7.g How well

        Not   1   2   3   4   5   6   7   8   9   10   Very

     How _____

     _____

8.   *Advocacy and Engagement*

8.a How well

        Not   1   2   3   4   5   6   7   8   9   10   Very

     How _____

     _____

8.b How well

        Not   1   2   3   4   5   6   7   8   9   10   Very

     How _____

     _____

8.c How well

        Not   1   2   3   4   5   6   7   8   9   10   Very

     How _____

     _____

8.d How well

        Not   1   2   3   4   5   6   7   8   9   10   Very

     How _____

     _____

CHAPTER 3

Supervising the Learning Community

INTRODUCTION

In this chapter we take up a metaphor for the context of supervisory practice—the learning community. This metaphor for the school has come increasingly to the fore as schools have struggled to meet the rising expectations of the state and federal governments and the public at large. In the literature, the primary focus is on the professional learning community of teachers. Our treatment, however, begins with the students as necessary and authentic members of the school as a learning community. Their learning is at the core of what the school stands for. Furthermore, their sense of being a community is no longer a given; it must be actively co-constructed by both the learners and the professionals in the school. After our treatment of the students as an integral part of the learning community, we then turn to the teachers and the recent development of their work as continually involving learning. The key to the learning of both student and teacher subcommunities in the school is reflective practice—the activity of reflecting on whether the activity one is engaged in is producing the intended results.

Learning through reflective practice represents a new view of teacher learning. Therefore, we spend time attempting to map the particulars of what learning through reflective practice looks like, so that supervisors may better understand how to facilitate it in their work with teachers. Toward the end of the chapter we turn to how a learning community might get off the ground. There we explore how the initial steps in the building of a learning community might be structured and how supervisors can support these initial building efforts.

SOME BACKGROUND

Community is a problem for students. The external social and cultural supports within which individuals and communities forged a relatively stable identity and life course, within which communities established customs and patterns, traditions and norms for guiding their collective life together have disappeared for all but a fraction of the human race. Lacking those supports, individuals and communities have to engage in a much more active and flexible creation of themselves and their social relationships.[1] Lacking more stable norms and traditions, individuals and communities are engaging in more and more short-term, pragmatic agreements about their personal and social relationships. This takes place not only in the workplace and the political arena but also in the family. One hears references to the postmodern family home as a busy train station where both children and parents check in for brief moments to catch their breath and touch base before rushing off to their next commitments or activities, whether that is serving on the local school committee, flying off to a corporate meeting on the opposite coast, coaching Little League, taking the weekly exercise class, driving Laura to her soccer game, or taking Larry to his Cub Scout meeting.

Schools face the fallout from this thinning of family and community ties in the attendant loss of social capital. Parents work longer hours, often dropping their children off for preschool and picking them up from the after-school program on their way home from work. Other children bring to school additional debilitating conditions, such as severe poverty, the effects of family dysfunction, neighborhood violence, and substance abuse in the home, further depleting social capital. Finally, schools also have an increasingly multicultural student body to accommodate, often recent immigrants and second-language learners. The accumulated impact of these influences works against the schools' mission to prepare young people for participation in social, civic, and political life.[2] The school reform agenda has all but neglected this aspect of schooling in its unrelenting focus on academic achievement.

Nevertheless, schools as well as all other institutions in conditions of postmodernity or late modernity, have to face the challenge of *constructing* community. Community is no longer a given to which we simply adjust. Community in the postmodern world is a much more fluid, pragmatically constructed, multidimensional phenomenon. Postmodern communities are constituted by their diversity, find enrichment through pluralism, engage members in pragmatic processes of self-government that promote both personal growth and at least minimal community commitment as inescapably mutually interdependent responsibilities.

LINKING COMMUNITY TO LEARNING: COMMUNITY FOR LEARNING

Given the increasingly common experience in many schools of student diversity and the growing indications from research that a student's culture, class, and gender affect not only what the student learns but also the student's readiness to learn,

---

[1] Anthony Giddens, *Modernity and Self-Identity: Self and Society in Late Modern Age,* Stanford, CA: Stanford University Press, 1991.
[2] John I. Goodlad and Timothy J. McMannon (eds.), *The Public Purpose of Education and Schooling,* San Francisco: Jossey-Bass, 1997; and T. H. Marshall, *Class Citizenship and Social Development,* Chicago: University of Chicago Press, 1964.

schools facing the demands of the policy community for school improvement are realizing that there is no "one size fits all" collection of instructional strategies. Teachers need to know, for example, how the student's native language nuances the meanings that English words and phrases have; how social class attitudes affect the values attributed to various cultural phenomena, such as authority, style, and gender roles; how gender socialization affects the student's ability to enter into collaborative learning arrangements. In other words, students use their lifeworlds, their everyday worlds outside of school, as the interpretive landscape for what they are learning in school, as well as normative sources for classroom behavior. This does not destroy the possibility for common learning in a classroom, but it does initially make it problematic. If classroom instruction ignores, or worse, disparages that lifeworld, then learning is impeded. If, on the other hand, teachers communicate an acceptance of the diversity that is in the classroom, attempt to understand each student's background and to relate the lesson to that background, students will feel included, connected to the learning tasks of the class. Those classrooms that require each student to talk about her or his background, that expect each student to respect the diverse backgrounds represented in the class, and that explicitly connect the classroom learning to elements in that background will have begun to create a sense of community, which is valuable in itself and as a support to the learning agenda of that class. From this perspective, then, we may speak of the importance of community for schools to be able to respond to the national and state agendas for improved student learning for all.

COMMUNITY AS CURRICULUM

Besides the importance of students' experiencing a sense of community as a healthy environment for learning their academic lessons, there are other reasons for schools to develop a greater sense of community. Given the present fragmentation of civil society under the pressures of increasing diversity, a diversity caused by immigration but also heightened by the spread of identity politics, by the rapidity of technological change, and by the erosion of traditions and other stable sources for community identity, the social purposes of schooling require new attention. In the past, it was generally assumed that schools were the place where children from different racial and cultural and social class backgrounds would mingle and learn to get along, would not only tolerate difference but would learn and embrace a common identity. Aside from a standard course in civics, students would be gradually socialized through the daily interactions with the dominant culture as it was taught and as it was transmitted through the general environment of the school. The agenda of school renewal, by its silence on the social purposes of schooling, seems to take this prior assumption of socialization by osmosis for granted. Conditions of late or postmodernity challenge the wisdom of this inattention to the social purposes of schooling. Rather, those conditions suggest that schools need to be far more proactive in teaching students how to construct and reconstruct community. Those conditions suggest that there needs to be a curriculum *of* community, a curriculum that intentionally and explicitly attends to the building up of knowledge, skills, and dispositions which constitute the work of becoming and sustaining a community.[3]

Teachers and administrators are challenged to map out the various opportunities for learning how to be a community whether those learning opportunities are to be found in the academic program, in co-curricular activities, or through a broad array of institutional structures and processes. The curriculum of community is not one course, or a cluster of courses. Rather, it is a sequence of multiple learning activities spread out over the whole K–12 curriculum, some of which take place in the classroom through deliberations of how the class will comport itself; some of which are explicitly connected to learnings in the academic subjects, such as geography, history, literature, science, world languages, and art; some of which take place on the playground, in the cafeteria, or on the school bus; some of which may be learned in group communication exercises run by the guidance department or homeroom teachers, some of which may be learned in school-sponsored special events for grandparents and parents.

The curriculum of community is taught by the establishment and maintenance of a school honor code; by frequent reference to schoolwide core values; by the daily engagement of student conflict-resolution teams; in activities conducted by the student government and student court; in school-sponsored community service activities; through big brother–big sister arrangements; through peer tutoring programs; through the dramatization of student issues in dramas, musical comedies, and artistic displays; through special assemblies where civic community issues are deliberated. The curriculum of community is explicitly taught in all the co-curricular activities of the school as well, through the exercise of teamwork, and contributing to a sense of pride in the school. The adults in the school could develop a notebook of actual and potential learning activities that make up the curriculum of community, which they agree will be taught by everyone in the school, including the support staff, cafeteria workers, and custodians, applying those learnings consistently in the design of various interactions they have with children at various grade levels in developmentally appropriate ways. Every year, faculty, staff, students, and parents could add new suggestions to the notebook of learning activities.

Obviously, this curriculum will be constructed over several years by the educators and staff at the school, with the help of parents, district professionals, and students themselves. It will grow out of a commitment to make the school a humane and socially nurturing environment in which the pursuit of academic learning will go hand in hand with social learning. The curriculum will build on the very basic experiences of people being present to one another, learning to trust one another, to talk to one another and share stories. It will progress to more intentional and explicit focus on the active establishment and maintenance of a culture and of structures that support community.

The curriculum of community flows from understanding community in late modernity as a complex, multidimensional, fluid, contested, and pragmatic

---

[3]Robert J. Starratt, "Community as Curriculum," in Kenneth Leithwood and Philip Hallinger (eds.), *Second International Handbook of Educational Leadership and Administration,* London: Kluwer, 2002, pp. 321–348.

phenomenon. It is built upon and sustained by relationships of interpersonal mutuality, by a mutual presence to a shared common work or activity, by shared responsibilities and rights of membership, and by mutual commitments of loyalty. This curriculum recognizes that community has to be actively constructed every day by the members of that community, for the agreements of today may sow the disagreements of tomorrow. It also recognizes that a contemporary community inescapably involves diversity and the politics of identity, and so it builds in structures and processes to negotiate and honor difference, to find common ground as well as time and space for a variety of interests. In all this, it insists on processes of deliberation. Finally, this curriculum explicitly attends to the institutionalization of communal self-governance, thereby sowing the seeds for more adult participation in a democratic community.

In community, individuals learn the very basic disposition to being a social human being in sharing the experiences of everyday life. Gabarino suggests that the single most important resource to promote resiliency in children is a relationship with at least one caring adult. Ideally, that is the parent–child relationship.[4] Additional experiences with caring adults in school only add to the development of resiliency in children. There they learn trust. There they learn the basic human responses of being present to the other, paying attention, listening, feeling empathy, as well as the experiences of interdependence and responsiveness. Add experiences of friendship and cooperation with other children and that sense of self-efficacy continues to grow.

As the child grows in a supportive community, he or she discovers that there are rules by which the community governs itself, by which the community protects the rights of each member. These rules gradually communicate a sense of responsibility to respect other members in the community, and an understanding that everyone has to take responsibility for preserving and sustaining the community through those common agreements. Developmentally, children progress toward an understanding of communal self-governance, and as that understanding develops, the foundations of democratic governance can be introduced.

Ample evidence supports this position. When accompanied by a strong commitment to learning and when accompanied by steps that demonstrate this commitment to students, building community in schools leads to improved student performance.[5] Further, providing for the affiliative needs of teachers, parents, and students, and focusing on the common good, lead to improved student behavior, stronger bonds of collegiality among the faculty, and more productive relationships with parents.[6]

---

[4]James Gabarino, *Raising Children in a Socially Toxic Environment,* San Francisco: Jossey-Bass, 1995.

[5]See, for example, James Coleman and Thomas Hoffer, *Public and Private High Schools: The Impact of Communities,* New York: Basic Books, 1987; and Anthony S. Bryk and Mary E. Driscoll, *The School as Community: Theoretical Foundations, Contextual Influences and Consequences for Teachers and Students,* Madison, WI: National Center for Effective Secondary Schools, 1988.

[6]See, for example, Penny B. Sebring and Anthony S. Bryk, "Student-Centered Learning Climate," in Sebring et al., *Charting Reform in Chicago: The Students Speak,* Report sponsored by the Consortium on Chicago School Research, Chicago: University of Chicago, 1996.

But there are other reasons why community is important. Supervisors, for example, need to be clear about what they are doing to further the sense of community in their schools. The concern is not simply to facilitate the smooth running of their school, but to teach those life lessons needed to support a healthy public life. With this in mind, the promotion of school community should do more than foster bonds of friendship and respect among students, emphasize the satisfaction of working together to achieve a successful completion of a team project or competition, teach the benefits of collaborative learning, or develop a proud sense of membership in a collective identity. While promoting these desirable aspects of community, supervisors must also foster those political skills needed to participate in the contested process of setting public policy, to partake in adjudicating and arbitrating community conflicts over policy implementation, and to join those groups that concern themselves with managing the affairs of a self-governing polity. In other words, educating in and for community means not only developing satisfying relationships that embrace the wholeness of the persons involved, but also teaching the responsibilities of membership in community, the responsibilities of citizenship.

THE LEARNING COMMUNITY OF TEACHERS

As the influential study of Lieberman and Miller in the early 1990s documented, the majority of teachers inhabited a culture of classroom isolation.[7] Although that has begun to change, Day and Harris maintain that isolation remains the standard condition for most teachers, even today.[8] For those teachers there is little or no time for reflection. Their learning opportunities are haphazard, fragmented, and discontinuous. Reflecting on the classroom experience alone, like bowling alone,[9] is no fun, especially when it may reveal shortcomings and the need to change. Lacking opportunities to share their reflections with other teachers, teachers seldom ask or recognize *why* certain teaching practices work and others do not. Their practice is not publicly accessible for analysis. Clearly, they cannot be said to belong to a learning community.

Nevertheless, these same teachers are faced with the demands of the state to hold themselves accountable for the high quality of learning for all their students. The benchmarks for high-quality learning are expressed in more rigorous state curriculum standards. The measure of learning the material contained in those standards is now assessed by exams, the results of which are made public.

As Richard Elmore contends, these new demands require schoolwide instructional expertise that is beyond what the majority of schools can deliver.[10] Part of the

---

[7]Ann Lieberman and Lynne Miller, *Teachers, Their World and Their Work,* New York: Teachers College Press, 1992.

[8]Chris Day and Alma Harris, "Teacher Leadership, Reflective Practice, and School Improvement," in Leithwood and Hallinger (eds.), Kluwer, pp. 957–977.

[9]Robert Putnam, *Bowling Alone: The Collapse and Renewal of American Community,* New York: Simon & Schuster, 2000.

[10]Richard Elmore, *Building a New Structure for School Leadership,* Washington, DC: Albert Shanker Institute, Winter 2000.

problem is that the depth of subject-matter knowledge demanded by state standards is beyond what most teachers have mastered. If the teachers (as well as school administrators) cannot pass the state exams their students are taking, how can they be expected to prepare their students to take them? The other part of the problem is that teachers have not been asked to come together and agree upon what might constitute good instructional practice in teaching this more demanding curriculum so that all students learn it well. The schools are currently facing a teaching-capacity deficit, and this deficit can be corrected only by a continuous, schoolwide and districtwide effort aimed precisely at building that capacity.

This pressure on schools has been relentless for the past 20 years. The response has been to reinvent the school as a learning community. Teachers, supervisors, and administrators have had to relearn what they need to understand and practice to meet the demands of these more rigorous expectations. They have had to do this without any clear and surefire solutions on the horizon. They have had to reinvent themselves and master the new knowledge and skills that will generate improved student learning for all, especially for those previously underperforming segments of the student body. In the process, they had to move from a relatively superficial provision of equal *opportunity* to succeed to a rigorously tested accountability *for* student success. The focus moved from standardized teaching to high-quality, measurable student learning. Schools were to be evaluated on results rather than good intentions.

Some of the early research shows that, with a combination of administrative and teacher leadership, schools that have reinvented themselves as learning communities have begun to show improved results on state and local assessments.[11] As the culture of the school gradually—and usually painfully—transitions from one of teacher isolation, autonomy, and low accountability to one of teacher collaboration, team learning, and shared accountability, the professional morale of teachers grows alongside an increased sense of collective efficacy.[12]

THE LEARNING PROCESS IN A LEARNING COMMUNITY

For supervisors to carry on their work with teachers in this change toward a collaborative culture, it is important for them to understand the changed perspective on teacher learning when it is situated in a learning community. Day and Harris, as well as Lieberman and Miller, explain how teachers in a learning community learn through reflective practice in a community of practice.[13] In the past, the model for teacher learning was based on the assumption of the need for some external stimulus, such as required reading of a journal essay, a presentation by an outside expert, a graduate course at a nearby university, attendance at a seminar or workshop outside the district. Teacher learning was often tied to professional development or

[11]Richard DuFour and Robert Eaker, *Professional Learning Communities at Work: Best Practices for Enhancing Student Achievement*, Bloomington, IN: National Education Service, 1998.
[12]Ann Lieberman and Lynne Miller, *Teacher Leadership*, San Francisco: Jossey-Bass, 2004.
[13]Day and Harris, op. cit.; and Lieberman and Miller, op. cit.

in-service activities, frequently chosen by administrators. This deficit model of learning assumed that the teacher would be exposed to new ideas and then encouraged to try out the new ideas in the classroom. While some of this external stimulation or guidance may still be necessary, the emerging understanding of teacher learning places learning much closer to the daily practice in the classroom. This learning has been labeled "reflective practice" by Donald Schön,[14] and has almost become the mantra of the learning community. In their work with individual teachers or teams of teachers, supervisors need to become adept at encouraging and facilitating reflective practice. What follows is an attempt to interpret that concept.

PRIMARY AND SECONDARY REFLECTIVE PRACTICE

We can distinguish between *primary* and *secondary* reflective practice. Primary reflective practice happens in the actual activity of teaching something to a group of students. Secondary reflective practice takes place after the teaching activity, as a teacher reflects back on the lesson and asks what worked and what didn't work in the prior class; secondary reflective practice can also take place before the teaching activity, as a teacher thinks back on what has worked well when teaching the upcoming lesson in the past, and plans the teaching activity to come.

Primary reflective practice is a dynamic dialogue between the guiding ideas and hunches of the teacher and the actions of teaching; the actions modify as well as express the ideas, and the ideas illuminate both the positive and negative outcomes of the teaching activity. The teacher initiates and guides the activity of instruction with certain ideas, such as the idea of gravity (the topic of the curriculum unit), and the idea of curiosity as a motivator for student learning. As the students' engagement in the lesson unfolds, the teacher is receiving perceptual and verbal feedback on the effects of the instruction by observing students' responses. Those feedback messages may suggest, for example, that the motivational ideas work well for most of the students, but not all of them, and therefore the ideas about motivation have to be modified. The feedback messages may suggest that the teacher needs to appeal to more sensory experiences of the learners for them to begin to grasp the notion of gravity. By modifying the ideas embedded in the initial instructional activity, the teacher then adapts the activity. This is done in an attempt to discover whether a new or modified idea suggested by the feedback and now embedded in a changed instructional activity results in improved learning. Such as activity could be an experiment that requires more student hands-on contact with the material instead of having the teacher demonstrate the experiment. Thus, as the class unfolds, the dialogue between ideas and activities goes on as the teacher monitors the effects of the activities on student learning.

Reflective practice begins by being alert to what one is attempting to teach, how one is actively engaging the students through instructional activity, how students

---

[14]Donald A. Schön, *The Reflective Practitioner: How Professionals Think in Action,* New York: Basic Books, 1983.

are responding to this instructional activity, and whether it is enabling them to perform the desired learning. This process of ideas guiding action is accompanied by
reflective monitoring, which continues to guide the action in an unfolding dynamic
flow of reflective activity in which the practice and reflection are simultaneously
talking to one another as the teaching activity unfolds. This is primary reflective
practice.

Primary reflective practice then becomes the source for subsequent reflective
practice, either as reflection on the teaching activity after the recently completed
class or as reflection about how to modify that teaching activity in future classes.
That is what is meant by secondary reflective practice.

As regards primary reflective practice, there is no guarantee that the monitoring
of the fit between ideas and actions in the internal dialogue of reflection will *necessarily* help the situation. The reflector, the teacher, may be limited in her or his ability to reflect—because of limitations in understanding of the subject matter, because
of limitations of instructional versatility, because of limited understanding of the
students in the classroom, or because of limitations in the emotional maturity that
would enable reasonably accurate self-criticism. Some or all of these limitations
will affect how the teacher interprets the feedback messages from students, and how
the teacher responds to the feedback. Usually, a more experienced teacher will have
overcome many of those limitations. However, if the reflective practice takes place
in an isolated individual teacher, then the chances for overcoming those limitations
are lessened.

When that reflective practice takes place with other teachers in a form of
secondary reflective practice on a prior lesson, then the sharing of insights, knowledge of students, knowledge of the curriculum material, and versatility in designing
effective learning activities will provide a larger emotional and intellectual landscape against which to view one's individual practice.

This collegial sharing is the key to the necessity for and power of a learning
community. As groups of teachers grow accustomed to the experience of listening
to others talk about their teaching and about the complexities of student learning,
they will grow more comfortable in sharing their classroom experiences. They will
begin to recognize a shared calling to transform their work in progressively small,
but significant, ways that generate increased learning for all their students. Their
sharing of secondary reflective practice with other teachers will begin to affect their
primary reflective practice, in their ability to be self-critical of instructional activity
that doesn't work, and in their ability to imagine and enact other instructional protocols that are more successful in promoting student learning.

This shared reflective practice is the core work of a learning community: to
share in these kinds of exercises of secondary reflective practice so that their
instructional practice and student learning will improve. This sharing in secondary
reflective practice helps all the teachers make what is tacit knowledge *explicit*
knowledge, enables them to name the practices that work and *know why* as well as
to name the practices that do not (always) work and *know why*. Making that knowledge more explicit enables teachers to use that knowledge more intentionally in
their practice.

As will happen again and again, however, teachers will find that conditions change, children from different backgrounds and with different needs arrive in their classrooms, and potentially more powerful learning supports become available. Any or all of these contextual variables will require additional shared reflective practice to meet new instructional challenges in their classrooms. Their own learning will (or should) never stop.

As Wenger has helped us understand, this kind of learning is not to be disparaged; rather, it is the natural way communities of practice learn.[15] Even though professionals have to master a core body of knowledge—usually in university-based degree programs—the problems and issues they encounter in the practice of their profession have a unique and complex mix of variables for which their university courses did not prepare them. They have to bring the more abstract bodies of knowledge from their university programs to help them interpret what is in front of them, but they will also have to build up a certain amount of trial-and-error experience that they can call upon, as well as to consult more experienced members in their unit to develop a realistic and reasonable response to the situations they are encountering for the first time.

Supervisors, sensitive to the power of teachers reflecting together to generate new knowledge and new instructional strategies, can encourage and support this collegial reflective practice. The supervisor initially may have to facilitate and coach the teachers as they venture forth from their relative isolation to engage in reflective conversations. However, supervisors should avoid micromanaging these initial attempts. Once that group of teachers gets comfortable with each other, they will quickly be able to manage on their own. The supervisor's job then changes to cheerleader, arranger of schedules to facilitate teachers' working together, and periodic participant at points where the group would benefit from a review of the progress they have been making. These periodic reviews can provide the basis for an alternative form of supervision, allowing the supervisor to fulfill the bureaucratic requirement of documenting teachers' progress.

One important aspect of reflective practice the supervisor should continually attempt to advance is the teachers' ability to name the causes of the problems they are trying to understand, and to say why their responses to the problem are working or not working. The ability to place their practice against the theoretical and research landscape about teaching, learning, human development, and cultural differences will increase their ability to use these interpretive frames for further reflection on and redesign of their practice.[16] Furthermore, as the culture of collaboration develops among the teaching faculty, this kind of team learning can take a variety of forms, some involving teams tackling problems in the vertical articulation between various

---

[15]Etienne Wenger, *Communities of Practice: Learning, Meaning, and Identity,* Cambridge: Cambridge University Press, 1998.
[16] See this helpful essay on adult cognitive development: Norman Sprinthall and Lois Theis-Sprinthall, "The Teacher as an Adult Learner: A Cognitive-Developmental View," in Gary A. Griffin (ed.), *Staff Development, The Eighty-Second Yearbook of the National Society for the Study of Education,* Chicago: University of Chicago Press, 1983, pp. 13–35.

subjects from grade to grade, some involving teams that redesign curriculum units horizontally across a specific grade cluster. In all of these cases, teachers will be exploring solutions to problems embedded in their practice.

With this understanding of the centrality of collegial reflective practice to the continual learning of the learning community, supervisors should also encourage teachers to coach their students in similar reflective practices in their academic as well as social learning. As we insisted at the start of this chapter, students and their learning ought to be at the heart of the learning community. Why should they not benefit from the very reflective practice by which their teachers are learning? By connecting shared reflection to the students' learning process, teachers can redesign their assessment of student work to include student discussions of what they are learning and how that learning can be useful in their own lives.

BUILDING A LEARNING COMMUNITY

The effort of building a learning community, given the dominant culture of teacher isolation, has to be endorsed and supported through the school system. It has to be the central policy of the governing boards of education, tied to a 5- or 10-year plan with specific targets for each year, endorsed by the central office staff, and supported by the teacher unions and local school administrators as well as by the majority of teachers. In other words, building a learning community cannot be one of five projects that a school system initiates in a given year. Rather, it has to be the large, overarching initiative that coordinates the various ingredients that contribute to a vibrant learning community within the large context of school renewal and shared accountability for improved learning for all students. Superintendents and principals, in their executive capacity, will have to exercise strong leadership in mounting and sustaining this effort. Supervisors (including principals when they are wearing their supervisor's hat) in their day-to-day interactions with teachers and teams of teachers will be crucial support staff for this effort.

SUMMARY

In this chapter we have reviewed the ideas connected to the current interest in the learning community as the core image energizing school renewal. We have attempted to correct a one-sided view of the learning community as exclusively focused on the learning by teachers by insisting that students be included as the primary learners in the learning community we call school. Furthermore, community itself is seen as problematic for students, and therefore needs to be addressed as a more structured part of the school's curriculum. In addressing the larger issue of school reform, schools have attempted to reinvent themselves as learning communities. Since many of the issues involved in school reform have no easily available external solutions, teachers themselves must generate the solutions within their local context from the talents and resources within the school faculty through the process of shared reflective practice. What that looks like and how it might change the culture of isolation to one of collaboration that would support even further teamwork engaged us in the final section of the chapter.

SOME REFLECTIONS

1. Can you think of three to five examples of teachers being sensitive to the various cultures represented in the students in a class? How does that sensitivity contribute to the curriculum of community?
2. What kind of explicit teacher strategies build a sense of teamwork among students working on class projects?
3. To encourage teachers to talk with other teachers about student learning, supervisors need to model such talk. Provide three examples of how supervisors might engage teachers in talk about students learning.
4. Discuss three to five ways supervisors and administrators might rearrange the weekly class schedule to provide time for teachers to engage in secondary reflective practice.

CHAPTER 4

Supervision as Moral Action

INTRODUCTION

Educational leadership has come to be appreciated as comprising more than technical proficiency at various administrative functions such as decision making, coordinating the initiatives of several departments via block scheduling, reading a spreadsheet for budgetary analyses, and so forth. It is seen as involving more than professional competency, such as understanding the new pedagogical approaches to constructivist learning, or creating an integrated strategic plan for faculty development over five years. Educational leadership has come to be seen as including moral awareness and moral commitments as well. The work of supervisors is likewise seen as including moral dimensions. This chapter explores those moral dimensions. Rather than attempting an exposition of moral principles supervisors are supposed to follow, we situate the moral activity of supervisors in relationships, relationships with teachers, most importantly, and relationships with students and with the intrinsically moral activity of learning.

First, we look at the practice of supervision as sometimes having a moral underside to it, an underside whose moral dimensions need to be made explicit. We then proceed to explore the institutional position of supervisors and their contribution to promoting a moral community at the school. While supervisory work is embedded in the multilayered moral life of the school, it is perhaps in acknowledging and supporting the moral character of learning itself that supervisory work finds its most consistent grounding.

SOME BACKGROUND

Many stories told by teachers of their experiences of "being supervised" are anything but uplifting.[1] Again and again teachers tell of being placed in win–lose situation and of experiencing powerlessness, manipulation, sexual harassment, and

[1]See *Impact,* New York State Association for Supervision and Curriculum Development, vol. 19, no. 1 (Fall 1983). The whole issue is devoted to dealing with these less than altruistic motives. Arthur Blumberg raises penetrating questions in his treatment of the "cold war" between teachers and supervisors in *Supervisors and Teachers: A Private Cold War,* Berkeley, CA: McCutcheon, 1974. See also Joseph Blase and Jo Blase, *Breaking the Silence: Overcoming the Problem of Principal Mistreatment of Teachers,* Thousand Oaks, CA: Corwin Press, 2003

racial and ethnic stereotyping. At best, their encounters with supervisors lead directly to evaluative judgments based on the skimpiest of evidence. At worst, these encounters can destroy autonomy, self-confidence, and personal integrity. Unfortunately, supervision as practiced by some supervisors is not only nonprofessional, it is dehumanizing and unethical.

The most traditional exercise of supervision is the formal observation of a teacher in his or her classroom. Despite some semblance of clinical supervision, most encounters result in the supervisor's making evaluative judgments about the appropriateness and effectiveness of various teaching behaviors. These judgments are usually recorded and placed in the teacher's file. Classroom observations that start out with preconceived formulas for what constitutes good practice tend not to be very helpful.[2] Moreover, the supervisor's underlying but unspoken assumptions about teaching and learning frequently defeat the supervisory experience right from the start, because they tend to be simplistic and reductionistic. Teachers' decision making, whether flawed or appropriate, is based on an awareness of an extremely complex, multilayered field of human beings in dynamic interaction over extended periods of time. Supervisors who observe that group of human beings interacting in one slice of time cannot be aware of all that is going on.[3] Evaluation of teachers' performance is a very complex and imperfect art that, in practice, few have mastered.

Beyond professional issues are other attitudes and behaviors that undermine supervisors' activities. These have to do with the desire to dominate and control others; with insecurities that must be covered over by aggressive and controlling actions and words; and with racial, sexual, and ethnic stereotypes that prevent genuine communication and mutual respect. Some older teachers are disdainful of younger supervisors; some older supervisors are disdainful of younger teachers. A supervisor of color raises problems for a white teacher; white supervisors raise problems for teachers of color. Women supervising men and men supervising women have to deal with agendas beyond the explicit professional agenda. When racial and cultural differences are mixed with gender differences, the possibilities for misunderstanding and harm are multiplied.

The expanding literature by women about the challenges of being a woman teacher deserves much greater attention within the field of supervision. As more and more women teachers find their voice and explore ways of being more fully themselves in their work, rather than acting according to the roles they have been socialized to assume, supervisors need to be much more sensitive to this growth process.[4] For some women, this exploration of new personal terrain is a moral challenge. Male supervisors may be unprepared for this emerging phenomenon among women teachers. Our advice would be to begin the dialogue with women

---

[2]Susan Stoldowsky, "Teacher Evaluation: The Limits of Looking," *Educational Researcher,* vol. 13, no. 9 (November 1984), pp. 11–18.

[3]Jane Juska, "Observations," *Phi Delta Kappa,* vol. 72, no. 6 (February 1991), pp. 468–470.

[4]Nell Noddings, "Feminist Critiques in the Professions," in Courtney Cazden (ed.), *Review of Research in Education,* vol. 16 (1990), esp. pp. 406–416; Madeleine R. Grumet, "Women and Teaching: Homeless at Home," *Teacher Education Quarterly,* vol. 14, no. 2 (1987), pp. 39–46.

about what is afoot. This valued, growing female voice points to a need for more women supervisors.

When these negative issues dominate the supervisory experience, they subvert any possibility of open, trusting, professional communication and can lead to manipulative words and actions on the part of the supervisor, the teacher, or both. Sometimes the supervisor and the teacher are not aware that they are being offensive to each other. Sometimes one consciously seeks to control, dominate, or intimidate the other. Often teachers go through the motions, play a superficial role, act as though everything is perfectly understandable, and keep feelings and honest communication at a safe distance. More often than not, supervisory encounters take place without either teachers or supervisors revealing their true feelings toward each other or toward the game they are playing. It is simply an organizational ritual that must be completed to satisfy some political or legal necessity. In the above instances, supervision is the opposite of moral action, implying hypocritical, dishonest, disloyal, vicious, or dehumanizing intentions. Sometimes supervision is immoral simply because it wastes so much time of so many people.

THE MORAL GROUND RULES OF SUPERVISORY PRACTICE

If supervision is to be moral action, it must respect the moral integrity of the supervisor and the supervised. That is to say, the exchange between the supervisor and the teacher must be trusting, open, and flexible to allow both persons to speak from their own sense of integrity and to encourage each person to respect the other's integrity. The exchange must begin with an honest discussion of what will be helpful for the teacher and the students. For this to happen, supervisors need to explore those conditions necessary to establish and maintain trust and honesty and open communication. This means that supervisors need to discuss the ground rules ahead of time. Hence, supervisors need to explore with teachers what procedures will be followed, what rights and responsibilities will be defined, who controls what, whose needs are being served, the purpose of the exchange, and so on. This discussion in itself is a kind of moral action, a negotiation of guidelines to be followed so that fairness and honesty can be maintained. These exploratory discussions on how to initiate and maintain a genuine exchange constitute the heuristics of moral action.

Beyond setting the parameters and guidelines, there is the exchange itself, an engagement of another person in all his or her complexity, fragility, and ambiguity. Embedded in the process of making contact with that other person are the moral imperatives of acceptance, honesty, respect, and care. These constitute the moral activity of empowerment, the willingness to let people be who they are, and beyond that willingness, an appreciation of what they have to contribute. These moral imperatives are not experienced as some abstract, Kantian principles, reference to which deductively leads to specific conclusions. Rather, they are intuitive, instantaneous responses to the other person in the ebb and flow of the interaction. After the fact, through reflection, both supervisor and teacher can understand the moral aspects of those responses.

PROMOTING A MORAL COMMUNITY

Besides concern for the empowerment of individual teachers, supervisors have a responsibility to nurture the moral environment of the individual school. In fact, both moral concerns support each other. Everyday life in the school contains within it many moral challenges, but often supervisors do not know how to name them. Often institutional practices in the school convey a sense of impersonality. Communications contained in faculty memos, announcements to the students over the intercom, or administrative changes in student disciplinary policies can convey paternalistic, authoritarian, or adversarial attitudes. School practices—in grading and testing, in assigning students to tracked curriculum groups, in choosing textbooks and assembly speakers—can be questioned in terms of fairness, equity, respect for cultural pluralism, and other moral criteria. The imposition of uniform class schedules, the labeling of some children as "gifted" and others as "disabled," the practice of suspending students from class and from school attendance, the absence of important topics and points of view in textbooks, the process of calculating class rank, the absence of alternatives in student assessments, the criteria for student and faculty awards—these and other institutional procedures carry moral implications, because they advantage some students and disadvantage others.

In schools, standard operating procedures tend to take on a life of their own. Instead of regarding these procedures as human constructs put in place to serve a larger purpose, school personnel tend to allow means to become ends, to allow procedures to define the way things have always been and the way they are supposed to be. When institutional procedures become more important than the human beings the institution is supposed to serve, then the danger for moral mischief spreads. The institutional environment becomes inimical to human life. Values such as uniformity, predictability, efficiency, obedience, and conformity can tend to override other values, such as freedom of conscience, creativity, diversity, inventiveness, risk taking, and individuality. Individuals should not be forced to serve institutional procedures when those procedures violate human values. Institutional procedures should serve human beings. When they do not, they should be changed.

To speak of supervisory action as necessarily moral, but at the same time to restrict that activity exclusively to activity with individual teachers, is to ignore the institutional context of teaching and supervising and its potential for demoralizing, in the literal sense, the teaching–learning situation. It is also to ignore the supervisor's position within the institution. The supervisor's position differs from the teacher's institutional position. The teacher's primary responsibility is to the students: to see that they learn what the teacher and the school community have determined they should learn. The supervisor's responsibilities are more to the total community: to see that schoolwide goals are being achieved. Institutional arrangements impinge very directly on the teaching–learning situation, and individual teachers are not in a position to change them.

Supervisors, however, enjoy a multiplicity of institutional opportunities to initiate and sustain conversations among various groups within the school community. They can challenge the appropriateness of institutional practices that unfairly affect various segments of the community.[5] Supervisors function at a variety of institutional levels, and their activities intersect with a variety of offices. Because they are relatively free to structure their day, they can attend a variety of administrative and faculty meetings to bring these institutional moral concerns before the community. To ignore these issues is to allow institutional practices and policies to disempower teachers and students, to thwart the very work supervisors carry on with individual teachers.

THE MORAL IDEAL OF TEACHING

We will not argue for the need of supervisors to encourage the moral commitment of teachers, as though that is lacking on the part of teachers. On the contrary, the action of supervision takes place within an existing moral environment created by the professionalism of teachers. We will better understand the moral dimensions of supervision by a close look at the moral dimensions involved in the ideal of teaching, an ideal to which the large majority of teachers subscribe and which makes up the core of their general concept of professionalism.[6]

When we first think about professionalism, our attention is drawn to issues of competence. Professionals are experts, and this expertise entitles them to be autonomous. But expertise is not enough to earn one the mantle of professionalism. Though society often refers to expert safecrackers, hairdressers, gamblers, and baseball players as being professionals, the reference is colloquial. Being a professional has to do with something else besides being competent. Society, for example, demands not only that physicians, physicists, teachers, and other professionals be skilled but also that their skills be used for good intentions. Professionals enjoy privileges because they are trusted. It takes more than competence to earn trust. One might refer to this "something else" as professional virtue.[7]

What are the dimensions of professional virtue? At least four are related to this discussion:[8]

a commitment to practice in an exemplary way

a commitment to practice toward valued social ends

a commitment not only to one's own practice but to the practice itself

a commitment to the ethic of caring

[5]For a more extensive discussion of this responsibility of supervisors, see Robert J. Starratt, "Building an Ethical School: A Theory for Practice in Educational Leadership," *Educational Administration Quarterly,* vol. 27, no. 2 (May 1991), pp. 195–202.
[6]Magdalene Lampert and Christopher M. Clark, "Expert Knowledge and Expert Thinking in Teaching: A Response to Floden and Klinzing," *Educational Researcher,* vol. 19, no. 5 (June–July 1991), pp. 21–23.
[7]This discussion of professional virtue follows Thomas J. Sergiovanni, *The Moral Dimensions of Leadership.* San Francisco: Jossey-Bass, 1992, pp. 52–56.
[8]The first two dimensions are from Alastair McIntyre, *After Virtue,* Notre Dame, IN: Notre Dame University, 1981. The third is from Albert Flores, "What Kind of Person Should a Professional Be?" in Albert Flores (ed.), *Professional Ideals,* Belmont, CA: Wadsworth, 1988. The fourth is from Nel Noddings, *Caring: A Feminine Approach to Ethics and Moral Education,* Berkeley, CA: University of California Press, 1984.

The four dimensions of professional virtue provide the roots for developing a powerful norm system that, when combined with the norm system that defines the school as community, can transform supervision as it is now practiced. For this reason establishing the virtuous side of professionalism should be a high priority for supervision.

A commitment to exemplary practice, for example, means practicing on the cutting edge of teaching, staying abreast of the latest research in practice, researching one's own practice, experimenting with new approaches, and sharing one's craft insights with others. Once established, this dimension results in teachers' accepting responsibility for their own professional growth, thus greatly reducing the need for someone else to plan and implement staff development programs for them. The focus of professional development shifts from "training" to providing opportunities for self-renewal, for interacting with others, for learning and sharing. Much of what happens in this kind of professional development is informal and built into the everyday life of the school. Teachers accept a greater share of the responsibility for planning and carrying out both formal and informal activities and programs.

The second dimension of professional virtue, a commitment to practice toward valued social ends, represents a commitment to place oneself in service to students and parents and to agreed-upon school values and purposes.

The third dimension of professional virtue, a commitment not only to one's own practice but also to the practice of teaching itself, forces teachers to broaden their outlook. Such a commitment requires that teaching be transformed from individual to collective practice. In collective practice, for example, it would not be acceptable for one teacher to teach competently in the company of others having difficulty, without being concerned, without offering help. It would not be acceptable to have special insights into teaching and not to share them with others. It would not be acceptable to define success in terms of what happens in one's own classroom when the school itself may be failing.

The fourth dimension, a commitment to the ethic of caring, places the professional in a caring relationship with the client. In other words, the professional rejects impersonal, condescending, manipulative, demeaning ways of treating the client. Whatever service the professional provides to the client is provided with care for the full humanity of the client.

THE MORAL CHARACTER OF LEARNING AND TEACHING

A deeper look at the professional virtues of teaching leads toward an exploration of the virtue or moral character in learning itself. In other words, while teaching has its virtues, it also derives its moral character from the moral character of the very learning it seeks to nurture and promote. What follows is an attempt to uncover that deeper moral character of learning and of teaching.[9] To probe that moral character,

[9]This section is adapted from an earlier essay by Robert J. Starratt, published as "Grounding Moral Educational Leadership in the Morality of Teaching and Learning," *Leading and Managing,* vol. 4, no. 4 (1998), pp. 243–255.

we have to move beyond a more familiar understanding of learning and indeed of knowledge itself, and turn toward what is emerging as a new understanding of knowledge and therefore of learning. This new understanding is grounded in the intrinsic *relationality* of reality. Learning then begins to look more like a dialogue between the learner and the reality under study. From there, we move to a view of scholarship, or the pursuit of knowledge, as both an intellectual and moral activity. We next consider the morality of knowledge application, or the morality of the social uses of knowledge. We try to illuminate this understanding of the moral character of learning and teaching by describing two contrasting approaches to teaching in response to the policy agenda of school reform.

If we can understand as supervisors that the nature of learning itself is intrinsically a moral activity, then supervisors' involvement with teachers as they promote that moral activity of learning partakes of that intrinsically moral character.

BASIC ASSUMPTIONS: RELATIONAL LEARNING VS. ISOLATED LEARNING

One of the most profound flaws in modernity was the gradual emergence of an aggressive assertion of the necessity of the autonomous individual. This assertion eventually developed into a philosophical, political, and economic theory and became firmly entrenched as an ideology of individualism, an unquestioned dogma that the individual, in order to be fully human, had to assert his independence from family, community, nature, God, cosmos. The individual had to stand alone against the cosmic, political, and religious landscape; to admit any intrinsic dependence on that landscape was to negate, it was believed, the individual's uniqueness, the particular destiny, the freedom to be the one-of-a-kind person he was entitled to be. (We use the masculine here intentionally, for obvious reasons.) That ideology had profound consequences for understanding how such an isolated individual could know the world from which the individual stood decidedly apart. It led to Descartes' struggle to build a logical basis for knowing even that he existed; his *cogito, ergo sum* (I think, therefore I exist) was the act of an isolated individual who had to be the sole explanation of his own knowledge, since his standing apart from the world left him no secure bridge or connection to that world. Descartes' radically isolated knower became the starting point for most of the subsequent epistemologies of modernism. Somehow the mind of this isolated, separated knower had to be predisposed to know the world objectively whether through innate ideas or through logical and perceptual mechanisms whose forms naturally conformed to the logical and conceptual forms of objective realities grasped through reason and the methodologies of science. Much of cognitive science today is still wrestling with what is basically the epistemological question inherited from Descartes.[10] New understandings of

---

[10]Jerome Bruner, "The Transactional Self," in J. Bruner and H. Haste (eds.), *Making Sense: The Child's Construction of the World,* New York: Methuen, 1987, pp. 81–96.

knowledge and learning that have emerged in the past century have helped us overcome the isolation of the knower.

The new sociology of knowledge places the knower inside culture, inside a
tapestry of already constructed knowledge and language maps, frameworks,
threads, logics, methodologies.[11] The knower knows by receiving knowledge
already constructed for the knower by the community, which enfolds the knower.
This understanding of the embeddedness of the knower is enriched through the
insights of philosophers and scientists well versed in quantum physics and various
branches of the new biology.[12] They offer a different epistemology by changing the
assumptions about the human individual knower. The individual knower is not
isolated from what he or she knows. The human knower is already implicated in
nature. The human mind is embedded in the cosmic field; the energy flowing in that
field is flowing in the human mind, in the human brain, in the history of the culture
and of the language. That culture, that language, that mind, that brain, these minds
and these brains are all connected in space and time with everything that ever was,
that is now, and that will be. The universe, in each of its parts and in its unity,
reflects an underlying intelligence. It appears to know what it is doing, whether we
are talking about astrophysics or subatomic physics, about the evolution of life
forms and their genetic and biochemical intelligence, about the evolution of animals
and humans and their forms of intelligence as social beings; about the evolution of
culture and civilization and their forms of linguistic, scientific, philosophical, artistic and religious intelligence.

If knowledge is not a particular something that an isolated individual somehow
steals or coaxes or conjures from a hostile or indifferent nature, then what is it? To
overcome the riddle of knowledge, we must overturn one of the basic assumptions
that has led to the riddle in the first place, and that is the assumption of an isolated
knower, separated from the natural world he or she is trying to know. Dewey, Whitehead, Polanyi, Bateson, and many others[13] suggest that we begin with the assumption
that the individual human being is not isolated from nature but is in relationship to all
of nature. Being in relationship to the natural world means being in multiple

---

[11]E. Doyle McCarthy, *Knowledge as Culture: The New Sociology of Knowledge,* London: Routledge, 1996.
[12]Robert M. Augros and George N. Stanciu, *The New Biology: Discovering the Wisdom in Nature,* Boston:
New Science Library, 1987; Gregory Bateson, *Mind and Nature: A Necessary Unity,* New York: Dutton, 1979,
and *A Sacred Unity: Further Steps to an Ecology of Mind,* R. E. Donaldson (ed.), New York: HarperCollins,
1991; Loren Eiseley, *The Immense Journey,* New York: Vantage Books, 1957, and *The Star Thrower,* New
York: Times Books, 1978; James Lovelock, *Gaia: A New Look at Life on Earth,* Oxford: Oxford University
Press, 1979; Ilya Prigogine and Isabelle Stengers, *Order Out of Chaos: Man's New Dialogue with Nature,*
New York: Bantam, 1984; George A. Seilstad, *At the Heart of the Web: The Inevitable Genesis of Intelligent
Life,* New York: Harcourt Brace, 1989; Frederick Turner, *Rebirth of Value: Meditations on Beauty, Ecology,
Religion and Education,* Albany: State University of New York Press, 1991; Alfred North Whitehead, *Science
and the Modern World,* New York: Macmillan, 1925; Danah Zohar and Ian Marshall, *The Quantum Society,*
London: HarperCollins, 1994.
[13]John Dewey, *Experience and Nature,* La Salle, IL: Open Court, 1929; John Dewey, *The Quest for Certainty:
A Study of the Relation of Knowledge and Action,* New York: Putnam, 1929; Michael Polanyi, *The Tacit
Dimension,* Garden City, NY: Doubleday, 1966; Whitehead, op. cit.; Bateson, *Mind and Nature* op. cit.

relationships simultaneously: relationships such as gravity, the food chain, weather patterns, political and cultural institutions; relationships of energy exchange, of love and fear, of aesthetic and economic dependencies. Knowledge is what emerges from the intentional exploration of those relationships, whether those relationships are benign or problematic.

Knowledge is a dialogue between the intelligences found in the natural and social worlds and the intelligences of individual knowers. Being embedded in relationships with the natural and social world implies mutual involvement and respect for those relationships. It implies a language or languages by which a dialogue takes place. The knower and the known speak to one another, resist one another, attract one another, threaten one another, seduce one another, puzzle one another. Since they exist continuously in relationship to one another, there is no question of the knower living independently on some higher plane above the known. They are intertwined, implicated in each other's existence. This holds for relationships of love and relationships of enmity; relationships between humans and songbirds, and humans and the HIV virus; relationships between spouses and relationships between jailers and prison inmates, relationships with weeds in my backyard and with eruptions on the sun's surface. Unless the experiences of these relationships issue in a dialogue of mutual understanding at some minimal level, then there is no knowledge.

KNOWLEDGE AS FAMILIARITY AND RESPECT LEADING TO RESPONSIBILITY

Knowledge, in other words, can be understood from the standpoint of relationality, from an ontology not of isolated beings, but of beings in a field, the energy of which grounds, creates, and sustains relationality. Looked at this way, we may speak of knowledge as the achievement of a certain mutual familiarity or intimacy. If we postulate that knowing is somewhat like loving, that the approach to the object of knowledge requires a profound respect for and sensitivity to its integrity, then knowing means acknowledging the relationship between the knower and the known, being responsible *to* and *for* the known—then we have a different understanding of knowledge. From this perspective, knowing is not only a meeting between intelligences, it is also an implicit moral act. In that moral act of knowing, the knower accepts the responsibility of coming to know the known carefully—that is, full of care for the integrity of the known. That implies avoiding a careless approach to the relationship, to the dialogue, so that the knower knows the known as it truly is, or at least as truly as present circumstances allow. It means putting aside one's own sense of superiority or importance, leaving one's own self-centered agenda aside, submitting oneself to the message of the subject, willing to be humbled by the complexity of the known. It also means that the knower, when she or he shares her or his knowledge of the known, represents the known as accurately and as sensitively as circumstances allow. That sharing becomes an invitation to another to approach the known with similar reverence and care.

THE MORAL CHARACTER OF SCHOLARSHIP

This careful and caring ethic is elaborated in the traditions and rituals that surround the work of scholars. Scholarship is meant to be trusted by the public, because the scholar is assumed to be committed to the fullest and clearest understanding of what he or she is studying, and to the most honest and undistorted representation of that knowledge as circumstances allow. Scholars cannot report their findings in dishonest ways, bending their conclusions to fit a preconceived theory to which they have personally committed their reputation. Their job is not to tell the public what it wants to hear, but to "let the facts speak for themselves." Insofar as their findings are presented in interpretive frameworks, they acknowledge those frameworks' influence on the intelligibility of the findings. Where their speculations go beyond the findings of their research, they announce them as such. Scholars are obliged to treat their knowledge carefully, for they recognize that the search for and disclosure of knowledge is a moral as well as an intellectual enterprise.

For the scholar, the knowing process involves a care-full attention to the known. It involves listening to the muted and subtle messages being sent by the known. It means bringing the initial interpretation of these messages back to the subject of study, asking repeatedly, "Did you mean this, or did you mean that? Are my methods of attending to you getting in the way of what you want to say to me? Am I starting from the wrong assumptions when I interpret you this way? Is this what you really mean?" Again and again, the scholar checks the evidence, compares the messages, listens with the heart as well as the mind. As Polanyi suggests, scholars try to get to know the subject so well that they develop an intuitive, tacit knowing of the complexity of the subject, so that they know without being able to say precisely how they know until further reflection points to the logic of the conclusion.[14]

Most scholars exhibit a fascination with their field of study, and within it, those special areas of their research. The fascination flows over into affection. They "love studying this stuff." They love their learning into knowledge and understanding. Some say disparagingly that scholars are "married to their work." For scholars, the relationship between themselves and their subject is so gratifying, so thrilling, so fascinating, that it becomes their whole world.

The scholars' love for what they are studying does not necessarily imply that their relationship with that subject is not frustrating, painful, disagreeable. The otherness of the subject will intrude on the scholar's plans and timetable. The subject will go silent, refusing to provide any knowledge about itself for weeks. The subject will also appear to contradict itself, or at least contradict the preliminary conclusions drawn by the scholar. The subject will refuse to cooperate with the technology the scholar is using to poke around its insides. The scholar will rant and rave at the subject, accusing the universe of perfidy in allowing this aberration to exist, complaining that the subject is intentionally deceitful.

---

[14]Polanyi, op. cit.

THE SOCIAL RESPONSIBILITY OF KNOWLEDGE UTILIZATION

Beside the knowledge of the other as it is in itself and in relationship to me, knowledge also reveals the relationships between the properties of various things.

We know the properties of types of steel, types of gasses, types of acids. We know that certain gasses when heated will melt steel; that certain acids will corrode steel. We know that steel is "stronger" than wood, that a steel axe can cut through wood. We know that certain laws protect citizens' rights. We know that termites can eat wood. We understand the relationship between traffic lights, pedestrian walkways, and the flow of traffic. We discover that certain microbes will help diffuse an oil spill. We know that a certain circumference of pipe will allow only a certain volume of water to flow through it at any time. Rarely, however, are these isolated, one-to-one relationships. For example, water will flow through pipes according to conditions of pressure, as well as conditions of gravity; water will not flow through a pipe going uphill unless it is pumped, or unless the water source is already at a height above the hill. Microbes cannot be introduced into a water system to dispel an oil spill unless the water is sufficiently warm to sustain the life and activity of the microbes. Laws against libel limit laws protecting free speech.

The knowledge that we acquire reveals not only the relationships we have to the world but also how the world works, or how, with some inventiveness, we can make it work. Knowledge not only teaches reverence for the world, it also reveals the actual or potential working relationships of the world.

Knowledge is useful for our work, individually and collectively, in the world. That work involves not only our "career"; it involves our work as a member of a family, as a neighbor, as a citizen, as a homebuilder, as a member of multiple organizations, as a member of the human race, as an intelligent animal in the natural environment. Often our "work" is indeed focused on our career. That is where, for many, they make their public contribution to the world. That work involves our intelligence, our artistry, our energy. It also involves a basic sense of obligation, obligation not simply to one's employer to give an honest day's work for a day's pay, but an obligation to the world—however amorphous our definition of that term might be—to make a contribution, to respond to some minimal sense of stewardship.

There are, unfortunately, many examples of unscrupulous people who use their knowledge in exclusively self-serving ways. Almost every day the media carry reports of people and companies violating the trust of their profession or their craft: insider trading, tax fraud, bribery of public officials, shoddy field testing of medicines, misleading manipulation of experimental research results, cost-cutting procedures that endanger the lives of automobile drivers, violations of health code regulations in food-processing plants, refusal of insurance companies to honor the terms of their policies, violations of construction safety codes, willful violations of workers' workplace safety regulations, molesting of children by teachers. The public is outraged precisely because of the public trust in the integrity of professionals. Their position of superior knowledge and expertise leads us to place significant aspects of our lives in their hands. Their crimes are more serious than crimes of passion—the fight in the tavern, the drug-crazed street robber. Professionals violate our trust, our respect for their role as public servants when they use their profession to break the law and to defraud the customer. The unfortunate cynicism toward lawyers and doctors, business executives and politicians, teachers and clergy is not only a measure of the public's disappointment at their behavior; it is also a measure of our continued high expectations of the moral ideal of their professions.

TWO TEACHERS WITH DIFFERENT UNDERSTANDINGS OF LEARNING

When we think now of how knowledge is approached in schools, we find two different kinds of teachers. Let us call one teacher Stan Dards and the other Connie Strukt. Stan Dards assumes that knowledge is objectively out there awaiting a knower, assumes that the student is independent and separated from what he or she knows, assumes that learning is simply a matter of appropriating that knowledge, either by memorization of its formulation in the textbook or by performing lab experiments that will lead to the development of correct research skills and to answers already prescribed in the textbook. Knowledge is a question of getting and knowing how to get the right answers. The right answers are what the experts know and have told us is what we need to know about the matter. The process of explaining what lies behind the "right answer" is almost always neglected in Stan's classes. Covering the syllabus is equated with mastering the objective knowledge contained in the state curriculum standards. Depending on how many right and wrong answers a student comes up with in the course of a semester, a student receives a grade, indicating "how much" of the syllabus he or she has learned, how much he or she knows. When students take the high-stakes test, their "achievement" is expressed in the number of right answers achieved on the test.

Stan Dards explains to his class that they are involved in a high-stakes process. They have to prepare for a state exam that will determine whether they are promoted or held back. Success in the state exam will mean that they have what it takes to be productive citizens in future endeavors. If they work hard, stay focused, work at the daily assignments and correct their mistakes as soon as they are aware of them, if they stay up with the flow of the course, they will be successful. To help them prepare for the state exams, Stan Dards will provide them with many exercises that pose questions similar to the ones they'll have on the exam. They'll have a chance to practice answering questions like the ones on the test.

Stan Dards's weekly lesson plans are carefully matched to the state curriculum standards for the academic level of his students. He provides drills, spot quizzes, team competitions throughout the week to make sure students have sufficient time on task learning the material contained in the curriculum standards. His students practice test-taking skills as well, learning how to narrow down the possible responses to multiple-choice questions, and how to construct a preliminary outline for an essay-type response on the test.

Connie Strukt's classroom teaching reflects an enthusiastic fascination with the material being studied. Students sense that she actually enjoys "messing around with this stuff." She communicates such enthusiasm for the material under study that even normally resistant students go along so as not to hurt her feelings. Connie invites the students to enter the world of the subject matter, whether that be chemistry, mathematics, or poetry. Entry into that world, however, is not as a tourist; rather, they enter into a world where they are dramatically implicated, where they are in relationship with what they are learning, where they become responsible for and to what they know.

Connie Strukt also advises her students about the process involved in preparing for the high-stakes state exams. She points out, however, that the curriculum standards, while helpful in highlighting important and interesting things to learn, represent an artificial construction of a sequence of learnings that, in being divided into separate curriculum strands, tend to conceal the many relationships between the strands of knowledge. She spends time preparing for the high-stakes tests, but within a context of learning as an exciting and soul-expanding journey. Her weekly lesson plans have one eye on the curriculum standards and another eye on creating a dialogue with the subject matter, seeking to stimulate a fascination with the intelligence embedded in whatever they are studying. By encouraging a dialogue between their intelligence and the intelligence in the realities they are studying, she is helping her students engage the methodologies needed to carry on the dialogue—methodologies of measuring, observing, imaginatively exploring alternative scenarios, seeking evidence of various types of relationships, uncovering the logic behind a relationship.

Connie knows that this kind of dialogue between intelligences is the way that knowledge is constructed. She also realizes that students are constructed by knowledge, even as they construct knowledge. Assuming that knowledge is grounded in relationality, then knowledge will reveal how the knower is in relationship to the known. Learning about chemical compounds not only illuminates the ecology of the immediate environment but also reveals how their own bodies work. Learning about the Second World War re-places them in relationship to their own willingness to die for their country, in relationship to nonviolence as a desirable ethic, in relationship to weapons of mass destruction, in relationship to the actual sufferings of civilian populations, in relationship to the reality of genocide, in relationship to political fanaticism, in relationship to the geopolitics of current history. Connie encourages her students both to take responsibility *for* what they know and to be responsible *to* what they know. Learning for right answers is replaced with learning how to live in some kind of harmony with their natural and social world. There is no one right answer to that larger agenda. The knowledge students absorb, however, continues to illuminate their relationship to their natural and social world, and to reveal how those relationships make demands on them and on their generation.

Connie also provides them with experiences in the use of their knowledge to analyze and respond to problems in the real world. For example, through computer simulations, she sets her students to work on an engineering problem, on an investment strategy, on a census-taking issue. Again using case studies and computer simulations, she presents students with problems from the world of public health, environmental protection, food-processing technologies, genetic research. In social studies, Connie has students construct family histories using stories from relatives still alive, letters from deceased relatives, old newspaper stories, family picture albums. She requires them not only to trace their genealogies, but also to attempt to understand the human and civil rights issues their forebears faced, the technologies available to them for various survival tasks, their cultural enjoyments and artifacts.

In the process of learning the curriculum standards, Connie teaches the students how to use their knowledge, how to apply what they know to real people and real situations. In the process, she teaches them how to honor the tools of generating knowledge and applying knowledge, how to report their findings with integrity; how to avoid going beyond the evidence and to announce speculation when it is being employed. Furthermore, she requires them to apply their knowledge and imagination to explore ways to improve the situation under study. How might the public health department better monitor the processing of food or the levels of bacteria in the water supply? How might companies change their policies toward whistle-blowers to encourage early detection of serious production problems? How might human rights abuses in developing countries be more effectively treated in international law? Connie encourages her students to use their knowledge in the service of people in the local community and subsequently has them reflect how it feels to use their knowledge as a service to others, rather than simply as a means to getting a grade on a test. She wants her students to learn that their talents are given to them primarily to serve the community, and only secondarily to be used for their own advantage.

The practice of using and applying their knowledge will be accompanied by a continuous stream of admonitions, such as these: Knowledge brings responsibility. If we do not use our knowledge to improve people's lives, then what good is it? Respect the integrity of what you know and how you came to know it. Respect the craft of language and rhetoric. Respect the audience who receives your knowledge reports by providing them illustrative examples and precise language and occasional humor for when they get drowsy.

Her major sermon to the students is this: You do not have the moral option to choose not to learn. Choosing not to learn is choosing not to know what you will need to know in order to make a contribution to the world. Your chosen ignorance may be the occasion of an accident, the loss of life, the failure of an important project, the frustration of a community's dream, the disappointment of people who were counting on you to perform. An organization's or a community's achievement of excellence depends not only on the quality of its most talented members, but upon the intelligent cooperation of people like you and me. The shoddy or incompetent work of anyone diminishes the achievement of the whole. We have achieved as a civilization whatever level of greatness, whatever level of excellence, whatever level of good order because countless people like you and me knew what to do when it counted most. They were prepared. That's why learning what you learn in school is not only a privilege, it is a duty to yourselves and to your community and to your future children and grandchildren.

These portraits of Stan Dards and Connie Strukt are obvious imaginary constructs employed to contrast two different understandings of learning, and therefore, of the moral character of teaching. Stan Dards would not be looked upon by most as a weak teacher. In fact, he represents what many educators, parents, and policy makers consider good teaching to be all about. Connie Strukt, however, may be as successful as Stan in preparing her students for the test by immersing them in intelligent dialogue with their subjects, a dialogue which would enable them to respond to the test with greater confidence and agility. On the other hand, much of what Connie teaches does not appear on any high-stakes test, but does appear to be of enormous value both to the students and to the state's future welfare. The states need more Connies in the classroom if their efforts to improve the intellectual rigor of the curriculum are to bear fruit. Teachers like Stan simply employ the new state curriculum standards to encourage the same unreflective, alienating kind of learning that currently exists in schools. The moral character of learning—both for the healthy constructing of ourselves and for the reverential reconstructing of our world—is equally important to the intellectual mastery of knowledge. We suggest that neither aspect of learning—its intellectual or its moral character—can be authentically engaged without the other.

SUMMARY

Supervisors need to take a good look at existing relationships with teachers to see whether any "underside" issues are getting in the way of authentic working relationships. Supervisors, by virtue of their position within the organization of the school or school system, may exercise significant influence over the building of a moral community at the school. This would entail their taking a closer look at the organizational structures and processes of the school to see whether they serve some students well, but disadvantage others, and thus are a source of injustice. A moral community needs to look at itself critically from time to time to see that it practices what it preaches. Supervisors are in a good position to call attention to these institutional problems.

Looking at their involvement with teachers, supervisors need to acknowledge the moral activity of teachers, not only their exercise of professional virtue, but the grounding of that virtue in the moral character of learning and teaching. Supervisors may legitimately ask, however, how they are supposed to interact with teachers about this character of teaching and learning. Suppose, for example, that there are many Stan Dards on the faculty of the school. We have suggested that supervisors need to ground their authority at least as much in the accepted norms of the community, in the common or core values that the community espouses. It would seem that discussions about the moral character of learning and teaching need to be raised with the community of teachers, rather than be superimposed on a classroom observation of one teacher. Supervisors need to encourage teachers to share ideas and stories about how they perceive their professional virtue, how they describe in narratives their own commitment to the integrity of learning. Those kinds of exchanges among the teachers at large will encourage other teachers to reflect on the moral character of their teaching. Teachers might begin to put together a looseleaf notebook of examples of when they brought out the moral character of learning in their classrooms. That notebook could be placed in a conspicuous location in the teachers' room. Once teachers grow comfortable talking about the topic, supervisors might encourage them to set up some internal benchmarks of accountability for including attention to the moral dimensions of learning in their weekly lesson plans. With that community grounding of the discussions, that kind of legitimizing of concern for the moral dimensions of learning, supervisors would then be enabled to carry the discussion forward as an authentic concern of the community.

It is our belief that teachers experience their work as driven by a moral ideal. That ideal activates and validates their integrity as human beings. That ideal is embedded in their understanding of teaching as a profession. It is what teachers are called to do; it is their vocation.

Because teaching and learning are moral activities, supervision partakes of their moral qualities. Supervision is supposed to support, nurture, and strengthen the moral ideals embedded in teaching. Supervision as a professional activity, therefore, is intimately tied to both the knowledge expertise of the teacher and the moral responsibility of the profession of teaching. The supervisor must understand the complexities of teaching, its multilayered and multidimensional artistic knowledge base. Beyond appreciating that complex knowledge base and being able to converse with teachers about it, the supervisor is obliged to participate with teachers in the task of bringing youngsters to the condition of learning. The supervisor does this by supporting the teachers' search for improved responsiveness to their students.

That support will clearly bring the supervisor's professional knowledge base into play. In subsequent chapters we will deal with various aspects of that knowledge base. Supervision as moral activity, however, involves more than the supervisor's knowledge; it involves the supervisor's ability to engage teachers at a level of moral discourse that mirrors the moral responsibility teachers model for their students. Ultimately, what teachers try to accomplish with their students is not simply the acquisition of knowledge, although that is central to their task; teachers also want the experience of knowing they have opened up students to an appreciation of life, an experience of themselves as connected to a world that is challenging and complex, filled with beauty and pain and joy.[15]

Underneath all the specifics of what they are teaching, teachers basically want to share a deep part of their lives with youngsters, the joy and fascination that they experience in understanding and engaging the world through a variety of perspectives. Teachers are happy enough when their students score well on exams; however, they are most fulfilled when their students delight in what they are learning. It is at this level that a supervisor engages teachers in the moral dimension of teaching. At this level supervisors engage in one of the fundamental aspects of empowerment.

SOME REFLECTIONS

1. Reflect on the outstanding teachers you have had during your schooling. Were they like Stan Dards or Connie Struct? What qualities made those teachers special? Did they embrace a moral ideal in their teaching?
2. Try engaging a colleague at school in a conversation about the intrinsic morality of learning. Where does the conversation go? What does that conversations suggest about the possibility of such conversations between supervisors and teachers?
3. Talk to some students about their favorite classroom experiences. Do their stories reflect any aspects of the moral nature of learning treated in this chapter?
4. Can you recall any learning experiences in your schooling which brought you into any kind of felt relationship to the material under study, when a learning experience challenged you to look at yourself differently, brought you into a profound insight about life, caused a deep sense of appreciation of something or someone—when learning brought you some deep satisfaction beyond getting a good grade? What was the stimulus that sparked those kinds of learning?

[15]For other testimonies of this moral commitment to the human growth of students, see Tracy Kidder, *Among Schoolchildren,* New York: Avon, 1989; Philip Lopate, *Being with Children,* New York: Poseiden, 1975; Jay Mathews, *Escalante,* New York: Holt, 1988; Jo Anne Pagano, *Exiles and Communities: Teaching in the Patriarchal Wilderness,* Albany: State University of New York Press, 1990; Robert Fried, *The Passionate Teacher,* Boston: Beacon Press, 1995; and Robert J. Starratt, *Centering Educational Administration: Cultivating Meaning, Community and Responsibility,* Mahwah, NJ: Erlbaum, 2003.

CHAPTER 5

The Supervisor's Educational Platform

INTRODUCTION

Throughout the book we are emphasizing the link between supervision and the involvement of teachers in the restructuring of the core work of the school. By distinguishing between what we term Supervision I and Supervision II, we want to draw attention to a different way of being a supervisor and to a different process that encourages and supports the reflective practice of teachers. Supervision II appears to be the more effective way to elicit teachers' involvement in the restructuring agenda. Supervision II encourages teachers to draw on the collective wisdom of their craft and to collaborate on the redesign of student learning activities that progressively engages students in the active production and performance of knowledge. The collaborative reflection on the complexities of the teaching–learning work enables teachers to explore the conceptual maps they use to define and shape the curriculum they teach.[1] In this chapter, we suggest that this reflective practice needs, at some point, to engage each teacher's educational platform. Unless teachers and supervisors uncover their platforms, they will not establish a base of mutual understanding that is necessary to ground their collaborative efforts.

SOME BACKGROUND

Besides the technical understandings that emerge from a blend of intuition and conceptual schemata, there is a floor of beliefs, opinions, values, and attitudes that provides a foundation for practice. These beliefs, opinions, values, and attitudes make up what has been called a "platform."[2] Just as a political party is supposed to base its decisions and actions on a party platform, so too educators carry on their work, make decisions, and plan instruction based on their educational platform. When a teacher is asked why a child was disciplined in a certain way, he or she frequently

---

[1]Donald A. Schön, *The Reflective Practitioner.* New York: Basic Books, 1983.
[2]Decker Walker, "A Naturalistic Model for Curriculum Development," *School Review,* vol. 80, no. 1 (1971), pp. 51–65.

will respond with a generalization about how all children should be disciplined. When asked about the social usefulness of learning a certain lesson, a teacher frequently will frame his or her explanation according to a set of more general beliefs about the socialization of children.

A teacher's platform is rarely explicit. Neither is it static or one-dimensional. It is derived from life experiences, from formal education, and especially from trial-and-error experience in classrooms. Teachers are not accustomed to pausing before walking into their first class of the day and recalling the elements of their platform. Rather, their platform is seen in action, in their patterns and habitual ways of interacting with students.

Whether or not a platform position is right or wrong is not the issue here. Knowing *what* the platform position is, understanding the relationship between teaching practices and platform elements, perceiving inconsistencies between the spoken platform and the platform in practice, appreciating differences between one's own platform and that of another—these are the points of emphasis in this chapter. Both teacher and supervisor need to know what their respective platforms are. They need to examine where they agree and where they differ and whether the differences are so substantial as to inhibit the collaborative work of redesigning the teaching–learning process. In the effort to encourage reflection in practice, teachers and supervisors need to take the time to articulate their platform. Most teachers tend to resist the exercise simply because they are not used to making their platform explicit. They simply act according to the feel of the situation. Yet when they do write out their platform, they experience the satisfaction of naming what they do and why they do it. Greater sense of task identity and task significance strengthens motivation, satisfaction, and commitment to one's work.[3]

What follows are several examples of at least partially developed platforms. In practice, a teacher's platform might take more of a narrative, or more of a disjointed style, than the examples below. What is presented here is more of a skeletal form, which tends to focus on the primary emphasis of the platform.

THE BASIC COMPETENCY PLATFORM

1. The purpose of schooling is to ensure a minimal competency in prescribed skills and understandings for all children. Enrichment of students' learning beyond these minimum competencies is an important but secondary aim of schooling.
2. Schools can make a great difference in the achievement of these minimum competencies; people who do not achieve them end up as unproductive citizens living on the margins of society.

[3]J. Richard Hackman and Greg R. Oldham, "Motivation Through the Design of Work: Test of a Theory." *Organizational Behavior and Human Performance,* vol. 16 (1976), p. 256.

3. Present and future civic and employment demands point to the absolute necessity of acquiring basic competencies. Mastery of these competencies will assist
the person in other areas of personal and social growth.

4. The educator's job is to construct a highly organized environment to promote
the gradual mastery of basic competencies in reading, writing, computation,
and scientific processes. This implies a careful definition of learning objectives
for each major unit of an intentionally sequenced series of learnings, careful
assessment of entry-level skills and understandings with built-in correction of
start-up deficiencies, careful monitoring of student progress with built-in remediation phases, a requirement of mastery before moving on to the next unit, and
a sequential progression to broader and deeper levels of mastery of the competencies as defined by graduation requirements.

5. Almost all students, except a small percentage of children with severe disabili-
ties, are capable of mastery levels of learning in these minimum competencies,
given sufficient time and appropriate instruction.

6. The most significant factor in learning is "time on task." This means that much
of class time will be spent on drills and exercises that strengthen the target competency, that additional time will be afforded to those students needing it, and
that daily homework will be assigned on the target competency.

7. While one approach to learning a competency may be initially stressed,
alternative methodologies will be employed for students experiencing
difficulty.

8. Higher-level learnings and cultural enrichment activities will tend to receive
less attention, especially in the earlier grades, except for those students who
have achieved mastery of the minimum competencies.

9. Classroom discipline will be controlled more by the intense concentration on
the learning task than by the teacher's imposition of punishments and repetition
of rules.

10. All the reward systems of the school should serve to promote academic
achievement as the highest priority. Rewards for other desirable behaviors or
achievement should be secondary to this priority.

THE DEMOCRATIC SOCIALIZATION PLATFORM

We have to start with the nature of learning. To learn is to develop understanding
which leads into and grows out of action. Learning means to discover a sense of
agency by which we define and construct ourselves, but this is always done with and
through others. Learning involves the mutual creation of a public sphere in which
the development of my own autonomy is matched by the obligation to contribute
to the well-being of the whole. Learning thus involves the making of a public world,
as much as learning to create the processes which sustain it, as learning the
substantive values by which it is to take shape. The motivation to learn involves
realizing the distinctive qualities of the self as agent with and through others. The

learning conditions for the unfolding self are social and political: my reality requires your recognition and your capacities demand my support.[4]

1. The primary aim of education is to enable the individual to function in society. Assuming a democratic society, the school should promote not only those qualities necessary for survival (employment, getting along with people, managing one's financial affairs, being a responsible family person, etc.) but also those qualities necessary for a healthy democratic society (political involvement that seeks the common good, willingness to displace self-interest for a higher purpose, skills at community building and conflict resolution, an understanding of how the political process works and how to influence public policy, etc.).

2. The school should intentionally arrange itself so that learning takes place primarily in a community context. Students should be taught to collaborate on learning tasks rather than to compete with one another. Team projects, peer tutoring, group rewards, and discussion of community problems should have priority even while the development of individual talents is encouraged. Individual talents, however, should be prized more for what they contribute to the community than for the exclusive enrichment of the individual.

3. Learning is best nurtured in a community context. Language skills are developed by regular and varied group communication. A sense of history and culture is nurtured by a focus on the group's history and culture. Psychological needs such as self-esteem and assertiveness are best met through active involvement in the community. Acceptance of differences and the development of individuality are negotiated best when there is a sense of community. Values, laws, and social customs are best taught within the context of the community.

4. The educator stands within the learning community and yet holds a special place of authority. The educator facilitates and directs the learning tasks of the younger members of the community but allows the agenda of community dynamics to intrude on the more academic tasks when the need arises.

5. Teachers and students function best when they work in relatively small, relatively self-contained, relatively autonomous learning communities. Hence those schools with large enrollments should be broken down into manageable learning communities that allow for closer and more continuous contact between a team of teachers and their students.

6. The curriculum should be controlled by a set of schoolwide learning outcomes for each year, but the learning community should have considerable autonomy in the ways it achieves these outcomes. The teams of teachers should be accountable for promoting required learnings but should be allowed to devise the particular learning activities that best address the students in their communities.

[4]These observations on the nature of learning are adapted from John Nixon, Jane Martin, Penny McKeown, and Stewart Ranson, *Encouraging Learning: Towards a Theory of the Learning School,* Buckingham, England: Open University Press, 1996, pp. 50–52.

7. Wherever possible, the learning communities should be involved with the larger civic community through parental involvement, by using the civic community as a learning laboratory, by discussing problems in the civic community, and by promoting the value of community service.

THE URBAN TEACHER PLATFORM

You have to understand the environments my kids come from. Many come from the projects, single-parent families, predominantly welfare children; others are first-generation immigrants, half of those are ESL students; some come from the older tenement communities, remnants of the ethnic neighborhoods, solid working-class families looking for discipline and security in the school. So what do I think are the three most important educational goals for me and my kids? First is discipline—by that I mean learning to follow the rules, learning self-control, impulse control. These kids grow up in neighborhoods where they see everything—murders, rapes, drugs, prostitution, shakedowns by local gangs or single entrepreneurs—what we call the bully—many of them girls. Lots of disorder in their lives, unpredictability, a kind of low-level haphazard chaos. So when they come into my class, they have to learn what it's like to be in an orderly place—quiet, predictable, where consequences follow choices—where they know they are cared for, but they also know there is no nonsense, no jiving the teacher. You do your work, you get acknowledged; you don't do your work, you suffer the consequences—do it after school, and then get it from your parent when you go home, because I've called.

So discipline is first. Then the habit of putting in the effort—the work ethic, learning that you don't get something for nothing. You want to get me off your back, you do the work—every day, do the homework, do the drills. Weekly tests tell you how you're doing. Below a "C" and your mother gets a call and you stay after school. I believe these kids can do the work I assign—all of them. But they come from environments either where the work ethic isn't a big deal. Or, with my kids from the tenements, their parents work hard and they have the work ethic, but not a "school work" ethic. Kids in their neighborhood all talk about how they hate school. Often both parents work, some on two jobs, and they don't push their kids. There are exceptions, but I'm on the phone all the time with parents. Kids have got to learn that work in the adult world is not much fun either. But if they are to develop any self-respect, they have to be able to take on any assignment, however unpleasant or uninteresting and put their backs into it. So that's number two—learn how to work hard consistently at what you're given to do.

Third is what used to be called manners. These are middle school kids, going through the beginning of the rebellious years. It's not just learning to say "please" and "thank you"; it's learning to respect other people, because they're human beings like you. Being a mother of an eleven-year-old, I know what the girls are going through. The boys are simply cruel in the way they treat them. Of course, the girls can be terribly insulting to the boys. So I'm always at them. While they're in my classroom, I will not tolerate name-calling, stereotyping, certainly not bullying by anyone. I spend time after school almost every day with two to five kids, working through a disagreement, a fight, a name-calling incident. I'm proud of what I accomplish with most of my kids. Their parents tell me about the good effects they see in their kids.

What do I believe about my kids as learners? I see them as struggling to survive without a lot of the supports that I had. I think in order to be a good student, you have to believe that studying hard at school leads to something, believe that there's something, some reward for putting up with the daily grind of school. For many of these kids, they don't see how school connects to anything meaningful in their lives. For the girls, who are maturing into young womanhood earlier now, relationships, boyfriends, family, and parenting are big realities for them. For the boys, it's sports, hobbies, gangs, getting into trouble for the fun of it. For both girls and boys, school is something imposed on them. So as learners, as young people who have potential to become young scholars with interest in pursuing a college degree, most of my kids don't see that in their future. Those who do look toward some kind of career seem to think mostly about something in the service industries. The only aspect of schoolwork that many have an interest in is computers and the Internet. I try to use that as a vehicle for teaching a lot of my basic curriculum.

My usual teaching strategies with these kids? First, as I indicated earlier, these kids need structure, discipline, hard work. Since this is a more traditional middle school, I teach everything except art and music. So I line up lots of activities to fill the day. Writing exercises on sentence structure, vocabulary drills, map exercises for geography, science workbook exercises on classification and measurements, math workbook drills. Sometimes we set up teams to see which team gets the highest score. The kids like that a lot. I keep them busy all the time. They're glad to get out of my clutches, but they learn to do the work, and sometimes even enjoy it.

THE ECOLOGICAL PLATFORM

1. The primary reality is neither the individual nor human society, but the entire ecosphere. Hence, the survival demands of the ecosphere and the concomitant implications for human society should constitute the primary focus of schooling.
2. Human culture can be understood analogously in ecological imagery. Human beings live within a culture as organisms in a natural environment of food chains, cycles of life, and rhythms of seasons. Human beings understand themselves as human through the rituals, traditions, artifacts, and relationships that are elements of a living culture. Hence schools, besides teaching the primary systems and structures of the ecosphere, should teach the cultural ecology by which human survival and development is possible.
3. The individual does not stand outside of the natural or cultural environment; rather, the individual is embedded in the natural and cultural environment. Human fulfillment does not mean escaping from this environment but discovering harmonious ways to live with those two environments. Learning itself is a discovery of one's relationship to and embeddedness in the cultural and natural environment.

4. The social purposes of schooling are not so much to achieve technical control over nature or to master the culture in the service of some instrumental purpose, but to overcome those social practices and social arrangements that destroy the natural and cultural environment. This is achieved by exploring those public policies and practices that sustain and respect the natural rhythms and patterns of nature and culture. Ethnocentric, nationalistic, sexist, racist, and all other exploitative relationships deny the unity and integrity of the natural and human environment. When society harms the environment, it literally harms itself; similarly, when society damages the natural bonds between human beings, it damages itself. People are inextricably embedded in their cultural bonds; those bonds support humanity and feed the human spirit. People's understanding of who they are collectively is embedded in their culture.

5. Knowledge, then, is not something one individual achieves or possesses; it is the achievement and heritage and energy of all human beings. When one knows something, one knows it as one's culture names it. One knows something because the relationships that are grasped in knowledge contain oneself as much as one contains those relationships. Human beings always know much more than they can articulate because most knowledge is tacit and is experienced at subliminal levels of intuition. The human body knows at least as much as the human mind does; the mind has different ways of articulating that knowledge than the body does.

6. Relationships to the environment and culture are known through experience. Using a language to describe those relationships frames those relationships in ways that distort as well as clarify. Language is not a neutral tool for expression; language carries interpretations constructed and imposed by the culture. Hence part of the task of schools is to make explicit the point of view embedded in taken-for-granted cultural understandings. Everyday language contains many class, sexist, rationalistic, economic, and ethnocentric distortions, which in turn reveal distortions and disharmonies between human beings and the natural environment, within the culture and within human beings themselves.

7. The classroom itself represents an artificial cultural ecology that distorts how youngsters view the natural environment, how they view themselves, how they view science and rationality. Current school curricula promote values that are antithetical to both the survival of the ecosphere and the cultural unity and integrity of the human race. Hence the pedagogy employed and the curriculum and the assessment of learning must be transformed to reflect the survival demands of both the natural and the human environment.

TWO VIEWS OF KNOWLEDGE AND LEARNING

Gee has identified two major influences on teachers' and supervisors' platforms.[5] One perspective, developed by the Project Zero researchers at Harvard, focuses on

[5]James Paul Gee, "On Mobots and Classrooms: The Converging Languages of the New Capitalism and Schooling," *Organization, Self-Organization,* vol. 3, no. 3 (1996), pp. 385–407.

the type of knowledge and skills found in "experts" or scholars of various academic disciplines.[6] This tacit platform reveals a view of learning, of the knowledge to be learned (the curriculum), of appropriate teaching, of the social uses of knowledge, and of the primary aims of education. The work of the Harvard researchers continues a long tradition in education, namely, that the purpose of schooling is to introduce young people into the rudiments of the academic disciplines, to bring them gradually to a level of the "novice expert." At this level, students would (1) exhibit the ability to speak and write about the central conceptual frameworks or systems of ideas in a field—say, mathematics, or economics; (2) understand and be able to use the core methodologies of inquiry, or knowledge production; (3) be able to explain various uses to which the knowledge in that field may be put; and (4) be able to present that knowledge of the field in a variety of formats (through charts and diagrams, metaphors, narratives, written expositions). Such an approach to the tasks of learning has available the rich sources of knowledge contained in what might be called the accepted canon of each discipline. It can structure the tasks of learning much the way scholars in the field have structured their learning by imitating the research methodologies employed by the scholars as well as the methods of reporting their findings (through statistics, research reports, charts and diagrams, or research narratives).

A second perspective is provided by the work of cognitive psychologists such as Brown and Campione,[7] and Bereiter and Scadamalia.[8] They argue that in the real world, problems are encountered that do not fit neatly into a single academic framework. Rather, they are embedded in complex situations that require many perspectives to be engaged in the process of addressing that problem. Real-world problem solving requires teams of people who have various types of expertise, none of which by themselves are able to resolve the problem. For example, a community attempting to clean up a toxic waste site or looking to renovate an abandoned factory network along the riverfront in a rundown section of its city, or a community's effort to attract new industries and provide jobs and a stronger tax base all use teams of experts. Thus, these educators advocate an approach to learning that involves teams of young learners using a methodology called a jigsaw. Each member of the team goes off to research one aspect of a problem and then comes together to teach the others on the team how his or her information can be used to address a piece of the puzzle. Using the ad hoc expertise of the whole team, the students propose a response to the problem. Gee maintains that this approach to learning is much more in line with the postmodern world, in which knowledge is not a static body of information to be mastered discretely discipline by discipline. Rather, knowledge is seen as more transitory, more something constructed within a defined context in response to a particular problem or issue. As students proceed to new problems in different contexts, they have to gather new information, create useful formats for bringing

[6]Martha Stone Wiske (ed.), *Teaching for Understanding: Linking Research with Practice,* San Francisco: Jossey-Bass, 1998.

[7]Ann L. Brown and J. C. Campione, "Guided Discovery in a Community of Learners," in K. McGilly (ed.), *Classroom Lessons: Integrating Cognitive Theory and Classroom Practice,* pp. 229–270. Cambridge, MA: MIT Press, 1994.

[8]Carl Bereiter and M. Scardamalia, *Surpassing Ourselves: An Inquiry into the Nature and Implications of Expertise,* Chicago: Open Court, 1993.

that information to bear on a situation, and align that approach with the formats that others have created using different information. Thus, knowledge and its creative alignment with other varieties of knowledge is something that is always new, always being constructed to respond to specific situations.

A platform based on this perspective would reflect a different understanding of the aims of education, a different understanding of the nature of learning, of the curriculum, of the social purposes of the schooling, and of the core strategies of teaching.

ELEMENTS OF A PLATFORM

In stressing the importance of explicating the platform, we realize that many teachers will find the exercise difficult. Their platform statements may or may not come out as clearly as the ones given here. On the other hand, the effort to elucidate the platform can help teachers become more reflective about their practice. Such reflection can help teachers puzzle their way through instructional problems which their intuitions cannot solve. It also enables teachers to acknowledge some inconsistencies in their practice that, although not previously acknowledged consciously, may have created an occasional sense of dissatisfaction. Recognizing such inconsistencies opens up the space for changes in practice.

Furthermore, platform clarification brings greater, more explicit intelligibility to what teachers do in class every day. It gives teachers names and words for telling their story. It enables them to talk with greater clarity among themselves, with parents, and with supervisors about what they do. The examples above provide some idea of what a platform entails. In general terms we can say that a platform contains about eight elements. All platforms need not contain all these elements; some may be expressed more in narrative form, some in a sequence of terse sentences; some may be better expressed in pictures or cartoons. Furthermore, platforms need not be cast in stone. From year to year, new elements will be added or some will be stressed more than others. The important thing is to have a sense of what one's platform is, rather than to construct a prize-winning statement for the school board.

General Elements of a Platform

1. *The aims of education.* Set down, in order of priority, the three most important aims of education—not simply education in the abstract, but education for the youngsters in your school system.
2. *Views of knowledge.* Some will emphasize the academic disciplines as bodies of knowledge objectively "out there" to be mastered in order to understand how the world works. Other teachers will acknowledge that knowledge is what knowers actively produce in dialogue with the "public" knowledge of the school's curriculum. Gradually, that actively produced knowledge will come to look more and more in agreement with the curriculum knowledge, as the testing regime

shapes and conditions the students' construction of knowledge into "correct" knowledge. Other educators see knowledge as much more a pragmatically and socially constructed knowledge which is useful for a specific context, but which will be reconstructed for different practical problems in different contexts. It is learning how socially to construct useful knowledge that is the more important "curriculum," rather than the content of the knowledge produced in any given pragmatic contest. Others, finally, will view knowledge as completely dominated by the interpersonal relations of the persons sharing the knowledge and the power relations between them. In relationships of disproportionate power, in which the subordinated person identifies with the superordinate person, knowledge is what the dominant person declares it to be; in relationships of equal mutuality, knowledge comes to be what the parties agree it is.

3. *The social significance of the student's learning.* Some teachers emphasize vocational learning; some, the learning of how to be a good citizen; some, the acquisition of the cultural heritage of Western civilization. Others might deemphasize the content of the curriculum in favor of the useful skills students acquire, such as seeking clear evidence, entertaining competing points of view, developing a work ethic, arguing for or representing a position clearly and persuasively. Still others would assert that youngsters in school learn how to participate as members of various worlds—the cultural world, the world of nature, the social world, and the political world.

4. *The image of the learner.* Often metaphors will capture how the teacher thinks of a learner: an empty vessel; a mind; an information processor; a constructor of knowledge for practical applications to life; a novice scholar; a gifted, mediocre, or slow learner; a philistine; an artist; a mystery. Some will classify learners as possessing high intelligence; others will claim that intelligence is itself learned, not given. We tend to view learners as developing humans who create themselves and the trajectory of their lives through learning.

5. *The image of the curriculum.* Some would say that the curriculum is the doorway into the worlds of nature, culture, and society. Others would see the curriculum as representing the cumulative record of what humankind has learned about the way the world works. Some would say that the curriculum provides a uniform script containing all the knowledge necessary for carrying on one's role in life; others would go farther and claim that the curriculum should also teach youngsters how to improvise upon the script for their own authentic playing of their part in life, as well as to improve the script for others. Critics of the accepted canon of the curriculum would argue that it contains the privileged knowledge that enables those in power to stay in power. Others would simply say that the curriculum is the stepping-stone to getting into and succeeding in a university. We tend to see the curriculum as what is learned, as the meaning that learners make out of exposure to the subjects studied in school.

6. *The image of the teacher.* What is a teacher? Is a teacher an employee of the state, following the educational policies and practices dictated by the local, state, and federal government? Or is a teacher a professional specialist whom a community employs to exercise his or her expertise on behalf of youngsters?

Or is a teacher a spokesperson for tradition, passing on the riches of the culture? Or is a teacher a political engineer, leading youngsters to develop those skills necessary to reform their society? We emphasize the teacher's role as facilitator and guide of student learning.

7. *The preferred pedagogy.* Will the teacher dominate the learning experience? Some assume that inquiry learning is the best way to teach. Others assume that each discipline lends itself better to some forms of pedagogy than others. Some would opt for much more student-initiated learning, while others favor group projects. Although there may be some reluctance to focus on *one* pedagogical approach to the exclusion of all others, teachers tend to settle on two or three as the more effective approaches.

8. *The preferred school climate.* This element brings various environmental considerations into play, such as the affective tone to schoolwide and classroom discipline, feelings of student pride in the school, faculty morale, the openness of the school community to divergent lifestyles, expressive learnings, and individualistic ways of thinking and behaving. Some would describe an environment reflective of a learning community: open, caring, inquisitive, flexible, collaborative. Some would opt for order and predictability. Others would prefer a more relaxed climate, perhaps more boisterous but also more creative and spontaneous. This element is very much related to what is valued in the curriculum and to the social consequences of learning.

It becomes obvious to teachers when they test out their assumptions for each of the elements discussed above that there tends to be an intrinsic logic to them. That is, there tends to be a consistency between assumptions about the nature of the learner and the preferred kind of teacher–student relationship, which in turn relates logically to teachers' beliefs about the aims of education. As educators clarify their assumptions, beliefs, and opinions under each of these eight categories, the platform they use in practice should become apparent to them. That is to say, educators usually make practical decisions about professional practice based upon convictions, assumptions, and attitudes that are not clearly or frequently articulated. Nevertheless, they do influence, some would even say dominate, actions. By bringing these convictions, assumptions, and attitudes out into the open for their own reflection, educators can evaluate internal consistency and cogency. They can also check whether they are satisfied with their platform, or whether they have not taken important factors into consideration. By clarifying the underlying intelligibility of their actions, educators might see a need to grow in specific areas to increase their effectiveness as well as to broaden their capacities.

THE SUPERVISOR'S PLATFORM

The above analysis of key elements in a platform deals with an educational platform. This educational platform focuses on what one believes ought to happen in a process of formal education. It could belong to a teacher, a student, an administrator, or a supervisor. The supervisor can elaborate his or her own educational platform, but it becomes complete when the supervisor adds his or her beliefs about the activity of supervising. Two categories that concern supervision are the following: the purpose of supervision and the preferred process of supervision.

1. *The purpose or goal of supervision.* Some would say that the purpose of supervision is to weed out the weak and encourage the competent, one teacher at a time. Others would say that supervision, in the present context of school renewal, should aim at improved student achievement on standards-based tests. Thus, supervisors should work with groups of teachers to get them to map all their instruction to curriculum standards. Others would say that supervisors should attempt to get all the teachers in the school to collaboratively focus on enhancing quality learning for all students within state curriculum guidelines first, and within local curriculum guidelines in addition. This view of the purpose of supervision would engage teachers in a collaborative, multiyear effort to generate multiple and adaptive teaching protocols that engage each student in quality learning activities.

2. *The preferred process of supervision.* Some would say that the state policy agenda of renewal leaves them no choice but to take a hierarchical, authoritative approach to supervision. Teachers have no choice but to focus on improving student achievement on state tests through careful attention to the state curriculum standards. Supervisors have to monitor each teacher's class test scores and apply remediation procedures to those teachers whose students do poorly. This means tight control over professional development options, focusing only on those directly related to strategies to improve test scores. It means, as well, holding teachers accountable, setting up early warning systems for teachers of underperforming classes. Other supervisors would say that the process of supervision must start by communicating to teachers the belief that teachers as a group can deal efficaciously with the state school renewal agenda. This supervisor would be collegial and encourage collegial teacher initiative, imagination, and teamwork. This supervisor would provide resources of time, finances, and professional development expertise to support teachers' cooperative work to develop responsive teaching protocols for the diverse student needs, as all seek to be responsive to the state curriculum guidelines.

Again, the point of clarifying one's convictions and unspoken assumptions about the nature of supervision is to open the door for growth, for the sharing of ideas, and for supervisory performance grounded in basic beliefs. Ideally, these last two elements of the supervisor's platform should be written down before one reads this book, and again after one has read the book. If the analysis of supervision presented between these covers has an effect, it would show up in the differences between the two platform statements.

APPROACHES TO PLATFORM CLARIFICATION

A useful exercise for supervisors and a whole school's faculty might be to identify the tacit platform behind the state's agenda of school reform. Are the aims of education spelled out in predominantly economic terms, in functional utility terms, in the more traditional commitment to the academic disciplines, or to the formation of a democratic community? Is the learner a passive recipient of a prepackaged curriculum, or an active and collaborative learner who creates or constructs ever richer and more complex clusters of knowledge? Is the teacher a civil servant expected to follow detailed curriculum plans and instructional protocols, carefully mapping all instruction to the anticipated material on high-stakes tests, or is the teacher a professional who continually adapts classroom activities to the diverse abilities of the students while addressing the curriculum guideline laid down by the state? Does the assessment of student learning reveal a superficial understanding of learning as recall, as the ability to narrow down several possible answers to the one or two "right" answers?

By interrogating the tacit platform behind the state's school renewal agenda, teachers and supervisors can identify the level of responses being demanded of them and of the students. This clarification of the policy environment and its demands enables the local school to decide how to meet these demands while at the same time deciding how to add value in ways that respond to the particulars of the community.

Many teachers may find the initial efforts at platform clarification very frustrating. It is not something they do often, and there can be a feeling of awkwardness. Yet everyone has an unexpressed platform. Were a sensitive observer to follow a teacher around for a day or two on the job, it would be relatively easy to guess that teacher's beliefs about how youngsters learn best, about what is important to learn, about good teaching and inferior teaching, and so on. People's actions usually reveal their assumptions and attitudes quite clearly.

Two different approaches offer supervisors and teachers a way to construct their platforms. One approach would be to work with all the teachers or a group of them in a staff development format. The other approach would entail a supervisor and a teacher working in a one-on-one situation.

Group Approaches to Educational Platform Development

In a staff development framework, supervisors can work with a group of teachers. Some explanation of what platforms are and how platform clarification might assist their practice should be given. Examples of platforms should then be provided. Teachers would then write out their own platform. They should be encouraged to try out a unifying image or metaphor around which all their platform elements might cluster. David Hunt, in his work with teachers, has found that metaphors help teachers bring out the theory embedded in their practice.[9] Metaphors of teaching, such as guiding a journey, conducting an orchestra, pulling rabbits out of a hat, mining gold, tending a garden, captaining a ship, and directing a play, contain beliefs and assumptions about learning, curriculum, social purposes of schooling, and pedagogy. Many others find the orderly process of filling out where they stand on the eight elements of the platform the most convenient beginning for the exercise. After the first draft, they may want to rearrange and amplify. Putting

---

[9]David E. Hunt, *Beginning with Ourselves,* Cambridge, MA: Brookline Books, 1987.

words onto paper may then enable them to see their guiding metaphor. Teachers can also check the internal consistency between elements of the platform and note points to pursue with themselves or with others during subsequent exercises. Others will prefer a less structured approach, letting their assumptions come out as they are felt and recognized, rather than having to force them into categories with which they are uncomfortable.

Some find it helpful to find a quiet place to write down their reflections. Normally, these thoughts will come out in no particular order of priority. Once teachers have written down the elements of their platform, they can with further reflection begin to group them in clusters and place them in some order of importance. Almost everyone with any experience in education, however, will feel several times during this exercise the need to qualify and add nuance to those general statements: "Which teaching strategy I'd use in a given situation depends a lot on a youngster's background. But by and large, I'd choose this approach." "While I'd place my major emphasis on mastery of basic intellectual skills, I still think it's important to spend some time teaching kids good manners." "I almost always prefer to start a lesson with a colorful advance organizer. That usually stirs up the pupils' curiosity. But there are times when I run plain, old-fashioned memory drills."

Others will find the writing exercise too tedious and will seek out a colleague with whom to discuss this whole question. The free flow of shared ideas frequently stimulates the process of clarification. In those instances, a tape recorder may help for subsequent transcription of the conversation. Others may find a combination of dialogue and writing the better way. Still others may refer to a formal statement of goals that the school or system has in print to begin the process. By studying the goals and *probing the assumptions behind them,* the teacher may discover areas of disagreement or agreement.

However teachers go about clarifying their platform initially, two other steps will prove helpful. After the first tentative statement of the platform, the teachers should compare their platform with those of two or three colleagues, to test out areas of agreement or disagreement. Sometimes this may lead to modification of their own platforms. It may also lead to a greater acceptance of diversity of perspectives. It certainly will help teachers to build teamwork. Knowing the biases behind one another's approach will enable teachers to work together in areas where they agree or might complement one another.

When the teachers have discussed their platforms together, they should then compare them with the school's or the system's platform. That may not exist in a written document, but, as in their own cases, it exists implicitly in the operational policies of the school or school system. They may find some genuine discrepancies between what the school's goal statements profess and what the school practices. Bringing those discrepancies to light, in itself, would be a service to the school. The purpose of examining the expressed and unexpressed (but operative) platforms of the school, however, is aimed more at a comparison between the school's platform and the teachers' platforms. If they find striking divergences between them, then the teachers and supervisors will have to seek some means of reconciling the discrepancies, modifying one or the other to make them more compatible.

The point of this exercise is not to introduce frustration and cynicism but, on the contrary, to reduce it. If supervisors and teachers are to work toward restructuring the educational process in their schools and school systems, then this exercise may be a good place to begin. As Michael Fullan suggests, school improvement and classroom improvement necessarily overlap, and teachers must be involved with both levels of improvement.[10]

The group activity with platforms can continue on to a variety of discussions. Teachers may use the discussions as a basis for considering curriculum restructuring as well as new configurations for instructional space and time arrangements. They may also use the sharing of their platforms as a launching pad for discussions about including other student learning outcomes that their present teaching is ignoring or slighting, or other ways of evaluating student learning. These follow-up discussions will depend on the particular context and frame of mind the teachers are in, or on perceived student or professional needs within the school. Discussions about platforms among groups of teachers, while worthwhile in themselves, also can lead to a variety of additional staff development initiatives.

Individual Use of Platform Development

Supervisors can also use the group platform exercise to work with individual teachers. Discussions about the teacher's platform enable both supervisor and teacher to clarify what teaching episodes mean to the teacher. Such discussions can enable teachers and supervisors to interpret and explore possibilities within such teaching episodes and series of episodes. Making one's platform explicit also enables both supervisor and teacher to explore discrepancies between the teacher's platform in theory and the platform in use. That is to say, in particular instances, teachers may act in class in contradiction to their stated platform. Supervisors and teachers then have to discuss the apparent discrepancy and see whether such practices need to be changed to conform to their stated platform. The emphasis here is not so much on correcting faults, however, as it is on clarifying the intelligibility and intentionality of the teacher's work with youngsters. As teachers become more reflective about their work, under the influence of exercises like platform clarification, they will grow in their sense of consistency and in their responsiveness to students as well. Moreover, through discussions about the teacher's platform, supervisors will be working out of a framework of collegial conversation with the teacher based on the teacher's language and perspectives, rather than a framework of some generalized format for teaching. Such a basis of understanding between supervisor and teacher facilitates ongoing positive conversations, which teachers can feel comfortable with because they are dealing with their own agenda rather than a bureaucratic agenda of filling out forms containing categories constructed by someone else.

---

[10]Michael G. Fullan, "Staff Development, Innovation, and Institutional Development," in Bruce Joyce (ed.), *Changing School Culture Through Staff Development,* Alexandria, VA: Association for Supervision and Curriculum Development, 1990, pp. 3–25.

SUMMARY

In this chapter, we have taken up the concept of the educational platform. When examples of educational platforms were given, it became apparent that a platform is made up of those basic assumptions, beliefs, attitudes, and values that are the underpinnings of an educator's behavior. It also became apparent that the platform tends to shape the educator's everyday practice. By encouraging teachers to clarify their platform, supervisors can stimulate a variety of teacher reflections on their practice. Some of these reflections can take place in a group setting, generating possibilities for restructuring the work of the school. Other reflections on practice in the light of the platform can take place on an individual basis. Such reflection can provide some common language and understanding between supervisor and teacher out of which can grow new insight into teaching and new possibilities for student learning.

SOME REFLECTIONS

1. Since the whole chapter suggests a major reflective exercise, we begin with these questions: What did you learn from completing a draft of your education and supervisory platform? Is your supervisory platform consistent with the platform most of the teachers hold about curriculum, learning, and teaching?
2. How consistent is the school district's enacted platform—through its policies and procedures—with the teachers' platform in your school? Does the evidence suggest what, if anything, needs to be done about this?
3. Are some educational and supervisory platforms more attractive to you and your colleagues? If the answer is yes, which ones and why did you choose them? Gather with colleagues who agree. With which educational and supervisory platforms do you disagree?

PART TWO

Foundations for Supervision

CHAPTER 6

Teaching and Learning

INTRODUCTION

In more traditional times, supervisors were expected to visit classrooms and observe what the teacher was doing, often noting whether the teacher's actions conformed to a list of activities assumed to be related to superior or good teaching. Currently, supervisors need to attend at least as much to what students are doing as to what teachers are doing. This shift of focus is occasioned by the massive changes in the policies driving school renewal. The school renewal effort focuses much more on what students know, understand, and are able to do as measured by performance standards that are related to curriculum standards. Dissatisfied with the continuing evidence of the gap between students who perform well in schools and the large numbers who do not, national and state governments have issued zero tolerance policies on student low performance.[1] These governments now demand evidence of quality understanding of curriculum material for *all* students. Most of the academic discipline-based professional organizations have likewise weighed in with their own proposals that *all* students should be able to reach deep understanding in the academic disciplines. A strong consensus has emerged among educational reformers that the measure of a good school has to go beyond the kind of teaching and learning that results only in performing well on statewide tests. Thus, while maintaining a close eye on the teacher's skills in the classrooms, supervisors have to attend to the evidence that all students in the class are learning at a level of developmentally appropriate, deep understanding of the curriculum.

Because of this focus on student learning, this chapter will emphasize the teachers' focus on providing multiple opportunities for students to learn. Likewise,

---

[1]Peter W. Hill and Carmel A. Crevola, "The Role of Standards in Educational Reform for the 21st Century," in D. D. Marsh (ed.), *Preparing Our Schools for the 21st Century,* Alexandria, VA: Association for Supervision and Curriculum Development, 1999, p. 118; United States Department of Education, No Child *Left Behind* Act of 2001, DC.

in the next chapter on curriculum, the focus will be on the students' engagement in performing the curriculum, and the teachers' designing of the curriculum to effect that engagement. These two chapters will overlap in significant ways because the focus on student active learning ties the enactment of the curriculum and the acts of teaching together much more organically. Furthermore, since assessment of learning is so crucial to the act of learning itself, assessment appears more intrinsic to teaching as well as to enacting the curriculum. Thus, teaching, learning, curriculum, and assessment are seen as interpenetrating realities to which supervisors must attend as an organic whole as they seek to make sense of what is actually going on in classrooms.

SOME BACKGROUND

How we think about curriculum matters. We can think about curriculum-as-planned, as-taught, as-learned, and as-tested. For example, the curriculum can be thought of as a body of knowledge codified by the academic disciplines and translated into course syllabi, textbooks, and demonstration materials. This is the *curriculum-as-planned*. Teachers take the curriculum-as-planned and adapt it to their own perspectives, supplement it with commercial or personal materials, emphasize some elements, and give less attention to others. They may have developed clever ways to teach certain parts of the curriculum; other parts they teach with less creativity and verve. This is the *curriculum-as-taught*.

Students encounter the curriculum-as-taught, misunderstand or misinterpret certain parts of it, relate other parts of it to their prior knowledge (which itself is limited and fallible), memorize certain parts to be repeated verbatim on exams, are absent from class on some days when crucial concepts are treated, and are oblivious to the significance or meaning of certain other parts. Some students find the material interesting, while others find it boring but tolerable in the short run. Still others have not learned the previous material well enough to build bridges to the new material. This is the *curriculum-as-learned*. It will be different for every student in the class, even though the majority of students may have acquired a sufficient common vocabulary of the material to talk about it with the teacher.

Students are then tested on what they have learned. The tests cover only selected parts of the curriculum thought to be representative of the material that should have been learned. Often tests are constructed to measure simple recall of information and definitions. Other tests are constructed with some easy questions, some moderately complicated questions, and some difficult questions that can only be understood by students functioning at the metacognitive level. Some tests attempt to find out what the students do not know, others to find out what they know well. Many tests are constructed on the conviction that achievement is reflective of the so-called normal curve of intelligence and that the job of the test is to sort out the brighter from the less bright, so that the teacher's grade sheets can reflect this normal curve. Many teachers have learned that too many high grades are interpreted by parents and administrators as a sign of insufficient rigor and that too many low

grades are interpreted as a sign of unrealistically demanding (and unfair) expectations. This is the *curriculum-as-tested*.

To be sure, in this system creative and stimulating pedagogical techniques may
be encouraged, and some personal interpretations by students may be allowed, especially in literature, social studies, and the fine arts. (Creative algebra, on the other
hand, is almost as unthinkable as a creative fire drill.) Despite concessions for creativity and interpretation, by and large the curriculum content and the methodologies associated with distinct subject matters are established by curriculum experts,
to be taught and learned as they are presented in textbooks and outlined in the
school's or district's syllabus.

DEEP UNDERSTANDING FOR ALL STUDENTS

This traditional understanding of the curriculum and the teaching of it have been
altered by the importance given to the curriculum-as-learned. Now the emphasis is
on the success of *all* students in acquiring a deep understanding of the material.
Under the traditional system a school could maintain the easy assumption of the normal curve of achievement: 10 to 20 percent of the students receive an A; around 30
percent receive a B; around 30 percent receive a C; the rest receive either a D or an
F. Now, however, that is unacceptable. Virtually all students are expected to achieve
at an A or a B level. It is further assumed that, if they do not, there is something
wrong with the way the material is being presented and taught. The explanations that
students don't care, that they are lazy and unfocused, no longer settle the issue. It
must be asked *why* they don't care, *why* they are unfocused, *why* they are apathetic.
The answers to these questions imply that the school (not simply one particular
teacher) has failed to entice them to care, has failed to explain or present the material in ways that facilitate cognitive clarity and attention, has failed to stimulate and
excite in students the curiosity and involvement needed to connect with the material
and tasks at hand. The curriculum is no longer considered exclusively as what has
been institutionally constructed for the relatively passive, uncontaminating reception
by the students; now the curriculum is seen primarily as what works for these students on this day in this context, as this part of a broader understanding-in-process of
a larger framework of knowledge. Today's curriculum is what the students can learn
today, with an eye on its connection to yesterday's and tomorrow's learning.

The emphasis is on the activity of the students as they attempt to construct the
knowledge and understanding implied in the curriculum unit. Whereas in the traditional system the emphasis in classroom learning seemed to be on the students' ab-
sorbing what the teacher was saying or demonstrating, now the emphasis is on the
students' actively interacting with the material at hand to *draw out* the knowledge
and understanding called for by the curriculum task. In this way, students from an
early age learn attack skills and inquiry strategies to make sense out of new material. They build up a repertoire of problem-solving alternatives, habits of looking at
material from several points of view, processes of building on earlier understandings to piece together a new puzzle. This does not mean that the teacher never

provides a demonstration or an overview or a theoretical explanation. Instead, the emphasis is on teaching the students to become more independent learners. Even in cases where the teacher does provide the initial demonstration, researchers have shown that students must work over that instruction in their own minds, using previously understood categories and skills to reconstruct for themselves what the teacher is trying to show.[2] Students cannot be said to understand what the teacher was demonstrating without such active internal processing. Moreover, it is only by developing their mental images of the material by making applications, by providing explanations, by giving multiple examples of the concept or principle involved, and by connecting that to larger networks of meanings that lasting or deep understanding is achieved. This is a different understanding of learning; rather than attempting to remember what someone else told them, students must work over the material, and work at it in a variety of formats, and produce a variety of performances.[3]

Research is showing that students have a wealth of prior learnings and experiences that they call on to grasp new material.[4] Teachers, however, seldom encourage students to call on that prior learning, nor do they teach students specific strategies for making those connections. As a result, youngsters attempt a hit-or-miss process of making connections, often distorting or misinterpreting the material at hand. By carefully listening to students as they explain how they arrived at certain conclusions, teachers can come to understand the common errors children make on their way to figuring something out.[5] Their "wrong" answers are frequently "correct" when one understands the premises under which they have been working. Teachers need to consider youngsters' descriptions of their academic performances to understand how the patterns of their thoughts are formed and shaped.[6]

Children are constantly constructing their world out of the conversations of their parents and friends, and out of the meanings and associations picked up in their everyday experience in school and at home. This internalized world picture, in turn, shapes their subsequent perspectives and interpretations. Schoolwork often asks them to realign those perspectives with new understandings. Unless a teacher is somehow aware of how a child is making sense of the world, he or she may not know how the prior understandings of that particular child are distorting or preventing the appropriation of the new material.

---

[2]See Bonnie Shapiro's research in *What Children Bring to Light: A Constructivist Perspective on Children's Learning in Science,* New York: Teachers College Press, 1994. See also the illuminating essays of teachers doing research on their teaching in Marilyn Corchran-Smith and Susan L. Lytle (eds.), *Inside/Outside: Teacher Research and Knowledge,* New York: Teachers College Press, 1993.

[3]See the work of David Perkins and his associates at Harvard Project Zero, as elaborated in his *Smart School: Better Thinking and Learning for Every Child,* New York: Free Press, 1992. John Bruer underscores the importance of challenging students to develop their own understandings as they grapple with knotty problems. See his *Schools for Thought: A Science of Learning in the Classroom,* Cambridge, MA: MIT Press, 1993.

[4]For an illustrative example of such research with kindergarten children, see Irmie Fallon and JoBeth Allen, "Where the Deer and the Cantaloupe Play," *The Reading Teacher,* vol. 47, no. 7 (1994), pp. 546–551. See also the research reported in Corchran-Smith and Lytle, op. cit.

[5]Shapiro, op. cit.

[6]Again, the accounts of teacher research documented in Corchran-Smith and Lytle, op. cit., are instructive.

AUTHENTIC TEACHING AND LEARNING

A shift of major proportions appears to be occurring in our understanding of teaching and learning, namely, that authentic learning goes well beyond the passive intake of information to active engagement of the learner in producing or reproducing knowledge and understanding. Recent research is showing that authentic learning does not take place until the learner has come to an understanding of the material by organizing information into meaningful categories and into networks of categories, by having to explain what the material looks like from different perspectives, by providing various examples, by applying the understanding to new problems or contexts, and by evaluating the significance of new information in the light of this understanding. Even then a student's understanding is incomplete. It must be complemented by placing that understanding within the perspectives of an academic discipline, then showing how that understanding is related to other understandings considered essential in that field. The understanding is more mature when it can be connected to the world beyond the school, when it can be used to explain or explore issues in the civic community, and when the student can discuss his or her understanding with an adult audience in that larger community.[7]

The focus on the student as the active producer of knowledge has been pushed even further. Some well-documented research indicates that children can move to the metacognitive level in their learning. That is to say, they can discover the very processes by which they come to learn something. They can reflect on what they have been learning to grasp how they came to learn the material, by seeing the methods they have used to construct bridges from earlier knowledge to new material, and by coming to understand the process of knowing (metacognition). Groups of youngsters engaged in the jigsaw method of peer teaching can be guided to discuss how they came to the understandings they were trying to communicate to one another.[8]

David Perkins calls this attention to metacognition "the metacurriculum," thereby situating this form of learning as the crowning achievement of the students' active learning process.[9] He cites the following examples of attention to the metacurriculum:

- encouraging students to think about the kinds of questions they would pose for themselves when faced with new material (e.g., What is this? How does it work? What is this like?)

---

[7]See the work of the Center on Organization and Restructuring of Schools, as reported in Fred M. Newmann and Gary G. Wehlage, *Successful School Restructuring,* Madison, WI: Center on Organization and Restructuring of Schools, 1995.

[8]L. Baker and A. L. Brown, "Metacognitive Skills and Reading," in P. D. Pearson (ed.), *Handbook of Reading Research,* vol. 2, New York: Longman, 1984, pp. 353–394; A. L. Brown and A. S. Palinscar, "Reciprocal Teaching of Comprehension Strategies: A Natural History of One Program for Enhancing Learning," in J. D. Day and J. G. Borkowski (eds.), *Intelligence and Exceptionality: New Directions for Theory, Assessment, and Instructional Practices,* Norwood, NJ: Ablex, 1987.

[9]Perkins, op. cit., p. 101.

- encouraging students to describe their general problem-solving strategies (e.g., divide a problem into subproblems)
- getting students to use terms such as hypothesis and sources of evidence as they try to make sense out of new material
- understanding that what is accepted as evidence varies across subject matters (formal proof in mathematics, experimental results in science, argument from the text and historical context in literary criticism, etc.)

This practice of reflective learning, usually carried on verbally with other students and the teacher, provides the foundation for the appropriate transfer of learning in new situations and for developing the general skills of learning how to learn. When it is carried out within a collaborative context, students also learn the important lesson of relying on the cumulative intelligence of the group, where everyone has some important insight or perspective to contribute, oftentimes correcting an oversimplification or distortion of understanding presented by other individuals in the group or filling in some unattended spaces in the group's thinking. The presence of the teacher allows for challenges to the misconceptions or distortions still remaining in the group's deliberations. The point is that the activity does not begin with the teacher's explaining the metacognitive content and skills; instead, the students are asked to come up with their own understandings, thus developing the habit of processing their work for the metacognitive scaffolding around it.

Fred Newman and Gary Wehlage add another dimension to the metacurriculum by insisting that this knowledge have some value beyond the school, beyond the simple achievement of competence.[10] Student learning should issue in more public products or performances that have aesthetic, pragmatic, or personal value. Students should be able to apply their understanding in public performances in their communities and to discuss these performances with adults in the community, using the understanding of the frameworks and methods of the disciplines. The concentration and effort required to produce something worthy of public scrutiny will necessarily deepen the students' appropriation of the metacurriculum. Barbara Presseisen refers to this aspect of higher-order thinking as *conation*, the motivating influence of doing a task when learning applies to the real world of the student.[11]

In order for students to develop the habits required for their full attention to the activity of learning, many researchers who deal with the metacurriculum stress a division of the learning activity into three stages: (1) the anticipatory activities, (2) the learning exercise itself, and (3) the follow-up activities.[12] In the anticipatory stage students are asked to recall earlier learnings about both content and learning procedures, which are connected to the learning at hand. These will serve as a bridge to the new material. The new material will be introduced with initial probing questions to begin focusing on the nature of the problems to be encountered. Again, students

---

[10]Newman and Wehlage, op. cit., pp. 9–11.

[11]Barbara Z. Presseisen, "Thinking Skills in the Curriculum," in James W. Keefe, and Herbert J. Walberg (eds.), *Teaching for Thinking*, Reston, VA: National Association of Secondary Principals, 1992, p. 4.

[12]This is a summary of several suggestions contained in essays in Keefe and Walberg, op. cit.

will be asked to recall a variety of attack skills that can be employed as they seek to make sense of the task. This is sometimes called a rehearsal of the learning activity. If grouping and collaboration are called for, specific responsibilities and subtasks are clarified, as well as the expected results of the exercise.

In the learning activity itself, students will engage the material by setting up the task, identifying the key components of the new materials, asking questions of the material, and applying various previously acquired categories, such as cause–effect analyses, comparison–contrast analysis, explanatory hypotheses, species/genus categories, narrative structural elements, the influence of contextual variables, cultural values and ideologies, taxonomies, sources of evidence and weighing of evidence, and appropriate boilerplate formulas and equations. As the learners come to a deeper understanding of the new material and make sense of it, they move toward the completion of the task, whether it is to write an expository paragraph in plain language about the material, to report on the conclusion of an experiment to peers working on other experiments, to evaluate a political debate, to compare two poets or painters, to write an interpretation of a historical event that had been reported from three different perspectives, or to argue the public policy merits of a proposal for a new sewage treatment plant in the community. Before completing the task, they might review an explicit or tacit checklist, asking themselves such questions as these: Do my results relate to the definition and purpose of the exercise? What procedures did I follow? Did I skip any steps in the analysis or argumentation? Is my report well organized so that the main points are clear? Is my presentation grammatically correct and stylistically graceful? Self-checks such as these allow for revision of the jagged edges of a report and further cement the cognitive grasp of the learning.

In the follow-up activities, students should be called upon to explain their conclusions or findings, defend the methods they used to derive their conclusions, or explain how their findings relate to the larger field or academic discipline (e.g., as illustrating a general principle, or as filling in some information or perspective missing from, but consistent with, earlier learnings about the discipline). Other students should be asked to evaluate the group's report, and the group should be expected to comment on the appositeness of those evaluations. Finally, they should be asked to explain what they learned in the exercise, in terms of both subject matter and the learning processes employed, and explain what use their learning might have for the real world and for them personally. When appropriate, they should be asked to speculate about future applications of their learning to other new learning tasks.

In the elaboration on the above, it may seem that these three stages of the metacurriculum are more appropriate for doctoral students in their final year of completing their dissertation, but not for students in elementary and middle schools. Yet research is showing that students of these ages are capable of thinking their way through these activities—not with the complex vocabulary of adults, but nonetheless still reflecting the underlying metacognitive processes.[13]

---

[13]See the remarkable achievements of formerly low-achieving minority students in the learning projects designed by Ann Brown and her colleagues, as reported in Ann L. Brown and Joseph C. Campione, "Students as Researchers and Teachers," in Keefe and Walberg, op. cit., pp. 49–57.

THE CONTEXT OF THE LEARNER

While the recommendations coming from the research on successful, or smart, schools provide invaluable insights into the process of learning, we have to situate the recommendations within an understanding of the various contexts of the learner. These contexts involve the long-standing and deeply personal influences on the self-perception, the expressive style, the language, the social perspectives, and the sense of family and group belonging of the learner. The students' race, ethnic identification, social class, gender, and family background, therefore, are major influences on basic attitudes toward school, toward authority, toward the so-called mainstream culture, and toward the traditional academic tasks of classroom learning. If it is important to link new learning tasks to prior experience and to the real-life circumstances of the learner, then a school setting that conveys little regard for, or in fact shows disregard for, race, culture, ethnicity, language community, or social class differences will not succeed in bringing students to other than superficial compliance with academic demands.

Signithia Fordham and John Ogbu, for example, have documented how school success for an African-American student is judged by his or her African-American peers as "acting white."[14] For many African-American youngsters, then, especially in early and mid-adolescence, complying with the academic demands of teachers and school authorities to get high grades and placement in honors programs is equated with adopting white, middle-class language and culture, with acting superior to their peers. Hence, many African-American youngsters engage in cultural resistance in schools, insisting on speaking "Black English" and in staying together in exclusively African-American groups. Hispanic or Latino students likewise perceive a disparagement of their cultural and linguistic heritage, as do Asian students, often to a lesser extent. When one adds class differences to the cultural differences, then culturally different students from impoverished families face a school environment that is dominated by white middle-class culture and attitudes that, subtly or directly, label them as "other," and thus inferior.[15] Add to this the even more consistent and less acknowledged absence of the feminine voice and perspective in the curriculum, and it becomes clearer that the learning context of a female, minority, poor child is perhaps the least attended to in the schools.

---

[14]Signithia Fordham and John U. Ogbu, "Black Students' School Success: Coping with the Burden of 'Acting White,'" *Urban Review,* vol. 18 (1986), pp. 161–176.

[15]See the penetrating analysis of the Teach for America project by Thomas Popkewitz, "Policy, Knowledge, and Power: Some Issues for the Study of Educational Reform," in Peter W. Cookson and Barbara Schneider (eds.), *Transforming Schools,* New York: Garland, 1995, pp. 415–455. Popkewitz's insights are confirmed by the research of critical ethnographers who study the antagonisms between students' home cultures and the school-imposed mainstream culture which often attempts to delegitimize the students' home culture. Cf. Bradley A. Levinson, Douglas E. Foley, and Dorothy C. Holland (eds.), *The Cultural Production of the Educated Person: Critical Ethnographies of Schooling and Local Practice,* Albany: State University of New York Press, 1996; also, Paul E. Willis, *Learning to Labor: How Working Class Kids Get Working Class Jobs,* Famborough, England: Saxon House, 1977.

The solution is to train teachers to be more attuned to the lifeworld of these children and to relate the learning tasks to that lifeworld in such a way that that lifeworld is honored and respected in all its human dimensions. The problem is that teachers bring the same cultural and class baggage to their work as does the general population. Teachers by and large represent the mainstream of American culture and see their job as bringing these children into the mainstream. What they usually do not realize is that they convey to their students that the mainstream is better, superior, more legitimate than the student's lifeworld. Moreover, the textbooks, the testing and grading system, the behavioral norms of the school—just about all institutional aspects of the school—convey a similar message. That is why we have stressed early in this book the importance of community as a necessary and essential environment for learning. Teachers will need to partner with parents and leaders of the minority communities to understand the realities of the students' lifeworld, both the different values and assumptions embedded in that context and the struggles involved in dealing with joining the mainstream while attempting to maintain and protect all that is good in their own cultural communities.

On the basis of that understanding, teachers can build bridges between their students and the learning agenda of the schools. This will involve incorporating more multicultural components in the curriculum as well as creating reference points between the students' lifeworld and the material under study. It will also mean supporting learning performances that use the lifeworlds of the students as an arena for legitimate research (e.g., the economics of the housing projects, the history of immigration in their communities [including the oral history of grandparents, grand uncles and aunts, etc.], the classical poetry of their language community, the art and dance of their cultural community, the political struggles of their communities, the geography of the country of origin of their forebears, and the contribution of women in their cultures). If the school is a community of learners, then teachers will allow themselves to be taught by their students and by their students' parents, and will be able to reinforce the comparisons among the struggles and heroics of several cultures. "Being different," then, becomes a way of contributing to an enlarged sense of community among people who are seeking ways to live in harmony, where differences as well as deeper unities are honored.

IMPLICATIONS FOR TEACHING

The focus on active student learning and on the curriculum-as-learned obviously will present new challenges to teachers. To be sure, excellent teachers have already been engaged in the kind of facilitating pedagogy that enhances active student learning and deep understanding of the curriculum. They have done so, by and large, in school systems that continue to encourage a model of teaching that promotes student passivity in learning, with the resulting alienation from and apathy toward the work of learning. The evidence of the failure of the schools to bring about in the majority of students the kind of deep understanding and metacognition called for by the public and by scholars is quite conclusive. The blame should be shared by school boards, by parents, and by textbook publishers, as well as by school administrators, teachers, and professors preparing teachers for their work. Righting the situation will require a broad-based effort by the school board, the textbook publishers and technology specialists, the school administrators, the universities, and, of course, the teaching profession itself.

For the moment, let us assume that all other stakeholders in the school are willing to support teachers' efforts to restructure the learning environment. In such an ideal situation, what kind of teachers are we looking for?

Ideally, schools need teachers who

- are committed to the principle that all children can succeed at learning and who will do all in their power to bring that about.
- are convinced that significant learning is achieved only by the active engagement of the learner in the production or performance of multiple expressions of authentic understanding.
- are committed to collaborating with other teachers in the school to build a flexible, responsive, and dynamic learning environment that engages every student.
- know the content of the academic disciplines they are teaching as well as the methodologies of inquiry of those disciplines.
- know the components of the metacurriculum—the aspects of higher-order thinking; the major conceptual frameworks, models, and methodologies of the disciplines—and can recognize productions and performances that authenticate learners' relative proficiency in the metacurriculum.
- have executive control of a wide variety of instructional protocols and strategies for opening up the curriculum to youngsters.
- can design a variety of learning activities, for individuals as well as groups, that will maximize autonomous, active involvement with the material.
- are sufficiently sensitive to the "home culture" of all their students so as to encourage learning activities that engage that culture in developmentally appropriate ways.
- continually monitor students' work through dialogue and action research so as to assess whether an individual student is experiencing difficulties, to discover what the source of those difficulties is, and to respond in ways that will facilitate the mastery of the learning tasks.
- are committed to working with parents as partners in supporting the learning tasks in which their children are engaged.
- can evaluate in both formative and summative procedures a variety of assessment performances and portfolios.

Obviously, this profile of the kind of teacher needed for the work of restructuring requires a transformation of the professionals currently working in the classrooms of most schools in the country. The job of supervisors is to encourage teachers to work together as colleagues in their own transformation. Supervisors will not be able to legislate this transformation; it must be achieved by the teachers themselves. Again, we come back to the important foundation of community as the environment for change. If, in the formation of a professional community, the teachers come to some agreements about working together to develop approaches to stimulate more authentic student learning, then the climate for their own transformation will be set. Supervisors need to facilitate the formation of this kind of professional community.

STANDARDS FOR AUTHENTIC PEDAGOGY

Newmann and Wehlage offer a concise definition of what they term "authentic pedagogy."[16] By this they mean the kind of teaching that leads to authentic learning or performance. Authentic student learning is the result of active engagement of the student with the material of the curriculum. Authenticity calls for student accomplishment to reflect (1) the construction of knowledge (2) through disciplined inquiry (3) to produce discourse, products, and performances that have meaning beyond success in school.[17] The criteria of authenticity require students to show successful analysis of the material, an understanding of the disciplinary concepts that ground the essential meanings of the discipline, and elaborated performances that are concerned with the world beyond the school. Newmann and Wehlage's standards for authentic pedagogy are summarized in Table 6–1.

TABLE 6–1. Standards for Authentic Pedagogy: Instruction.

Construction of Knowledge

Standard 1. Higher-Order Thinking: Instruction involves students in manipulating information and ideas by synthesizing, generalizing, explaining, hypothesizing, or arriving at conclusions that produce new meaning and understanding for them.

Disciplined Inquiry

Standard 2. Deep Knowledge: Instruction addresses central ideas of a topic or discipline with enough thoroughness to explore connections and relationships and to produce relatively complex understanding.

Standard 3. Substantive Conversation: Students engage in extended conversational exchanges with the teacher and/or their peers about subject matter in a way that builds an improved and shared understanding of ideas or topics.

Value Beyond School

Standard 4. Connections to the World Beyond the Classroom: Students make connections between substantive knowledge and either public problems or personal experiences.

Source: Fred M. Newmann and Gary G. Wehlage, *Successful School Restructuring,* Madison, WI: Center on Organization and Restructuring of Schools, 1995, p. 17. Used with permission.

---

[16]Newmann and Wehlage, op. cit., p. 17.
[17]Ibid., p. 11.

Newmann, Secada, and Wehlage propose a three-pronged strategy for assessing authentic pedagogy: assessing tasks that teachers give students to complete, assessing the dynamics of teaching and learning, and assessing the work students actually do.[18] They then provide research-based standards and scoring criteria for assessing tasks, teaching and learning, and student work. The protocols for assessing tasks are provided in Appendix 7–1. Teaching–learning and student work protocols are available from the Wisconsin Center for Educational Research.

Newmann and Wehlage's categories—construction of knowledge, disciplined inquiry, and value beyond school—appear deceptively simple, but they provide for a wide expression of teaching strategies and interventions. Their focus on the student's role in the production of knowledge and understanding stands in sharp contrast to the previously assumed, more passive role of the student in receiving curriculum "delivered" by the teacher. Their approach emphasizes the teacher's understanding of how students process the academic tasks before them and of the students' prior knowledge that can be built on to introduce new material. In this approach the student is the main actor. In contrast, the teacher is much more of a director, who connects various forms of structured activity into cohesive wholes that are consistent with the frameworks and methodologies of the academic disciplines, who continually raises questions about matters not being addressed by the learners in their inquiry activities, and who gets students to reflect on what and how they are learning.

The effectiveness of teachers in this system is enhanced by the kind of networking that they engage in with their colleagues. Working collaboratively, they can explore new approaches, discuss problem areas, look into research findings, engage in their own research to find out what students are thinking and feeling about their work, and make use of resources such as the Internet and CD-ROM databases.

CONCERN WITH OUTCOMES

Carl Vigeland tells of a discussion several golf afficionados were having about the perfect golf swing. In comparing different golfers, someone mentioned Lee Trevino's swing. The others objected that Trevino's swing was hardly classic. Trevino's defender retorted, "Look where the ball ends up; the ball tells you who has the best swing." Indeed, in his prime, Trevino could put the ball where he wanted it more consistently than other golfers who appeared to have a more perfect swing.[19] The moral of this story for teachers is that no matter how imaginative or "perfect" their teaching plan seems, the key is whether all students are learning successfully. Teachers have to be able to read the readiness and interest and prior learning of their students so well that they get them successfully involved all the time.

---

[18]Fred M. Newmann, Walter G. Secada, and Gary G. Wehlage, *A Guide to Instruction and Assessment: Vision, Standards and Scoring,* Madison: Wisconsin Center for Educational Research, 1995.
[19]Carl Vigeland, *Stalking the Shark,* New York: Norton, 1996, p. 23.

Obviously, Trevino did not win every tournament he played in; neither will teachers always succeed. That is why they have to keep studying their game, getting better at it, practicing a variety of approaches until they develop the kind of mastery that enables them to consistently hit the mark with their students.

The moral applies equally well to students. A student may not appear particularly flashy or creative. He or she may not follow the model problem perfectly, and the style and methods used may be unorthodox. But look at the results. Do the results indicate a profound and personalized grasp of the deep structures and frameworks of the material under study? Trevino's coach had enough sense to see where Trevino put the ball, even though his swing was not picture-perfect. The good teacher will have enough sense to understand the learning strategies and processes that enable a student to produce an answer true to the mark, even though his or her learning style may be different or unorthodox, or even slightly outrageous.

The emerging view of teaching reveals a much closer attention to the kinds of questions students are asking of the material in the curriculum, an active engagement of the students in generating questions which they might pursue as a class and as small inquiry teams. On the basis of questions generated by the students and the teacher, the teacher spends a good amount of time (often with other teachers at the same grade level) planning and designing learning activities, often in dialogue with students to see whether they think the activities make sense. This planning involves asking questions such as these: What do students already know that will help them connect to this new material? What in the students' life experiences would help them connect to this material? Are there some students with hobbies, interests, or special talents who might be called upon to lead the rest of the students to engage the material? These kinds of questions help the teacher build metaphorical and cognitive scaffolding around the new learning units so that students will be able to generate new knowledge from their prior knowledge and experience. Thus, the work of teaching includes this all-important front loading of careful planning and design. Supervisors should want to explore this altogether crucial aspect of the teacher's work in their conversations about the work of the classroom. What follows are examples of front-loading activities of teaching.

TEACHING FOR UNDERSTANDING

A group of Harvard educational researchers and teachers from several schools in the Boston area have engaged in a multiyear project called Teaching for Understanding. They have developed a framework for thinking about how to teach for understanding which embodies a thoroughly performative view of understanding. David Perkins from Harvard University explains four broad principles that provide both teachers and learners a sense of what this performance approach to understanding involves.[20]

---

[20]David Perkins, "What Is Understanding?" in Martha Stone Wiske (ed.), *Teaching for Understanding: Linking Research With Practice,* San Francisco: Jossey-Bass, 1998, pp. 52–54.

1. Learning for understanding occurs primarily through reflective engagement in approachable but challenging understanding performances.
2. New understanding performances are built on previous understandings and new information provided by the instructional setting.
3. Learning a body of knowledge and know-how for understanding typically requires a chain of understanding performances of increasing challenge and variety.
4. Learning for understanding often involves a conflict with older repertories of understanding performances and their associated ideas and images.

These educators developed a framework for bringing the above principles into the daily work of the classroom (see Figure 6–1). The four activities in the framework point to the all-important planning that grounds this kind of teaching.

1. The *Generative Topic* is the large umbrella topic or theme, which generates all the various subtopics that teachers and students decide they wish to explore. The generative topic should lead to crucial learnings in one or more of the academic disciplines and provide opportunities for students to make multiple connections to real-life issues. It helps if these topics have been or are controversial, with various points of view, and force students to formulate a position and defend it. Teachers

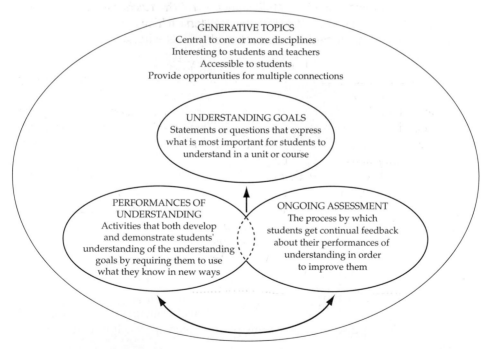

FIGURE 6–1. The Teaching for Understanding Framework.
Source: From Tina Blythe and Associates, *The Teaching for Understanding Guide,* San Francisco: Jossey-Bass, 1998, p. 19. Reprinted with permission of John Wiley & Sons, Inc.

and students need to spend the necessary time developing the topic in order to get the students sufficiently hooked on the topic or some aspects of it.

2. *Understanding Goals* state what is most important for the students to understand in the unit. These goals will be sufficiently broad as to encourage a wide variety and levels of performances of understanding of them.

3. *Performances of Understanding* indicate how the student is expected to demonstrate his or her level of mastery of the understanding goals. The understanding performance is not a one-shot event. Rather, they see understanding developing and becoming more complex over several performances. Thus, the learning unit will involve multiple performances moving from the simpler initial performances to more advanced performances through to the more complex culminating performances. Furthermore, the progressively complex performances will allow for sufficient variety to engage the various intelligences of the students.

4. *Ongoing Assessment* is the process of continual feedback about the performances. This assessment involves self-assessment, peer assessment, teacher assessment, and assessment, on occasion, by others in the community. Students gain understanding not only through performance, but also through reflection on their performance. Often it is in the assessment that the deeper insight occurs, which leads to a revision or development of a richer, more sharply focused performance of understanding. Both students and the teacher need to establish ahead of time the criteria for assessment, criteria which are tied to the understanding goals and are publicly applied to all performances.

These frameworks are then developed into graphic organizers (see Figure 6–2 and Figure 6–3 for examples), which are planning instruments for teachers to map out how they see the unit developing over the course of several weeks.

While this work may be interpreted as the work of curriculum planning and development, it is also presented here as an indication of the front loading of the teaching act. Teaching is not an isolated series of acts or behaviors; rather, teaching is an ongoing activity stretching across time, an activity whose beginning may be identified with the work of brainstorming a generative topic with students, whose continuation is further focused through the planning out of the unit using such tools as the graphic organizer, and whose partial culmination comes in the dialogic assessment of the culminating performances of the students. Supervisors need to take into account the full complexity of teaching conceived as this kind of extended, intentional activity. The Teaching for Understanding project provides a comprehensive outline of a curriculum, and will be reviewed in the next chapter when we look at some curriculum frameworks supervisors and teachers might employ as they develop rich and powerful learning activities for and with students.

Blythe and associates provide a checklist for teachers to evaluate whether and how they are teaching for understanding (see Figure 6–3). Supervisors might discuss such a checklist as the criteria they might use for their common discussion of what is happening in the classroom.

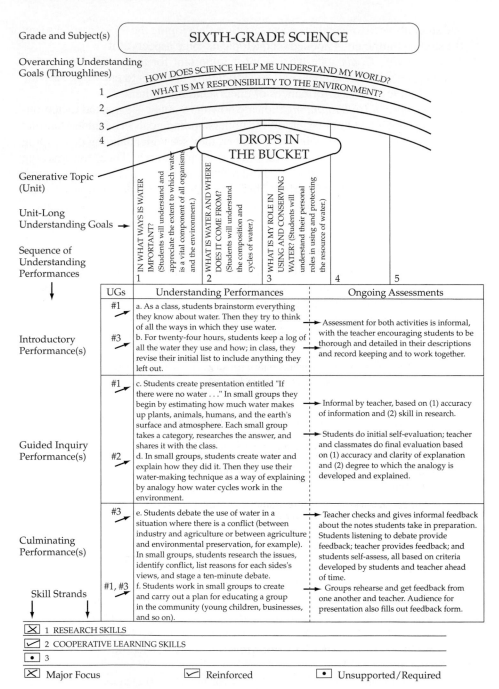

FIGURE 6–2. Sample Graphic Organizer for a Sixth-Grade Science Unit.
Source: From Tina Blythe and Associates, *The Teaching for Understanding Guide,* San Francisco: Jossey–Bass, 1998, p. 100. Reprinted with permission of John Wiley & Sons, Inc.

YOU KNOW YOU ARE TEACHING FOR UNDERSTANDING WHEN . . .

The learning is generative:

☐ Instruction is focused around a few central topics.

☐ The topics are personally significant for you and your students.

☐ Students are actively engaged in their work.

☐ An atmosphere of genuine inquiry pervades the classroom.

The understanding goals are clear and explicit:

☐ Overarching goals or throughlines are explicitly stated and posted in the classroom.

☐ Goals for particular units are closely related to overarching goals.

☐ You and your students regularly discuss and reflect on unit-long and overarching goals to help students make the connection between what they are doing and why they are doing it.

Students are working on performances of understanding almost constantly:

☐ Students work actively in varied formats: pursuing projects and reflecting alone, collaborating and conferencing in small groups, and interacting in whole groups.

☐ Students are thinking and making that thinking visible in the contexts of performances of understanding that challenge their misconceptions, stereotypes, and rigid thinking.

☐ Students can explain why they are doing what they are doing.

☐ You spend your time coaching , conferencing, leading, participating in discussions, and sometimes lecturing.

☐ The room is filled with student work, both finished and in progress.

☐ Responsibility and authority for the work is shared between you and your students.

The assessment is ongoing:

☐ Students engage in cycles of drafting, reflecting, critiquing, responding to, and revising their own and others' work.

☐ You and your students share responsibility for assessment.

☐ Everyone assesses work according to stated criteria and standards for quality, which are closely related to the understanding goals.

☐ Assessment is often casual, conversational, and spontaneous; periodically it is more formal, recorded, and planned.

☐ Self-reflection occurs frequently, in a variety of forms.

FIGURE 6–3. Checklist for Teaching for Understanding.
Source: From Tina Blythe and Associates, *The Teaching for Understanding Guide,* San Francisco: Jossey–Bass, 1998, p. 105. Reprinted with permission of John Wiley & Sons, Inc.

UNDERSTANDING BY DESIGN

Another example of the front-loading work of teaching can be found in the stimulating work of Grant Wiggins and Jay McTighe, which, like the work described in the immediately preceding section, pursues a rich and complex understanding of the notion of understanding. Their work treats teaching, learning, curriculum, and assessment as parts of an organic collective activity of teachers and students, and therefore some of it will be treated in this chapter and some in the following chapter, where we take up curriculum and assessment. Wiggins and McTighe probe the meanings of the word "understanding," and they come up with six facets of understanding which taken together make up a large, complex understanding of understanding. When we truly understand, they claim, we

- can *explain:* provide thorough, supported, and justifiable accounts of phenomena, facts, and data.
- can *interpret:* tell meaningful stories; offer apt translations; provide a revealing historical or personal dimension to ideas and events; make it personal or accessible through images, anecdotes, analogies, and models.
- can *apply:* effectively use and adapt what we know in diverse contexts.
- have *perspective:* see and hear points of view through critical eyes and ears; see the big picture.
- can *empathize:* find value in what others might find odd, alien, or implausible; perceive sensitively on the basis of prior or direct experience.
- have *self-knowledge:* perceive the personal style, prejudices, projections, and habits of mind that both shape and impede our own understanding; be aware of what we do not understand and why understanding is so hard.[21]

As we shall see in the next chapter, this understanding of understanding overlaps with but differs from that offered by Mansilla and Gardner in the Teaching for Understanding project.[22]

Wiggins and McTighe offer effective and self-referencing aspects of understanding which appear missing (but not necessarily precluded) from the Teaching for Understanding project. Like their counterparts in Teaching for Understanding, Wiggins and McTighe provide for differing levels of depth in the six facets of understanding, beginning from the most superficial, which they call the *naïve;* moving up to an incomplete but insightful level, which they call the *intuitive;* thence to a more personalized grasp, which they call the *developed;* thence to a more subtle and richer mastery, which they call the *in-depth;* and finally, to a thorough, elegant, and inventive account, which they call the *sophisticated.* They exhibit a fine

---

[21]Grant Wiggins and Jay McTighe, *Understanding by Design.* Alexandria, VA: Association for Supervision and Curriculum Development, 1998; *The Understanding by Design Handbook,* Alexandria, VA: Association for Curriculum Development, 1999.

[22]Veronica Boix Mansilla and Howard Gardner, "What Are the Qualities of Understanding?" in M. S. Wiske (ed.), *Teaching for Understanding: Linking Research to Practice,* San Francisco: Jossey-Bass, 1998, pp. 161–198.

sensitivity to developmental aspects of learning and teaching when they use an analogy drawn from basketball. The overarching goal is to get the beginning students of basketball to play a full game of basketball as a team. But the coach dissects the various skills and understandings required by that overarching goal, and works from the most basic skills to the more advanced skills. He or she works on chunks of performances, such as dribbling the ball, and then passing the ball, and then shooting the ball, and then putting the three skills together in more complex practice sessions. All the while, the coach provides feedback on various chunks of performance, insisting on more practice on dribbling with the left hand, then on passing with two hands off the running dribble. The coach designs the activities at practice with the whole performance in mind. The coach understands that younger boys and girls will not have the physical strength and agility of their teenage counterparts, so their performance will be expected to be rough around the edges.

Wiggins and McTighe make the point that teachers need to understand how a particular understanding so glibly referred to in the textbooks came to light in the first place (Galileo's musings about the relationship between the sun and the earth; Newton's musings about the activity of atoms). Students need to go through the struggles of the initial discoverers and inventors of knowledge to come to a deeper understanding. They need to create their knowledge through a series of scaffolded exercises resembling some of what the original knowledge creator had to go through. Their initial insights will be fuzzy, partial, inarticulate. But students have to go through the cycles of inquiry, have to put in the work, so to speak, to gradually arrive at greater clarity and depth of understanding. They will have to spiral through the facets of understanding, move back and forth from what they know to how it might be applied, from applications to explanations of the results of applications, to interpretations of how the explanations can be reconciled with other things they know, to gain a larger perspective on the apparently conflicting interpretations.

The good teacher knows this about learning and will design learning activities that progressively and cumulatively draw the students into the performance of those larger units of understandings. The earlier chunks of performance will develop from the design of simpler exercises that require and develop less complex aspects of the six facets of understanding. All those activities will require performances which can be assessed by both the students and the teacher, using the six aspects of understanding, and those assessments become part of a new cycle of learning designs aimed at the larger goals of understanding, again reflecting the six facets of understanding at a higher level.

Wiggins and McTighe emphasize the importance of "hooking" the students in their first encounter with the subject matter through provocative statements or questions, through instant immersion into an aspect of the material that appears to contradict a previously held certainty (e.g., the shortest distance between two points is not a straight line), through presenting clashing points of view, through starting an argument, staging a dramatic moment, providing experiential shocks. These hooks should lead to an initial presentation of the learning outcomes of the unit, and those outcomes can be presented in the form of large questions, the answers to

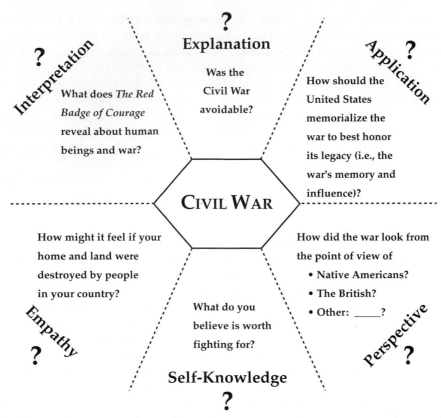

FIGURE 6–4. Curriculum Application of Six Facets of Understanding.
Source: From *The Understanding by Design Handbook,* G. Wiggins and J. McTighe, Alexandria, VA: Association for Supervision and Curriculum Development, 1999, p. 118. Reprinted by Permission. The Association for Supervision and Curriculum Development is a worldwide community of educators advocating sound policies and sharing best practices to achieve the success of each learner. To learn more, visit ASCD at www.ascd.org.

which they are called upon to discover (see, for example, Figure 6–4). Those questions could embody the six facets of understanding:

- *Explanation:* How would you possibly explain why such and such happened?
- *Interpretation:* How could these intelligent, well-intentioned people come up with such different interpretations of the same event?
- *Application:* If we were to bring this case to trial, how would different sides gather evidence?
- *Perspective:* Compare and contrast the geography of these two countries.
- *Empathy:* How would you write your family history if this happened to your family?
- *Self-knowledge:* What does it mean to say that you are the kind of person you are because of this?

The teacher can also use the six facets of understanding to design learning activities:

- *Explanation:* What kind of data, problems, experiences must students encounter in order to construct an explanation?
- *Interpretation:* What events, texts, ideological or political groups, public personalities will provide grist for the interpretation?
- *Application:* What kind of authentic situations and audiences will suggest a way to apply what they know?
- *Perspective:* What activities and sources will generate multiple points of view?
- *Empathy:* What direct or simulated experiences might force students to viscerally connect with others?
- *Self-knowledge:* What experiences or activities will help students reflect on what they do not know, or to identify one of their blind spots or stereotypes?

At this point, it may become evident how much this approach to teaching is based in the teacher's knowledge of students and dialogue with the students about their interests and concerns. On the one hand, there is no question of throwing out the required academic curriculum. For teachers facing a critical public demanding accountability for promoting student learning of state-mandated curriculum standards, this is not an option, and it really never was. Wiggins and McTighe suggest, however, that teachers need to think underneath the state standards to get at the important enduring understandings which ground the knowledge and skills called for in the curriculum standards. We will go into that more in the next chapter.

In the front-end planning for teaching, the teacher begins to develop the learning activities that connect students to the academic curriculum by imagining the kinds of initial student performances that will lead them to the kinds of understandings sought for in the academic curriculum. The teachers' work is, in one sense, the reverse of what had been traditionally supposed. In the traditional supposition, teachers studied the academic disciplines in their own education and coupled that understanding with the curriculum material designed by the school district and by textbook publishers, which was organized into the scope and sequence of material to be covered (the curriculum-as-planned); the teacher then communicated that curriculum in classroom explanations, illustrations, model problems, exercises, drills, group activities (the curriculum-as-taught). The student absorbed what the text and the teacher said, and repeated what the book and the teacher said in a variety of assigned exercises (the curriculum-as-learned); the teacher then designed a test around selected pieces of the curriculum-as-taught to see whether the student could come up with the right answers contained in the text and the teacher's explanations (the curriculum-as-assessed).

Using the process described by Wiggins and McTighe, however, the teacher begins with the curriculum-as-learned or as-understood according to the six facets of understanding in one or several combinations. The teacher designs initial performances with expectations that students will have difficulties, but with the expectation that the ongoing activities of self-assessment, peer assessment, and the teacher's own assessment will enable them to carry out additional performances of understanding with increasing clarity and complexity. All along, the teacher has an idea of *the what* and *the how* of the final performance (a joining of the curriculum-as-learned and the curriculum-as-assessed). So the teacher moves from a notion of the curriculum-as-learned and as-assessed in the final performance, to an exploration of the curriculum-as-practice and rehearsal. With this in mind, the teacher then goes to work on the curriculum design (as series of performances, feedback loops, explanations, assessments, more performances, etc.) Only then does the teacher move to the curriculum-as-taught, but the teaching takes place *within* the curriculum being practiced and rehearsed, not before it. As the teacher learns whether his or her design of the activities leading to performances actually brings the students to the desired level of understanding across the six facets of understanding, then the curriculum-as-planned—a series of unit designs—begins to take an intelligible shape, for it then becomes a clear sequence of learning, appropriate to the development, the readiness, the prior understandings of material expressed in previous performances, and expresses a logic of the construction of knowledge.

As we suggested toward the end of the section on teaching for understanding, supervisors working within this framework of teaching would need to discuss with the teacher all this front-end work as well as the actual classroom teaching to have a clearer picture of the organic activity of teaching.

RESEARCH ON BEST PRACTICE

In their research on the work of national, academic discipline–based professional associations, Zemelman, Daniels, and Hyde have discovered a strong consensus not only about what schools should be teaching and how youngsters should be learning, but also about how teachers might best structure their teaching and their classrooms.[23] They cite six practices common to teachers, mainly from the Midwest, who are successful in teaching to the new standards.[24] These six ways of structuring their teaching and their classroom practices tend to confirm the recommended practices of teaching implied in both the Teaching for Understanding project and the Understanding by Design perspectives:

1. *Integrative Units.* These involve multiweek chunks of curriculum around large themes or topics, which enable teachers to deal with many curriculum areas, such as math, biology, history, art, ecology, and health. This allows youngsters to learn discrete things within a larger framework that provides meaning and connections. While this practice is easier in elementary grades where teachers tend to be involved in all learning areas, there is evidence that high school teachers can schedule themselves in back-to-back classes or work with block scheduling several days a week to involve students in more integrative learning units.

---

[23]Steven Zemelman, Harvey Daniels, and Arthur Hyde, *Best Practice: New Standards for Teaching and Learning in America's Schools,* 2nd ed., Portsmouth, NH: Heinemann, 1998.
[24]Ibid., pp. 183–216.

2. *Small Group Activities.* Teachers involve students in collaborative learning in pairs, threes, ad hoc groups, and long-term teams. Some of this work involves jigsaw-type processes of teaching one another; some involves critiquing one another's work; some involves study teams competing against other study teams; some involve students cycling through learning centers within the classroom for 20 to 40 minutes each day.

3. *Representing to Learn.* Originally built around the "writing to learn" design, the activity has expanded to using a variety of representations to focus attention, raise questions, clarify insights, visualize what one is trying to learn. These representations include drawing a picture, using Venn diagrams, jotting down speculations or hypotheses, brainstorming possible solutions, rephrasing the central question, diagramming relationships, mapping potential causes and effects or intervening influences. These representations open up spaces for teachers and students to talk one-on-one to clarify questions, to get focused or refocused, to clear away unnecessary side-street distractions in a student's thinking. Successful teachers get students to keep learning logs, sketchbooks, or idea maps so that they can review them frequently to see where students are moving in the learning process.

4. *Classroom Workshops.* This represents a chunk of time (30 minutes to an hour) when students can *do* the subject: read a story, study an historical source document, complete an art project, write a creative piece. An essential quality to the classroom workshop is that students get to choose what they will do during that time. If a student finishes a project before the time is up, she or he is expected to begin another project during the remaining time. During the workshop, the teacher moves around and conducts brief, one-on-one conversations with individual students. These kinds of workshops require original tone setting with the group and establishing the ground rules all agree to live by.

5. *Authentic Experiences.* This practice involves teacher–student dialogue about their interests, about topics connected to their lives, to the real world. This includes activities that require students to connect with current events in the news media. In some instances, it means connecting the learning with the multiple intelligences students bring to the work, or connecting the work with family or local community people. Authentic experiences require student self-assessment of their learning, as well as assessment by members of the community. Some teachers use video cameras as tools to pursue learning projects or to express the results of learning projects.

6. *Reflective Assessment.* This is the practice of having students keep records of what they are doing and learning, records such as portfolios of their best work. These records enable a student to confer with her or his teacher and discuss the work; they enable a teacher to combine instruction with assessment. The ongoing self-assessment continues the activity of learning so that students can check frequent mistakes and take steps to correct them, or so that students may see how their work has been one-dimensional and now must move into a more complex and challenging set of performances.

Again, the focus on what the student does is striking. These are supposed to be examples of best practices of *teaching,* but they are about how the teacher involves the student in active learning. One might ask, Does the teacher ever do "direct teaching"? To be sure, there is time for some whole-class instruction. At the beginning of some projects, teachers may need to provide demonstrations about using equipment or other learning resources. There are also many opportunities for mini-lessons for small groups of students who are having difficulties with their learning projects. Nevertheless, this newer appreciation that the primary work of the school is student involvement in active learning places the teachers' work of structuring student learning activities and providing feedback, some coaching, some motivating, some encouragement during times of stress, in a fresh perspective.

Much of the new research on teaching leads to the conclusion that teaching is much more than following a script and supervision is much more than making sure that those scripts are being followed.[25] As teaching becomes more and more context-specific and subject-matter-dependent, supervision becomes more contextually constructed and teacher-dependent. There is no template held by supervisors to which teachers must try to fit themselves. What makes sense is not something that can be determined beforehand and presented as a script. Instead, what makes sense in teaching must be constructed from within the act of teaching itself. For example, much depends on the teacher's understanding of the subject matter he or she is teaching; as this subject-matter understanding changes, so does what makes sense. Subject-matter knowledge consists of the facts, concepts, principles, and theories underlying the structure of the discipline. "Pedagogical content knowledge" counts too.[26] This kind of knowledge refers to the teacher's ability to transform subject-matter understandings into learning activities that make sense to students.

To this list we add that supervision will increasingly be viewed as a role-free process. For teachers to be active participants in knowledge and collaborators in creating new knowledge about teaching and learning, they must assume roles not only as co-supervisors with principals and other administrators but also as co-supervisors with other teachers. Indeed, the future will show that supervision involving principals and other administrators as lead people will be less important than collegial supervision involving peers.

SUMMARY

An overriding theme of this chapter is that supervisors must consider the bottom line at all times, that is, whether all students are successfully engaged in learning. As we will see in later chapters,

---

[25]See, for example, Lee S. Shulman, "Knowledge and Teaching: Foundations of the New Reform," *Harvard Educational Review,* vol. 57, 1987 pp. 1–22; and S. M. Wilson and A. E. Richart, "150 Different Ways of Knowing: Representations of Knowledge in Teaching," in J. Calderhead (ed.), *Exploring Teachers' Thinking,* London: Cassell, 1987.

[26]Shulman, op. cit.

successfully engaging all students in learning involves both supervisors and teachers in an ongoing quest to improve not only specific instructional strategies but also

- working relationships both vertically and horizontally among teachers.
- partnerships with parents.
- the utilization of space, time, and technology within the school.
- the way the learning community supports experimentation.
- the moral commitment to learning.
- the professional development opportunities of teachers.

For now, it may be clear that supervisors have to pursue their own professional development as they shift from Supervision I to Supervision II. The research literature on student learning and teacher action research is growing rapidly, and there is much to absorb as supervisors attempt to gain a deeper appreciation of the change in focus from teacher work to student work. As this professional development for supervisors continues, we believe that a much deeper appreciation of the complexity of teaching will emerge, and with it a greater appreciation of how teachers intuitively are moving in the right direction.

To help you think about student learning, its assessment, and teacher practices in a thoughtful way, we have provided several frameworks. Table 6–1, for example, includes a set of standards that teachers alone or together can use to assess authentic pedagogy. Suggestions are provided for helping teachers and supervisors develop curriculum and teaching repertoires that embody a commitment to teaching for understanding.

SOME REFLECTIONS

1. How many of the six practices of successful teachers cited in the section "Research on Best Practice" can be found in your school? What percentage of the teachers use one or more of these practices? What does that tell you about the educational platform of the teachers at your school?
2. Has the shift from passive student learning to active student learning taken place at your school? If so, have student attitudes toward learning changed?
3. If you were a supervisor in your school, which ideas from this chapter would you use, and how would you go about using them? Explain your answer using your supervisory platform as a rationale.

CHAPTER 7

Supervisors Engaging Curriculum Through Assessment

INTRODUCTION

This chapter continues the focus of the previous chapter on the supervisor's role in enhancing the core work of the school, teaching and learning. As we saw in the previous chapters, national and international efforts at school reform have tended to focus on student learning of more demanding subject matter and the proof of that learning by performance on state and national tests. This focus has profoundly altered the work of supervisors, requiring them to look with the teachers at what students are actually learning, at how to assess that learning, at how to refashion teaching in the face of student underperformance. The chapter initially discusses how the state imposition of performance-based accountability standards has radically changed the way teachers teach the curriculum and assess how the students perform the curriculum.

With that major change noted, the chapter turns to the curriculum-as-assessed, and explores how assessment has become much more organically integrated with the curriculum-as-planned, as-taught, and as-learned. This shift implies a shift in the conversations supervisors have with teachers, and how they collectively view areas of needed professional development. Several aspects of authentic assessment are reviewed as helpful perspectives to apply to this work. The chapter concludes with an appendix from the work of Newmann, Secada, and Wehlage that illuminates the scoring of authentic assessments.

SOME BACKGROUND

Both nationally and internationally, governments are demanding that students be held accountable for mastering high standards of academic performance. Teachers and school officials are expected not only to provide equal opportunity to learn the curriculum, but also to see that it is learned, and learned well, by all students. As Richard Elmore has commented:

> With increased accountability, American schools and the people who work in them are being asked to do something new—to engage in systematic, continuous improvement in the quality of the educational experience of students, and to subject themselves to the discipline of measuring their success by the metric of students' academic performance. Most people who currently work in public schools weren't hired to do this work, nor have they been adequately prepared to do it either by their professional education or by their prior experience in schools.[1]

A performance-based, constructivist view of learning; a legislated, standards-based view of curriculum content; a view of intelligence, not as fixed, but as something a learner develops; and a concomitant understanding of teaching as a more complex, flexible, and multidimensional process, now require supervisors and teachers, both novice and veteran, to engage the teaching–learning process with much more sophisticated perspectives. This view of accountability is now the dominant policy perspective.

ASSESSMENT WITHIN MANDATED ACCOUNTABILITY

Assessment has been viewed, often cynically, as the tail that wags the dog. What is assessed is what gets taught. What is assessed becomes or defines the curriculum. Now, however, we see a twist on that observation. The curriculum is also what you do when the assessment shows that students are not learning the first draft of the curriculum-as-planned and the curriculum-as-taught. The response is no longer to deliver the same curriculum, but to refashion the curriculum into new learning activities, with new scaffolding and more clearly articulated rubrics for assessing the next performance of those students who are not learning the lesson on the first bounce. Again, experienced teachers do this kind of curriculum development. The supervisor, however, can be an important support person for teachers, especially novices, in their on-the-spot bafflement over why students are not grasping the material, and can coach teachers in the process of fact-finding and brainstorming various ways to be more responsive to learners.

In response to this legislated accountability, school systems and individual schools have become more data-focused—that is, focused on test results. Using test results, educators are targeting those areas of curriculum standards in which student performance does not measure up. That leads to a more careful look at potential deficiencies in the curriculum-as-taught, as well as problems with the curriculum-as-learned. Despite complaints to the contrary, the effect on student underperformance has begun to show, especially in the elementary and middle grades.

[1]Richard F. Elmore, *Bridging the Gap Between Standards and Achievement: The Imperative for Professional Development in Education,* Washington, DC: Albert Shanker Institute, 2002, p. 1.

A DEEPER VIEW OF ASSESSMENT

The emphasis on assessment of student learning, however, seems to suggest a more complex agenda for teachers and supervisors, one that opens up new perspectives on both teaching and learning. Assessment of the curriculum-as-learned is a multifaceted activity that can be integrated into many aspects of the teaching–learning process. Traditionally, assessment was seen primarily as what happened after the teacher taught and after the student learned what was taught. And indeed, that is the way it is being treated in the data-driven school-improvement process. As Grant Wiggins suggests, however, assessment should enter into the very early stages of teaching a unit of the curriculum.[2] Assessment of the impact of a planned lesson should be going on simultaneously with the teaching of the lesson plan (similar to the reflection-in-practice discussed in Chapter 3). Assessment of student learning should begin in the first five minutes of every class and continue informally throughout every class. In other words, assessment of the curriculum-as-taught and the curriculum-as-learned should not have to wait until they are supposedly completed.

The key to this richer understanding of assessment is the element of *feedback*. As in the learning of any physical skill, the initial efforts are only partially successful. Learning the proper balance while riding a bicycle is usually preceded by several falls or near collisions with the sidewalk. Learning to respond to the feedback from the inner ear and the patient coaching of a parent enables the prospective Lance Armstrong to gradually learn the leans and shifting of the body's center of gravity to master the skill of bicycling. This applies to learning to play the piano as well as learning to play computer games. The closer the feedback to the activity, the faster the gradual mastery of the skill.

CONSTRUCTIVIST TEACHING AND LEARNING

Lauren Resnick's approach to knowledge-based constructivist teaching and learning presents additional insight into the self-monitoring feedback connection to learning.[3] Studies of reading comprehension and learning from texts reveal that good readers employ identifiable skills, including making inferences, making comparisons, connecting relationships with other texts—skills reflecting a kind of talking back to, or arguing with, the text. However, while these skills are learnable, they have to be taught and taught so that the learner applies them systematically until they become second nature. These skills, however, cannot be taught in a decontextualized, prepackaged form. Rather, they are taught more in a coaching fashion as the student engages in talking back to the text, asking it questions, arguing with it. In

---

[2]Grant Wiggins, *Educative Assessment: Designing Assessment to Inform and Improve Student Performance,* San Francisco: Jossey-Bass, 1998.

[3]Laurent B. Resnick and Megan Williams Hall, "Learning Organizations for Sustainable Educational Reform," *Deadalus,* vol, 127, no. 4 (1998), pp. 89–118.

other words, as the student practices reading, the teacher guides and provides feedback in the form of suggesting questions to ask the text, challenging unsupported inference without any plausible evidence, recalling previous texts that gave the student problems. In effect, the teacher is teaching the reader how to engage in making sense out of printed material through a reflective, self-monitoring, and self-correcting process. The knowledge the student constructs has to be knowledge about something, a knowledge that is generated by a disciplined construction of meaning that flows from a disciplined dialogue with the material under study. The feedback, anchored in the logic of the dialogue, channels the learning of the learner in a verifiable, or at least reasonable, sequence of learning performances.

When that learning performance is situated within the context of curriculum standards, the process of assessment, begun at the start of learning a new curriculum unit and shaped through scaffolding and rubrics, enables the learner to construct a meaningful performance of those curriculum standards. The performance is not a rote memory performance. Rather, it is a performance that reflects an authentic engagement of the subject matter on its own terms, as well as in relationship to the sense-making abilities of the learner. The performance belongs to the individual learner, reflecting her or his voice, but it is performance of understanding of the curriculum in some or many of its complex elements and internal and external relationships. Thus, the continuous feedback from the learner's self-monitoring as the learner engages the subject matter is seen as an essential ingredient of authentic learning. That feedback guides the performance of the learning in more and more complex expressions.

REFLECTIVE PRACTICE

With this much richer understanding of assessment as a continuous reflective practice of the learner that guides and channels the learning process, supervisors and teachers are in a position to explore multiple ways to enrich and deepen the learning process for all their students. Implied in this collaborative work is the teachers' growing sensitivity and responsiveness to the feedback from the students' responses to the learning activities the teacher has prepared. Teaching requires the same self-monitoring by the teacher in order to engage the students in authentic learning—a continuous minute-by-minute assessment of their responses as the lesson unfolds. This assessment is guided by the teacher's knowledge of each student in the class, by the knowledge of the subject matter, and by the rubrics established for assessing student performance. To the beginning teacher, this level of simultaneous awareness will seem daunting, if not impossible. However, experienced teachers are able to develop this awareness at various levels of effectiveness. These teaching skills of self-monitoring, reflective practice are learned over time, but not without some coaching from an expert teacher or from a supervisor or both. Such coaching will help the teacher translate his or her understanding of the subject matter into a variety of learning activities that respond to various readiness levels and to design appropriate rubrics for assessing various levels of student performances of their learning.

We are now in a position to explore additional elements of authentic assessment as they might support the externally imposed accountability for learning. To briefly recapitulate, we have come to see that assessment as an activity continuous with the activity of teaching and learning is a powerful tool for promoting high-quality student learning for both the successful and the underperforming student. *Feedback from within the practice* of attempting to master something, as well as feedback from the teacher in the form of coaching specific learning skills, what many have called the learning-how-to-learn curriculum, gradually channels the learning process into performances of learning that can stand up to demanding assessments. These more formalized assessments should be understood as yet another feedback mechanism for both the teacher and the learner to gauge where the student is or is not progressing in the performance of the curriculum standards. This is to identify all forms of assessments as assessments *for* learning, not simply *of* learning.

A MORE THOUGHTFUL ASSESSMENT SYSTEM

As we have stressed earlier, the curriculum-as-planned, the curriculum-as-taught, and the curriculum-as-learned should be woven together tightly. The same is true for the curriculum-as-tested (or assessed). We prefer the word "assessed" rather than "tested" because of the many negative connotations associated with tests and testing. Assessment suggests multiple approaches to the inquiry of what was learned. The term "authentic assessment" signifies that the assessment is close to the planned and taught curriculum as well as to the learned curriculum. Authentic assessment usually involves the completion of a whole task, one that reflects the complex and multileveled learning that has been necessary to produce the product for assessment.

Just as the supervisor needs to review the kind of learning activities the teacher designs to engage the students with the curriculum, so too should the supervisor review the kind and quality of assessments of student learning the teacher requires. In fact, the assessments alone will reveal much about the curriculum-as-planned and the curriculum-as-taught, as well as about the curriculum-as-learned.

To understand how the supervisor's attention to issues of assessment can be sharpened, we will first look at some postulates offered by Grant Wiggins and then move on to examples of student self-assessment. This will lead to considerations of the teacher's assessment of the curriculum-as-taught and the curriculum-as-planned.

Grant Wiggins, one of the leaders in promoting authentic assessments, offers nine postulates for a more thoughtful assessment system.[4] His postulates assume an approach to teaching that stresses the active engagement of the student with the curriculum material. They apply not only to end-of-semester exams but also to shorter assessment tasks.

---

[4]Grant Wiggins, *Assessing Student Performance,* San Francisco: Jossey-Bass, 1993, pp. 47–67.

Postulate 1: Assessment of thoughtful mastery should ask students to justify their understanding and craft, not merely to recite orthodox views or mindlessly employ techniques in a vacuum.

Here Wiggins would have students be required to explain or defend their product, whether a term paper or lab report.

Postulate 2: The student is an apprentice liberal artist and should be treated accordingly, through access to models and feedback in learning and assessments.

Students need models of excellence and an opportunity to imitate those models. This implies cycles of exposure to a model of excellence, practice of the model, feedback, and refinement of the work. Whatever assessment products the student creates should exhibit an appropriate level of excellence that has already been modeled in their earlier learning activities.

Postulate 3: An authentic assessment system has to be based on known, clear, public, nonarbitrary standards and criteria.

This postulate implies that students know in advance the scoring criteria and have seen models, whether papers or videotaped performances. Advanced placement exams provide such scoring rubrics so that students will know ahead of time the criteria for the scores to be given.

Postulate 4: An authentic education makes self-assessment central.

This implies that self-assessment is a frequent, normal occurrence. For major pieces of work, students could be asked to hand in a self-assessment with their work.

Postulate 5: We should treat each student as a would-be intellectual performer, not as a would-be learned spectator.

This postulate does not deny that we want students to be capable critics of artistic, political, or scientific performances. It asserts that the emphasis in our assessments, however, should be on the students' creating a product or a performance of their own.

Postulate 6: An education should develop a student's intellectual style and voice.

This implies that work will be returned not only for grammatical or methodological mistakes, but also if that work is boring, disorganized, bland, without some fingerprint of the student. Peer readings and critiques of reports can help here.

Postulate 7: Understanding is best assessed by pursuing students' questions, not merely by noting their answers.

This postulate suggests that students should be judged by the questions they raise, their criticisms of accepted opinions, their probing for the unattended to, and their asking for an alternative view.

Postulate 8: A vital aim of education is to have students understand the limits and boundaries of ideas, theories, and systems.

In assessments, we should have students be able to point to the partiality or tentative nature of knowledge or systems of knowledge so as to avoid the absolutizing of any particular discipline. This can be done by exposing them to the history of the disciplines or by indicating the disputed areas in those disciplines.

Postulate 9: We should assess students' intellectual honesty and other habits of mind.

This implies self-assessment, as well as an expected candor about what students really know and what they are faking. Assessments that attend to this postulate would have students document their project from its inception, describing the difficulties and successes along the way. In group projects, this would require students to say what they have learned with the help of others in the group.

ASSESSMENT AS PART OF CURRICULUM

As we ponder Wiggins's nine postulates, we come to realize that assessment is not primarily something done after the learning has taken place in order to assign a grade. It does serve that purpose, but that purpose should be secondary. Assessment is part of the teaching and learning process itself. Models of the expected performance provide students with a clearer understanding of the task to be achieved as they engage the matter at hand. The teacher's continuous monitoring of student learning at every stage enables the students to check their emerging understandings in the mini-performances of each stage of completing the larger learning task of the curriculum unit. Through frequent conversations with peers in cooperative learning projects, students will be picking up additional clarifications and new insights as their own learning continues to unfold. This points to another important element in the learning process—talk. When learners talk with the teachers and their peers about what they are learning, the very talking about it surfaces insightful learning, as well as misunderstandings, making their learning publicly available for feedback. Finally, the summative performance of the curriculum unit provides the opportunity for important feedback and reflection on the learning performed in the assessment.

Educators tend to think that learning has taken place *only* when the students get the task right. More often, however, learning takes place when they do not get it right. When they do not get it right, students have to figure out what they need to do to learn. That review of learning often leads to crucial insights into the correct procedure, the clearer expression, the deeper relationship to patterns that have not been recognized. The history of science is instructive here. Most successful scientific breakthroughs occur after many false starts and misguided hunches in the laboratory. The same holds true for many artistic works. The masterpiece or successful composition takes place only after many revisions of unsatisfactory attempts.

Learning involves moving forward by inches, and often only after many false starts. Progress is a matter of making mistaken connections that are corrected only after trying them out and finding that they do not work or that they make only superficial sense. Understanding is initially partial, muddy, disjointed. It becomes sharper as the learner clears away the unrelated associations, the unworkable applications, the confusion of one thing for another. Learning progresses only by stumbling, groping in the darkness, muddling through until it is time to quit for the day, and coming back the next day for more of the same.

While all of this is going on, the learner is extremely vulnerable. After all, no one wants to appear stupid in front of others and certainly not to oneself. As a result, the learner often fakes it, trying to maintain the impression that he or she knows the material at hand.

This vulnerability is exposed by the teacher in such often-asked questions as, Who is having trouble understanding this? or Is this clear now so we can move on? The problem here is that most youngsters are reluctant to admit that they are confused. Teachers must convince them that it is normal to find learning difficult and that the asking of questions should be the expected protocol rather than the exception. Unfortunately, teachers can become impatient when youngsters ask a lot of questions; they sometimes send the unspoken message that questions are not really welcomed. Many teachers have forgotten how they felt as young students—afraid of being considered stupid by their peers, let alone by their teacher. It is true that teachers feel pressured to cover the material and therefore become impatient when the class gets slowed down by two or three youngsters who are struggling to keep up. Finding flexible ways to assist these students while keeping the others moving forward is not easy, especially when teachers are working with supervisors who expect relatively uniform teaching procedures to be sufficient for the whole class or who expect that a certain percentage of students will fail as a matter of course.

Research by Ames,[5] following up on work by C. I. Diener and Carol Dweck, has indicated that children adopt early on in their school experience either a *performance motivation* or a *learning motivation*.[6] Those with a performance motivation concentrate on finishing the task, getting a high grade, and winning teacher and parental praise. Those with a learning motivation derive satisfaction from the learning experience itself, finding it intrinsically rewarding to solve new problems or work on new material. When faced with problems they cannot solve, the two groups tend to interpret the cause of their failure differently. The performance-motivated students tend to say that they are not smart enough and that there is nothing they can do about it. Consequently, they tend to give up easily. The learning-motivated students tend to keep working at the problem, trying other approaches. For them, it is not a matter of a lack of intelligence. The performance-oriented group tends to present a static view of intelligence (you either are smart enough or you are not); the learning-oriented group tends to think of intelligence developmentally or incrementally. Ames's research shows that the static view of intelligence and the performance motivation are taught inadvertently starting in the early grades. Her research shows that altered classroom protocols can develop in the students a deeper learning motivation and a belief that intelligence can be built incrementally, as they work through successively more satisfying solutions to the learning task.

These findings point out the need to use frequent informal assessments to determine which students are succeeding and which are having problems in carrying out a particular learning task. Teachers must listen sensitively to students'

[5]Carol A. Ames, "Motivation: What Teachers Need to Know," *Teachers College Record,* vol. 91 (1990), pp. 409–421.
[6]C. I. Diener and Carol S. Dweck, "An Analysis of Learned Helplessness: Continuous Changes in Performance, Strategy, and Achievement Cognitions Following Failure," *Journal of Personality and Social Psychology,* vol. 36 (1978), pp. 451–462.

explanations of their difficulties and their way of approaching the task. They must also devise alternative approaches to clarifying a topic or task. These on-the-spot assessments can significantly reduce the remediation required after more formal assessments reveal the unattended misunderstanding. Moreover, a student who clears up a misunderstanding while the learning is in progress should not subsequently receive a negative grade on the formal assessment. This is part of the formula of working for the success of all children in the learning task.

Nevertheless, more formal assessments are still necessary. With the current emphasis in schools on the active production of student understanding, all assessments should be aimed at high-quality learning. Testing for the simple recall of information will no longer serve this focus on learning. Instead, assessments, both formal and informal, should focus on the performance of some intellectual task.

In preparing formal assessments, teachers should review examples of acceptable and superior performances, brainstorming ahead of time two or three student responses that would satisfy some or all of these criteria for each question in the assessment. After students have engaged in the performance assessment, teachers might again review those criteria to see whether the assessment did, in fact, draw out various characteristics of higher-order thinking and understanding.

SELF-ASSESSMENT

Let us turn to Wiggins's postulate dealing with student self-assessment. The following example may help supervisors realize how rich a source of teaching and learning such exercises involving the curriculum-as-learned can be.

Consider a class setting, say, a self-contained high school poetry class with one teacher and 24 students. The class has just concluded a comparison of two poems. Previous classes have dealt with aspects of poetry, such as mood, figures of speech, rhythm, unity, image, and symbol. The students have read a variety of poems and have done some analysis using these critical concepts. The objective of today's class is to have students use these critical concepts to compare two poems and to argue why one poem is "better" than the other. This objective fits into the larger goal of the course, which is for students to learn to discriminate between superior and inferior literary expression.

Toward the end of the class, the teacher feels satisfied that most of the students have demonstrated a good grasp of the analytical concepts and have applied them well in arguing for the superiority of one poem over the other. In an attempt to further reinforce the learning and to test out her impressions that the class has achieved the instructional objectives, she says, "Now let's all pause a minute and reflect on what it is we learned today. What new thing struck us? What have we understood with greater clarity? How does what we've done today fit with what went on before? Of what practical use was this whole experience, anyway?"

The following answers come back. Listen for one or more of the six facets of understanding.

- "I learned that it makes a difference when you read a poem out loud. I could *hear* how superior that first poem was to the other one."

- "I learned that you can still like an inferior poem—I mean, yeah, the first poem is a better poem, by all the measures we apply to it, but I like the second poem because it expresses a feeling about being alone that I've had many times. Just because a poem is a mediocre poem doesn't mean it's no good at all."
- "I learned that I had to read both poems at least four times before they made any sense to me. It seems that with poetry, kinda like music, you gotta acquire a kind of familiarity with it before it really says anything to you."
- "I learned that all this art stuff isn't entirely a matter of feeling, you know, all from inside someone's fantasy. There's something to it, some kind of intelligence. And you can talk about poetry intelligently, instead of simply leaving it to subjective feelings of like or dislike."
- "I learned that I have no poetic imagination. I never thought those kinds of thoughts. And I'm wondering how one gets to be a poet—are you born that way, or can you develop poetic imagination?"
- "I'm really having a hard time understanding what makes a poem 'unified.' It's a word that seems to me to mean perfect, or perfection. Like a perfect circle or something. So if a poem has unity, then it must mean that every word, every line is in a perfect place. But who could ever decide that? Maybe I need to see examples of *really* unified poems and some that are a little off-center and maybe I'll catch on."
- "I learned that it feels good to discover that a lot of people agree with my conclusions. Before the class started, I wasn't sure whether my picking the first poem as better was the right answer, you know. But when other people gave the same reasons as I had, I really felt good, because I figured—yeah, for the first time—that I'm understanding all the stuff we've been doing on poetry."

The teacher then continues the class by picking up on one student's question about what makes a poem unified. Other students are asked to come up with responses to the question, and a disjointed class discussion ensues about poetic unity. The teacher cites another student's comment that poetry is like music, and asks how one would know that a song is unified. That leads to further examples, and the class moves into a distinction between narrative unity and a unity of impression, which then leads to the deeper question of whether the poem itself is unified, or whether it creates a sense of unity in the reader. The teacher then asks the class whether they have experienced their life as a unity each day. This leads to several humorous responses, and the teacher challenges them to write a poem about an experience that conveys to them a sense of completeness.

This example illustrates a range of student learnings that reflect not only the achievement of the teacher's objectives but also the many idiosyncratic, ancillary learnings that always occur. The example points to the importance of taking time to let students reflect on what they have learned. Obviously, the students in this poetry class have relatively high levels of motivation and of verbal and abstractive abilities. Students in third or fourth grade will come up with simpler responses, to be sure. But getting them into the habit early of evaluating what they are learning will pay enormous dividends as it develops into ongoing reflective habits of mind and a genuine satisfaction over knowing that they are making progress.

Students' evaluation of their appropriation of the curriculum can lead to both cognitive and affective results. By reflecting on their grasp of the learning task, they can clarify what they know. Frequently, simple recall of the class material or unit will reinforce a student's grasp of the material. When this reflection is done in a nonthreatening environment, students can also clarify and admit what they have not yet grasped or understood. They can trace back the instructional sequence until they get to the point where the teacher or the textbook lost them. This clarification of what one does not know will often lead to a desire to learn that material.

On the affective level, students can be encouraged to review what they have learned, not so much for intellectual understanding but simply for enjoyment. The youngster who felt the need to read the poems many times was discovering how poems are meant to be enjoyed. This kind of enjoyment is not limited to those subjects within the humanities. A sensitive biology teacher or a physical education teacher can lead students into a kind of repetitive appreciation of what they have learned. Sometimes that leads to genuine wonderment.

On either a reflective or an affective level, student evaluation of this learning can lead to ownership. Recognizing what they have learned, what it means, how it is related to what they have learned before, how they can use it, what a sense of excitement or enjoyment comes with that mastery of a skill or discovery of a surprising piece of information—all of this leads students to appropriate that learning as theirs. Once appropriated, the learning tends to be effective, which is to say that the student owns it and can use it in many ways in the immediate future. Unfortunately, many teachers fail to take the time to encourage this sense of ownership. What they miss by not encouraging student self-evaluation is the genuine satisfaction of knowing how much their students have actually absorbed and the fascination of observing the individual subtleties in learning that manifest themselves through such feedback. Moreover, much of the formal evaluation the teacher engages in does not pick up the obvious clues that students put forth in their self-evaluation. A supervisor who helps a teacher to initiate student self-evaluation may have provided a stimulus for instructional and program improvement more effective than several semesters of in-service lectures on the topic.

In the example of the poetry class, the teacher used a spontaneous assessment of the students' learning to carry the lesson forward, to get them to probe for deeper understandings of the material. She was also able to employ their self-assessments to relate the material to their own personal experience, then to use that for writing their own poetry. In this example, one can see how easily spontaneous assessment can flow into curriculum elaboration. Assessment becomes part of the curriculum-as-taught and as-learned.

Barbara Means indicates that in the near future, low-cost, portable, computerized devices will be available to students for use in the classroom, at home, in community-based learning projects.[7] These devices can be connected to local, regional, and global networks, thereby enabling students to interact with and

---

[7]Barbara Means, "Technology in America's Schools: Before and After Y2K," in Ronald S. Brandt (ed.), *Education in a New Era,* Arlington, VA: Association for Supervision and Curriculum Development, 2000, pp. 185–210.

manipulate information for a variety of assigned learning projects. Students' learning performances will be entered in to these computerized devices to which teachers will have access. Thus, teachers will be able to monitor and assess students' progress or lack of it and, through the school computer network, provide feedback to students. Furthermore, students will be able to view other students' work for comparison with their own project, for engaging in discussion of difficult material in the assignment, and for helping other students who are stuck or blocked in their learning efforts. Such computer-assisted learning projects will also provide teachers with a record of the students' work over time, thus facilitating summative assessments of students' work. Technological tools for capturing and scoring student work may enable teachers to link class assessments with large-scale district or state assessments.

AUTHENTICITY IN ASSESSMENT

Besides the informal or formal assessment, teachers must design a more independent form of assessment to which the student must be held accountable. Tests often contain one or more faulty design features that end up sending the wrong message about the nature and purpose of school learning.[8] What we are looking for are *authentic* tests. Another of Wiggins's postulates on authenticity can help us here. Wiggins states in Postulate 3 that an authentic assessment system has to be based on known, clear, public, nonarbitrary standards and criteria. Among his criteria for authenticity are the following:

- The assessment task is like the problems faced by adult citizens, consumers, or professionals in the field.
- The assessment includes contextual factors found in real life, such as access to resources, variable time windows and restraints, and clear contextual parameters (e.g., audience, budget, and purpose). This criterion attempts to eliminate the false certainties of decontextualized learning.
- The assessment task presents real problems, not formulaic, boilerplate responses. Real problems require the application of various kinds of knowledge and skills and the prioritizing and organizing of stages of the work.
- The assessment is a *learning* task. There has been thorough preparation for performing the task; there is built-in self-assessment and self-adjustment by the student; the task may be discussed, clarified, and even modified by discussion with the assessor. There is concurrent feedback and the possibility of self-adjustment during the test. The results of the assessment (the judgments of the assessor) are open to discussion and possible revision. After completion of the assessment, teachers and students will discuss whether and why the assessment was a good assessment.

---

[8]See Richard J. Stiggins, "Revitalizing Classroom Assessment: The Highest Instructional Priority," *Phi Delta Kappan*, vol. 69, no. 5 (January 1988), pp. 363–368, for a commentary of teachers' faulty construction of classroom assessments.

- The assessment requires students to justify and explain answers or choices. Each student is expected to understand what he or she knows and to elaborate on that knowledge.
- The assessment is one of many assessments that look for consistent patterns of work, for habits of mind across various performances.

THE FORCE OF PRIOR ASSUMPTIONS

Behind any evaluation activity are values and assumptions about the nature of teaching and learning and the curriculum. Contrast the above criteria for authenticity with another set of assumptions and beliefs, listed below, which seem to stand behind the test protocols of many teachers.

- Knowing or understanding something means giving this particular response to that question.
- This curriculum design or this text contains the most legitimate, or the only legitimate, approach to this area of knowledge (e.g., modern Latin American history seen from a North American perspective), and therefore a test of the students' knowledge of this approach indicates that he or she knows something true or objective or valid about that area of knowledge.
- Using the language of public discourse in evaluation is the best means of measuring what the student has learned (rather than using poetry or music or graphics to measure it).
- Teachers and other school officials have the competency to decide the criteria for evaluating and ranking students.
- Learning primarily involves learning what others have discovered (and seldom the way they discovered it), and so evaluation monitors learning on that level.
- There is always a causal connection between learning and instruction (rather than learning and the *students'* search, inquiry, practice, trial and error, or logical deduction); hence, evaluation of learning implies an evaluation of instruction.
- The proper place for most learning is a classroom, and so evaluation never compares classroom learning (with all its constraints) with learning in other settings.

The point of listing these is to encourage supervisors to create distance from the evaluation activity so that both they and the teacher can perceive the value assumptions that are embedded in their evaluation procedures. Because these assumptions rarely surface for discussion, they remain a strong, constant shaper of teacher tests and assessments. Bringing teachers together to explore alternative approaches to authentic assessment will enable them to work together to reshape their assessment practices. If a healthy sense of community among teachers has begun to be developed, then the foundation of professional trust will support the difficult efforts in changing these deep-seated assumptions.

SUMMARY

We hope by now it will be clearer what kind of fundamental changes are in the wind, both nationally and internationally, as educators and policy makers chart the course for schools for the 21st century. As we have seen in the last two chapters, major changes in traditional views of education have occurred. They can be listed as follows:

- All children can and must learn at a much higher standard of performance than has been previously accepted. What was expected for top students is now expected for all.
- The whole school community must be mobilized to support this first principle of success for all, including the school board, the central office staff, the school administration, the teachers, the parents, and the students themselves. No longer can accountability for success or failure be placed exclusively on the shoulders of individual teachers, when the schoolwide conditions and supports and incentives for high-quality learning are not present.
- The work of students, their active engagement with the curriculum, and their performance of the curriculum are seen as the core business of the school. The teachers' role is to assist, guide, facilitate, coach, direct, stimulate, encourage, motivate, assess, and remediate this work. The essential focus of school restructuring is on improving the quality of student learning performances.
- A corollary of the above is that the teachers' focus is on the curriculum-as-learned, namely, the students' production and performance of knowledge and understanding, contextualized (1) by the students' gender, culture, stage of development, class, family background, learning style, interests, and prior experience; (2) by the real-life variables associated with the learning tasks; and (3) by the methodologies and conceptual frames of the academic disciplines. This focus displaces the more passive memorizing of the curriculum-as-taught. What counts is the knowledge of the student, not the knowledge on the page of the textbook.
- Testing and assessment procedures will reflect this different understanding of and approach to student learning, in order to promote authentic performance and production of the curriculum-as-learned.
- Schools will be reorganized around this core work of learning and the facilitation of learning in such a way that resources of professional staff, daily, weekly, and yearly schedules, space, student groupings for learning, home–school partnerships, community resources, administrative arrangements, budgets, and assessments will be refashioned to support and maximize student learning.
- The work of supervision, then, becomes more complex and more subtle. Authority, responsibility, and accountability will be shared with teachers. While a concern for improving individual classroom performance will be retained, a greater emphasis will be placed on the collaborative work of recreating a more user-friendly, learning-friendly school environment that will support more flexible and more responsive teaching and more consistently high-quality learning for all students.

In an appendix to this chapter, we have included an extensive treatment of standards and scoring criteria of authentic assessments. Again, the elaboration of this form of curriculum-as-assessed indicates the close links with the curriculum-as-learned and the curriculum-as-planned.

SOME REFLECTIONS

1. Can you name two or three teachers you know who exhibit the habit of continuous assessment simultaneously with their teaching of a class? Talk to them about the skills required

to be aware of various students in the class who might be having difficulty with the lesson and how they respond to their difficulties. Ask them how that has an impact on the quality of student learning.

2. Ask two or three teachers to share with you the various forms of assessment of student learning they employ and how they provide feedback to students on the good qualities of their performances as well as the deficiencies. Try to get a sense of whether the assessment is considered an integral part of the learning process.

3. Can you identify teachers in your school whose assessments and scoring of assessments resemble those recommended by Newmann and his associates (as presented in Appendix 7-1)? Ask them to talk about how the assessment structures the way they teach.

Appendix 7-1
Standards and Scoring Criteria
for Assessment Tasks

Overview and General Rules

The main point here is to estimate, for a given task, the extent to which the teacher communicates to students expectations consistent with the standards. To what extent does successful completion of the task require the kind of cognitive work indicated by each standard?

The seven standards reflect three more general standards for authentic achievement, as follows:

Construction of knowledge:	Organization of information
	Consideration of alternatives
Disciplined inquiry:	Disciplinary content
	Disciplinary process
	Elaborated written communication
Value beyond school:	Problem connected to the world beyond the classroom
	Audience beyond the school

A. If a task has different parts that imply different expectations (e.g., worksheet/short answer questions and a question asking for explanation of some conclusions), the score should reflect the teacher's apparent dominant or overall expectations. Overall expectations are indicated by the proportion of time or effort spent on different parts of the task and by criteria for evaluation stated by the teacher.

B. Scores should take into account what students can reasonably be expected to do at the grade level.

Source: Fred M. Newmann, Walter G. Secada, and Gary G. Wehlage, *A Guide to Authentic Instruction and Assessment: Vision, Standards and Scoring,* Madison: Wisconsin Center for Educational Research, 1995, pp. 80–85. Reprinted with permission.

Standard 1: Organization of Information

The task asks students to organize, synthesize, interpret, explain, or evaluate complex information in addressing a concept, problem, or issue.

Consider the extent to which the task asks the student to organize, interpret, evaluate, or synthesize complex information, rather than to retrieve or to reproduce isolated fragments of knowledge or to repeatedly apply previously learned algorithms and procedures. To be scored high, the task should call for interpretation of nuances of a topic that go deeper than surface exposure or familiarity.

3 = high
2 = moderate
1 = low

When students are asked to gather information for reports that indicates some selectivity and organizing beyond mechanical copying, but are not asked for interpretation, evaluation, or synthesis, give a score of 2.

Standard 2: Consideration of Alternatives

The task asks students to consider alternative solutions, strategies, perspectives, or points of view as they address a concept, problem, or issue.

To what extent does success in the task require consideration of alternative solutions, strategies, perspectives, and points of view? To be scored high, the task should clearly involve students in considering alternatives, either through explicit presentation of the alternatives or through an activity that cannot be successfully completed without examination of alternatives implicit in the work. It is not necessary that students' final conclusions include listing or weighing of alternatives, but this could be an impressive indicator that it was an expectation of the task.

3 = high
2 = moderate
1 = low

Standard 3: Disciplinary Content

The task asks students to show understanding and/or use of ideas, theories, or perspectives considered central to an academic or professional discipline.

To what extent does the task promote students' understanding of and thinking about ideas, theories or perspectives considered seminal or critical within an academic or professional discipline, or in interdisciplinary fields recognized in authoritative scholarship? Examples in mathematics could include proportion, equality, central tendency, and geometric space. Examples in social studies could include democracy, social class, market economy, or theories of revolution. Reference to isolated factual claims, definitions, algorithms—though necessary to inquiry within a discipline—will not be considered indicators of significant disciplinary content unless the task requires students to apply powerful disciplinary ideas that organize and interpret the information.

3 = Success in the task clearly requires understanding of concepts, ideas, or theories central in a discipline.
2 = Success in the task seems to require understanding of concepts, ideas, or theories central in a discipline, but the task does not make these very explicit.
1 = Success in the task can be achieved with a very superficial (or even without any) understanding of concepts, ideas, or theories central to any specific discipline.

Standard 4: Disciplinary Process

The task asks students to use methods of inquiry, research, or communication characteristic of an academic or professional discipline.

To what extent does the task lead students to use methods of inquiry, research, communication, and discourse characteristic of an academic or professional discipline? Some powerful processes of inquiry may not be linked uniquely to any specific discipline (e.g., interpreting graphs), but they will be valued here if the task calls for their use in ways similar to important uses within the discipline.

> 3 = Success in the task requires the use of methods of inquiry or discourse important to the conduct of a discipline. Examples of methods of disciplinary inquiry would include looking for mathematical patterns or interpreting primary sources.
> 2 = Success in the task requires use of methods of inquiry or discourse not central to the conduct of a discipline.
> 1 = Success in the task can be achieved without use of any specific methods of inquiry or discourse.

Standard 5: Elaborated Written Communication

The task asks students to elaborate on their understanding, explanations, or conclusions through extended writing.

This standard is intended to measure the extent to which a task requires students to elaborate on their ideas and conclusions through extended writing in a discipline. Expectations for elaborated communication can vary between disciplines. We indicate criteria for mathematics and social studies.

> 4 = Analysis/Persuasion/Theory.
> *Mathematics:* The task requires the student to show his/her solution path and to justify that solution path, that is, to give a logical argument, explain his/her thinking, or to justify results.
> *Social studies:* The task requires explanations of generalizations, classifications, and relationships relevant to a situation, problem, or theme. Examples include attempts to argue, convince, or persuade and to develop or test hypotheses.
> 3 = Report/Summary.
> *Mathematics:* The task requires some organization of material. The student is asked to give clear evidence of his/her solution path but is not required to give any mathematical argument, to justify his/her solution path, or to explain his/her thinking.
> *Social studies:* The task calls for an account of particular events or series of events ("This is what happened"), a generalized narrative, or a description of a recurrent pattern of events or steps in a procedure ("This is what happens"; "This is the way it is done").
> 2 = Short-Answer Exercises.
> *Mathematics:* The task requires little more than giving a result. Students may be asked to show some work, but this is not emphasized and does not request much detail.
> *Social studies:* Only one or two brief sentences per question are expected.
> 1 = Multiple-Choice Exercises.
> Fill-in-the-blank exercises (answered with less than a sentence).

Standard 6: Problem Connected to the World Beyond the Classroom

The task asks students to address a concept, problem, or issue that is similar to one that they have encountered, or are likely to encounter, in life beyond the classroom.

To what extent does the task present students with a question, issue, or problem that they have actually encountered, or are likely to encounter, in their lives beyond school? In mathematics, estimating personal budgets would qualify as a real-world problem, but completing a geometric proof generally would not. In social studies, defending one's position on compulsory community service for students could qualify as a real-world problem, but describing the origins of World War II generally would not.

Certain kinds of school knowledge may be considered valuable as cultural capital or cultural literacy needed in social, civic, or vocational situations beyond the classroom (e.g., knowing how a bill becomes a law, or how to compute interest on an investment). However, task demands for culturally valued, "basic" knowledge will not be counted here unless the task requires applying such knowledge to a specific problem likely to be encountered beyond the classroom.

When students are allowed to choose topics of interest to them, this might also indicate likely application of knowledge beyond the instructional setting. But tasks that allow student choice do not necessarily connect to issues beyond the classroom. To score high on this standard calls for clarity that the question, issue, or problem which students confront resembles one that students have encountered, or are likely to encounter, in life beyond school.

3 = The question, issue, or problem clearly resembles one that students have encountered, or are likely to encounter, in life beyond school. The resemblance is so clear that teacher explanation is not necessary for most students to grasp it.

2 = The question, issue, or problem bears some resemblance to real-world experiences of the students, but the connections are not immediately apparent. The connections would be reasonably clear if explained by the teacher, but the task need not include such explanations to be rated 2.

1 = The problem has virtually no resemblance to questions, issues, or problems that students have encountered, or are likely to encounter, beyond school. Even if the teacher tried to show the connections, it would be difficult to make a persuasive argument.

Standard 7: Audience Beyond the School

The task asks students to communicate their knowledge, present a product or performance, or take some action for an audience beyond the teacher, classroom, and school building.

CHAPTER 8

Developing Teacher Leadership

INTRODUCTION

The national agendas of school renewal and increased accountability for improved learning for all students changed the context for supervision. We link the agendas of school renewal and accountability because we see the accountability agenda as shaping the school renewal agenda. Accountability for quality learning for all students will necessarily drive the forms that school renewal takes, namely, those forms that demonstrably improve learning for all students. Presently, schools are expected to do more—in some instances, much more—with static or diminished financial resources. This changed context has placed greater emphasis on developing the human and professional resources already within the school system, which in turn has brought to the fore a focus on teacher leadership. This chapter explores some contemporary understandings and expressions of teacher leadership within both structured models of school improvement as well as more unstructured collaborations among teachers around student performance assessment. We go to some lengths in the chapter to elaborate on a form of teacher leadership that is mostly ignored or treated superficially in the literature, namely, teacher leadership as it is exercised in teachers' own classrooms with their student learners. With that as a firm base, teacher leaders can move beyond the classroom to engage other teachers in discussions of student learning. This chapter ends by exploring how supervisors and teacher leaders may hold the key to significant school renewal.

SOME BACKGROUND

The preceding chapters have progressively moved the supervisory process into the heart of the educational enterprise: teaching, curriculum, and student learning. The supervisory process is seen not so much as the performance of bureaucratic functions such as rating teacher and student performance according to prescribed behaviors, but as facilitating both teacher and student progress in the learning tasks at hand. We have moved into the essential meaning of Supervision II. However, the more we explored what Supervision II might mean, the more it became apparent that the process of supervision could not be tied to any one role or position. It could be exercised by a principal, a district supervisor, a lead teacher, a teaching colleague, and indeed, by a student. What is essential to the process is reflection on the significance of what is happening.

As a process, supervision involves a "standing over," a "standing above," to achieve a larger or deeper view of the educational moment, to gain a vision of the whole as it is reflected and embodied in its parts. In short, supervision is not so much a view of a teacher by a super-ior viewer; it is a super-vision, a view of what education might mean at this moment, within this context, for these particular people. Perhaps more accurately, the process of supervision is the attempt by a segment of the community of learners to *gain* this super-vision of the educational moment within their reflective practice, so that their insight into the possibilities of that moment can lead to the transformation of that moment into something immensely more satisfying and productive for them.

What becomes more apparent in the exploration of the significance of Supervision II is that the process requires an open, flexible, inquiring attitude. The process is not directed at judging behaviors according to a fixed, seemingly objective set of standards. Rather, the process leads to the construction of understanding and practical judgment, which leads to tentative, experimental choices that the participants see as responsive to the particulars of the context in which they find themselves. The participants, in their reflective practice, decide whether those choices are appropriate and productive for them. This is not to say that those pragmatic choices, guided by reflective practice, will be perfect. On the contrary, teaching and learning are carried forward in the reflective give-and-take concerning, in this particular situation, what works and what does not, what makes sense and what does not, what facilitates student performance and what does not. Neither the teacher, the students, nor the supervisor knows ahead of time what will result until they engage the material in a specific way.[1] They are constantly constructing the teaching-learning moment. Supervision is the attempt to see that teaching–learning moment in all its multidimensionality and all its possibility.

THE SUPERVISOR AS A PROFESSIONAL

Although it is possible and desirable for students to participate in this process of supervision, the responsibility for the more formal exercise of supervision is a professional responsibility of members of the educational staff—teachers, administrators, and professional support staff. To exercise this professional responsibility, those

---

[1]Michael Huberman, "The Social Context of Instruction in Schools," Paper presented at the Annual Meeting of the American Educational Research Association, Boston, April 1990.

engaged in the supervisory process need to have some sense (by no means ever complete) of the substance of the super-vision. In other words, they have to have some vision of an ideal educational moment or an ideal educational tapestry woven of many threads. One's educational platform is usually the unspoken foundation of such a vision, namely, a sense of how children learn, a sense of what is most valuable to learn, a sense of the social significance of what is learned, a sense of the ways to orchestrate learning, a sense of the importance of community and self-governance and social character in learning and for learning. Many teachers possess this vision tacitly, but the vision becomes narrowed by the daily routine of fragmented learning tasks. Through collaborative, reflective conversations in a supervisory process, teachers can regain that super-vision for themselves and for their students.

As professional educators, those who engage in supervision need to have a larger sense of the purposes of schooling. They have to bring to the supervisory process a sense of how *this* educational moment of *these* students and *this* teacher might embody the larger purposes of *this* school, given its neighborhood context, the socioeconomic realities of the community, the cultural makeup of its families, and the human potential and social capital such a community represents. Such an educational awareness does not come with state certification. It requires a sustained effort to be present to the cultural and social realities of the students, an attempt to understand what their world feels like and means to them. It also requires empathetically an understanding of the learning task from the inside, as it were, not simply as a proposition on a page in a textbook or course outline. Supervisors must imagine a variety of ways of entering into and working at the learning task. They must be willing to learn by trial and error what teaching strategies work in a particular instance. When one approach does not work, then both supervisor and teacher should say openly, "This isn't working. Let's try another way of looking at this."

Gaining super-vision through the reflective practice of teaching is not a deductive, logical, linear type of reasoning, moving from a clearly spelled-out vision to a three- or four-step process that ends up choosing a specific learning activity. Rather, it is a highly specific involvement with the task at hand that is illuminated by an intuition of how it is working, and by further intuitions flowing from the exchanges with the students that enable the teacher to see that this is an instance of the larger purpose or value that the school is promoting. The super-vision flows out of the task, rather than from a temporary pause in the level of reasoning. The experienced teacher knows the super-vision tacitly in the particularity of the task, as Michael Polanyi would say.[2]

Such intuitions, however, come only with time, experience, and reflection. Having a sense of these complex realities is not easily gained. It requires intelligent inquiry, reflective assessment, and deep familiarity with the material being taught. It also requires a critical assessment of the institutional barriers to teaching and

[2]Michael Polanyi, *The Tacit Dimension,* Garden City, NY: Doubleday/Anchor, 1967.

learning, given all the contextual variables just mentioned. In other words, the work of supervision is intellectual work—not exclusively intellectual work, but certainly work that must be enlightened by an effort to understand, to develop intelligible frameworks for interpreting what happens between teachers and students and for proposing how it might happen more felicitously. It should not be characterized as work that relies on checklists of supposedly correct teacher behaviors, or on assumptions of superior knowledge granted by administrative position, or on a romanticized personal experience as a teacher. The practice of Supervision II places challenging demands on those who exercise it.

The practice of Supervision I tends to promote incremental changes within the status quo. Hence relatively uniform formulas define "good teaching." A relatively superficial notion of what constitutes academic knowledge suffices as a measure of effectiveness. A complacency with institutional arrangements of classroom schedules, physical arrangements of the learning space, procedures for grading and promotion, and so forth, assumes that teaching and learning must take place within these boundaries. A view of knowledge as something that exists independently somewhere—in the textbook, in the library, in the teacher's head—and is to be communicated to the students, all of whom will receive it as some uniform package suitable for testing, informs the way Supervision I judges and rates the work teachers do.

The practice of Supervision II challenges all these assumptions. But these assumptions cannot be challenged unless one is prepared to argue intelligently for their displacement. When we say, then, that Supervision II requires a larger professional commitment, we mean that it requires a profound grasp of child and adolescent development, a commitment to a studied understanding of teaching and learning, a new view of the variety of settings and stimuli that can nurture learning, a new awareness of the complexity of student assessment, a revised concept of professional authority as a necessary complement to hierarchical legal authority, an understanding of adult learning, and an imaginative sense of the possibilities for flexible redesign of the process of schooling itself.

Supervision II requires those who implement it to shift from the traditional roles defined by Supervision I to those of facilitator, policy innovator, resource finder, inventor, collegial experimenter, intellectual, critic, coach, institutional builder, community healer, visionary. Supervision II views the work with individual teachers and groups of teachers as but one aspect of a large, communal effort of transforming the school into a learning community.

In earlier editions of this book, we tended to treat supervisory leadership as the domain of the administrator–supervisor or central office supervisor. We recognize now that teachers are supervisors in their own right—supervisors of students' production and performance of knowledge. In Chapter 4 we saw how much of the morality of supervisory work derives from its involvement with the intrinsically moral enterprises of learning and of teaching. In this chapter, we similarly propose that much of the leadership of supervisor–administrators and central office supervisors derives from their involvement with teacher leaders of student learning and the nurturing of that kind of teacher leadership.

EMERGING PERSPECTIVES ON TEACHER LEADERSHIP

Over the past 20 years or so there has developed a gradually maturing sense of what teacher leadership might mean. Some of it can be traced to the increased interest in improved professional status for teachers.[3] As the work of teaching came to be seen in its complexity and multidimensionality as requiring both logic and intuition, as well as a scholarly knowledge of the subject matter and the autonomy and discretion to translate that into various pedagogical strategies and learning activities suited to particular students in this and that classroom, there emerged a deeper sense of the professional demands of teaching.

Others stressed the importance of teachers' participation in the democratic governance and administration. If teachers engaged in participatory decision making with administrators, then there would be greater ownership of those decisions, and indeed, greater wisdom as well in those decisions. This viewpoint tended to place teacher leadership as being engaged in schoolwide management committees.[4]

Still others, linking teachers' core work with schoolwide leadership, saw the importance of teams of teacher leaders involved with curriculum decisions and the school's exploration of newer curriculum supports, such as computer software and math manipulables. Administrators, despite the call for them to be instructional leaders, were simply unable to devote the time and focus such leadership required, because of the immediacy of the daily administrative demands on their time. Others saw teachers leading other teachers by running seminars on new instructional practices or on collaborative projects.[5] From these perspectives, however, teacher leadership seems exclusively to mean the leadership of other teachers in improving their technical skills. In these instances, it would appear that the internal faculty would replace the external consultant who used to be invited in to march the faculty through some instructional improvement strategies. Teacher leaders would be considered to hold more legitimacy when they were addressing their colleagues, but underneath, the process would tend to be the same.

---

[3]Linda Darling Hammond and Gary Sykes (eds.), *Teaching as the Learning Profession: Handbook of Policy and Practice,* New York: Longman, 1983; Lee Shulman, "From Minsk to Pinsk: Why a Scholarship of Teaching and Learning," *Journal of Scholarship of Teaching,* vol. 1, no. 1 (2000), pp. 48–52; Donovan R. Walling (ed.), *Teachers as Leaders: Perspectives on the Professional Development of Teachers,* Bloomington, IN: Phi Delta Kappa Educational Foundation, 1994.

[4]Karen Seashore Louis, Sharon D. Kruse, and associates, *Professionalism and Community: Perspectives on Reforming Urban Schools,* Thousands Oaks, CA: Corwin Press, 1995; Thomas J. Sergiovanni, *Building Community in Schools,* San Francisco: Jossey-Bass, 1994.

[5]Bruce S. Cooper, "When Teachers Lead," in Terry A. Astuto (ed.), *When Teachers Lead,* University Park, PA: University Council for Educational Administration, 1993, pp. 7–13; Leonard O. Pellicer and Lorin W. Anderson, *A Handbook for Teacher Leaders,* Thousand Oaks, CA: Corwin Press, 1995; Patricia A. Wasley, *Teachers Who Lead: The Rhetoric of Reform and the Realities of Practice,* New York: Teachers College Press, 1991.

More recently, teacher leadership is being linked more closely to school renewal.[6] Here, the take on leadership is more connected to the ongoing, core work of teaching for improved student achievement and success, but now it is also linked to collaborative efforts with other teachers, to reflective practice with other teachers, to the cultural shift toward becoming a learning community of teachers. Before we explore this newer view of teacher leadership, we want to pause and look at teacher leadership in its most natural setting—the classroom—for this is perhaps the aspect of teacher leadership most ignored or superficially assumed in the scholarly writing about it.

TEACHER LEADERSHIP IN THE CLASSROOM

For the moment, we want to focus on teacher leadership in the classroom setting. Consider the typical situation on the opening day of school. The teacher, in most cases, does not know the students and the students do not know the teacher. Many of the students do not want to be there; they would rather be outside playing with their friends or pursuing a hobby. The students know that they are in a relative position of powerlessness. The teacher can make their lives miserable—piling on the homework, telling their parents when they get in trouble, meting out detentions and other forms of punishment. After the first or second grade, however, most students know that they can, to some extent, make the teacher's life difficult, or at least frustrate the teacher's attempt to totally control what goes on in the classroom. They can pass notes, throw spitballs, drop their books on the floor, ask silly questions, copy homework, misrepresent their teacher to their parents, and engage in other obstructionist forms of resistance. Good teachers know that. They also know that the youngsters are vulnerable to criticism and failure, are unsure of themselves, are easily embarrassed, and are in need of the approval of their classmates.

The leadership challenges for the teacher on the opening day of school are numerous. The teacher has to invite the students to believe that their time together can be satisfying, enjoyable, exciting, and rewarding. The teacher has to communicate

---

[6]Eric Camburn, Brian Rowan, and James E. Taylor, "Distributed Leadership in Schools: The Case of Elementary Schools Adopting Comprehensive School Reform Models," *Educational Evaluation and Policy Analysis,* vol. 25, no. 4 (2003), pp. 347–373; Michael A. Copland, "Leadership of Inquiry: Building and Sustaining Capacity for School Improvement," *Educational Evaluation and Policy Analysis,* vol. 25, no. 4 (2003), pp. 375–395; Frank Crowther, Stephen S. Kaagan, Margaret Ferguson, and Leone Hann, *Developing Teacher Leaders: How Teacher Leadership Enhances School Success,* Thousand Oaks, CA: Corwin Press, 2002; Gordon A. Donaldson, *Cultivating Leadership in Schools: Connecting People, Purpose, and Practice,* New York: Teachers College Press, 2001; Chris Day and Alma Harris, "Teacher Leadership, Reflective Practice, and School Improvement," in Kenneth Leithwood and Philip Hallinger (eds.), *Second International Handbook of Educational Leadership and Administration,* London: Kluwer, 2002, pp. 957–977; Ann Lieberman and Lynne Miller, "Teaching and Teacher Development: A New Synthesis for a New Century," in Ronald S. Brandt (ed.), *Education in a New Era,* Alexandria, VA: Association for Supervision and Curriculum Development, 2000, pp. 47–63; Joseph M. Sawyer, *Teacher Leadership as a Strategy for Implementing Change,* Unpublished doctoral dissertation, Boston College, 2005.

to the children that they are cared for and respected in their own right. The teacher has to be able to mix the distribution of "warm fuzzies" with gentle demands for responsibility and accountability. The teacher has to convince the youngsters that they can derive deep personal satisfaction, both individually and as a class, in the production of quality work. The teacher has to convince them that this is significant, valuable work they will be attempting together. The teacher has to get to know the strengths and shortcomings of each student so that those strengths can be developed and those shortcomings minimized, bringing out the leadership qualities of the students themselves so that they can develop the self-confidence and pride that comes with achievement. The teacher has to communicate a belief in these youngsters, an expectation that they can do high-quality work and that together they can become an outstanding class, a class that others in the school will take notice of and admire. The teacher, in other words, has to turn around potential hostility, apathy, and resistance into enthusiasm, collective self-confidence, interest, and pride in accomplishment.

Scan the book titles on corporate leadership in any bookstore and you will see references to these very same challenges: serving the customer well; managing by values; leading through human development; managing with courage and conviction in an age of uncertainty; leading with a vision of the possible; co-operating to compete; working it out; disciplining without punishment; arousing the heart; discovering the soul; developing the power to be extraordinary; discovering values to humanize the way we work; managing chaos; implementing management by meaning; providing knock-your-socks-off service; imagination engineering.

Many teachers are reasonably good technicians. They can come up with a good lesson plan, develop three or four ways to get across a concept, and devise a sophisticated grading scheme. Teacher leaders are good technicians, too, but they are also a lot more. They bring to their work with youngsters an excitement about learning, a belief in the sacredness of each child and in his or her untapped potentialities, an obvious caring for each child, and a commitment to create satisfying possibilities for the achievement of each child. Youngsters in their classes perceive this caring and respond readily to it. To be sure, there will be some students whose home experiences may have been so damaging as to require lots of time and effort to create the requisite trust. Teacher leaders take the long view with these children and eventually find ways to tease them into involvement.

Teacher leaders tend to focus on the profound significance of what students are doing and, by implication, on the profound significance of their own work as teachers. In Chapter 5 we discussed the notion of the educational platform. Here, we can say that the teacher leader's platform will be based on at least a tacit understanding that their work with youngsters is involved with the ongoing self-creation of each student. Likewise, the teacher leader somehow knows that in the learning experiences of the students in that classroom, the culture is being recreated, the human experiment is again becoming self-conscious, and a little piece of human history is moving from drift and accident to a clearer conscious direction. The teacher leader understands that work in the classroom is involved with what John Dewey termed the transformation of experience—where raw experience moves toward intelligent understanding and this understanding is put at the service of intelligent action on both an individual and a group basis.

Without necessarily using the above terminology, we know that the teacher leader works out of these understandings and commitments when we observe the deep satisfaction of the teacher when the student looks up from his or her work and says, "That's it, isn't it? I got it! I never thought I could do it," or "I get it now, I know how it works" or "We did it! Wait till we show our parents!" Those are the moments the teacher leader works for and the moments he or she continually reminds the students of.

The teacher manager tends to be someone who arranges the students' work around the mastering of the syllabus. The achievement of good grades on standardized or teacher-made tests provides the necessary evidence for the teacher manager that the work has been accomplished. The teacher leader, on the other hand, goes beyond the mastery of the common syllabus and good grades on tests to push for a more personal and profound appropriation of the material under study. He or she will ask the student, "What does this mean to you, in terms of how you define yourself, in terms of your relationship to the community or to nature?" Furthermore, the teacher leader tries to bring the whole class to a reflective appreciation of the significance of learning in its own right—as a sacred activity, as an emancipatory activity, as an activity that bonds them to each other and to their world. For the teacher leader, the student performance of knowledge is not simply the production of right answers. It involves a sense of personal appropriation, of personal reconstruction, as something that bears the stamp of the student's lived experience, as something needed by the community, as something worthy of celebration.

To be sure, this description of the teacher leader is idealized. Yet we all know teachers who have approached this ideal. A little reflection reveals that these teachers did indeed lead the class to an unusually high level of performance, not simply in achieving the standard requirements of learning the school syllabus, but in achieving a sense of both individual and group pride in the work done together and in the improved sense of self-esteem and self-confidence of the class. These teachers possessed those same qualities of leadership we recognize in other leaders in other fields of endeavor.

David Berliner offers the insight that teachers perform many executive-type functions in the classroom.[7] For instance, teachers engage in planning, in communicating goals, in regulating the activities of the workplace, in creating a pleasant atmosphere for work, in educating newcomers to the work group, in relating the work of the site to other units in the system, in supervising workers and other staff, and in motivating those being supervised and evaluating the work performance. Berliner comments that teaching requires ongoing management of the workplace by a talented executive. His analysis is consistent with the shift in understanding already alluded to in earlier chapters in this book, namely, that the students are workers involved in the production and performance of knowledge. Teachers facilitate

---

[7]David Berliner, "The Executive Functions of Teaching," *Instruction,* vol 43, no. 2 (1983), pp. 38–40.

(manage, if you will) this work. This executive work of teachers becomes leadership when it is suffused with a view of the learner as a bearer of unlimited and heroic possibilities as well as a view of learning as a transformative and sacred activity, not only for the individual student but for the community of learners. That vision transforms the technical work of teaching into something special, which is what any kind of leader does: elevate the conception of the work to a deeper significance than it previously had; connect the work to something intrinsically important for the carrying on of human life. That new sense of the significance and meaning energizes the workers more enthusiastically and wholeheartedly to transform the work itself.

Our insistence that we begin by grounding teacher leadership in the teacher's leadership of his or her students rests on the conviction that teaching demands an autonomy and discretion that is unique to the profession. Lee Shulman brings out the need for teacher autonomy and discretion as he describes the multiple demands teachers face in their classroom.[8] Teachers are expected to diagnose every student's learning readiness as well as learning handicaps or weaknesses for every new unit of the curriculum, in order to provide the appropriate stimulus and motivator for the learning involved. Shulman points out that when one student is having difficulty completing the reading project, for example, there could be any number of reasons for the difficulty: an ignorance of a basic phonic rule; a failure to apply the phonic rule even though already known; a misunderstanding of the point of the story; a confusion of the vocabulary with a similar-sounding word in the student's first language; an emotional upset at home the night before; a distraction caused by a classmate who was fooling around; a misunderstanding of the directions for the project given the day before; and so forth. The teacher has to spend sufficient time with that student to figure out what is causing the difficulty in order to respond with the appropriate guidance.

Teachers have the added challenge of balancing mastery of skills and understandings by every student with the demand to cover the syllabus in a limited amount of time. Moreover, they are to attend to the needs of mainstreamed students and bilingual students, with the often cumbersome record keeping required for administrative oversight. They are responsible for detecting the signs of child abuse; protecting all the children from the possibility of infection by an undisclosed student in the classroom with AIDS; teaching impulse control and providing appropriate sanctions for violations of classroom rules; teaching basic ethical principles, such as fairness, respect, and honesty; and balancing a firm application of the rules and of academic accountability with the common fact that youngsters have their bad days when they are feeling out of sorts with everything and everybody. In other words, teachers not only have to know their stuff, but also have to be responsive to the messy and unpredictable swirl of emotions, surprises, disasters, and multifaceted levels of realities being experienced by their students.

---

[8]Lee S. Shulman, "Autonomy and Obligation: The Remote Control of Teaching," in L. S. Shulman and G. Sykes (eds.), *Handbook of Teaching and Policy,* New York: Longman, 1983, pp. 484–504.

Teacher leaders somehow manage, most of the time, to provide the individual attention and motivation while leading the class to high-quality learning. They do not lead by providing uniform teacher protocols for every group of students every day in class. Rather, their work is characterized by versatility, inventiveness, improvisation, caring, laughter, multiple methodologies simultaneously employed for various subgroups in the class, willingness to throw away a lesson plan on the spot when it is not working, instantaneous restructuring of class activities when the moment presents itself. The teacher leader keeps his or her finger on the pulse of the class to determine the way students are responding to the day's learning activities. This is not to say that the teacher forgets about the mandated curriculum outcomes; on the contrary, the effort to have every student achieve those outcomes is precisely why the teacher leader adapts the flow of classroom activities. The teacher leader knows that each child will come to those learning outcomes in individual and personal ways and is continually seeking for the door that will open their minds to the lessons being attempted.

Because of that essential need for autonomy and discretion in the structuring and restructuring of the classroom work, teacher leaders who subsequently may attempt to exercise leadership with their colleagues know ahead of time how crucial that autonomy and discretion are for their colleagues as well. Hence, in their work with other teachers, they will present any specific protocols as requiring a multitude of adaptations and applications, for they know that there is no magic teaching formula that works for all children on the same day nor for any child on two consecutive days. Teacher leaders explore a variety of approaches to the subject matter, some of which may, at one time or another, prove useful. The larger lesson teacher leaders teach their colleagues is to trust in the ability of their students to do high-quality work once they are motivated and to trust in the mutual exploration with the teacher of how to do the work. Unlocking that potential of their students will always be different for different youngsters. Teacher leaders can help their colleagues to develop the ability to improvise on the spot, rather than to follow a model of teaching that does not work for several of the students in their class. Obviously, such improvisation will develop over time, with practice, through trial and error, with greater understanding of the subject matter and of the many ways youngsters come to knowledge. As Wasley also brings out, teacher leaders find that they grow in the exchange with their colleagues as they explore together alternative ways of approaching a learning unit.[9]

TEACHER LEADERSHIP IN COMPREHENSIVE SCHOOL REFORM

As indicated above, there is a growing consensus among scholars of teacher leadership that teacher leadership is the key to ongoing school reform. In some instances, there are national models of school reform that place teams of teachers in

[9]Patricia A. Wasley, *Teachers Who Lead: The Rhetoric of Reform and the Realities of Practice,* New York: Teachers College Press, 1991.

strategically important positions of influence during the change process. In a study of distributed leadership generated by a school's participation in one of these externally developed models of comprehensive school reform (CSR)—the Accelerated Schools Project, America's Choice, and Success for All—Camburn, Rowan, and Taylor found that these models *required* leadership from multiple and diverse members of the staff.[10] In other words, the models required that new leadership roles around improving instruction and student learning be added to existing administrative leadership roles, roles such as instructional coach or facilitator, or group leader. Usually, these roles were clearly defined and networked with other roles within the model. Furthermore, the models called for explicit training for leadership in these roles. The cultivation of leadership among teachers within these CSR models is intentional and structured, unlike the haphazard emergence of teacher leadership at various local school sites, described, for example, in Crowther et al.[11] The CSR models recognize the importance of adding leadership resources for the improvement of student learning, and provide for and assume that teachers are capable of the leadership required of them.

Lieberman and Wood describe another national reform effort, the National Writing Project (NWP), which has been most successful in developing teacher leaders.[12] Through participating in the NWP, teachers learn to become better teachers of writing and place themselves in a position to lead other teachers toward increased competency in teaching writing. The summer institute of the NWP is structured around building a learning community and, through a variety of activities, building teacher leaders. At the conclusion of the summer institute, teachers graduate with the title of teacher consultant. They return to their schools and classrooms but also participate in local, regional, and national leadership work. Lieberman and Wood identified the dynamics teachers experienced at the NWP summer institute that seemed to foster their leadership, some of which follow:

- Every teacher, no matter what his or her background or philosophy, is viewed as having something of value to contribute.
- Teachers commit themselves to learning from others.
- Teachers dialogue about and critique one another's writing.
- Teachers take ownership for their own learning.
- Teachers grow in their reflection on teaching through reflecting on their learning.
- Teachers rethink their professional identity, linking it to participating in a professional community.[13]

---

[10]Camburn, Rowan, and Taylor, op. cit.

[11]Crowther, Kaagan, Ferguson, and Hann, op. cit.

[12]Ann Lieberman and Diane R. Wood, *Inside the National Writing Project: Connecting Network Learning with Classroom Teaching,* New York: Teachers College Press, 2003.

[13]As reported in Ann Lieberman and Lynne Miller, *Teacher Leadership,* San Francisco: Jossey-Bass, 2004, pp. 39–42.

These powerful learnings enable the teachers to return to their classrooms to be leaders of student learning. Energized by the successful responses of their students, they have the confidence to carry on conversations with other teachers about the results of their work with students.

These national models of school improvement through enhanced teacher leadership do not displace administrative leadership, but rather, see the effort at school improvement as requiring a distributed leadership throughout the school, with individuals and teams all on the same page regarding the clear goals of improved and high-quality student learning, yet each doing a part, often a unique and indispensable part, to contribute to those goals. Furthermore, this distributed leadership is not designed as a sleek, efficient machine. Rather, it is the leadership of a community that engages, necessarily, it would seem, in a certain amount of redundancy, with various teams reinforcing the ideas and initiatives of others through their specific contributors.

These qualities of distributed leadership reflect a growing consensus within the educational community as well as within the business and public service communities that the demands of life in the 21st century require organizations of all kinds to transform their manufacturing and bureaucratic images of how they should function to images around learning and collaboration. We cite but a few of these perspectives:

> The postmodern era suggests a conception of organizations as process and relationships rather than as structures and rules, with conversation as the central medium for the creation of both individual meaning and organizational change.[14]
>
> The ability to collaborate—on both a large and small scale—is one of the core requisites of postmodern society. . . . [W]ithout collaborative skills and relationships it is not possible to learn and to continue to learn as much as you need in order to be an agent for social improvement.[15]
>
> Every enterprise has to become a learning institution [and] a teaching institution. Organizations that build in continuous learning in jobs will dominate the twenty-first century.[16]

The emphasis on the school as a learning community and the role of supervisors within those learning communities has been developed in Chapter 3. We can now begin to see how the learning community is the natural ground for the expression and development of teacher leadership. We have seen how the work of the learning community requires shared reflection on the activities of teaching and learning, shared discussion of the purposes and outcomes of teaching and learning, shared critique of organizational obstacles to teaching and learning, and shared

[14]Larry Sackney, Keith Walker, and V. Hajal, "Principal and Teacher Perspectives on School Improvement," *Journal of Educational Management,* vol. 1, no. 1 (1998), pp. 45–63.

[15]Michael Fullan, *Change Forces: Probing the Depths of Educational Reform,* London: Falmer Press, 1993, pp. 17–18.

[16]Peter F. Drucker, *Managing for the Future: The 1990s and Beyond,* New York: Truman Talley Books, 1992, p. 108.

exploration of potential instructional interventions that lead to transformational learning for every student. In this chapter, as in Chapter 3, we have stressed that the learning community and teacher leadership are *means* for enhancing student learning, *not ends* in themselves. The interaction of and with students in classrooms and in class-related projects is the primary reference for all deliberations of the learning community and all teacher leadership activity. As was mentioned in Chapter 6, the ongoing work of teachers has three points of emphasis, namely, a better understanding of each student's learning needs and capabilities, a better understanding of the subject matter of the curriculum and its relationship to many facets of the real world, and the development of a greater repertoire of student learning activities that will connect the students' needs and interests with the curriculum material and its relationships to the real world (i.e., instructional versatility and efficacy). Those points of emphasis should shape the focus of the learning community and the activities of the various teacher leaders within that community.

Having emphasized the above focus, we must now present another important aspect of teacher leadership and the reflection on practice that energizes it. Day and Harris suggest that, given the present context of externally imposed definitions and agendas of school reform, which encourages teachers to measure the efficiency of their own classroom practices against that agenda, teachers need to maintain a broad vision about their work.[17] They go on to quote Zeichner and Liston:

> Teachers cannot restrict their attention to the classroom alone, leaving the larger setting and purposes of schooling to be determined by others. They must take active responsibility for the goals to which they are committed, and for the social setting in which these goals may prosper. If they are not to be mere agents of others, of the state, of the military, of the media, of the experts and the bureaucrats, they need to determine their own agency through a critical and continual evaluation of the purposes, the consequences, and the social context of their calling.[18]

This form of shared teacher reflection points to the necessary view of schools as sites for social justice, democratic community, and authentic learning. Schools tend to be structured to accommodate the mainstream communities of a society. They tend to treat nonmainstream communities (recent immigrants, second-language learners, racial and religious minorities, people with handicapping conditions, poor people on welfare, for example) as groups that have to be brought into or up to the culture and practices of the mainstream. Their not-being-mainstream is viewed as a disadvantage, a handicap, an unfortunate condition that the school must remedy. For most children who belong to these communities, schools present obstacles to their learning through a one-culture-fits-all definition of curriculum and one-size-fits-all instructional schedules, textbooks, testing protocols, and grading systems. Teachers need to be advocates and spokespersons for these children and take a special interest in seeing that they succeed, that they have an equal opportunity to learn what the state holds them accountable to learn.

---

[17]Day and Harris, op. cit.
[18]Kenneth M. Zeichner and Daniel P. Liston, *Reflective Teaching: An Introduction,* Mahwah, NJ: Erlbaum, 1996.

Teachers also need to resist the imposition of a free market interpretation of the schooling process, and the exclusive equation of learning with standardized test scores. Unfortunately, the business community and the media seem to think that schools can be run like businesses, with a focus on the bottom line, which is equated with scores on standardized tests. This marketization of learning is a gross over-simplification and distortion of what learning means, and an oversimplification of the conditions of schooling. It tends to reduce learning to the accumulation of a portfolio for gaining admission to the prestigious universities and to high-profile jobs, and to miss the important side of learning as the gradual transformation of an unformed identity and an immature person into someone who knows where he or she came from, what communities he or she belongs to and has responsibilities for, how to find various types of human fulfillment, and what is worth striving for.

This concern brings us to a view of teacher leadership that proposes a richer framework for appreciating what teacher leaders aspire to and can accomplish. Frank Crowther and his associates have been studying teacher leaders for the past decade and have come up with significant empirical findings about teachers who have accomplished significant results for their schools not only by mobilizing their fellow teachers, but also by involving segments of the community in support of proj-ects that transform student learning, while also having a significant impact on the local community.[19] Crowther and his associates maintain that this kind of teacher leadership, though by no means universal, is more widespread than the national media might suggest. In their studies of teacher leaders in a variety of settings and two countries, they have developed a Teachers as Leaders framework, which we summarize in Exhibit 8–1. Crowther and his associates readily admit that few teacher leaders demonstrate all six descriptors at any one time, but the framework does capture the collective qualities of the teacher leaders they encountered. They find that their teacher leaders believe that education is about student learning, about intellectual, moral, emotional, and spiritual growth and development. Teaching is all about supporting that learning. Furthermore, teacher leadership ties school and community together on behalf of learning and advances social sustainability and

---

Teachers as leaders
1. convey convictions about a better world.
2. strive for authenticity in their teaching, learning, and assessment practices.
3. facilitate communities of learning through organizationwide processes.
4. confront barriers in the school's culture and structures.
5. translate ideas into sustainable systems of action.
6. nurture a culture of success.

Exhibit 8–1. Teachers as Leaders Framework.
Source: Adapted from Frank Crowther, Stephen S. Kaagan, Margaret Ferguson, and Leone Hann, *Developing Teacher Leaders: How Teacher Leadership Enhances School Success*, Thousand Oaks, CA: Corwin Press, 2002, pp. 4–5.

[19]Crowther, Kaagan, Ferguson, and Hann, op. cit.

quality of life for a community. Their experience is that when teacher leaders encourage all other teachers to play a significant part in leading a schoolwide effort, then great things are possible.

Many of the teacher leaders Crowther and his associates encountered addressed structural obstacles within their schools that limited quality learning for their students. They also addressed conditions in the community (unemployment, substandard housing) by creating learning opportunities in the school that would break the cycle of dependency and depression. While many of these teacher leaders worked in schools serving poor or marginalized communities, many of them were also found in communities serving relatively privileged families. While the former engage directly in promoting a sense of participatory capacity and of taking charge of their destinies for their students and the community, the latter teacher leaders frequently engaged their already privileged students and the community in discussions about their responsibilities to participate in groups seeking social justice for others. In both cases, these teacher leaders seemed profoundly aware that student learning should be related to the present-day social conditions of their society.

These teachers generate "new meaning and in so doing enhance the community's quality of life."[20] While Crowther and his associates do not elaborate on this statement, they seem to connect learning to the creation of new identities that have new meaning. Teachers offered hope to and developed the latent potential in the youth and their communities, giving them a sense that they were somebodies who could take charge of their individual and collective lives. The work of these teacher leaders was not simply professional work; it was profoundly moral work, work that asserted human dignity, caring, and courage. Their work might legitimately deserve to be called transformational.

These teachers, however, did not take on the work of transforming student learning single-handedly. In their studies of teacher leaders, Crowther and his associates always found a principal and other administrators who were supportive and encouraging. Even though the generative ideas may have originated with the teachers, they built up a team effort with the local administrators. Crowther and his associates speak of a parallel leadership, where administrators provide political, financial, and organizational support, and teachers do the "close-to-the-ground" work of transforming the learning process in classrooms and in class-related projects in collaboration with other teachers. One of the most precious resources within the school is time—time to learn; time to teach, assess, provide feedback, and remediate; time to work with other teachers to analyze student work, diagnose student learning problems, design new learning protocols and classroom arrangements; time to work with administrators on the realignment of school structures and procedures with more supportive conditions for quality learning; time to work with parents on home–school collaboration. Although there was never enough time, administrators in these studies managed to carve out additional minutes and hours from the daily, weekly, and monthly school schedule for the important work of

[20]Ibid., p. 29.

high-quality learning, and the slow redesign of the whole school in support of that learning. As an interesting aside, the researchers note that their teacher leaders were collaborating with administrators in work that in theory and in practice had been *reserved to administrators alone*. Indeed, this seems to be the enormous shift that has been taking place in the field.

Lieberman and Miller echo this sentiment as they trace recent developments in the teaching profession as it has evolved "from individualism to professional community . . . from technical work to inquiry . . . from control to accountability . . . from managed work to leadership. . . . Teacher leadership is no longer appointed or anointed by the principal; it is considered a necessary part of being a teacher."[21] Indeed, teacher leadership is coming to be seen primarily as involving the core work of the profession, namely, teaching and learning. Earlier, DuFour and Eaker had asserted that schools would not improve unless teachers would exercise a collective leadership in performing their core work—the enhancing of student learning.[22] In a way, they redefined teacher leadership as *the community of teachers working together to do their job well*. Roland Barth sounded the same theme when he said that for schools to become places where all students learn, then all teachers must become leaders.[23] Teacher leadership, then, is much more a collective, collaborative leadership than an individual leadership, even though it might originate with one individual teacher embracing the challenge to improve.

That core work begins in their classrooms as they lead the learning of their students. On the basis of that leadership, teachers engage one another in a collaborative effort to improve learning throughout the school. That effort to improve learning throughout the school becomes intermingled with administrative leadership as teachers and administrators explore more supportive schoolwide arrangements for improved student learning. Notice the organic relationship to the base of classroom leadership, as those concerns push outward in a greater collective effort to improve learning schoolwide.

TEACHER LEADERSHIP AS RELATIONAL

One of the keys to teacher leadership, as implied by the discussion above, is the ability to build working relationships and coalitions. Day and Harris suggest that the forging of close working relationships with other individual teachers through which mutual learning takes place is perhaps the most important dimension of teacher leadership.[24] Leithwood, Jantzi, and Steinbach call attention to those personality

[21]Ann Lieberman and Lynne Miller, "Teaching and Teacher Development: A New Synthesis for a New Century," in Ronald S. Brandt (ed.), *Education in a New Era,* Alexandria, VA: Association for Supervision and Curriculum Development, 2000, pp. 47–63.

[22]Richard DuFour and Robert Eaker, *Professional Learning Communities at Work: Best Practices for Enhancing Student Achievement,* Bloomington, IN: National Education Service, 1998.

[23]Roland S. Barth, *Learning by Heart,* San Francisco: Jossey-Bass, 2001.

[24]Day and Harris, op. cit.

characteristics that teachers identify in their teacher leaders, traits such as fairness, commitment to the school community, and concern for the morality of decisions, as well as being a humane person and being open, honest, and genuine.[25] Clearly, the teachers in that study valued the way their teacher leaders related to them. Those relational qualities enabled teachers to work with them with relative comfort and enthusiasm.

Although relationships with other teachers are obviously crucial, we want to call attention to the classroom base of teacher leadership, where relationships with students are crucial to the advancement of student learning. That's where teacher leadership starts, but not where it ends. Feeling secure in the role they have played in students' success some teachers may serve well in mentor roles with beginning teachers, or in leading a faculty committee dealing with curriculum articulation between grades. On the other hand, a teacher may have wonderful relationships with her or his students, but may not be very comfortable with leading the work of peers. Nevertheless, that teacher may be open to listening and participating in group work with other teachers. The leading of a team in the more formal sense, however, is not as crucial to teacher leadership in the way we are talking about it now; what is crucial is the willingness to join with one or more other teachers to engage in the continuous work of analyzing student work, diagnosing and naming student learning problems, and exploring ways to improve student learning. Leading committees may be a role that never materializes for some teacher leaders, but the continuing work of collaborating with other teachers on improving instruction and student learning will still be the legitimate definition of their leadership.

This does not mean that school systems should not try to identify and train teachers who can lead groups in the formal sense. That remains a significant task that has been largely unaddressed by schools and school systems, especially for those middle-range leadership roles that call for guiding a significant ingredient of the school renewal plan over the course of a two- or three-year period. Furthermore, given the significant turnover of school leaders, planning for the development of a continuing source of leaders for the school and school system is an even larger issue left unattended in the field. Nevertheless, school system administrators should view teacher leadership as encompassing the whole spectrum of possible leadership roles, seeing all the roles as *collectively* important and, indeed, indispensable. Where teacher leadership will count most, however, is where "the rubber hits the road," namely, in the classroom of every teacher. A school system can have a sophisticated array of formal leadership positions for teachers, but if teacher leadership does not extend down into every classroom, then the engine of school renewal for improved student learning will continue to sputter.

[25]Kenneth Leithwood, Doris Jantzi, and Rosanne Steinbach, "Fostering Teacher Leadership," in Nigel Bennett, Megan Crawford, and Marion Cartwright (eds.), *Effective Educational Leadership,* London: Open University Press, 2003, pp. 186–200.

IMPLICATIONS FOR SUPERVISORS

Kim Marshall suggests that it is time to rethink teacher supervision and evaluation.[26] He suggests that supervision should be linked to a broader, schoolwide strategy for improving teaching and learning. Among those strategies are some which we have already alluded to in this chapter, such as having teachers work in teams to evaluate student work and to develop common curriculum unit plans and common interim assessments. The formal observations of classes would be almost entirely replaced by brief, though frequent, walk-through class visits linked now to the work of teacher teams to improve student learning. Marshall is not the first, nor will he be the last, to suggest that the traditional practice of classroom supervision, teacher by teacher, consumes an enormous amount of time with negligible payoff. On the other hand, there are those who, specifically with the intention of developing the kind of broad teacher leadership we have described in this chapter, find the clinical cycle of supervision particularly helpful.[27] There is no need to choose one supervisory strategy and abandon all others. In some cases, the careful targeting of clinical supervision may be the perfect instrument to build a working relationship with a teacher, especially a less experienced teacher, that will lead to the building of those leadership qualities necessary for the success of all the students in his or her classes. With a trusting relationship established through the intense work of clinical supervision, the teacher may be encouraged to network with a group of other teachers who could be a continuing resource for generating good questions and good ideas relating to student learning.

Nevertheless, Marshall makes an important point. Too often, principals and department chairs feel obliged by the bureaucratic requirement of their school system to visit X number of classrooms a semester and write reports of those visits, even when they know how ineffective and artificial this activity is. Furthermore, some teacher unions will insist on supervision by the book, wanting every teacher to be measured by the same standard. Marshall suggests that supervisors need to take the leadership here and negotiate a certain flexibility for a variety of alternative ways to fulfill the quality-control function of supervision, while enhancing the professional development of teachers through in-house teamwork. Such alternatives to the traditional supervisory protocols are suggested in subsequent chapters of this book.

As has been suggested again and again, teachers do not become leaders on their own. They sometimes have very good mentors early in their careers who help them develop the strengths they need to continue professionally. They sometimes have very supportive principals who believe strongly in the leadership potential of teachers, and who go out of their way to provide the time and resources for their development. There is little doubt that ongoing, focused professional development

---

[26]Kim Marshall, "It's Time to Rethink Teacher Supervision and Evaluation," *Phi Delta Kappan,* vol. 86, no. 10 (2005), pp. 727–735.

[27]Laura Wagner Smith, "Building Teacher Leadership Capacity," in Patricia E. Holland (ed.), *Beyond Measure: Neglected Elements of Accountability,* Larchmont, NY: Eye on Education, 2004, pp. 71–99.

programs are called for, some of them rather basic in terms of how to work in groups, how to overcome communication problems in groups, and so forth. The summer institutes sponsored by the National Writing Project provide training in team sharing as well as in the technical side of teaching writing. Other professional development programs attempt to get teachers focused on the basic purposes and values behind their work. Others look at some technical issues, such as how to eliminate the less important material in the curriculum to provide time for the more important material.

In their text, Crowther and his associates provide detailed exercises that a school might try out to stimulate the latent leadership of teachers.[28] From the testimony of the teacher leaders they encountered, they were led to believe that many teachers would readily respond to the opportunity to engage in communal leadership within their schools. Their exercises are based on the belief that teachers are capable of doing great things when they work together. It is in the working together, collaborating in leadership action, rather than in assigning leadership titles, that the leadership work gets done.

As with the national school renewal models, very specific leadership training should be provided for those teachers who are asked to fill strategic leadership positions in a long-range change process. One basic leadership training usually occurs during the first two or three years of their careers, as beginning teachers are encouraged to reflect on how they lead their class to significant learning. It is in those early years that teachers learn those executive functions that Berliner and Schulman speak about, whereby they learn how to lead students to significant learning. In short, there is no particular formula all supervisors should follow, for the context and particular history of the schools they work in will vary.

SUMMARY

As pressure mounted on schools and school systems to accept greater responsibility for high-quality learning of all students, it became increasingly apparent that the leadership of principals and central office supervisors and directors had to be complemented by a broadly based, collective teacher leadership. In some instances of externally developed models of school renewal, various teacher leadership positions were built into the model, with training provided for those teachers who would occupy roles such as design coaches, literacy coordinators, and curriculum coaches. In other instances of local school initiatives, teacher teams within grade clusters or subject-matter departments were created to discuss examples of student work, to develop rubrics for assessing student work, to develop exemplars of various levels of student work, and to design common assessments. This latter work was seen as changing the school culture of teacher isolation to one of teacher collaboration, leading toward the emergence of a collective teacher leadership.

As we have seen in this chapter, there is a progression in the development of teacher leadership. It starts within the teacher's own classroom and then can begin to be linked to the leadership of other teachers. As that second form of teacher leadership matures, some teachers will be ready

---

[28]Crowther et al., op. cit.

for a more structured or formal type of leadership activity. In all these cases, the role of the supervisor will be to support the appropriate development of the necessary leadership. The point behind this whole chapter is similar to Marshall's, though perhaps more ambitious: Spend most of your supervisory energies in supporting and enhancing teacher leadership at whatever level the situation calls for. This, we believe, is the most significant exercise of supervisory leadership. This, we believe, moves supervision into a more transformational leadership role. Whereas supervision previously was envisioned as primarily a management control function, now it has its own leadership part to play in the renewal of the school through its promotion of teacher leadership.

SOME REFLECTIONS

1. Think of three to five teachers in your school whom you would consider classroom leaders—that is, leaders of student learners. What are some of their leadership qualities and strategies? How does the student engagement in learning differ from that in other classrooms? Does their leadership extend to other teachers? How do they differ individually in their leadership? How could the school best employ their leadership in other ways?

2. Think of administrator–supervisiors in the school system. How many define their leadership role as one of controling, managing, and telling? How many define their leadership role as facilitating, supporting, and listening? How do teachers tend to respond to each of those groups?

3. Reflect on the general pattern of the local teachers' union. How would the union respond to the notions about teacher leadership presented in this chapter? Think of ways the system could work with the union to promote teacher leadership for improved student learning.

4. Are those teacher leaders you identified above subject to the same evaluation procedures as other tenured teachers? If you were in charge, how would you supervise them?

PART THREE

Supervision, Evaluation, and Renewal

CHAPTER 9

Classroom Supervision and Evaluation: Perspectives for Practice

INTRODUCTION

The purpose of this chapter is to provide readers with a foundation of ideas for understanding and practicing classroom supervision and evaluation. Key to this foundation is knowing the difference between professional knowledge and scientific knowledge. Professional knowledge is *created in use* as professionals practice. Professionals are constantly researching their practice and are committed to a posture of reflective practice. As their best, professionals join with others in forming communities of practice, which allows them to share their practice and to help each other understand it better.

Scientific studies and the knowledge they produce help explain what is going on but do not in themselves produce practices. Scientific knowledge is created and codified outside the school and then applied to school problems. In applied sciences, the knowledge base of the field is considered to be superordinate to the practitioners, serving to tell them what to do. Professional knowledge, by contrast, is considered to be subordinate to the practitioners, serving to inform their intuitions. This on-the-spot creation of knowledge and practice found in the professions, particularly in schools, is best understood and put to work to improve the academic success of schools when continuous learning and the sharing of what is known become a central value.

SOME BACKGROUND

With this chapter, we begin examining the issues and practices of classroom supervision and teacher evaluation. The chapters in this section are based on the assumption that principals, staff developers, and other designated supervisors have critical roles to play in providing both the social and the structural supports that enhance student learning, and the leadership pathways that can be used to directly influence student learning. The pathways, as shown in Figure 1–1, include improving the school's instructional capacity; improving the quality of teaching, curriculum, and the climate for learning; and improving the extent to which students are engaged in the academic and civic life of the school. Key in traveling each of these pathways is the importance of teacher learning—not just any learning, but learning that is continuous and that is situated in real contexts of teaching.

If learning is to be continuous and embedded in the daily practice of teachers, then supervisors will have to take the view that teaching to learn and learning to teach at the same time must become a way of life in the school. Sometimes teachers engage in teaching to learn and learning to teach with the help of designated supervisors, and sometimes they work alone. In Supervision II, the kind of supervision we advocate in this book, this powerful combination of practicing and learning to practice at the same time best takes place with the help of colleagues.

We are at an important crossroad. Our tradition in school improvement has been to invest in organizational structures that monitor what teachers do and how they do it. We have preferred this micromanagement of teaching and learning over strategies that emphasize improving teacher quality. As Linda Darling-Hammond explains: "the century-old U.S. decision to invest in large highly specialized school organizations that design and monitor teaching rather than in knowledgeable teachers who could make decisions themselves has led to a system that fails at the most critical tasks of teaching."[1] In the next five chapters, we argue that bringing together teaching and learning to teach into one seamless practice is an important step in the development of supervision as a profession committed to continuous learning.

LOOKING AHEAD. Including "Evaluation" in the title of this chapter may raise concerns for some readers. After all, for most of its history, supervision designed to help teachers improve and supervision designed to assess how well they are doing were viewed as responsibilities best kept separate. Reasons given for this separation make sense. Evaluating teachers can dampen, if not betray, the collegiality and trust that are needed for teacher learning to take place. In debating this point, you might find it helpful to outline what you feel are arguments for keeping the two separate and arguments for bringing them together. Despite the concerns you identify and the concerns we raise above, we believe that the problem is not teacher evaluation itself but how it is conducted and used.

Too often, for example, teacher evaluation means the rating, grading, and classifying of teachers using some locally standardized instrument as a yardstick. Generally, the instrument lists traits of teachers assumed to be important, such as "the teacher has a pleasant voice," and certain tasks of teaching considered to be critical, such as "the teacher plans well." The evaluator usually writes in comments as, increasingly, does the teacher.

This evaluation instrument is filled out after a classroom observation of the teacher. The observation visit is usually preceded by a conference, which varies

---

[1]Linda Darling-Hammond, *The Right to Learn: A Blueprint for Creating Schools that Work,* San Francisco: Jossey-Bass, 1997, p. 20.

from a brief encounter to a session where lesson plans, objectives, and teaching strategies are discussed. Sometimes a postobservation conference follows, wherein comments and ratings are discussed and negotiated. Usually, the teacher-evaluation procedure is concluded when both parties sign the instrument. The instrument is then forwarded to the district archives. This teacher-evaluation procedure may occur once or twice a year for the tenured teacher and more often for novices. Many teachers report having been observed in the classroom only a handful of times, and some report almost never being observed after achieving tenure. The same things are observed year after year.

In an effort to correct this problem, some states have passed laws that require a much more intensive evaluation, often using state-provided standardized instruments. Texas and Florida are examples. The instruments comprise teaching behaviors claimed to be linked to the teaching-effectiveness research or to other models of effective teaching. Because of this claimed link to research, the instruments are considered scientific and objective. As we point out later, the systems turn out to be neither scientific nor objective and the teaching-effectiveness research upon which they claim to be based is often misrepresented.

HOW SCIENTIFIC ARE SUPERVISION AND EVALUATION?

The aim of this chapter is to explore issues and perspectives that affect the way classroom supervision is researched, taught, and practiced. By and large neither teachers nor administrators and supervisors are very satisfied with present procedures. Indeed, many supervisors privately view these procedures as lacking in credibility. What are the likely effects of participating in a system of supervision characterized by such doubts? Too often the system takes on a certain artificial or mechanical quality, a routine functioning that becomes an end in itself.

- From the supervisor's perspective: "Evaluation time has come and gone. I have observed all the teachers and completed my follow-up conferences. The proper paperwork has been filed. Now we can get back to preparing students to pass the state tests."
- From a teacher's perspective: "Evaluation time has come and gone. I have demonstrated all the required teaching behaviors in the lesson I taught and have survived the conferences with my supervisor. Now we can get back to preparing students to pass the state tests."
- From another teacher's perspective: "I have demonstrated all the required teaching behaviors in the lessons I taught. My supervisor was pleased and gave me straight A's on nearly all the indicators on the evaluation instrument. My conferences were pleasant, but I would have liked more feedback about my teaching that would help me get better. Now that this is over, we can get back to preparing students to pass the state tests."

In these examples, the process of classroom supervision is disconnected from the purposes the teachers have in mind, the planning they are doing, and the teaching itself. The second teacher's response is a good example. How helpful will getting straight A's be in building the capacity of this teacher?

When supervisors and teachers are involved in this kind of supervision, teachers come to view the process as "showboating" and supervisors come to view the process as a bureaucratic requirement they have to complete.

Some schools practice classroom supervision by remote control. This view, practiced by Supervisor A (described in Chapter 1) assumes that if the focus is on supervision through development of a materials-intensive curriculum, usually linked to a detailed curriculum syllabus or detailed predetermined objectives, then teachers can be supervised from a distance. Teaching behavior becomes more predictable and reliable as standards, teaching objectives, and materials become more structured, and standardized. This is especially true if high-stakes tests are used to measure the extent to which objectives and standards are met. The decisions that teachers make about what and how to teach are controlled by the standards and objectives they pursue, the materials they use, the curricula they follow, the assignments and tests they give, and the schedules they follow. Alternatively, teachers might be free to make curricular and teaching decisions but are held accountable for the scores of their students on standardized tests. In this scheme they wind up making predictable decisions about curricula and teaching that are aligned with test objectives. In too many ways the test itself becomes the curriculum and the testing program itself becomes a system of supervision that winds up controlling what both teachers and supervisors are to do and how to do it. Not only can teacher and supervisor discretion be compromised by remote control supervision but students also have little say over such matters. It is as if student interest did not count. Further, because of the tendency to teach all standards and objectives as if they were equally important, it becomes difficult to enrich the curriculum in ways so that different students become especially competent in different, but equally important, areas. One size fits all.

Seeking to control classroom practices by remote control raises nagging questions. How can supervisors be sure that teachers are indeed performing prescribed duties up to standard? What evaluation methods can be used to answer this question? The problem is that methods of classroom observation and evaluation are too often shrouded in scientism not found even in the more legitimate sciences. Yet most teachers and supervisors privately believe that *teaching is far more an artistic enterprise than a scientific one.*

In the next several chapters we examine approaches to supervision and evaluation that are more consistent with how teachers think and what they do and with the complexities involved in the work of teaching and learning. Basic to the discussion is the view that supervision should be a process and sometimes a set of skills available to teachers and principals alike. This theme was discussed in Chapter 1.

Let's begin by examining some issues that affect how supervision is received and practiced. Among them are how to avoid a rationalistic bias, how to differentiate between measurement and evaluation, how to ensure comprehensiveness, and how to measure up to standards of credibility.

AVOIDING A RATIONALISTIC BIAS

Practices of classroom supervision and evaluation need to reflect the realities of human nature and the realities of teaching. Instead of being sensitive to human nature and teaching, however, classroom supervision and evaluation typically play to images of scientism. Many of us dream of building a body of knowledge, a method of inquiry, and patterns of practice that will provide the basis for a profession of teaching and a clinically oriented supervision comparable with that of architecture and medicine or perhaps the performing arts professions.[2] We believe that it is possible for supervision and teaching to become established and recognized fields of inquiry and professional practice. These are admirable goals. But the question is: Are we going about this process the right way? Presently, theorizing and model building are patterned too closely after the physical sciences. Unfortunately, this patterning is simplistic. The problems addressed, the theorizing, how research is conducted, the conclusions drawn, and the building of practice models based on this inquiry are not sufficiently complex or comprehensive to be considered scientific by the established scientific community. Nor do they meet the standards of scientific and professional rigor that characterize the established professions. Ignoring this reality leads to the development of *rationalistic* theories and practices.

According to Terry Winograd and Fernando Flores, "The rationalistic tradition is distinguished by its narrow focus on certain aspects of rationality which . . . often leads to attitudes and activities that are not rational in a broader perspective."[3] Further, rationalistic theories and models are not viewed as credible given the realities of practice and as a result, tend to lead to bad science by being either elaborations of the obvious or by dealing with trivial questions.[4] When such models are used anyway, teaching suffers and teachers and supervisors experience frustration, combined with a loss of confidence in what sound theory and research about teaching and learning can provide.

Building generic models of teaching and supervisory practice based rigidly on the process–product teaching effectiveness research is an example of rationalistic rather than rational thinking. This research reveals that the explicit, or direct, teaching model is an effective way to teach basic reading and computational skills and simple subject-matter mastery to elementary school children. But assuming that this method represents a singular definition of "effective teaching" and thus prescribing this kind of teaching as the means by which all learning should take place is hardly a rational approach to teaching practice. Yet consultants, workshop specialists,

---

[2]See, for example, Thomas J. Sergiovanni, "Expanding Conceptions of Inquiry and Practice in Supervision and Evaluation," *Educational Evaluation and Policy Analysis,* vol. 6, no. 3 (1984), pp. 355–363; and *Leadership: What's in It for Schools?* London: Falmer Press, 2001, for a discussion of the nonrational and complex world of schooling within which supervision takes place.

[3]Terry Winograd and Fernando Flores, *Understanding Computers and Cognition,* Norwood, NJ: Ablex, 1986, p. 8.

[4]Charles Taylor, *Philosophy and the Human Sciences: Philosophical Papers,* vol. 2, London: Cambridge University Press, 1985.

contributors to widely circulated professional publications, and others have been quite successful in convincing many policy makers and professionals that explicit teaching is indeed the same as effective teaching. One popular example of rationality gone awry is the adoption by school districts, and in some cases by entire states, of teacher-evaluation checklists and other instruments composed of items primarily or exclusively based on this research. This results in uniform use of an instrument that might be appropriate for a limited range of teaching and learning outcomes but may be invalid for other teaching and learning outcomes.

Whether we are talking about the process–product teaching-effectiveness research or about some other body of knowledge, the indicators of effectiveness used are an artifact of how the researchers decided to define effectiveness in the first place. Had they defined effectiveness differently, different indicators would have been discovered. The indicators, therefore, are not entirely independent or objective, but a function of human decisions. Imagine what the consequences of redefining effectiveness would be in schools and, indeed, states that use evaluation instruments based on the original teaching-effectiveness research. Since the instrument behaviors would no longer be "valid," teachers originally thought to be "winners" might well now be "losers" and vice versa. Winning and losing in teacher evaluation is never entirely objective but always in part an artifact of the evaluation system used.

In Chapter 10, "Using Standards in Supervision," we discuss and provide examples from Charlotte Danielson's "A Framework for Teaching" as an alternative.[5] Though at first glance the framework looks like a one-best-way list that applies to all teachers and situations, and although her framework is frequently misused when applied indiscriminately, it is, in fact, a set of principles and practices of teaching that represent a bank of effective practices. Specific principles and practices vary in usefulness or appropriateness depending upon the specifics of the teaching situation under study. Frameworks move us forward not by determining what we should do but by informing our decisions about what to do and by providing a standard of quality for doing it. Once we decide that certain principles and practices make sense for a teaching and learning situation, Danielson's framework provides helpful rubrics for determining the extent to which teachers measure up to standards of quality ranging from "unsatisfactory" to "distinguished."

What changes are needed in the ways we think, inquire, and practice if teaching and supervision are to become less rationalistic and more rational? First, our views of how schools work and how life in classrooms unfolds need to change. Different views lead to different supervisory and teaching practices. Teaching, for example, is often thought of as a tightly connected process that resembles the throwing of teaching "pitches" into a learning outcome strike zone. There is always the danger that some pitches will miss the zone and thus be declared balls rather than strikes. Therefore, supervision, within this view, focuses on increasing the likelihood of teaching

[5]Charlotte Danielson, *Enhancing Professional Practice: A Framework for Teaching,* Alexandria, VA: Association for Supervision and Curriculum Development, 1996.

strikes being thrown. The emphasis is on programming and monitoring the practice of teaching to ensure that the process unfolds in a reliable and predictable manner. The problem with this view is that it does not reflect the realities of practice.

PATTERNED RATIONALITY

When teaching is conceived as pitching, making detailed goals and objectives explicit is considered critical. But teachers typically do not think and act in accord with discrete goals and objectives as much as they do in value patterns. Reading teachers, for example, are as concerned with the students' ability to synthesize and extend as they are with the mastery of reading fundamentals. They recognize that both goals need to be pursued in a manner that makes the experience of reading a joyful activity. But the two goals are often in competition. Too much emphasis on one can negatively affect the other. It does not make sense to most teachers, for example, to separate the sounding out of words from what these words are and mean to readers in context and vice versa. The issue for teachers is how to achieve a balance between and among competing values; the rationality that is appropriate is not linear or bureaucratic but pursues a pattern of outcomes. Some experts refer to this as *patterned rationality*.[6] Since teachers are concerned with outcomes that produce a sensible pattern, it is difficult to ask them to think specifically in terms of this outcome or that or even several outcomes discretely.

A surfing metaphor is much more descriptive of how teachers think and act. Teachers ride the wave of the teaching pattern as it uncurls. In riding the wave, they use various models of teaching and learning not rationalistically to prescribe practice but rationally to inform intuition and enhance professional judgment. A rational science of supervision and teaching places more emphasis on developing strategies that reflect a higher concern for values than goals, for patterns than discrete outcomes, and for learning how to ride the pattern of the wave of teaching.

When teachers do think about goals and objectives, they're just as likely to think about discovering them in the act of teaching as they are in setting them beforehand. Teachers adopt a more strategic than tactical view of goals and objectives. When "surfing," they gear their practice toward broad and often changing goals and rely heavily on assessing what was worthwhile after learning encounters have been concluded. Teachers are not likely to declare that something worthwhile did not count simply because they did not anticipate it beforehand. This reality is not sufficiently accounted for in more rationalistic models of teaching and supervision. Patterned rationality, strategic thinking, and discovery are important hallmarks of professional work. The complexities in how teachers think and act and the complexities in the teaching and learning issues they face is one good reason why *supervision must change from something we do* to *teachers to something we do* with *teachers*.

---

[6]Jean Hills, "The Preparation of Educational Leaders: What's Needed and What's Next?" UCEA Occasional Paper 8303, Columbus, Ohio: University Council for Educational Administration, 1982.

CONFUSING EVALUATION AND MEASUREMENT

Rationalistic thinking is encouraged by the confusion that exists between measurement and evaluation. Much of what passes as evaluation is not evaluation at all but measurement. How are the two different? Suppose, for example, you are interested in buying blinds for a window in your home. You would first need to know the size of the window. The window is 22 inches wide by 60 inches long. This set of figures is now your standard. You find some extra blinds in the attic. Using a ruler, you carefully measure the blinds and learn that none "measures up" to your standard. Though you had a role to play in this process, it was really the ruler that counted. Someone else using the same ruler would very likely have reached the same conclusion.

Though measurements need to be accurate and some skill is involved in the process, the standard against which measurements are weighed and the measuring device are more important than the person doing the measuring. Ideally, measurement should be "person-proof," in the sense that each person measuring should reach the same conclusion. Interrater reliability is highly valued. Thus in measurement-oriented evaluation systems, the role of the evaluator is *diminished*. Principals and supervisors are *less important* than the instruments and procedures they use and the training they get to learn how to use them properly. Further, when a measurement-oriented evaluation system is imported to a school or state, principals, supervisors, teachers, and the public forfeit the right to decide for themselves what is good teaching—what kind of teaching makes sense to them given their goals, their aspirations, the characteristics of their community, and so forth. Measurement-oriented evaluation systems, therefore, not only frequently result in rationalistic practices; they can also threaten one of the fundamental values undergirding schooling in America—the right to choose.

Evaluation, by contrast, is a distinctly human process that involves discernment and making informed judgments. Evaluation is never value-free or context-free. In our example above, once you have decided on the size of blinds needed, all subsequent decisions are a matter of preference, taste, and purpose. What effect do you want to create in the room you are decorating? Do you prefer wooden or metal blinds, a soft or bold look, warm or cool colors? How will the available options fit into the broader decorating scheme of the room? In matters of evaluation, interrater reliability is not highly valued. Instead, the evaluator's judgment, given desired effects, is what counts. Evaluation is a distinctly human rather than mechanical process.

One test for deciding whether a measurement-oriented or an evaluation-oriented approach to teacher evaluation makes sense is how you answer this question: Which of the two would be more responsive to the needs, requirements, and characteristics of the teaching and learning situation under consideration? A measurement-oriented system, for example, prescribes one set of teaching behaviors that are applied evenly to all students in all situations. An evaluation-oriented system requires teachers to make decisions about what to do and how to do it in light of their objectives and their estimates of the needs of the particular students they are teaching. Measurement has its place but in a growth-oriented system, evaluation should be the more common approach.

ISSUES OF COMPREHENSIVENESS

A good supervisory and evaluation system is one that is sufficiently comprehensive to serve a variety of purposes. At least three kinds of evaluation may be included:

- form-referenced teacher evaluation
- criterion-referenced teacher evaluation
- personally referenced teacher evaluation

As suggested above, the typical system now in place in most schools is measurement-oriented, seeking to establish the extent to which each teacher measures up to some preexisting form or scheme that defines effective teaching. This form is presumed to represent some minimum level of basic competence in teaching and is presumed to provide a yardstick for comparing one teacher or group of teachers with others who are being held to the same standard. Instruments used to measure alignment with the form represent a mold, template, or pattern. Teachers are expected to duplicate the form as they teach and are scored according to how close they come to this goal.

This *form-referenced teacher evaluation* may have an important role to play in school district evaluation systems, but it is always a limited one.[7] For legal and other reasons, school districts use form-referenced teacher evaluation to establish for the record that teachers have met minimum requirements. But once teachers have proved themselves by passing this test, it no longer makes sense to continue to require them to pass the same test again and again, year after year. Repeated use of form-referenced teacher evaluation for the same people not only is a poor use of supervisory time, but also focuses the evaluation on minimums rather than on discovery, experimentation, and growth. Further, continued use makes evaluation ritualistic rather than something that teachers consider meaningful and useful.

Form-referenced teacher evaluation is typically conducted using an instrument that records the presence or absence of teaching behaviors and teaching characteristics. The instrument is designed to track whether teachers, for example, are following accepted basic protocols. Reliability is very important to the success of form-referenced teacher evaluation. Each evaluation should be duplicated exactly by another evaluator. To achieve this reliabilty, architects of form-referenced teacher evaluation systems work hard to rule out judgments of goodness. Recording the presence or absence of behaviors, characteristics, or protocols, for example,

---

[7]The discussion of form-referenced, criterion-referenced, and personally referenced teacher evaluation approaches parallels Elliot Eisner's discussion of norm-, criterion-, and personally referenced student evaluation. See Elliot W. Eisner, *The Enlightened Eye: Qualitative Inquiry and the Enhancement of Educational Practice,* New York: Macmillan, 1991, pp. 101–103.

requires little judgment. It is a measurement task rather than an evaluation one. Ideally, form-referenced teacher evaluation should be "supervisor-proof."

In a comprehensive supervisory and evaluation system the emphasis should be on two other types of evaluation: *criterion-referenced teacher evaluation* and *personally referenced teacher evaluation.*[8] Criterion-referenced teacher evaluation seeks to establish the extent to which a teacher's practice embodies certain goals and purposes and values considered important to the school. Assume that the following questions reflect a particular school's shared purposes and values; an evaluation might ask: Does the teacher provide a classroom climate that encourages openness and inquiry? Do teachers accept students as individuals without question? Do teachers teach for understanding? Are students enrolled as "workers" and teachers as facilitators or managers of the teaching and learning environment? Do students have responsibility for setting learning goals and deciding on learning strategies? Is cooperation emphasized over competition? Is diversity respected? Different values lead to different norms, and different norms lead to different questions for guiding the evaluation. Charlotte Danielson's framework for teaching, referred to earlier in this chapter and more fully elaborated in Chapter 10, is an example of a set of guidelines that can be used to develop and conduct criterion-referenced evaluations.[9]

Criterion-referenced evaluation is in many respects a kind of inquiry that is constructed around the issues deemed important by teacher and supervisor. For this reason evaluation extends throughout the teacher's career. As time goes on, the nature of the questions that guide the evaluation should evolve from, Does the teacher's practice reflect a given value? to Are there better ways to do it? and What is the worth of the value in the first place? Criterion-referenced teacher evaluation does not lend itself to rigid and supervisor-proof instruments very well. Other forms of supervision such as clinical supervision, peer supervision, action research, reflective conversations about teaching standards and rubrics, examination of student work, and portfolio development are better options.

Personally referenced teacher evaluation emphasizes the teacher's personal goals and comparisons between past and present performance given these goals. Though external standards or norms might be used to help teachers focus on accepted dimensions of teaching, they should not be used to fix rigid baselines for making such comparisons. Instead, the purpose of personally referenced teacher evaluation is to help teachers understand and critically appraise their practice in light of their preferences, purposes, and beliefs. Personally referenced teacher evaluation also helps teachers gauge the progress they are making in achieving their goals. Frameworks for teaching, such as those proposed by Danielson, can help by suggesting goals that teachers might pursue.[10]

---

[8]See, for example, Eisner, *The Enlightened Eye,* p. 102, for a discussion of these concepts as applied to student evaluation.
[9]Danielson, op. cit.
[10]Ibid.

ISSUES OF CREDIBILITY

Credibility is an important issue in teacher evaluation, particularly if the evaluator goes beyond description to interpretation, identification of themes, and appraisal of worth. In using case-study methods to develop portraits of classrooms that lend themselves to evaluation, Elliot Eisner identifies three standards of credibility: structural *collaboration, consensual* validation, and *referential* adequacy.[11] The three sources of credibility apply as well to the evaluation of teaching.

- *The collaboration standard asks if multiple sources of information are used in providing descriptions, forming judgments, and reaching conclusions about a particular teacher's teaching.* Is classroom observation backed up with other sources of information? Such sources might include interviews with other teachers, examples of student work, photo essays, data descriptions of teacher–student interaction patterns, movement flowcharts, case studies of students, analysis of books read by students, student performance exhibits, a folio of tests, and homework assignments and other assignments given by the teacher. In supplying multiple sources of information about his or her teaching, the teacher must become a partner in the process. The teacher, after all, is in the best position to decide what sources of evidence are most appropriate to the particular form of evaluation.

- *The consensus standard seeks agreement among competent others that sources of evaluation information make sense, that descriptions are sound, that interpretations are compelling, and that the conclusions drawn are plausible.* The key partners to any agreement are, again, the teacher whose work is the focus of the evaluation and the person or persons (principal, other teachers, teams of teachers) assuming the supervisory role. If agreement is not reached at this level, third-party agreement may be necessary if conclusions need to be reached to resolve certain personnel matters such as retention or tenure.

  The consensus standard should not be confused with interrater reliability as understood in standards-referenced evaluation. The consensus standard seeks more holistic agreement about the adequacy of the evaluation process itself and about what it means for the teacher in question. For less contentious evaluation, all that is needed is a serious study of the evidence and the rendering of an opinion backed up by a simple statement of a paragraph or two. The art, drama, or film critic might serve as a helpful metaphor. The critic rates the subject and then provides a vivid assessment of that subject to validate that rating.

  When teacher and supervisor disagree and the consequences for employment or reputation or both are significant, the consensus standard may require two or more independent evaluations complete with detailed write-ups in the form of case studies. The studies are then compared. Each critic's opinion is considered, and the reasoning provided is assessed. The specifics of the case studies,

---

[11]Eisner, The Enlightened Eye, pp. 110–114. See also Elliot W. Eisner, *The Educational Imagination,* 2nd ed., New York: Macmillan, 1985.

the evidence gathered, the interpretations made, and other details need not overlap. In fact, they can be quite different. But for consensus to be judged to exist, the evidence needs to lead to the same conclusion. If consensus is not reached, a further step may be necessary. Different critics may be focusing on different aspects of the teacher studied and may bring different perspectives that lead to different conclusions. For this reason, evaluators or critics need to be brought together in conversation to discuss this possibility. If, as may happen in rare instances, differences cannot be reconciled by negotiation, the evaluation may have to be invalidated and the process repeated with different evaluators.

- *The standard of referential adequacy can be met by examining the nature of the evaluation write-up itself.* In assessing referential adequacy, Eisner asks if the description of events is rich enough and detailed enough so that others are able to see things and understand things that would be missed without the benefit of the write-up. According to Eisner, an evaluation write-up "is referentially adequate to the extent to which a reader is able to locate in its subject matter the qualities the critic addresses and the meanings he or she ascribed to them."[12] The evaluation, in other words, speaks for itself.

SUMMARY

In this chapter, we began an examination of the issues and practices of classroom supervision and teacher evaluation. We pointed out that key to the success of supervision is the extent to which teachers are learning and the extent to which this learning affects their practice in positive ways. The examination of issues is important because depending on how they are resolved, different supervisory practices are deemed appropriate. Among the issues discussed were the extent to which supervision and evaluation are viewed as scientific enterprises, how to avoid a rationalistic bias as we make supervisory decisions, as well as the importance of thinking in patterns, avoiding confusing evaluation with measurement, and sorting out different ways to conceptualize the supervisory process. In Chapter 11, we get closer to the practice of supervision by examining supervision as a form of professional development and renewal.

SOME REFLECTIONS

1. In the three examples of classroom supervision that we discussed, both of the teachers and the supervisor were eager to get classroom supervision out of the way so that they could "get back to preparing students to pass the state test." Would they feel the same way regardless of the kind of classroom supervision they were involved in? If you said no, what kind of supervision do you recommend? If you said yes, visit Chapters 12 and 13. These chapters discuss a number of alternatives, some of which may change your mind.
2. Suppose you are preparing a workshop for teachers and administrators on the theme of measurement and evaluation. You decide you want to use an example similar to, but not the same as, the decorating example used earlier in this chapter. What example would you use?

[12]Eisner, *The Educational Imagination,* p. 114.

CHAPTER 10

Using Standards in Supervision

INTRODUCTION

In this chapter, we examine standards for teaching and the role that they can play in supervision. We review standards for beginning teachers, standards for all teachers, and standards for teachers who seek board certification by the National Board for Professional Teaching Standards. By providing an array of standards from different sources, we hope to achieve a number of purposes:

1. to provide an overview of standards that can be used to construct a definition of effective teaching
2. to show how standards can be embedded in practice at different levels of quality and competence
3. to provide a bank of standards that can be used by teachers to examine their practice alone, together, or with their supervisors
4. to provide a bank of standards that schools can use in crafting teacher-evaluation systems

What about standards for the practice of supervision? At this writing, no set of standards for supervision has been fully developed and approved by either professional organizations or state governments. One reason is that supervision is first a function shared by individuals who are in many different roles. Principals and assistant principals, central office specialist, staff developers and coaches, teacher leaders and teachers are all examples of roles that have supervisory responsibilities. Sometimes the responsibilities of people overlap, and at other times the various roles have unique responsibilities. Sorting out the complexities inherent in a dual conception of supervision is not inviting.

Nonetheless, the field of supervision is now beginning to explore the use of standards. At this stage the approach that advocates seem to be taking is to welcome lots of different standards and then to work on inventing and using a process for paring the list down. Right now, for example, most people involved in the development of supervisory standards do not envision one best list. Instead, they seem to champion the establishment of a repository of standards from which supervisors, teachers, and schools may select those that make the best sense for a particular goal or purpose. Time will tell whether the supervisory standards we wind up with will be more of the same or will be a more helpful approach.

At this writing Steve Gordon is editing a book that proposes supervisory standards in 12 areas.[1] Gordon and his contributors are basing their work on a platform of assumptions that is intended to provide a kind of discipline and coherence that functions as a framework for action. Examples of key assumptions include the following:

- Instructional supervision is leadership for teaching and learning.
- Supervision is a function that should be provided not only by designated supervisors but also by principals, coaches, department chairs, team leaders, regular classroom teachers, and others who are responsible for teaching and learning.
- Standards adapted by a school or school district should be agreed upon by the school's entire professional community, with all providers of supervision being responsible together for helping meet the standards in question.
- The proposed standards should not always be standardized, nor should they be considered exhaustive. They should, instead, be considered the starting point rather than the ending point.

We also examine the Educational Leadership Constituent Council (ELCC) standards for both school site-based administrators and central office administrators.[2] Some of these standards deal with supervisory themes, but many do not. We ask the question: What responsibilities do those who assume different leadership roles have in providing good supervision? Then, using the version of the ELCC standards that the National Council for the Accreditation of Teacher Education (NCATE) uses to evaluate preparation programs for school administrators, we ask readers to match the standards to different role responsibilities. For example, which of the standards seems to best fit the principal's role and which of the standards seems to best fit the role of teachers and the role of teacher leaders?

---

[1]Steve Gordon (ed.), *Standards for Instructional Supervision: Enhancing Teaching and Learning,* Larchmont, NY: Eye on Education, forthcoming. Gordon and his contributors urge readers to join them in conversation about supervisory standards by visiting the Web site of the National Center for School Improvement, located at Texas State University in San Marcos, Texas (www.txstate.edu/ncsi). The Web site will provide a preliminary set of standards and the beginning of a conversation about their adequacy.

[2]The council includes the National Policy Board for Educational Administration, American Association of School Administrators, National Association of Secondary School Principals, National Association of Elementary School Principals, and Association for Supervision and Curriculum Development.

SOME BACKGROUND

We begin our exploration of standards in supervision with the practice of teaching and how teaching standards can help improve this practice. For example, practicing clinical supervision and engaging in other forms of supervision designed to improve teaching practice depend upon teachers' having a good eye for practice, a common language for sharing with each other what they see, the ability to transfer what is learned in one context to new contexts, and a developmental view of quality for assessing the adequacy of teaching.

- A good eye helps teachers see how one part of teaching is related to other parts, increasing their sensitivity to not just what is going on in a classroom but what events mean to different students, for different subjects, for different learning goals.
- A common language helps teachers communicate with each other and with supervisors about what they see, how they are doing, and what needs to be done next, creating common bonds and common understandings that help build communities of practice.
- Transferring what is learned from its original context to new and different situations helps teachers become independent learners and promotes steeper learning curves for teachers and their supervisors.
- A developmental view of quality helps teachers and supervisors understand good teaching not simply as an event that happens occasionally, but as a by-product of a career-long commitment to continuous learning.

Using standards in supervision can help develop all four of these qualities. But much depends upon whether we view standards primarily as templates or as frameworks.

TEMPLATES OR FRAMEWORKS

Lists are often used to help teachers develop a good eye, promote a common language, facilitate transfer, and cultivate a developmental view of quality. Teachers are given lists of things to do, lists of effective behaviors to emulate, and lists of quality standards toward which they should strive. Lists can be helpful. But despite their usefulness and popularity, lists can also be a problem for teachers and supervisors when they are routinely viewed as templates for an all-encompassing, one-best-way to do things. That is why frameworks are needed, too. While some standards for teaching may be singular and absolute, other standards make sense only if carefully matched to a teacher's goals and purposes, to subject-matter content standards, and to student learning situations. Once a standard is chosen for use from a broader framework, it should be placed in a developmental context by providing examples of teaching that would be appropriate for beginning but not accomplished teachers and vice versa.

In this chapter, we examine standards for teaching along with the ways teachers in schools can use these standards to improve teaching. Standards as frameworks help define what is good practice, help show how indicators of good practice relate to each other, help teachers and supervisors talk about the indicators of good practice in meaningful ways, and help teachers use the indicators of good practice to study their own teaching. Standards as frameworks provide an overview of effective teaching within which teachers can locate the problems, issues, and practices with which they are dealing in their own classrooms.

While frameworks should be anchored in theory, in the research on effective teaching and learning, and in the wisdom of practice gleaned from experience, they should be flexible enough to be responsive to the unique problems teachers face in their practice and to different subject-matter content, demands, and requirements that define the substance of what is being taught. As frameworks, standards for teaching should not so much prescribe what must be done as inform the decisions that teachers make about what to do and how to do it. They are the larger branches of a teaching tree that point the way to better practice. But no two teaching repertoires look exactly alike. Teachers may choose, for example, to ignore a standard at any given time if it does not apply to their teaching situation. But since standards and their indicators are not developed lightly and are anchored in disciplined research and inquiry, teachers should be able to defend the decisions they make as to what specific standards and when specific standards should or should not be included. Further, as frameworks, standards for teaching provide indicators of quality for judging how well teaching decisions and behaviors are embodied in practice.

Meeting standards for teaching and learning involves a continuous struggle to improve over the life of one's career. As will be pointed out in Chapter 11, Lauren Resnick and Megan Hall believe that learning to teach is an expandable repertoire of skills and habits.[3] Teachers as professionals do not just learn something and that's it. They are, instead, continuous learners whose roles include both teacher and learner, master and apprentice, as situations change. In this dynamic context, standards do not just stand still but are expandable as teachers learn and improve.

A FRAMEWORK FOR ENHANCING PROFESSIONAL PRACTICE

In the 1980s, the Educational Testing Service (ETS) began to develop a framework that states and local school districts could use in making teacher licensing and hiring decisions. The result was the creation of the PRAXIS series that includes PRAXIS I: Computer-Based Academic Skills Assessments, PRAXIS II: Academic Skills Assessment, and PRAXIS III: Classroom Performance Assessments. PRAXIS III is a research-based design for assessing a teacher licensure candidate's actual teaching skills and classroom performance. In preparing hundreds of assessors to use PRAXIS III for assessing new teachers, Charlotte Danielson realized its

[3]Lauren B. Resnick and Megan Hall, "Learning Organizations for Sustainable Educational Reform," *Daedalus,* vol. 27, no. 4 (Fall 1998), p. 110.

potential to be a powerful professional development tool for teachers at all stages of their careers. In her words:

> I witnessed the quality of the participants' [the PRAXIS III assessors being trained] conversation. It became clear that in their daily lives, educators have (or make) little opportunity to discuss good teaching. As participants watched videotapes and read scenarios of teaching during the assessor training, they had to determine how what they observed represented the application of the various criteria in different contexts. For example, they noticed that a kindergarten teacher's actions to help students extend their thinking were quite different from those employed by a chemistry teacher. And yet, both teachers might be extending their students' thinking; so both sets of action constituted examples of a particular criterion in different contexts.[4]

Danielson continues:

> Because of its impact on their own teaching, many PRAXIS III assessors reported that the experience of training . . . gave them a structured opportunity to discuss teaching with colleagues in a concrete and research-based setting. Such opportunities are indeed rare in schools. A participant's statement expresses the thinking of many: "By participating in the PRAXIS III training, I have focused more on my own teaching. I have become more thoughtful in my teaching and more concerned that my instructional activities fulfill my goals."[5]

Danielson concludes from this experience that structured conversations linked to PRAXIS III or other frameworks for teaching can be powerful ways to enrich the professional lives of teachers. From this experience Danielson developed her Framework for Teaching—a framework designed not just for beginning teachers but for experienced teachers as well. The framework for teaching involves 22 components of professional practice grouped into four domains: planning and preparing for teaching, the classroom environment, instruction, and professional responsibility. The components of professional practice are summarized in Table 10–1.

Danielson's work supports the distinction we make between templates and frameworks. Templates are easier for supervisors to use because they provide a single set of teaching behaviors that can be checked off as being observed in a lesson and sometimes rated for how well they were practiced. In templates, effective teaching results when more items from that set are checked off and when higher ratings are given for the ways in which the checked items are demonstrated. There is, however, no discussion about whether a particular item is relevant or not, no controversy about what particular items might mean or not mean in a given context, no grappling with issues of what is or is not appropriate for a particular objective, lesson, or group of students. The list is it! Different situations do not matter.

---

[4]Charlotte Danielson, *Enhancing Professional Practice: A Framework for Teaching,* Alexandria, VA: Association for Supervision and Curriculum Development, 1996, p. ix.
[5]Ibid.

TABLE 10–1. Components of Professional Practice.

Domain 1: Planning and Preparation

Component 1a: *Demonstrating Knowledge of Content and Pedagogy*
Knowledge of content
Knowledge of prerequisite relationships
Knowledge of content-related pedagogy

Component 1b: *Demonstrating Knowledge of Students*
Knowledge of characteristics of age group
Knowledge of students' varied approaches to learning
Knowledge of students' skills and knowledge
Knowledge of students' interests and cultural heritage

Component 1c: *Selecting Instructional Goals*
Value
Clarity
Suitability for diverse students
Balance

Component 1d: *Demonstrating Knowledge of Resources*
Resources for teaching
Resources for students

Component 1e: *Designing Coherent Instruction*
Learning activities
Instructional materials and resources
Instructional groups
Lesson and unit structure

Component 1f: *Assessing Student Learning*
Congruence with instructional goals
Criteria and standards
Use for planning

Domain 2: The Classroom Environment

Component 2a: *Creating an Environment of Respect and Rapport*
Teacher interaction with students
Student interaction

Component 2b: *Establishing a Culture for Learning*
Importance of the content
Student pride in work
Expectations for learning and achievement

Component 2c: *Managing Classroom Procedures*
Management of instructional groups
Management of transitions
Management of materials and supplies
Performance of noninstructional duties
Supervision of volunteers and paraprofessionals

Component 2d: *Managing Student Behavior*
Expectations
Monitoring of student behavior
Response to student misbehavior

Component 2e: *Organizing Physical Space*
Safety and arrangement of furniture
Accessibility to learning and use of physical resources

Domain 3: Instruction

Component 3a: *Communicating Clearly and Accurately*
Directions and procedures
Oral and written language

Component 3b: *Using Questioning and Discussion Techniques*
Quality of questions
Discussion techniques
Student participation

Component 3c: *Engaging Students in Learning*
Representation of content
Activities and assignments
Grouping of students
Instructional materials and resources
Structure and pacing

Component 3d: *Providing Feedback to Students*
Quality: accurate, substantive, constructive, and specific
Timeliness

Component 3e: *Demonstrating Flexibility and Responsiveness*
Lesson adjustment
Response to students
Persistence

Domain 4: Professional Responsibilities

Component 4a: *Reflecting on Teaching*
Accuracy
Use in future teaching

Component 4b: *Maintaining Accurate Records*
Student completion of assignments
Student progress in learning
Noninstructional records

Component 4c: *Communicating with Families*
Information about the instructional program
Information about individual students
Engagement of families in the instructional program

Component 4d: *Contributing to the School and District*
Relationships with colleagues
Service to the school
Participation in school and district projects

Component 4e: *Growing and Developing Professionally*
Enhancement of content knowledge and pedagogical skill
Service to the profession

Component 4f: *Showing Professionalism*
Service to students
Advocacy
Decision making

Source: Charlotte Danielson, *Enhancing Professional Practice: A Framework for Teaching,* Alexandria, VA: ASCD, 1996, pp. 3–4. © Charlotte Danielson, all rights reserved.

Different teacher intents do not matter. Different student needs and interests do not matter. It is the template that makes the decision, not the supervisor. Templates are supervision-proof, and this reality de-skills both teachers and supervisors. Many supervisors like templates because they make their job easier. But most supervisors know that when the template rules, it is less likely that teachers will be learning and less likely that their practice will improve.

Frameworks, by contrast, require much more work from everyone. Teachers and supervisors need to talk together, asking: What is intended by the teacher? Which indicators are most important in trying to understand these intents and in assessing the extent to which they are realized? What is unique about the students being taught that might influence which standards are most important? What is unique about the subject matter content being taught that might affect which standards should be emphasized and how they should be emphasized? Consideration needs to be given to how the indicators should be adjusted or sorted to accommodate all these situational variables. In some ways, the frameworks' indicators (or as Danielson calls them, components) represent ingredients that teachers may choose to use and choose to use in different ways in creating different, but equally effective, teaching and learning experiences for their students. Some ingredients may be more important on one occasion than on another.

> The framework for professional practice . . . provides a structure within which educators can situate their actions. The components are grounded in the assumption that even though good teachers may accomplish many of the same things, they do not achieve them in the same way. Therefore, a list of specific behaviors is not appropriate. Rather, what is needed is a set of commonalties underlying the actions, with the recognition that specific actions will and should vary; depending on the context and the individual.[6]

Danielson points out that the framework she proposes does not endorse a particular teaching style or approach to teaching. Different components of the framework might be emphasized in different ways in a Core Knowledge classroom as opposed to a Basic Schools classroom; in a Roots and Wings classroom as opposed to an Expeditionary Learning classroom; or an America's Choice classroom as opposed to a Montessori classroom. Rather than being a script, the framework helps teachers by forcing them to consider many possibilities and to discuss with their supervisors what makes sense in a particular situation, as well as how the various components might look in practice as situations vary. As Danielson states:

> The framework for teaching is grounded in the belief that . . . selecting instructional approaches rests absolutely with a teacher; this decision is a critical element of professionalism. Not all choices, however, are effective; not all are equally appropriate. Decisions about instructional strategies and learning activities involve matching the desired outcomes of a lesson or a unit (i.e., what the students are to learn) with the approaches selected. Not only should the instructional goals be worthwhile, but the

[6]Ibid., p. 17.

Read
187—195

methods and materials chosen should be appropriate for those goals and help students attain them.

Be able
to explain
to someone
else.

What is required, then, is that teachers have a repertoire of strategies from which they can select a suitable one for a given purpose. No single approach will be effective in every situation, for each set of instructional goals, or with all individuals or groups of students. These choices and decisions represent the heart of professionalism.[7]

Danielson's framework appears in Appendix 10–1. Only Domains 1 and 3, Planning and Preparation, and Instruction, are included as examples. Domains 2 and 4, Classroom Environment and Professional Responsibilities, are omitted.[8] Note that the framework includes a rubric comprising four levels of performance: unsatisfactory, basic, proficient, and distinguished. Many people prefer a simple numbering system (1 to 4, for example) to differentiate the four different levels of performance. A numbering system, they feel, scores in a more formative way in the sense that an assumption is made that becoming a successful teacher is a work in progress. Thus scores of 1 or 2 could just as well mean "having difficulty getting started" and "beginning to figure things out" as they do "unsatisfactory" or "basic."

USING THE FRAMEWORK

Think of a lesson you were teaching recently. Perhaps it was a lesson you taught today. As you review Danielson's framework, which of the components do you consider most important in analyzing your lesson, given your intents, the subject matter you wanted to cover, and the style of your lesson? Using the rubric provided, how would you score yourself on these indicators? Were there any that you would rate as being basic or unsatisfactory? With which two or three indicators did you feel you did the best? Mark them with an asterisk so that they stand out from the rest. What was special about your teaching in these areas? How would your ratings agree with those of a supervisor who was assessing your lesson? These are tough questions. What makes them so difficult is that you are being asked to rate yourself and to respond to these ratings alone. You do not have the benefit of talking things over with other teachers or a supervisor.

Suppose you could talk first with a trusted colleague. You describe the intents you had for your lesson, why you chose the strategies you did, and how the lesson fits into the larger picture of what you are trying to accomplish. You describe the students and how they have been responding to this general subject-matter theme. You talk about your own strengths and weaknesses with understanding the content you are teaching and in finding interesting ways to teach it. You talk about various ways you can tell if students benefited from the lesson and how they benefited. Your colleague shares his or her experiences, too, and that helps a lot. Together, you

[7]Ibid., pp. 17–18.
[8]See Danielson, op. cit., for the complete framework. See also http://sites.uen.org/archive_info/framework. html.

review the list of standards and their indicators in the framework, *choosing a hand-ful* of indicators that you feel would be most helpful to focus on.[9] You then use the rubric provided to rate yourself on the chosen indicators, sharing your ratings and reasons with your colleague. If you don't like the language used to label the rubric, change the labels to something else or use a number system such as 1 to 4. Your colleague asks you to give examples from what happened in the lesson. As the discussion continues, chances are you are getting a clearer picture of your lesson, of your strengths and weaknesses in teaching it, and of what you could do to improve. This learning will very likely help you as you prepare to visit this colleague's class-room in a few days.

Let's try using the framework to analyze the teaching of two other teachers. Teaching transcripts for both are provided below.[10] Let's begin with Joan Maxwell, who is teaching first-graders a lesson on the four seasons. Review the transcript, making a list of what you consider Joan's strengths and weaknesses. On the basis of your analysis, what strategies would you consider using to help Joan understand her lesson better and to make improvements? Now try the same thing using the frame-work for teaching. After reading the transcript again, use the relevant indicators from domains 1 and 3 of the framework to talk about Joan's teaching. How does using the framework in this way help you think about and understand this teaching? Now identify the level of Joan's performance on all the relevant components. Do any patterns emerge? On the basis of your analysis, what strategies would you con-sider using to help this teacher understand her lesson better and make improve-ments? How do these strategies differ from those that come to mind by reading the transcript without the benefit of the framework? Suppose that you were responsible for the summative evaluation of Joan Maxwell's teaching, and you used a teacher evaluation instrument patterned after the framework. What other kinds of informa-tion would you have to collect to help substantiate your ratings? What other kinds of information would you ask Joan to provide?

> Joan Maxwell has been teaching the first grade for seven years in a small rural com-munity school. Her students are children of primarily farm and ranch workers of lower middle-class background. Joan and her husband both received their degrees from a large university and now operate a lucrative business in the area. Joan is in-troducing a science lesson today; it's late fall and the children have been asked to bring in some leaves to show changes in leaf colors from season to season. The class has previously discussed seasonal changes and what weather patterns occur during these times.

[9]Choosing a handful of indicators instead of using the entire framework is important, because choosing helps focus attention on a manageable number of issues; does not overwhelm; and allows for a more authentic, in-depth conversation and analysis. Choosing enhances purpose and meaning. And choosing anchors the use of the framework to what is actually going on in the teacher's classroom. The teacher being helped has impor-tant roles to play. One of them is helping select the indicators for study.
[10]The transcripts are from Thomas L. Good and Jere E. Brophy, *Looking in Classrooms,* New York: Harper and Row, 1987. Excerpts from pp. 590, 592, 596, 597 and 598 from *In Classrooms,* 4th ed., by Thomas L. Good and Jere E. Brophy. Copyright © 1987 by Pearson Education. Reprinted by permission of the publisher.

TEACHER: Boys and girls, let's first review what we talked about last week when we were writing our stories about different seasons.

SHARI: (Calling out) Do we have to do this? Why can't we do something fun instead of doing something we don't like?

TEACHER: We can't always do things we enjoy. Carol, do you remember how many seasons we have in a year?

not good comment

CAROL: Three.

TEACHER: No, we wrote more stories than just three—think for a minute.

CAROL: Four. not very positive

TEACHER: All right, now can you name them for me?

CAROL: Fall, winter, summer . . .

TEACHER: Didn't you write four stories?

CAROL: I don't remember.

TEACHER: (forcefully, and with some irritation) You may have to go back and write them again. Who knows the fourth season? Can somebody in my special Cardinal group respond? John, you answer. not good

JOHN: Fall, winter, spring, and summer.

TEACHER: Good thinking! It helps us to remember seasons sometimes if we think about important holidays that come during them. Tim, in what season does Christmas come? — Should first review seasons w/everyone

TIM: (No response)

TEACHER: You weren't listening. I want you to put those leaves in your desk and not touch them again till it's time. Cory, when does Christmas come?

CORY: In the winter.

TEACHER: How do you know it's winter, Mark?

MARK: Because of the snow and ice and rain . . .

TEACHER: Does it snow here?

MARK: No.

TEACHER: How do you know it's winter, then?

MARK: (No response)

MARY: (Calling out) It snows at Christmas where I used to live.

TEACHER: Mary, if you have something to say, will you please raise your hand? (She does) Now what did you say?

MARY: Where I used to live it did snow, but not anymore.

TEACHER: Right! In some places it does snow and not others. Clarence, why wouldn't it snow here?

CLARENCE: Because it's too warm? not good

TEACHER: It's not warm here! I told you this before a couple of times. (Turns to Tim) I asked you once before to put those away and you can't seem to keep your hands on the desk, so I'm going to take them away from you and when we do our project you will have to sit and watch! Don't anyone else do what Tim did. Now, let's talk more about the fall season and get some good ideas for our story. What is another word for the fall season? Lynne?

LYNNE: Halloween.

TEACHER: I didn't ask you to give me a holiday, a word.

she's confusing the kids.

LYNNE: I can't think of it.

TEACHER: I'm going to write it on the board and see if Bobby can pronounce it for me.

BOBBY: (No response)

TEACHER: This is a big word, Bobby. I'll help you.

JUDY: (Calling out) Autumn!

TEACHER: (Turns to Judy) Is your name Bobby?

JUDY: No.

TEACHER: Then don't take other children's turns. Now, Bobby, say the word. (He does.) I think this is a good word to write in your dictionaries. Get them out and let's do it now.

JANE: I don't have a pencil.

TEACHER: That is something you are supposed to take care of yourself. Borrow one or stay in at recess and write it then. Let's look at these pictures of leaves as they look in the fall and spring. Mary Kay, can you tell me one thing that is different about these two pictures?

MARY KAY: The leaves are different colors.

TEACHER: Good. Tell me some of the colors.

MARY KAY: In spring, they are bright green.

TEACHER: Right. Joe, how about the other ones?

JOE: They are brown and orange and purple.

TEACHER: I don't see any purple—you've got your colors mixed up. Tony?

TONY: It's more red.

TEACHER: Yes. Steve, we are finished writing in our dictionaries; put it away. You can finish at recess with Jane. Some people in our class are very slow writers. Take out your leaves now. Mark, how does that leaf feel in your hand?

MARK: It feels dry and rough like old bread. (Class laughs.)

TEACHER: Don't be silly! How did it get so dry? Marilyn?

MARILYN: It fell off the tree.

TEACHER: Yes, a leaf needs the tree to stay alive. Is that right, Dave?

DAVE: You could put it in water and it would stay alive.

TEACHER: Not for long. Martha, what else can you tell me about these leaves?

MARTHA: I don't have one.

TEACHER: I don't know what to do about children who can't remember their homework assignments. You will never be good students if you don't think about these things. Mike, what do you see in the leaves?

MIKE: Lines running through.

TEACHER: We call those lines *veins*. Are all leaves the same shape?

MIKE: No, my leaf came from a sycamore tree and it has soft corners, not sharp ones.

TEACHER: That's good. I think you will be able to write an interesting story. Two holidays come during the fall; who can name one? Terri?

TERRI: Halloween.

TEACHER: That's one; Jeff, do you know another?

JEFF: (No response)

TEACHER: It comes in November and we have a school holiday.

JEFF: Easter?

TEACHER: No, that is in the spring; we have turkey for dinner this day.

CHORUS: Thanksgiving.

TEACHER: Now, do you remember, Jeff? I would like you to write about Thanksgiving in your story; then you won't forget again. Now we are ready to put on the board the vocabulary words that we will use for our story and pictures. (Teacher notices Shari, Jim, and Rick exchanging their books but she ignores their misbehavior.)

TEACHER: Ed, you come up here and Sally come up here and help me print our vocabulary words on the board. Ed, you print these four words (Hands him a list) and Sally, you print these four (Hands her a second list).

TEACHER: What are you kids doing in that corner? Shari, Rick, Jim, Terri, Kim stop fighting over those books. (All the children in the class turn to look at them.)

RICK: Mrs. Maxwell, it's all Kim's fault.

KIM: It is not. I wasn't doing anything. Shari, Rick, and Jim have been fooling around but I've been trying to listen.

TEACHER: Quiet down, all of you. You all stay in for recess and we'll discuss it then.

TEACHER: Okay, Ed, put your words up.

KIM: Not me!

TEACHER: Yes, all of you.

KIM: (Mutters to her friend.) It's not fair.

TEACHER: Kim, what did you say?

KIM: Nothing.

TEACHER: That's more like it.

TEACHER: Okay, Ed, put your words up.

ED: I've lost the list. . . . (Class roars with laughter.)[11]

The next teaching transcript features Linda Law teaching a social studies lesson to a group of bright ninth-graders. How do you size up this teaching episode? What are Linda's strengths and weaknesses? Do any patterns emerge in her teaching? What indicators from the framework would you emphasize as you plan your conversation with Linda? How does the framework help you be more helpful to Linda?

> Linda Law is teaching for a second year at Thornton Junior High School. The students at Thornton come from upper middle-class homes and Linda teaches social studies to the brightest group of ninth-grade students. Today she is deviating from her normal lesson plans in order to discuss the Tasaday tribe that resides in the Philippine Rain Forest.

TEACHER: Class, yesterday I told you that we would postpone our scheduled small-group work so that we could discuss the Tasadays. Two or three days

---

[11]Good and Brophy, *In Classrooms*, pp. 596–598.

[handwritten margin notes: "good motivation", "madly connected onward", "revised"]

ago Charles mentioned the Tasadays as an example of persons who were isolated from society. Most of you had never heard of the Tasadays but were anxious to have more information, so yesterday I gave you a basic fact sheet and a few review questions to think about. I'm interested in discussing this material with you and discussing questions that you want to raise. It's amazing! Just think, a Stone Age tribe in today's world. What an exciting opportunity to learn about the way people used to live! Joan, I want you to start the discussion by sharing with the class what you thought was the most intriguing fact uncovered. — *[handwritten: Should have asked for a volunteer]*

JOAN: (In a shy, shaky voice) Oh, that they had never fought with other tribes or among themselves. Here we are, modern people, and we fight continuously and often for silly reasons.

SID: (Breaking in) Yeah, I agree with Joannie; that is remarkable. You know, we have talked about human's aggressive nature, and this finding suggests that perhaps it isn't so.

SALLY: (Calling out) You know, Sid, that's an interesting point!

TEACHER: Why is that an interesting point, Sally?

SALLY: (Looks at the floor and remains silent)

TEACHER: Why do you think these people don't fight, Sally?

SALLY: (Remains silent)

TEACHER: Sally, do they have any reason to fight?

SALLY: No, I guess not. All their needs . . . you know, food and clothing, can be found in the forest and they can make their own tools.

[handwritten margin note: "good"]

Teacher: Yes, Sally, I think those are good reasons. Class, does anyone else want to add anything on this particular point? (She calls on Ron, who has his hand up.)

RON: You know what I think it is that makes the difference, well, my dad says it is money. He says that if these Tasadays find out about money, there will be greed, corruption, and war, all in short order.

TEACHER: Ron, can you explain in more detail why money would lead to deterioration in life there?

RON: (With enthusiasm) Well, because now there's no direct competition. It's people against nature and what one person does is no loss to another.

[handwritten margin note: "positive keep enthusiasm"]

TONY: (Calling out) Not if food or something is in short supply!

TEACHER: Tony, that's a good point, but please wait until Ron finishes his remarks. Go ahead, Ron.

RON: Well, money might lead to specialization and some people would build huts and others would hunt and exchange their wares for money, and eventually they would want more money to buy more things and competition would lead to aggressive behavior.

TEACHER: Thank you, Ron, that's an interesting answer. Now, Tony, do you want to add anything else?

TONY: No, nothing except that Ron's making a lot of generalizations that aren't supported. You know, the Tasadays might have specialized labor forces. Now there's nothing in the article I read about this.

TEACHER: That's good thinking, Tony. Class, how could we find out if the Tasadays have a specialized labor force?

MARY: (Called on by the teacher) Well, we could write a letter to Dr. Fox, the chief anthropologist at the National Museum, and ask him.

TEACHER: Excellent, Mary. Would you write a letter tonight and tomorrow read it to the class and then we'll send it.

MARY: Okay. (The teacher notices Bill and Sandra whispering in a back corner of the room and as she asks the next question, she walks halfway down the aisle. They stop talking.) *—Good Discipline.*

TEACHER: What dangers do the Tasadays face now that they have been discovered?

TOM: (Calling out) I think the biggest problem they face will be the threat of loggers, who are clearing the forest, and the less primitive tribes, who have been driven farther into the forest by the loggers.

TEACHER: Why is this a problem, Tom?

TOM: Well, they might destroy the tribe. You know, these less primitive tribes might attack or enslave the Tasadays.

TEACHER: Okay, Tom. Let's see if there are other opinions. Sam, what do you think about Tom's answer?

SAM: Well, I do think that those other natives and the loggers are threats, but personally I feel that the Tasadays' real danger is sickness. Remember how, I think it was on Easter Island, natives were wiped out by diseases that they had no immunity to. I think they might be wiped out in an epidemic.

TEACHER: What kind of epidemic, Sam?

SAM: Well, it could be anything, TB, you know, anything.

TEACHER: Class, what do you think? If an epidemic occurred, what disease would most likely be involved?

CLASS: (No response)

TEACHER: Okay, class, let's write this question down in our notebooks and find an answer tomorrow. I'm stumped, too, so I'll look for the answer tonight as part of my homework. I'm going to allow ten minutes more for this discussion, and then we'll have to stop for lunch. I wish we had more time to discuss this topic; perhaps we can spend more time tomorrow. In the last ten minutes, I'd like to discuss your questions. What are they? Call them out and I'll write them on the board.

ARLENE: I was surprised that the oldest of these people were in their middle forties and the average height was only five feet. It looks like living an active outdoor life, they would be healthy and big. What's wrong with their diet?

MARY JANE: I'm interested in a lot of their superstitious behavior. For example, why do they feel that to have white teeth is to be like an animal?[12]

lots of why's —good.

---

[12]Good and Brophy, *In Classrooms*, pp. 590–592.

ACCOMPLISHED TEACHING

For any profession to grow in what it needs to know and to be able to do, emphasis needs to be given to outstanding practice. In teaching, too often we come to see supervision and evaluation as remediations of deficiencies, as improving teachers who are just barely making it, and in other ways focusing on raising the floor in developing and increasing teacher competence. But supervision and evaluation are about excellence, too. What is best practice? How is it defined? What does it look like in practice? How can best practice be shared? How can we raise the ceiling by making best practice even better? These are the kinds of growing questions that the National Board for Professional Teaching Standards has been concerned with since its formation in 1987.

The National Board for Professional Teaching Standards provides a process of growth and assessment that leads to board certification. Board-certified teachers are considered among the nation's best. This demanding process validates a teacher's practice as compared with national standards. "Teachers who choose to seek national board certification complete a demanding demonstration of their knowledge and skills. At their schools they develop a portfolio including student work samples, videotapes of lessons, and reflective commentary about their progress and problems in helping students learn. All of this takes place in the classroom, with the focus on good teaching and student learning. Candidates take part in lengthy written assessment exercises, again measuring their performance against established standards."[13] The process and content of board certification differs depending upon the level (elementary school, middle school, or high school) and the subject matter specialty. But certification efforts are united by a common view of what accomplished teaching is like and how accomplished teachers approach their work. This view is reflected in five propositions and their indicators, summarized in Table 10–2.

Seeking board certification can be a very effective strategy for improving the quality of teaching across the board in a school. Much depends on whether a school or school district is able to provide incentives in the form of financial support for the application process and perhaps salary stipends for teachers who successfully complete the process and become certified. Benefits to the school result from the process itself and from having specially qualified teachers who can help with mentoring and other professional development activities. The process provides an opportunity for teams of teachers to work together in discussing and understanding the board standards and to help each other prepare the necessary documents required by the assessment process. And the process stretches those who are principals or other designated supervisors by increasing their own learning curves and calling on them to place teaching and learning at the center of their practice. Much depends on whether or not a school views this process as a sound investment in improving student learning.

[13]"Investing in the Future: What Policymakers Can Do," National Board for Professional Teaching Standards. Southfield, MI, undated.

TABLE 10–2. The Five Propositions of Accomplished Teaching and Their Indicators As Developed by the National Board for Professional Teaching Standards.

1. Accomplished teachers are committed to students and their learning.

   Accomplished teachers should be able to demonstrate that they
   - Make knowledge accessible to all students
   - Teach in ways that reflect the belief that all students can learn
   - Recognize differences among students and take those differences into account
   - Are responsive to student interests, abilities, skills, family circumstances, and peer relationships
   - Understand how students develop and learn
   - Are aware of and use widely accepted theories of cognition and intelligence in their teaching
   - Are aware of the influence of context and culture on behavior
   - Develop student capacity to learn and respect for learning
   - Foster student self-esteem, motivation, character, and civic responsibility
   - Instill respect for individual, cultural, religious, and racial differences

2. Accomplished teachers know the subjects they teach and how to teach those subjects to students.

   Accomplished teachers should be able to demonstrate that they
   - Have rich understanding of the subjects they teach, including how their subjects are created, organized, and linked to other disciplines
   - Are able to apply the subjects they teach to real-world settings
   - Use knowledge to develop critical and analytical capacities of students
   - Are aware of the preconceptions and background knowledge that students bring to their learning
   - Understand where difficulties are likely to arise and modify their teaching accordingly
   - Create many pathways for students to learn the subjects they are teaching
   - Help students learn to pose and solve their own problems

3. Accomplished teachers are responsible for managing and monitoring student learning.

   Accomplished teachers should be able to demonstrate that they
   - Create, enrich, maintain, and alter instructional settings to capture and sustain the interest of their students
   - Are able to use time wisely and effectively
   - Are adept at engaging students and adults to assist their teaching and at using the knowledge and expertise of their colleagues to complement their own
   - Command a range of teaching techniques, know when each is appropriate, and can implement them as needed
   - Are aware of and avoid using practices that are ineffectual or damaging in other ways
   - Are able to engage groups of students in a disciplined learning environment
   - Are able to organize teaching and learning to allow the school goals for students to be met
   - Know how to develop and help set norms for social interaction among students and between students and teachers
   - Understand how to motivate students to learn and to maintain their interest over time
   - Assess the progress of individual students as well as the class as a whole
   - Use multiple methods for measuring student growth
   - Can clearly explain student performance to parents

(Continued)

TABLE 10–2. (*Continued*)

4. Accomplished teachers think systematically about their practice and learn from experience.

   Accomplished teachers should be able to demonstrate that they
   - Are models of educated persons, exemplifying the virtues they seek to inspire in students (curiosity, tolerance, honesty, fairness, respect for diversity, and appreciation of cultural differences)
   - Have the capacities that are prerequisites for intellectual growth, including the abilities to reason, to understand multiple perspectives, to be creative, to take risks, to be experimental, and to adopt a problem-solving orientation
   - Draw on their knowledge of human development, subject matter, and instruction, and on their understanding of students to make good judgements about sound practice
   - Are familiar with and rely on the literature that supports effective teaching and on their own experiences as teachers and the experiences of their colleagues
   - Engage in lifelong learning and are able to encourage lifelong learning in their students
   - Critically examine their practice-seeking to deepen their knowledge, sharpen their judgement, and improve their teaching practice

5. Accomplished teachers are members of learning communities.

   Accomplished teachers should be able to demonstrate that they
   - Contribute to the effectiveness of the school by working collaboratively with other professionals on teaching and learning policy, curriculum development, and staff development
   - Can evaluate school progress and allocate resources in the light of state and local standards and objectives
   - Are knowledgeable about community resources that can be used for the benefit of their students and are skilled in employing those resources
   - Can find ways to work collaboratively and creatively with parents, engaging them productively in the work of the school

Source: Summarized from "What Teachers Should Know and Be Able to Do," National Board for Professional Teaching Standards, www.nbpts.org/about/coreprops.cfm. To order a complete set of the standards, phone 1-800-228-3224.

STANDARDS FOR SUPERVISION

As suggested in the opening paragraph of this chapter, the topic of standards for supervision is complex. This complexity is a result of the distribution of supervisory functions across a number of supervisory roles. Principals, for example, have important supervisory responsibilities, but so do teacher leaders and others. Deciding who is responsible for what is not always easy, nor is agreeing on what is best practice in supervision.

THE EDUCATIONAL LEADERSHIP CONSTITUENT COUNCIL (ELCC) STANDARDS

The use of standards is the latest attempt to define and describe what principals and other administrators should know and do. In 1996, for example, the Council of Chief State School Officers adopted the list of standards for school leaders provided by the Interstate School Leaders Licensure Consortium (ISLLC). Neil Shipman, an assessment expert, and Joseph Murphy, a highly respected professor of educational administration, describe the two-year effort as follows:

> Forged from research on productive educational leadership and the wisdom of colleagues, the standards were drafted by personnel from 24 state education agencies and representatives from various professional associations. The standards present a common core of knowledge, dispositions, and performances that will help link leadership more forcefully to productive schools and enhanced educational outcomes. Although developed to serve a different purpose, the standards were designed to be compatible with the new National Council for the Accreditation of Teacher Education (NCATE) Curriculum Guidelines for school administration—as well as with the major national reports on reinventing leadership for tomorrow's schools. As such, they represent another part of a concerted effort to enhance the skills of school leaders and to couple leadership with effective educational processes and valued outcomes.[14]

Beginning in 2003, NCATE has used a version of the ISLLC standards to assess the school administration preparation programs of universities seeking accreditation. This version, the Educational Leadership Constituent Council standards, was largely a reformatting of the ISLLC standards. The new standards differ by being performance-based. Not only must universities show they are addressing the right content, they must also provide compelling evidence that their students are able to perform in each of the standards areas at a required level of competence.

The new standards can be accessed at www.npbea.org/ELCC/ELCCStandards%20_5-02.pdf. You will need to have the standards downloaded in order to complete the exercise that appears in Appendix 10-2. This exercise examines how responsibility for the standards is distributed across a variety of school and school district roles. Before turning to Appendix 10–2, let's consider the issue of distribution of responsibility.

DISTRIBUTING RESPONSIBILITY FOR SUPERVISION

Though the ELCC standards are formally aimed at the responsibilities of principals and other designated administrators, the supervisory roles and functions are more broadly distributed and assumed by incumbents of many other roles. In the past, supervision was something that principals and others did to teachers. Today supervision is something done with teachers and, as a result, is much more effective.

In successful schools, collaborative cultures provide the norms and contexts for teachers to inquire into, reflect on, and improve their practice as individuals, as colleagues, and as members of communities of practice. Collaborative cultures require that supervisory roles and functions be the responsibility of teachers; of teacher leaders such as coaches, academic deans, grade-level and team leaders, department

---

[14]Council of Chief State School Officers, *Interstate School Leaders Licensure Consortium: Standards for School Leaders,* Washington, DC: Author, 1996, p. 3.

chairs, peer supervisors, and peer facilitators; of central office supervisors such as subject-matter and curriculum experts and professional development experts; and of principals and their assistants. In the language of distributed leadership: The functions of supervision are more effective in improving teaching and learning, teacher performance, and student achievement when responsibility for them is distributed across several roles. For this reason, successful schools are more likely to establish a collective responsibility for teaching, learning, and student achievement. Once collective responsibility becomes an accepted norm of the school, teachers will be more willing to help each other, to share their practice together, and to care about each other.

Two kinds of responsibility are necessary. One kind of responsibility comes from the obligations that teachers feel as a result of their membership in collaborative cultures and communities of practice. These obligations require teachers to be responsive to community norms. The second kind is the official responsibility that comes from the various roles that people assume. Every role has its responsibilities. Teachers, for example, are responsible for providing differentiated teaching and for being continuous learners. Students are responsible for giving their best efforts. Principals are responsible for providing the discretion, support, and help teachers need to be continuous learners. Parents are responsible for helping their children come to school ready to learn.

Let's now turn to Appendix 10–2. Presented here is an abridged version of the ELCC standards for school administrators.[15] These standards are arranged in the form of an inventory. This inventory, the ELCC Distributed Responsibility Inventory, asks the question, How important are each of the six ELCC standards to teachers, teacher leaders, principals and their assistants, and central office supervisors? Review the standards provided in the introduction to Appendix 10–2. Then, following the directions provided, use a five-point rating scale to indicate how important the six standards and their elements are to each of the four roles. Use your school as a frame of reference. Let's take standard 2, element 2.1, "Promote a positive school culture," as an example. What rating would you give your school for this standard? The mean sum distribution in one school might be teachers 4, teacher leaders 4, principals 4, central office 4. The mean sum distribution in another school might be teachers 1, teacher leaders 2, principals 5, central office 4. In the first school, responsibility for promoting a positive school climate is broadly distributed across the four roles. Each of the role groups feels that climate is an important responsibility that must be shared. In the second school, responsibility for promoting a positive school climate does not include teachers or teacher leaders very much. The principal and the central office have virtually all the responsibility.

If you gave a high rating to most of the elements for standards 1.0, 2.0, 3.0, 4.0, 5.0, and 6.0, you are describing a school culture in which collective responsibility for the success of the school is an established norm. Further, in the school that you

---

[15]The ELCC Distributed Responsibility Inventory is designed for your use in summarizing your ratings after you have examined the complete downloaded list of ELCC standards. See Appendix 10–2 for downloading details.

evaluated, the functions of supervision are more important than are supervisory roles. It is important, for example, for teachers to practice new learnings in their classroom with the help of other teachers, teacher leaders, and their principal.

IT'S ABOUT TEACHERS LEARNING

Anthony Alvarado, the former leader of District 2 in New York City and of the San Diego School District, believes that teacher learning is the key to improving student achievement. Simply put, Alvarado believes that students learn from teachers; therefore, if you want to improve student achievement, then you have to improve teaching. Laura Varlas reports that Alvarado believes, "timely classroom application is essential because that's where the real lessons are learned–where educators engage in professional growth rather than just receive professional training. Through trial and error and trial again, teachers accumulate the professional survival gear that is going to nourish success year after year. 'If you're an administrator [Alvarado said] you must know teaching inside and out. If you're not in classrooms most of the time, how can you improve them?'" Alvarado warned that it's not enough to know if a kid can or can't do something—you need to know *how* they are learning. Assessments always lead back to instruction.[16]

Teacher learning is a cousin to supervision and to professional development. If teachers are not learning, if their practice is not improving, then student achievement will not have improved and supervision will have failed. When teachers, supervisors, administrators, and others are working together within a collaborative culture, communities of practice will pop up all over the school and school district. It is these communities of practice that will help develop a collective responsibility for success.

These discussions of standards for teaching and learning and of standards for supervisory practice are aimed at placing matters of teaching and learning and matters of improving student achievement front and center as the driving forces for the practice of supervision.

SUMMARY

In this chapter we showed that using standards in supervision is a strategy that has great promise for building instructional coherence, helping teachers learn together, and improving student achievement. The critical issue is whether standards are understood as templates that narrow and unduly script the work of teaching and learning or as frameworks that point the way while allowing for teacher and for school-level discretion. Using the Danielson Framework for Teaching as an example, we showed how the dimensions of teaching that constitute the framework can be

[16]Varlas, Laura, "Banking on Teachers," *Education Update,* vol. 47, no. 1 (January 2005, p. 1.) "Banking on Teachers" is a report of Anthony Alvarado's views given in an address at ASCS's 2004 Conference on Teaching and Learning held October 15–17 in Dallas, Texas.

used as a one-best-way script or as a repository of items from which teachers and supervisors choose. As we stated: "Choosing a handful of indicators instead of using the entire framework is important, because choosing helps focus attention on a manageable number of issues; does not overwhelm; and allows for a more authentic, in-depth conversation and analysis. Choosing enhances purpose and meaning. And choosing anchors the use of the framework to what is actually going on in the teacher's classroom."

Though the ELCC standards are formally aimed at the responsibilities of principals and other designated administrators, the supervisory roles and functions are more broadly distributed and assumed by those in many other roles. We then asked the question, How are the ELCC standards distributed across all the roles involved in supervision? If, for example, the competencies, commitments, and requirements inherent in the standards help define this array of roles, then one sign that a school is developing a collective responsibility for student achievement and school improvement is that the distribution across the roles is fairly even. And that is a good sign. We then examined an abbreviated definition of the ELCC standards provided the ELCC Distributed Responsibility Inventory as a way to find out just how these responsibilities are shared by teachers, teacher leaders, principals, and central office supervisors.

SOME REFLECTIONS

1. Templates or frameworks, what is the difference? Of course, both are necessary if we value instructional coherence, but which of the two ought to be the basis for a school's primary strategy for aligning standards, curriculum, teaching, and assessment? Give reasons for your responses.
2. The Danielson framework has its uses and its abuses. Give examples of each.
3. Familiarize yourself with the idea of distributing responsibility for supervision in a school or school district. Now review the ELCC Distributed Responsibility Inventory. If you were to give the inventory to a principal, an assistant principal, a key supervisor at the central office, a department chair, and a literacy coach (all people that you know), how do you think they would respond? If the people you have chosen were all in the same school, what might you say about the distribution of responsibility for supervision in that school? Is responsibility broadly distributed or narrowly distributed? Does it matter? Why or why not?

Appendix 10–1. An Abbreviated Framework for Teaching: Domains 1 and 3

Element	Unsatisfactory	Basic	Proficient	Distinguished
DOMAIN 1: PLANNING AND PREPARATION				
Component 1a: Demonstrating Knowledge of Content and Pedagogy				
Knowledge of Content	Teacher makes content errors or does not correct content errors students make.	Teacher displays basic content knowledge but cannot articulate connections with other parts of the discipline or with other disciplines.	Teacher displays solid content knowledge and makes connections between the content and other parts of the discipline and other disciplines.	Teacher displays extensive content knowledge, with evidence of continuing pursuit of such knowledge.
Knowledge of Prerequisite Relationships	Teacher displays little understanding of prerequisite knowledge important for student learning of the content.	Teacher indicates some awareness of prerequisite learning, although such knowledge may be incomplete or inaccurate.	Teacher's plans and practices reflect understanding of prerequisite relationships among topics and concepts.	Teacher actively builds on knowledge of prerequisite relationships when describing instruction or seeking causes for student misunderstanding.
Knowledge of Content-Related Pedagogy	Teacher displays little understanding of pedagogical issues involved in student learning of the content.	Teacher displays basic pedagogical knowledge but does not anticipate student misconceptions.	Pedagogical practices reflect current research on best pedagogical practice within the discipline but without anticipating student misconceptions.	Teacher displays continuing search for best practice and anticipates student misconceptions.

(Continued)

Appendix 10–1. An Abbreviated Framework for Teaching: Domains 1 and 3 (Continued)

Element	Unsatisfactory	Basic	Proficient	Distinguished
Component 1b: Demonstrating Knowledge of Students				
Knowledge of Characteristics of Age Group	Teacher displays minimal knowledge of developmental characteristics of age group.	Teacher displays generally accurate knowledge of developmental characteristics of age group.	Teacher displays thorough understanding of typical developmental characteristics of age group as well as exceptions to general patterns.	Teacher displays knowledge of typical developmental characteristics of age group, exceptions to the patterns, and the extent to which each student follows patterns.
Knowledge of Students' Varied Approaches to Learning	Teacher is unfamiliar with the different approaches to learning that students exhibit, such as learning styles, modalities, and different "intelligences."	Teacher displays general understanding of the different approaches to learning that students exhibit.	Teacher displays solid understanding of the different approaches to learning that different students exhibit.	Teacher uses, where appropriate, knowledge of students' varied approaches to learning in instructional planning.
Knowledge of Students' Skills and Knowledge	Teacher displays little knowledge of students' skills and knowledge and does not indicate that such knowledge is valuable.	Teacher recognizes the value of understanding students' skills and knowledge but displays this knowledge for the class only as a whole.	Teacher displays knowledge of students' skills and knowledge for groups of students and recognizes the value of this knowledge.	Teacher displays knowledge of students' skills and knowledge for each student, including those with special needs.
Knowledge of Students' Interests and Cultural Heritage	Teacher displays little knowledge of students' interests or cultural heritage and does not indicate that such knowledge is valuable.	Teacher recognizes the value of understanding students' interests or cultural heritage but displays this knowledge for the class only as a whole.	Teacher displays knowledge of the interests or cultural heritage of groups of students and recognizes the value of this knowledge.	Teacher displays knowledge of the interests or cultural heritage of each student.

Element	Unsatisfactory	Basic	Proficient	Distinguished
Component 1c: Selecting Instructional Goals				
Value	Goals are not valuable and represent low expectations or no conceptual understanding for students. Goals do not reflect important learning.	Goals are moderately valuable in either their expectations or conceptual understanding for students and in importance of learning.	Goals are valuable in their level of expectations, conceptual understanding, and importance of learning.	Not only are the goals valuable, but teacher can also clearly articulate how goals establish high expectations and relate to curriculum frameworks and standards.
Clarity	Goals are either not clear or are stated as student activities. Goals do not permit viable methods of assessment.	Goals are only moderately clear or include a combination of goals and activities. Some goals do not permit viable methods of assessment.	Most of the goals are clear but may include a few activities. Most permit viable methods of assessment.	All the goals are clear, written in the form of student learning, and permit viable methods of assessment.
Suitability for Diverse Students	Goals are not suitable for the class.	Most of the goals are suitable for most students in the class.	All the goals are suitable for most students in the class.	Goals take into account the varying learning needs of individual students or groups.
Balance	Goals reflect only one type of learning and one discipline or strand.	Goals reflect several types of learning but no effort at coordination or integration.	Goals reflect several different types of learning and opportunities for integration.	Goals reflect student initiative in establishing important learning.

(Continued)

Element	Unsatisfactory	Basic	Proficient	Distinguished
Component 1d: Demonstrating Knowledge of Resources				
Resources for Teaching	Teacher is unaware of resources available through the school or district.	Teacher displays limited awareness of resources available through the school or district.	Teacher is fully aware of all resources available through the school or district.	In addition to being aware of school and district resources, teacher actively seeks other materials to enhance instruction, for example, from professional organizations or through the community.
Resources for Students	Teacher is unaware of resources available to assist students who need them.	Teacher displays limited awareness of resources available through the school or district.	Teacher is fully aware of all resources available through the school or district and knows how to gain access for students.	In addition to being aware of school and district resources, teacher is aware of additional resources available through the community.
Component 1e: Designing Coherent Instruction				
Learning Activities	Learning activities are not suitable to students or instructional goals. They do not follow an organized progression and do not reflect recent professional research.	Only some of the learning activities are suitable to students or instructional goals. Progression of activities in the unit is uneven, and only some activities reflect recent professional research.	Most of the learning activities are suitable to students and instructional goals. Progression of activities in the unit is fairly even, and most activities reflect recent professional research.	Learning activities are highly relevant to students and instructional goals. They progress coherently, producing a unified whole and reflecting recent professional research.

Element	Unsatisfactory	Basic	Proficient	Distinguished
Instructional Materials and Resources	Materials and resources do not support the instructional goals or engage students in meaningful learning.	Some of the materials and resources support the instructional goals, and some engage students in meaningful learning.	All materials and resources support the instructional goals, and most engage students in meaningful learning.	All materials and resources support the instructional goals, and most engage students in meaningful learning. There is evidence of student participation in selecting or adapting materials.
Instructional Groups	Instructional groups do not support the instructional goals and offer no variety.	Instructional groups are inconsistent in suitability to the instructional goals and offer minimal variety.	Instructional groups are varied, as appropriate to the different instructional goals.	Instructional groups are varied, as appropriate to the different instructional goals. There is evidence of student choice in selecting different patterns of instructional goals.
Lesson and Unit Structure	The lesson or unit has no clearly defined structure, or the structure is chaotic. Time allocations are unrealistic.	The lesson or unit has a recognizable structure, although the structure is not uniformly maintained throughout. Most time allocations are reasonable.	The lesson or unit has a clearly defined structure that activities are organized around. Time allocations are reasonable.	The lesson's or unit's structure is clear and allows for different pathways according to student needs.

(Continued)

Appendix 10–1. An Abbreviated Framework for Teaching: Domains 1 and 3 *(Continued)*

Element	Unsatisfactory	Basic	Proficient	Distinguished
Component 1f: Assessing Student Learning				
Congruence with Instructional Goals	Content and methods of assessment lack congruence with instructional goals.	Some of the instructional goals are assessed through the proposed approach, but many are not.	All the instructional goals are nominally assessed through the proposed plan, but the approach is more suitable to some goals than to others.	The proposed approach to assessment is completely congruent with the instructional goals, both in content and process.
Criteria and Standards	The proposed approach contains no clear criteria or standards.	Assessment criteria and standards have been developed, but they are either not clear or have not been clearly communicated to students.	Assessment criteria and standards are clear and have been clearly communicated to students.	Assessment criteria and standards are clear and have been clearly communicated to students. There is evidence that students contributed to the development of the criteria and standards.
Use for Planning	The assessment results affect planning for these students only minimally.	Teacher uses assessment results to plan for the class as a whole.	Teacher uses assessment results to plan for individuals and groups of students.	Students are aware of how they are meeting the established standards and participate in planning the next steps.
		DOMAIN 3: INSTRUCTION		
Component 3a: Communicating Clearly and Accurately				
Directions and Procedures	Teacher directions and procedures are confusing to students.	Teacher directions and procedures are clarified after initial student confusion or are excessively detailed.	Teacher directions and procedures are clear to students and contain an appropriate level of detail.	Teacher directions and procedures are clear to students and anticipate possible student misunderstanding.

Element	Unsatisfactory	Basic	Proficient	Distinguished
Oral and Written Language	Teacher's spoken language is inaudible, or written language is illegible. Spoken or written language may contain many grammar and syntax errors. Vocabulary may be inappropriate, vague, or used incorrectly, leaving students confused.	Teacher's spoken language is audible, and written language is legible. Both are used correctly. Vocabulary is correct but limited or is not appropriate to students' ages or backgrounds.	Teacher's spoken and written language is correct and clear. Vocabulary is appropriate to students' age and interests.	Teacher's spoken and written language is correct and expressive, with well-chosen vocabulary that enriches the lesson.

Component 3b: Using Questioning and Discussion Techniques

Element	Unsatisfactory	Basic	Proficient	Distinguished
Quality of Questions	Teacher's questions are virtually all of poor quality.	Teacher's questions are a combination of low and high quality. Only some invite a response.	Most of teacher's questions are of high quality. Adequate time is available for students to respond.	Teacher's questions are of uniformly high quality, with adequate time for students to respond. Students formulate many questions.
Discussion Techniques	Interaction between teacher and students is predominantly recitation style, with teacher mediating all questions and answers.	Teacher makes some attempt to engage students in a true discussion, with uneven results.	Classroom interaction represents true discussion, with teacher stepping, when appropriate, to the side.	Students assume considerable responsibility for the success of the discussion, initiating topics and making unsolicited contributions.

(Continued)

Appendix 10–1. An Abbreviated Framework for Teaching: Domains 1 and 3 (Continued)

Element	Unsatisfactory	Basic	Proficient	Distinguished
Student Participation	Only a few students participate in the discussion.	Teacher attempts to engage all students in the discussion, but with only limited success.	Teacher successfully engages all students in the discussion.	Students themselves ensure that all voices are heard in the discussion.
Component 3c: Engaging Students in Learning				
Representation of Content	Representation of content is inappropriate and unclear or uses poor examples and analogies.	Representation of content is inconsistent in quality: Some is done skillfully, with good examples; other portions are difficult to follow.	Representation of content is appropriate and links well with students' knowledge and experience.	Representation of content is appropriate and links well with students' knowledge and experience. Students contribute to representation of content.
Activities and Assignments	Activities and assignments are inappropriate for students in terms of their age or backgrounds. Students are not engaged mentally.	Some activities and assignments are appropriate to students and engage them mentally, but others do not.	Most activities and assignments are appropriate to students. Almost all students are cognitively engaged in them.	All students are cognitively engaged in the activities and assignments in their exploration of content. Students initiate or adapt activities and projects to enhance understanding.
Grouping of Students	Instructional groups are inappropriate to the students or to the instructional goals.	Instructional groups are only partially appropriate to the students or only moderately successful in advancing the instructional goals of a lesson.	Instructional groups are productive and fully appropriate to the students or to the instructional goals of a lesson.	Instructional groups are productive and fully appropriate to the instructional goals of a lesson. Students take the initiative to influence instructional groups to advance their understanding.

Element	Unsatisfactory	Basic	Proficient	Distinguished
Instructional Materials and Resources	Instructional materials and resources are unsuitable to the instructional goals or do not engage students mentally.	Instructional materials and resources are partially suitable to the instructional goals, or students' level of mental engagement is moderate.	Instructional materials and resources are suitable to the instructional goals and engage students mentally.	Instructional materials and resources are suitable to the instructional goals and engage students mentally. Students initiate the choice, adaptation, or creation of materials to enhance their own purposes.
Structure and Pacing	The lesson has no clearly defined structure, or the pacing of the lesson is too slow or rushed, or both.	The lesson has a recognizable structure, although it is not uniformly maintained throughout the lesson. Pacing of the lesson is inconsistent.	The lesson has a clearly defined structure around which the activities are organized. Pacing of the lesson is inconsistent.	The lesson's structure is highly coherent, allowing for reflection and closure as appropriate. Pacing of the lesson is appropriate for all students.
Component 3d: Providing Feedback to Students				
Quality: Accurate, Substantive, Constructive, and Specific	Feedback is either not provided or is of uniformly poor quality.	Feedback is inconsistent in quality: Some elements of high quality are present; others are not.	Feedback is consistently high quality.	Feedback is consistently high quality. Provision is made for students to use feedback in their learning.

(Continued)

Appendix 10–1. An Abbreviated Framework for Teaching: Domains 1 and 3 (Continued)

Element	Unsatisfactory	Basic	Proficient	Distinguished
Timeliness	Feedback is not provided in a timely manner.	Timeliness of feedback is inconsistent.	Feedback is consistently provided in a timely manner.	Feedback is consistently provided in a timely manner. Students make prompt use of the feedback in their learning.
Component 3e: Demonstrating Flexibility and Responsiveness				
Lesson Adjustment	Teacher adheres rigidly to an instructional plan, even when a change will clearly improve a lesson.	Teacher attempts to adjust a lesson, with mixed results.	Teacher makes a minor adjustment to a lesson, and the adjustment occurs smoothly.	Teacher successfully makes a major adjustment to a lesson.
Response to Students	Teacher ignores or brushes aside students' questions or interests.	Teacher attempts to accommodate students' questions or interests. The effects on the coherence of a lesson are uneven.	Teacher successfully accommodates students' questions or interests.	Teacher seizes a major opportunity to enhance learning, building on a spontaneous event.
Persistence	When a student has difficulty learning, the teacher either gives up or blames the student or the environment for the student's lack of success.	Teacher accepts responsibility for the success of all students but has only a limited repertoire of instructional strategies to use.	Teacher persists in seeking approaches for students who have difficulty learning, possessing a moderate repertoire of strategies.	Teacher persists in seeking effective approaches for students who need help, using an extensive repertoire of strategies and soliciting additional resources from the school.

Source: Domains 1 and 3 are reproduced from Charlotte Danielson, *Enhancing Professional Practice: A Framework for Teaching.* Alexandria, VA: Association for Supervision and Curriculum Development, 1996. © Charlotte Danielson, used with permission. Danielson can be reached at Educational Testing Service, Mail Stop 14-D, Rosedale Road, Princeton, NJ 08541.

Appendix 10–2
ELCC Distributed Responsibility Inventory

How important are the six Educational Leadership Constituent Council (ELCC) standards to teachers, teacher leaders, principals and assistants, and central office supervisors?

Introduction

Recognizing that all the ELCC standards may be important to all roles, we must note also that some of the standards are more important to some roles than to others. This inventory seeks to find out how perceived responsibility and importance for the six ELCC standards and their elements are distributed across four roles: teachers, teacher leaders, principals and assistants, and central office supervisors. For a complete copy of the ELCC standards, including the elements for each of the six standards, it will be necessary to download and review the complete set at www.npbea.org/ELCC/ELCCStandards%20_5-02.pdf.

The Standards

Standard 1.0: Have the knowledge and ability to promote the success of all students by facilitating the development, articulation, implementation, and stewardship of a school or district vision of learning supported by the school community.

Standard 2.0: Have the knowledge and ability to promote the success of all students by promoting a positive school culture, providing an effective instructional program, applying best practice to student learning, and designing comprehensive professional growth plans for staff.

Standard 3.0: Have the knowledge and ability to promote the success of all students by managing the organization, operations, and resources in a way that promotes a safe, efficient, and effective learning environment.

Standard 4.0: Have the knowledge and ability to promote the success of all students by collaborating with families and other community members, responding to diverse community interests and needs, and mobilizing community resources.

Standard 5.0: Have the knowledge and ability to promote the success of all students by acting with integrity, fairly, and in an ethical manner.

Standard 6.0: Have the knowledge and ability to promote the success of all students by understanding, responding to, and influencing the larger political, social, economic, legal, and cultural context.

Directions

As you review the six downloaded standards, note that each is accompanied by several elements that specify the dispositions and behaviors that are needed for the standard to be met. Only the broad titles for each element will be used here, however, as you assess how important that element is for the four roles (teachers, teacher leaders,* principals and assistants, central office supervisors).

Using a rating scale of 1 to 5, with 5 indicating a very important responsibility and 1 a responsibility that is not very important, evaluate the importance of each element for each

---

*Teacher leaders include such rules as grade-level chairs, team leaders, department chairs, coaches, and facilitators.

role. Now compute the mean sum ($\bar{X}$) for each of the four roles. If, for example, the sum for the role of teacher for the "Vision" elements (Standard 1—Vision) is 20, and since there are 5 elements, the $\bar{X}$ score is 4 (20 ÷ 5 = 4).

Standard 1—Vision
1.1 *Develop a vision*
       teacher _____ teacher leader _____ principal _____ central office _____
1.2 *Articulate a vision*
       teacher _____ teacher leader _____ principal _____ central office _____
1.3 *Implement a vision*
       teacher _____ teacher leader _____ principal _____ central office _____
1.4 *Steward a vision*
       teacher _____ teacher leader _____ principal _____ central office _____
1.5 *Promote community involvement in the vision*
       teacher _____ teacher leader _____ principal _____ central office _____

Standard 1.0 sums
       teacher _____ teacher leader _____ principal _____ central office _____

Standard 1.0 $\bar{X}$ sums
       teacher _____ teacher leader _____ principal _____ central office _____

Standard 2—Culture of Learning
2.1 *Promote positive school culture*
       teacher _____ teacher leader _____ principal _____ central office _____
2.2 *Provide effective instructional program*
       teacher _____ teacher leader _____ principal _____ central office _____
2.3 *Apply best practice to student learning*
       teacher _____ teacher leader _____ principal _____ central office _____
2.4 *Design comprehensive professional growth plans*
       teacher _____ teacher leader _____ principal _____ central office _____

Standard 2.0 sums
       teacher _____ teacher leader _____ principal _____ central office _____

Standard 2.0 $\bar{X}$ sums
       teacher _____ teacher leader _____ principal _____ central office _____

Standard 3—Management
3.1 *Manage the organization*
       teacher _____ teacher leader _____ principal _____ central office _____
3.2 *Manage operations*
       teacher _____ teacher leader _____ principal _____ central office _____
3.3 *Manage resources*
       teacher _____ teacher leader _____ principal _____ central office _____

Standard 3.0 sums
       teacher _____ teacher leader _____ principal _____ central office _____

Standard 3.0 $\bar{X}$ sums
       teacher _____ teacher leader _____ principal _____ central office _____

Standard 4—Community

4.1 *Collaborate with families and other community members*
            teacher _____ teacher leader _____ principal _____ central office _____
4.2 *Respond to community interests and needs*
            teacher _____ teacher leader _____ principal _____ central office _____
4.3 *Mobilize community resources*
            teacher _____ teacher leader _____ principal _____ central office _____

Standard 4.0 sums
            teacher _____ teacher leader _____ principal _____ central office _____

Standard 4.0 $\overline{X}$ sums
            teacher _____ teacher leader _____ principal _____ central office _____

Standard 5—Ethics

5.1 *Acts with integrity*
            teacher _____ teacher leader _____ principal _____ central office _____
5.2 *Acts fairly*
            teacher _____ teacher leader _____ principal _____ central office _____
5.3 *Acts ethically*
            teacher _____ teacher leader _____ principal _____ central office _____

Standard 5.0 sums
            teacher _____ teacher leader _____ principal _____ central office _____

Standard 5.0 $\overline{X}$ sums
            teacher _____ teacher leader _____ principal _____ central office _____

Standard 6—Context

6.1 *Understand the larger context*
            teacher _____ teacher leader _____ principal _____ central office _____
6.2 *Respond to the larger context*
            teacher _____ teacher leader _____ principal _____ central office _____
6.3 *Influence the larger context*
            teacher _____ teacher leader _____ principal _____ central office _____

Standard 6.0 sums
            teacher _____ teacher leader _____ principal _____ central office _____

Standard 6.0 $\overline{X}$ sums
            teacher _____ teacher leader _____ principal _____ central office _____

Source: Standards from National Policy Board for Educational Administration on behalf of the Educational Leadership Constituent Council, 2002, reprinted by permission. The standards are used as part of the NCATE accreditation process. Other members of the ELCC include the American Association of School Administrators, National Association of Elementary School Principals, National Association of Secondary School Principal, and Association for Supervision and Curriculum Development.

CHAPTER 11

Supervision as Professional Development and Renewal

INTRODUCTION

This chapter contrasts three levels of supervision: in-service, professional development, and renewal. All three levels are useful, but the second and third levels are more powerful strategies for teacher learning than is the first. A design for using the three levels of teacher learning in practice is provided. One purpose of this design is to show how effective supervision and increases in teacher learning are linked. Supervision is a cousin to teacher learning. Building the capacity of teachers is important because it is a key factor in improving student achievement. It is commonly stated that "as goes the principal, so goes the school." There is much truth to that statement, but even gifted principals can do only so much without teachers who know about teaching, care about teaching, are willing to help each other, and are committed to being continual learners.

SOME BACKGROUND

Clearly, the overarching purpose of supervision is to help teachers improve. The focus of this improvement may be on what the teacher knows, the development of teaching skills, as well as the teacher's ability to make more informed professional decisions, to be a better problem solver and to inquire into his or her own practice. Traditionally, improvement has been sought by providing *in-service* programs and activities. Well-intentioned supervisors are placed in the driver's seat, taking responsibility for the *what*s, *how*s, and *when*s of improvement as they plan and provide in-service programs they think will be best for teachers. In-service emphasizes training teachers in the best way to do something. Steps and scripts, in which one size fits all, are typically provided. In-service providers talk and teachers listen. Discussion may follow, but it needs to be on task as determined by the chosen training scripts. In recent years in-service has given way to *professional development*.

Here teachers play key roles in deciding the direction and nature of their professional improvement.

Frances Bolin, Judith McConnel Falk, and their colleagues[1] suggest that neither in-service nor professional development is expansive and penetrating enough to tap the full potential for teachers to grow personally and professionally. As Bolin writes:

> What would happen if we set aside the question of how to *improve* the teacher and looked instead at what we can do to encourage the teacher. . . . Asking how to encourage the teacher places the work of improvement in the hands of the teacher. It presupposes that the teacher desires to grow, to be self-defining, and to engage in teaching as a vital part of life, rather than as unrelated employment. This leads to looking at teaching as a commitment or calling, a vocation . . . that is not adequately contained in the term *profession* as it has come to be used.[2]

FRAMEWORKS FOR GROWTH

According to Bolin, when supervision shifts away from providing improvement experiences and opportunities, *renewal* begins to dominate. Supervision as renewal is more fully integrated into the everyday life of the school as teachers move from the backseat to the driver's seat by assuming more responsibility for their own growth. Learning and reflecting on one's practice become integral parts of the role of teacher. At its best, today's supervision trickles down from above as supervisors create collaborative cultures. As renewal, supervision also bubbles up from below as teachers commit to sharing their practice and to helping each other create communities of practice. Bringing collaborative cultures and communities of practice together creates powerful learning intersections. It is these learning intersections that make professional learning communities so powerful.

IN-SERVICE. In-service is a highly directive and structured process. Responsibility for in-service is usually in the hands of someone other than the teacher, and the emphasis is on the development of job-related skills through the provision of training and practice experiences. The workshop featuring a tell, sell, and practice format is often the vehicle for delivering in-service. When in-service is the sole or primary vehicle for promoting growth, teaching comes to be viewed as a job with teachers as workers who, it is apparently assumed, possess limited capacity or will to figure out things for themselves. Though teacher in-service has a long history, teachers do not always regard the process with enthusiasm. It is often too formal and bureaucratic and characterized by a high degree of administrative planning and scheduling. Too often, in-service serves less to provide growth and more to meet

---

[1] See, for example, the articles that appear in Frances S. Bolin and Judith McConnel Falk (eds.), *Teacher Renewal Professional Issues, Personal Choices,* New York: Teachers College Press, 1987.
[2] Frances S. Bolin, "Reassessment and Renewal in Teaching," in Bolin and Falk, op. cit., p. 11.

legal requirements of one sort or another. Program activities often are selected and developed for uniform dissemination without giving serious consideration to the purposes of such activities or to the needs of individual teachers. Structure, uniformity, and tight control from above result in a training rather than an education emphasis. We are not suggesting that in-service be abandoned, for it can be useful under proper circumstances. Workshops and inspirational speakers, for example, have important roles to play. We are suggesting, however, that a commitment to teacher growth requires much more than in-service programming.

PROFESSIONAL DEVELOPMENT. Professional development seems more in tune with the view of teaching as a profession. The emphasis is on the development of professional expertise by involving teachers in problem solving and action research. Teachers and supervisors share responsibility for the planning, development, and provision of staff development activities, and the focus is much less on training than on puzzling, inquiring, and solving problems.

From the supervisor's standpoint, professional development emphasizes providing teachers with the opportunity and the resources they need to reflect on their practice and to share their practice with others. Thirty-six years ago Herbert Thelen suggested that the most useful professional development programs are characterized by **"intensity of personal involvement, immediate consequences for classroom practice, stimulation and ego support by meaningful associates in this situation, and initiating by teacher rather than outside."[3]**

Anything supervisors can do to help develop and strengthen professional community among teachers will become an investment in promoting professional development. Supervisors, therefore, help both indirectly, by promoting opportunity and support, and directly, by collaborating with teachers as colleagues.

RENEWAL. Renewal focuses on the development of the personal and professional self through reflection and reevaluation. As Francis Bolin suggests, renewal implies doing over again, revising, making new yet restoring, reestablishing, and revaluing.[4] In renewal the emphasis is on the individual teacher and his or her personal and professional development.

Neither professional development nor renewal is imposed by the school upon the teacher; the teacher engages in these processes for himself or herself. In-service, on the other hand, typically assumes a deficiency in the teacher and presupposes a set of appropriate ideas, skills, and methods that need to be developed. In-service works to reduce the teacher's range of alternatives—indeed, to bring about conformity. Professional development and renewal assume a need for teachers to grow and develop on the job. Rather than reducing the range of alternatives, they seek to increase this range. Teacher growth is less a function of polishing existing skills or of keeping up with the latest developments and more a function of solving problems

---

[3]Herbert Thelen, "A Cultural Approach to Inservice Education," in Louis Rubin (ed.), *Improving In-Service Education,* Boston: Allyn & Bacon, 1971, pp. 72–73.
[4]Francis S. Bolin, "Reassessment and Renewal in Teaching," in Bolin and Falk, op. cit.

TABLE 11–1. Models of Teacher Development.

	In-service Training	Professional Development	Renewal
Assumptions	Knowledge stands above the teacher.	The teacher stands above knowledge.	Knowledge is in the teacher.
	Knowledge is, therefore, instrumental. It tells the teacher what to do.	Knowledge is, therefore, conceptual. It informs the teacher's decisions.	Knowledge is, therefore, personal. It connects teachers to themselves and others.
	Teaching is a job and teachers are technicians.	Teaching is a profession and teachers are experts.	Teaching is a calling and teachers are servants.
	Mastery of skills is important.	Development of expertise is important.	Development of personal and professional self is important.
Roles	Teacher is consumer of knowledge.	Teacher is constructor of knowledge.	Teacher is internalizer of knowledge.
	Principal is an expert.	Principal is a colleague.	Principal is a friend.
Practices	Emphasize technical competence.	Emphasize clinical competence.	Emphasize personal and critical competencies.
	Build individual teacher's skills.	Build professional community.	Build caring community.
	Through training and practice.	Through problem solving and inquiry.	Through reflection and reevaluation.
	By planning and delivering training.	By emphasizing inquiry, problem solving, and research.	By encouraging reflection, conversation, and discourse.

Source: Thomas J. Sergiovanni, *The Principalship: A Reflective Practice Perspective,* 5th ed. Boston, MA. Allyn & Bacon. Copyright © 2005 by Pearson Education. Reprinted by permission of the publisher.

and of changing as individuals. Growth occurs when teachers see themselves, the school, the curriculum, and the students they teach in a new light. The assumptions, roles, and practices associated with in-service training, professional development, and renewal as models of teacher development are summarized in Table 11–1.

Judith Warren Little proposes several principles that she believes should guide the thinking of supervisors as they design professional development opportunities and experiences for teachers. Professional development should

- offer meaningful intellectual, social, and emotional engagement with ideas, with materials, and with colleagues.

- take account of the context of teaching and the experience of other teachers.
- offer support for informed dissent as a means to evaluate alternatives and to scrutinize underlying assumptions for what is being proposed or done.
- place classroom practice in the larger context of purposes and practices of schooling.
- provide teachers with ways they can see and act upon the connections among students' experience, classroom practice, and schoolwide structures and cultures.
- prepare teachers to employ the techniques and perspectives of inquiry in an effort to increase their capacity to generate knowledge and to assess the knowledge claimed by others.[5]

Little offers these principles as alternatives to the one-size-fits-all in-service training models that, when used excessively, provide teachers with shallow and fragmented content and subject them to passive roles as they participate in scripted workshops. In professional development the teacher's capacities, needs, and interests are paramount. Teachers are actively involved in contributing data and information, solving problems, analyzing, and so forth. Supervisors are involved as colleagues. Together, principals and teachers work to develop a common purpose themed to the improvement of teaching and learning. Together, principals and teachers work to build a learning and inquiring community.

Milbrey McLaughlin argues that teachers should be empowered in ways that enable them to exercise more control over their classrooms. More control, in her view, is needed for teachers to make the changes in their practices that are necessary for them to teach more effectively.[6] McLaughlin found that teachers' participation in a professional community of like-minded colleagues had a significant effect on their ability to know better what to do in the classroom and to adapt their teaching strategies to more effectively meet student needs.[7]

G. Lichtenstein, M. McLaughlin, and J. Knudsen found that professional knowledge plays a central role in empowering teachers. They point out that the knowledge that counts in empowering teachers is not the stuff of the weekend workshop or the after-school in-service. The knowledge that counts in empowering teachers is the knowledge of the teaching profession in its broadest sense.[8]

PROFESSIONAL COMMUNITY. The ideal setting for teacher learning and for providing the professional development opportunities which enhance this learning is the school as a professional community. In professional communities, "learning

---

[5]Judith Warren Little, "Teacher's Professional Development in a Climate of Educational Reform," *Educational Evaluation and Policy Analysis,* vol. 15, no. 2 (1993), pp. 129–159.
[6]Milbrey McLaughlin, as cited in A. Bradley, "By Asking Teachers About 'Context' of Work, Center Moves to the Cutting Edge of Research," *Education Week,* March 31, 1993, p. 6.
[7]Milbrey McLaughlin and Joan E. Talbert, *Contexts that Matter for Teaching and Learning,* Stanford, CA: Stanford University, Center for Research as the Context of Secondary School Teaching, 1993, p. 18.
[8]G. Lichtenstein, M. McLaughlin, and J. Knudsen, "Teacher Empowerment and Professional Knowledge," in A. Lieberman (ed.), *The Changing Context of Teaching,* Ninety-First Yearbook of the National Society for the Study of Education. Chicago: University of Chicago Press, 1992.

and teaching depend heavily upon creating, sustaining, and expanding a community of research practice. Members of the community are critically dependent on each other. . . . collaborative learning is not just nice but necessary for survival. This interdependence promotes an atmosphere of joint responsibility, mutual respect, and a sense of personal and group identity."[9] Professional communities

- encourage teachers to reflect on their own practice.
- acknowledge that teachers develop at different rates and at any given time are more ready to learn some things than others.
- acknowledge that teachers have different talents and interests.
- give high priority to conversation and dialogue among teachers.
- provide for collaborative learning among teachers.
- emphasize caring relationships and felt interdependencies.
- call for teachers to respond morally to their work.
- view teachers as supervisors of learning communities in their own classrooms.[10]

These brief summaries suggest that the kind of supervision evolving today is much more focused on teaching and learning, much more central to the classroom, and much more collaborative than in the past.

In sum, the strength of professional communities (or professional learning communities, as they are often called)[11] is their powerful learning intersections. As explained earlier, that is the point where collaborative cultures created from above by supervisors and administrators meet communities of practice that bubble up from teachers below. Both are needed for either to be effective. No matter how hard supervisors try, collaborative cultures too often lead *only* to contrived collegiality. Andy Hargreaves views contrived collegiality as a set of formal procedures that come from above that encourage people to work together.[12] Communities of practice, by contrast, are created when teachers voluntarily share purposes, commit to help each other, and accept a collective responsibility for improving teaching and learning and even the school itself. They come to represent a shared practice. Ordinary groups of teachers function as a collection of individual practices. But without help from above, they, too, soon come to create contrived collegiality. Supervisory supports are not strong enough to encourage and empower a shared practice. As communities of practice depend on the development of collaborative cultures and other supervisory supports, so do collaborative cultures and other supervisory supports depend on a network of communities of practice being established within the

---

[9]A. L. Brown, "The Advancement of Learning," *Educational Researcher,* vol. 23, no. 8 (1994), p. 10.

[10]Thomas J. Sergiovanni, *Leadership for the Schoolhouse,* San Francisco: Jossey-Bass, 1996, p. 142.

[11]See for example, Richard DuFour and Robert E. Eaker, *Best Practices for Enhancing School Achievement,* Bloomington, IN: National Educational Services, 1998. See also Robert Eaker, Richard DuFour, and Rebecca DuFour, *Getting Started: Reculturing Schools to Become Professional Learning Communities,* Bloomington, IN: National Educational Services, 2002; Richard DuFour, *Principal as Staff Developer,* Bloomington, IN: National Educational Services, 1991. These publications are available for ordering at www.nesonline.com/Catalog/ItemList.asp?mode=p.

[12]Andy Hargreaves, *Changing Teachers, Changing Times,* New York: Teachers College Press, 1994.

school. Here is what Stephanie, a teacher at Adlai Stevenson High School in Lincolnshire, Illinois, has to say:

> I began to learn more about Stevenson's culture that summer [after I was hired]. One of the subjects I would be teaching was Advance Placement Psychology, so the AP Psychology team had a few meetings to discuss curriculum and methods of teaching. The unbelievable amount of support and guidance I received over the course of the school year was foreshadowed by the events of the summer. During the summer months and thereafter the other AP Psychology teachers, Laura and Laurie, walked me through how to teach the course on a day-by-day basis.

A key element of the Stevenson culture, as I see it, is the strong relationships between administrators and teachers, teachers with other teachers, and of course teachers with students. The first two types of relationships began over the summer months prior to classes' beginning. The first year of teaching is always going to be marked by challenges, but the added pressure of teaching an Advanced Placement course added another layer. In some ways, I found teaching AP easier than teaching regular [classes] because of all the help I received. Laura and Laurie both helped me master the content along with how to forge positive relationships with students. They were a great support system and helped to keep me grounded at times when I otherwise would have felt very overwhelmed. It is this type of relationship that makes me feel so lucky to be teaching at Stevenson. Stephanie states further: "I could not possibly count all the times I arrived at my desk to find a lesson plan or offers to help me. I think the main way new teachers learn is much more informal, through interactions with other teachers. I learned so much just from watching other teachers in the Social Studies office interact with each other and with their students. By observing other teachers, I was able to see what works for them and see how I can adapt what they do to use in my own classroom."[13]

SOME EVIDENCE

In reviewing the research on teacher learning and teacher effectiveness, Dennis Sparks and Stephanie Hirch of the National Staff Development Council note that effective teacher learning is

- focused on helping teachers become deeply immersed in subject matter and teaching methods;
- curriculum-centered and standards based;
- sustained, rigorous, and cumulative; and
- directly linked to what teachers do in their classrooms.[14]

[13]Thomas J. Sergiovanni, *Strengthening the Heartbeat: Leading and Learning Together in Schools*, San Francisco: Jossey-Bass, 2005, pp. 120–123.

[14]Dennis Sparks and Stephanie Hirch, "Strengthening Professional Development A National Study," *Education Week*, May 24, 2000, p. 45.

They believe that "we cannot expect teachers to use yesterday's training to prepare today's students for tomorrow's future."[15] In an earlier review, Sparks and Susan Loucks-Horsley listed the following as effective practices:

- programs conducted in school settings and linked to schoolwide efforts
- teachers participating as helpers to each other and as planners, with administrators, of in-service activities
- emphasis on self-instruction with differentiated training opportunities
- teachers in active roles, choosing goals and activities for themselves
- emphasis on demonstration, supervised trials, and feedback; training that is concrete and ongoing over time
- ongoing assistance and support available on request.[16]

Beatrice Birman, Laura Desimone, Andrew Porter, and Michael Garet surveyed a national sample of over 1,000 mostly math and science teachers who had participated in the federally funded Eisenhower Professional Development Program.[17] They sought to identify what approaches to professional development are most effective. The researchers identified three structural features that set the context for teacher development and three core features that characterize the processes that occur during a professional development activity. They are as follows:[18]

1. Structural features
   - *Form:* Was, for example, the learning experience designed as a study group, teacher network, mentoring relationship, research project, teacher resource center, peer inquiry, or other collaborative approach? Or was the learning experience designed as a traditional workshop or conference?
   - *Duration:* Was the learning experience designed for teachers to spend more time over a long period, or was the learning experience shorter and more limited in time span?
   - *Participation:* Did groups of teachers from the same school, departments, grade levels, or teams participate together, or did teachers from different schools participate individually?

2. Core features
   - *Content focus:* To what degree did the learning activity focus on deepening teachers' content knowledge in the subjects they teach?
   - *Active learning:* To what extent did teachers have opportunities to be actively involved in the analysis of teaching and learning? Did they, for example, view students work together or observe and discuss teaching together?
   - *Coherence:* To what extent did the learning activities encourage professional community of teachers that was linked to experiences consistent with their goals, school standards, and assessments?

---

[15]Ibid.

[16]Dennis Sparks and Susan Loucks-Horsley, "Five Models of Staff Development for Teachers," *Journal of Staff Development,* vol. 10, no. 4 (Fall 1989), p. 40.

[17]Beatrice Birman, Laura Desimone, Andrew Porter, and Michael Garet, "Designing Professional Development that Works," *Educational Leadership,* vol. 57, no. 8 (May 2000), pp. 28–33.

[18]Ibid., p. 29. See also Beatrice Birman, Laura Desimone, Andrew Porter, and Michael Garet, "Designing Effective Professional Development: Lessons from the Eisenhower Program" at Edpubs@inet.ed.gov.

In studying the dynamics of the three structural features and three core features and assessing their effects on improved classroom teaching, the researchers conclude: "Specifically our research indicates that professional development should focus on deepening teacher *content knowledge* and knowledge of how students learn particular content, on providing opportunities for *active learning,* and on encouraging *coherence* in teachers' professional development experiences. Schools and districts should pursue these goals by using activities that have greater duration and that include *collective participation.* Although reform forms of professional development [i.e. study groups, mentoring, peer inquiry, teacher networks] are more effective than traditional forms [i.e. workshops], the advantages . . . are explained primarily by the greater duration of the activities."[19] Longer activities, the researchers explain, are more likely to be content-focused, to involve active learning, and to contribute to coherence.[20]

Barbara Neufeld and Dana Roper point out that improving teaching in today's world requires changing the ways we have organized professional development and changing the content of professional development so that both better address the new learning needs of teachers. Neufeld and Roper argue that "professional development of the sort needed to help teachers teach for understanding requires both new ideas about what counts as professional development and new policies that provide the framework within which professional development can occur."[21] For professional development to succeed:

- it must be grounded in inquiry, reflection, and experimentation that are participant-driven.
- it must be collaborative, involving a sharing of knowledge among educators and a focus on teachers' communities of practice rather than on individual teachers.
- it must be sustained, ongoing, intensive, and supported by modeling, coaching, and the collective solving of specific problems of practice.
- it must be connected to and derived from teachers' work with their students.
- it must engage teachers in concrete tasks of teaching, assessment, observation, and reflection that illuminate the processes of learning and development.
- it must be connected to other aspects of school change.[22]

A DESIGN FOR PLANNING

When planning for professional development, consider the following questions: What are we trying to accomplish? What will teachers be able to know and do as a result of engaging in professional development? What aspects of good teaching will

---

[19]Ibid, p. 32.

[20]Ibid.

[21]Barbara Neufeld and Dana Roper, "Coaching: A Strategy for Developing Instructional Capacity," Washington, DC: Aspen Institute Program in Education, www.aspeninstitute.org, and Providence, RI: Annenberg Institute for School Reform, June 2003, p. 3 (www.annenberginstitute.org).

[22]Ibid. Neufeld and Roper point out that this list is summarized from Linda Darling-Hammond and Milbrey McLaughlin, "Policies that Support Professional Development in an Era of Reform," Phi Delta Kappan, vol. 76, no. 8 (1995), pp. 597–604.

be the focus of our learning efforts? How can we assess our progress as learners? In what ways can our professional development activities and procedures be improved? How shall we proceed from here? Who will be responsible for what? These are the kinds of questions that can help bring a sense of coherence to the planning process. They represent five important components that constitute a design framework for planning—intents, substance, performance expectations, approach, and responsibility. Let's examine each below.

Intents

Professional development programs and activities are often designed around such intentions as presenting information, helping teachers understand this information, helping teachers use this understanding in their teaching, and helping teachers to accept, and be committed to, these new approaches. *Presenting* information is a *knowledge*-level intent. For example, a program might be designed to introduce a group of science teachers to the concept and language of inquiry teaching. Promoting *understanding* is a *comprehension*-level intent. The intent here might be to help teachers understand how inquiry teaching might affect the way they presently plan and organize instruction. *Using* inquiry methods effectively in teaching a particular biology unit is an example of an *application*-level intent. Although each of these levels is necessary to help teachers learn how to teach in new ways, none is sufficient alone to ensure that they will teach in new ways on a regular basis. Teachers may be able to demonstrate such methods on demand but are not likely to use them once out of the spotlight unless they believe in, and are committed to, such methods. Becoming *committed* to inquiry methods as a useful approach to science teaching is a *value*-level intent. We need to be concerned with all four levels:

Knowledge level—I know it.

Comprehension level—I understand it.

Application level—I can do it.

Value level—I will do it.

Knowing what level to aim for and then focusing on that level are important insights and skills basic to the planning enterprise.

Substance

Louis Rubin has identified four critical factors in good teaching, each of which he believes can be improved through appropriate teacher growth and development activities:

the teacher's sense of purpose

the teacher's perception of students

the teacher's knowledge of subject matter

the teacher's mastery of technique[23]

Sense of purpose and perception of students are part of a teacher's *educational platform* and as such, represent values, beliefs, assumptions, and action theories a teacher holds about the nature of knowledge, how students learn, appropriate relationships between students and teachers, and other factors. We examined educational platforms in supervision in Chapter 5. One's educational platform becomes the basis for decisions one makes about classroom organization and teaching, and, indeed, once a platform is known, key decisions the teacher will make can be predicted with reliability.

A teacher who considers his or her purpose is only to impart information is likely to rely heavily on teacher talk and formal classroom arrangements. Likewise, a teacher who perceives youngsters as being basically trustworthy and responsible is likely to share responsibilities for decisions about learning with the class. If a supervisor were interested in reducing teacher talk and/or increasing student responsibility, he or she would have to contend with the critical factor of purpose and perception of teachers. His or her target is the restructuring of educational platforms of teachers.

In describing the importance of knowledge of subject matter, Rubin notes:

> There is a considerable difference between the kind of teaching that goes on when teachers have an intimate acquaintance with the content of the lesson and when the acquaintance is only peripheral. When teachers are genuinely knowledgeable, when they know their subject well enough to discriminate between the seminal ideas and the secondary matter, when they can go beyond what is in the textbook, the quality of the pedagogy becomes extraordinarily impressive. For it is only when a teacher has a consummate grasp of, say, arithmetic, physics, or history that their meaning can be turned outward and brought to bear upon the learner's personal experience. Relevancy lies less in the inherent nature of a subject than in its relationship to the child's frame of reference. In the hands of a skilled teacher, poetry can be taught with success and profit to ghetto children.[24]

Although content versus process arguments continue from time to time, both aspects of instruction are necessary for effective teaching. Our observation is that the less the teacher knows about a particular subject, the more trivial the teaching and the more defensive the pedagogy. By "defensive pedagogy," we mean dominance by the teacher and strict adherence to curriculum materials. But a teacher can have a great appreciation for a particular field of study and still not be able to communicate its wonder and excitement effectively. Mastery of technique, classroom organization and management, and other pedagogical skills make up the fourth critical dimension of effective teaching. Each of the critical factors in good teaching

[23]Louis J. Rubin, "The Case for Staff Development," in Thomas J. Sergiovanni (ed.), *Professional Supervision for Professional Teachers,* Washington, DC: Association for Supervision and Curriculum Development, 1975.
[24]Ibid., p. 47.

can be understood and developed as technical, clinical, personal, or critical teaching competence. These dimensions are the basis for deciding the substance of staff development programs. A comprehensive program is concerned with all four—the teacher's conception of purpose, sensitivity to students, intimacy with subject matter, and basic repertory of teaching techniques.

Performance Expectations

The major performance expectations for which teachers should be accountable are summarized in Exhibit 11–1. It is reasonable to expect that teachers *know how* to do their jobs and keep up with major developments. But knowing and understanding are not enough. Teachers also are expected to put their knowledge to work—to demonstrate that they *can do* the job. Still, demonstrating knowledge is a fairly low-level competency. Most teachers are competent enough and clever enough to come up with the right teaching performance when the supervisor is around. The proof of the pudding is whether they *will do* the job of their own free will and on a sustained basis. Finally, as professionals, teachers are expected to engage in a lifelong commitment to self-improvement. Self-improvement is the *will-grow* performance expectation. Self-employed professionals (doctors, accountants, and others.) are forced by competition and by visible product evaluation to give major attention to the will-grow dimension. Teachers have not felt this external pressure for continuing professional growth. Increasingly, however, school districts are making the will-grow dimension a contractual obligation, and indeed, teachers who are perfectly satisfactory in the know-how, can-do, and will-do performance expectations face sanctions (including dismissal) for less than satisfactory commitment to continuing professional growth. Further, in this age of standards and high-stakes testing, new pressures to perform at high levels are likely to emerge, encouraging even more attention to continuing professional growth.

- *Know How.* I know how to teach and help students learn. You can find out how much I know by talking with me.
- *I can teach effectively* and am able to get students to learn. You can find out how effectively I can teach by observing my teaching.
- *I will teach effectively,* and I will meet other responsibilities all the time, even when no one is looking. You can find out if I am doing the job consistently by looking at my lesson plans, the assignments I give my students, and the work that they do. You can also do walk-throughs of my classroom to gauge the character and climate of my class, to observe samples of my teaching, and to visit with my students.
- *I will grow* on the job. You can find out if I am continually learning by observing me, asking me to share my ideas with colleagues, and looking for changes in my teaching practice.

Exhibit 11–1. Performance Expectations for Teachers.

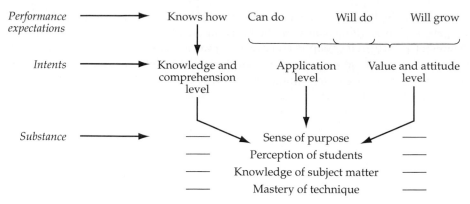

FIGURE 11–1. Building a Design for Teacher Growth and Development.

The relationships between performance expectations, intents, and substance are summarized in Figure 11–1. For example, in the know-how area, teachers are expected to know and understand purposes, students, subject matter, and techniques. In the can-do area, teachers apply this knowledge of substance to their classrooms. Will-do, however, requires not only ability to apply this knowledge but a commitment to its application over time. Teacher growth programs aimed at the will-do dimension must have "value and attitude" as well as application intents. If performance and commitment are to be sustained over time, teachers must see value in what they do and believe it is important to commit themselves. The will-grow dimension is equally dependent upon value and attitude intents. Thus supervisors working with teachers in the will-do and will-grow areas and who choose strategies suited only to knowledge and comprehension are not likely to be successful.

Approach and Responsibility

We have now discussed three of five design components for planning and providing teacher growth and development opportunities: intents, substance, and performance expectations. Two more remain: the *approach* used to provide this development and deciding who is *responsible* for what. These design components for planning professional development will be explored in the remainder of this chapter and in other chapters of Part III.

TRADITIONAL APPROACHES AND SUPERVISORY RESPONSIBILITY. Traditional approaches to staff development were discussed earlier in this chapter. Typically, they involve in-servicing teachers. They seem best suited when a problem can be defined as a deficit in knowledge of some kind. Effective traditional approaches typically are accompanied by clear objectives and rely on conventional, though well-executed, instruction. Teachers generally assume passive roles and are exposed to logically structured programs or activities. Techniques most often used are lecture, illustrated lecture, demonstration, and observation, often followed by guided discussion activities.

Traditional approaches seem well suited to routine information updating of the latest books, techniques, principles, and ideas relating to one's work. It is not assumed that a particular group is considering adopting something new, but that the group is only learning more about it. As intents change from learning to understanding, to applying, to integrating new things into one's repertoire of behavior, approaches will need to change if efforts are to be effective. The widespread use of traditional approaches to the virtual exclusion of other approaches would lead one to conclude that educators have an insatiable appetite for knowledge but are not interested in doing very much with this knowledge.

The locus of responsibility for traditional approaches to teacher growth and development is with the administration as it executes its personnel administration functions. Although traditional approaches have a place and should remain administrative responsibilities, alone they represent a minimum commitment to teacher growth and development.

INFORMAL APPROACHES AND TEACHER RESPONSIBILITY. Perhaps the most innovative and provocative approaches to teacher growth and development are those that rely on exploration and discovery by teachers. It is assumed that by providing teachers with a rich environment loaded with teaching materials, media, books, and devices, and that with generous encouragement and support from principals and supervisors, teachers will interact with this environment and with each other through exploration and discovery. Exploration and discovery can help many teachers find themselves, unleash their creativity, learn more about their own capabilities as people and teachers, and at the same time, pick up new teaching ideas, activities, and methods.

Earlier we noted that professional development is most meaningful to teachers when they are personally involved, have responsibility for setting the agenda, work collaboratively with others, and when learning has immediate consequences for classroom practice.[25] Informal approaches seem best able to meet these criteria, and because of their enormous potential, such approaches should play an important role in school district planning. Major responsibility for informal approaches rests with teachers. They can take a variety of forms: two teachers sharing ideas; a team or family of teachers working and planning together; teacher involvement in an in-building resource center; and participation in district or area teacher centers. Informal approaches should be encouraged and supported.

SHARED APPROACHES AND SHARED RESPONSIBILITY. Informal approaches are low-keyed, classroom-focused, teacher-oriented, and particularistic. Traditional approaches, on the other hand, are high-keyed, more formal, system- or school-oriented, and universal. A supervisory system of teacher growth and development, in contrast, assumes an intermediate position whereby designated supervisors enter into a relationship with teachers on an equal footing and assume an active role along with teachers. The teachers' capacities, needs, and interests are paramount, but

[25]Herbert Thelen, op. cit.

sufficient planning and structure is introduced to bridge the gap between these interests and school program and instruction needs.

Shared staff development approaches usually have the following characteristics:

1. Teachers are actively involved in contributing data, information, or feelings; solving a problem; or conducting an analysis.
2. Supervisors share in the contributing, solving, and conducting activities above as colleagues of the teachers.
3. In colleagueship supervisors and teachers work together as professional associates bound by a common purpose. The common purpose is improvement of teaching and learning through the professional development of both teacher and supervisor.[26] Neither the teacher's autonomy as a professional nor the supervisor's responsibilities as a professional are compromised in the process, since the relationship is based not on bureaucratic or personal authority but on the authority of shared commitments to professional improvement.
4. Staff development activities generally require study of an actual situation or a real problem and use live data, either from self-analysis or from observations of others.
5. Feedback is provided, by supervisors, by other teachers, or as a result of joint analysis, which permits teachers to compare observations with intents and beliefs, and personal reactions with those of others.
6. The emphasis is on direct improvement of teaching and learning in the classroom.

In the next chapter, we focus on clinical supervision and on coaching as ways to help teachers research their practice. Clinical supervision works with either a designated supervisor helping a teacher or with teachers helping each other. Clinical supervision and coaching are good examples of a balanced approach to supervision—informal enough to be responsive to the teachers' needs and interests and formal enough to ensure that agreed-upon standards of good teaching are also given attention. Coaching takes a number of different forms but at its root shares the posture of clinical supervision.

Supervision as professional development and renewal helps define the meaning of being a professional in schools. They embody the belief that learning in schools is not just for students but for everyone. This broad-based approach to learning resembles a system of nested learning communities. According to Lauren Resnick: "In nested learning communities, not only students but also all educational professionals are learners. Teachers, principals, central-office administrators form communities of adult learners who are focusing on improving their practice. . . . Schools

---

[26]Our definition of "colleagueship" follows Morris Cogan, *Clinical Supervision,* Boston: Houghton Mifflin, 1973, chap. 5. In contrast, the relationship between supervisor and teacher in traditional approaches is more clearly superordinate–subordinate, and in informal approaches the supervisor is more of a helper, facilitator, or passive supporter. In the intermediate approach the supervisor is neither dominating nor passive but is involved, side by side, with the teacher as a colleague.

become places where learning is the work of both students and professional educators. . . ."[27] Within these learning communities "ability is seen as an expandable repertoire of skills and habits, professionals are defined as individuals who are continually learning rather than as people who already know. Their roles include both teacher and learner, master and apprentice, and these roles are continually shifting according to context."[28] Supervision as professional development and renewal is an example of an emphasis on teacher learning that embodies the principle *teaching to learn and learning to teach at the same time*—a principle basic to the practice of Supervision II.

SUMMARY

In Chapter 11, we proposed a framework for teacher learning and supervision that allows for three broad strategies: in-service, professional development, and renewal. Though all three have merit, professional development and renewal are more powerful than in-service. Several practices of professional development and renewal are discussed. We also pointed out the importance of the view that teacher learning depends on a network of learning intersections emerging in the school and school district. Learning intersections are occasions when collaborative cultures from above meet communities of practice that emerge from below. A design for planning teacher growth and development was then provided. In Chapter 12, we move on to clinical supervision and coaching—approaches to professional development and renewal that incorporate many of the standards for quality teacher learning and improvement discussed in Chapters 10 and 11. Clinical supervision and coaching involve teachers working together to research their practice.

SOME REFLECTIONS

1. In this chapter we noted that there is a shift in emphasis in supervision from doing things *to* teachers to doing things *with* teachers. To what extent is this shift apparent in your school?
2. Richard DuFour, a well-known scholar–practitioner, has published and practiced widely in the area of professional learning communities. Several publications, written with Robert Eaker and Rebecca DuFour, that can help you understand the basics of developing professional learning communities are referenced in footnote 11 of this chapter. The publications are available for ordering online at www.nesonline.com/Catalog/ItemList.asp?mode=p. Consult DuFour's work carefully, and prepare a brief article for your school district monthly newsletter that summarizes his ideas about professional learning communities and how they work.

---

[27]Lauren B. Resnick and Megan W. Hall, "Learning Organizations for Sustainable Educational Reform," *Daedalus,* vol. 127, no. 4 (Fall 1998), p. 109.
[28]Ibid., p. 110.

CHAPTER 12

Clinical Supervision
and Coaching

INTRODUCTION

The purpose of this chapter is to examine clinical supervision and coaching as strategies for supervision. Both strategies are able to reach deep into the academic life of the classroom while at the same time focusing broadly on the learning needs of teachers and the learning needs of students. Together, the strategies are beginning to write a new script for what instructional leadership must look like if principals and other supervisors aspire to join with teachers to create communities of practice throughout the school. These communities of practice are one way to establish collective responsibility for teacher learning and for improved student achievement.

SOME BACKGROUND

Supervisory leadership is key to successfully traveling the three pathways to student achievement discussed in Chapter 1. This leadership depends upon a practice of supervision that reaches deeply into the culture of schools. This supervision is

- sometimes direct and other times indirect.
- sometimes centered in the classroom and other times centered out of class.
- sometimes focused on issues important to teachers and other times focused on issues important to others.
- sometimes aimed at helping teachers understand and improve their practice and other times aimed at gauging their effectiveness.
- sometimes collaborative and other times individual.

When supervision is direct, centered in the classroom, focused on teachers' issues, aimed primarily at helping teachers understand and improve their teaching, and collaborative, the term *clinical supervision* is often used. Experts agree that clinical supervision in a variety of forms has potential to accelerate the rates of learning for teachers and to significantly improve teaching and learning in our schools.[1] Still, we have a long way to go in realizing this potential. Clinical supervision is time-consuming and takes a lot of effort to do well under our current bureaucratic patterns of schooling. But supervisors and teachers who are serious about improving schools will find clinical supervision to be a powerful and appealing strategy worth the extra effort. Much will depend upon whether principals and other designated supervisors will invest in helping teachers assume more responsibility for supervising themselves than is now the case. Teachers learning together within communities of practice should be our goal.

In recent years school-based staff development has gained an important beachhead as a supervisory strategy. Like clinical supervision, it too reaches deep into the classrooms of teachers, helping them improve. Those who provide this site-based staff development are often called mentors, coaches, instructional coordinators, and lead teachers. Increasingly, site-based supervision is becoming classroom-based supervision.[2]

In this chapter we will use the term *coaches* to describe these in-class and in-school supervisors. Coaches and coaching are very important because they can provide teachers with needed support at the school site and in the classroom virtually every day. The use of coaches is based upon the belief that the line between teachers teaching and teachers improving their teaching needs to disappear.

- Today's teachers must teach and learn to teach at the same time.
- Teacher learning is not just an event, nor is teacher learning just a process. Teacher learning is a norm, too, a natural part of one's everyday teaching practice.

This stance puts teaching on a par with medicine and other more established professions—professions where practicing and learning how to practice better routinely go on at the same time. In the next section, we examine the first of our strategies, clinical supervision, in more detail.

Some may wonder about the use of the word *supervision* in education. For many, it has industrial overtones and implies some form of inspection, or "snoopervision." Since this is a chapter about coaching too, why not use the label "clinical coaching" instead? Abandoning the language of supervision, however, would mean abandoning an important part of education's library of ideas that developed over most of the 20th century. Many argue that supervision is an industrial import that features a hierarchical model of leadership in schools. But Edward Pajak,[3] a

---

[1] See for example, Carl Glickman, Stephen Gordon, and Jovita Ross-Gordon, *Supervision of Instruction,* 4th ed., Boston: Allyn & Bacon, 1998, p. 297.

[2] See, for example, Hayes Mizell, "Pioneers for Professional Learning," Remarks given at the initial meeting of the School-Based Staff Development Learning Community sponsored by the National Staff Development Council, Dallas, August 5, 2004. Information about the School-Based Staff Development Learning Community, including Hayes Mizell's remarks, can be accessed at www.psdc.org/connect/projects/schoolbased.cfm.

[3] Edward Pajak, *Honoring Diverse Teaching Styles: A Guide for Supervisors,* Alexandria, VA: Association for Supervision and Curriculum Development, 2003.

respected scholar in supervision with a historical bent, thinks otherwise. In his words:

> Some educators are reluctant to use the word "supervision," because they incorrectly associate it with a hierarchical relationship rooted in an industrial model of schooling. On the contrary, Edward C. Elliott, an early 20th-century educator, described supervision in schools as being closely related to "the democratic motive of American education."[4] He clearly distinguished "centralization of administrative power," which he said stifled creativity and individuality in school, from "*decentralized, cooperative, expert, supervision.*"[5] By the 1920s no fewer than five textbooks emphasized democracy as a guiding principle of supervision in education.[6]

Pajak notes that Raymond Callahan, an expert on the influence of industrial ideas in education, gives supervision a clean bill of health: "Callahan also explained that supervision distinguished itself from both administration and industrial logic in the 1930s by aligning itself with the process of curriculum development and a 'new organization, the Association for Supervision and Curriculum Development.'[7] It is in this traditional democratic spirit of supervision in education and its long-standing respect for creativity, cooperation, decentralization, and individual difference that this book is written."[8]

THE FOCUS OF CLINICAL SUPERVISION

Clinical supervision is a form of coaching. At times the clinical supervision coach may be the principal or other designated supervisor. At other times the clinical supervision coach may be the teacher across the hall or another peer. Sometimes only two people are involved. At other times several people are involved.

Morris Cogan cites two purposes of clinical supervision: "The first is to develop and explicate a system of in-class supervision that, in competent hands, will prove powerful enough to give supervisors a reasonable hope of accomplishing significant improvements in the teacher's classroom instruction. The second purpose is to help correct the neglect of in-class or clinical supervision and to establish it as a necessary complement to out-of-class ('general') supervision."[9]

---

[4]E. C. Elliott, *City School Supervision,* New York: World Books, 1914, p. 2, cited in Pajak, op. cit., p. 4.

[5]Elliott, op. cit., p. 78, cited in Pajak, op. cit., p. 4.

[6]See also F. C. Ayer and A. S. Barr, *The Organization of Supervision: An Analysis of the Organization and Administration of Supervision in City School Systems,* New York: Appleton, 1928; A. S. Barr and W. H. Burton, *The Supervision of Instruction,* New York: Appleton-Century, 1926; W. H. Burton, *Supervision and the Improvement of Teaching,* New York: Appleton-Century, 1927; J. E. Hosic, "The Democratization of Supervision," *School and Society,* vol 11. (1920), pp. 331–336; and C. R. Stone, *Supervision of the Elementary School,* Boston: Houghton Mifflin, 1929. Quote from Pajak, op. cit, p. 4.

[7]R. E. Callahan and H. W. Button, "Historical Change of the Role of the Man in the Organization: 1865–1950," in D. E. Griffiths (ed.), *Behavioral Science and Educational Administration,* Sixty-third Yearbook of the National Society for the Study of Education, Part II, Chicago: University of Chicago Press, 1964, cited in Pajak, op. cit., p. 5.

[8]Pajak, op. cit., p. 5.

[9]Morris L. Cogan, *Clinical Supervision,* Boston: Houghton Mifflin, 1973, p. xi.

In a similar vein, Robert Goldhammer refers to clinical supervision as follows:

First of all, I mean to convey an image of face-to-face relationships between supervisors and teachers. History provides the principal reason for this emphasis, namely, that in many situations presently and during various periods in its development, supervision has been conducted as supervision from a distance, as, for example, supervision of curriculum development or of instructional policies framed by committees of teachers. "Clinical" supervision is meant to imply supervision up close.[10]

General and clinical supervision are, of course, interdependent. Meaningful classroom interventions are built upon healthy organizational climates, facilitated by credible leadership, and premised on a reasoned educational program. Although general supervision is an important and necessary component of effective supervision, without clinical supervision and other forms of coachings, it is not sufficient.

Clinical supervision refers to face-to-face contact with teachers with the intent of improving instruction and increasing professional growth. In many respects, a one-to-one correspondence exists between improving classroom instruction and increasing professional growth, and for this reason, staff development and clinical supervision are inseparable concepts and activities. How does evaluation fit into this picture? Evaluation fits as a natural part of one's professional life and occurs continually. Every decision that teachers, administrators, and supervisors make is preceded by evaluation (often implicit) of some sort. Evaluation is valuing, and valuing is judging. These are natural events in the lives of educational professionals and, of course, are critical aspects of clinical supervision and other forms of staff development. In short, clinical supervision is a way in which teachers can collaborate to research their practice and improve their learning and their teaching. This researching of one's practice naturally involves evaluation. Clinical supervision, however, does not lend itself very well to summative evaluation.

SUPERVISORY PURPOSES

Before continuing with our discussion of clinical supervision, let's examine the various purposes of evaluation. This brief departure can help us understand that while clinical supervision and evaluation are inevitably mixed, not all kinds of evaluation threaten the kinds of relationships among teachers and between teachers and supervisors that are needed for clinical supervision to work well.

Evaluation can have a number of focuses, some of which are more compatible with events, purposes, and characteristics of supervision than others. Evaluation experts, for example, make an important distinction between *formative* and *summative* evaluation.[11] Teacher-evaluation procedures typically found in school can be

---

[10]Robert Goldhammer, *Clinical Supervision: Special Methods for the Supervision of Teachers,* New York: Holt, 1969, p. 54.
[11]Michael Scriven, "The Methodology of Evaluation," in Robert Stake (ed.), *AERA Monograph on Curriculum Evaluation,* no. 1, Chicago: Rand McNally, 1965. See also Benjamin Bloom, Thomas Hastings, and G. F. Madaus, *Handbook on Formative and Summative Evaluation of Student Learning,* New York: McGraw-Hill, 1971.

classified as summative. Evaluation that emphasizes ongoing growth and development would be considered formative. Consider the following distinctions:

1. Summative evaluation of teachers has a certain finality to it—it is terminal in the sense that it occurs at the conclusion of an educational activity. Summative evaluation of a teacher's performance suggests a statement of worth. A judgment is made about the quality of one's teaching.
2. Summative evaluation is a legitimate and important activity that, if done carefully, can play a constructive role in a school's total evaluation strategy.
3. Formative evaluation of teachers is intended to increase the effectiveness of ongoing educational programs and activity. Evaluation information is collected and used to understand, correct, and improve ongoing activity.
4. With respect to teaching, formative evaluation is concerned less with judging and rating the teacher than with providing information which helps teachers learn more about their disciplines, about how students learn, and about teaching.
5. In the strictest sense, formative and summative evaluation cannot be separated, for each contains aspects of the other. It is useful nevertheless to speak of a formative focus and a summative focus to evaluation.[12]

The focus of clinical supervision should be on formative evaluation. The supervisor is interested first and foremost in improving teaching and increasing teachers' personal development. Does this emphasis conflict with demands that teachers be held accountable for their actions? We think not. A formative evaluation emphasis is consistent with holding teachers accountable in a professional but not bureaucratic sense. Professional accountability is growth-oriented and implies a commitment to consistent improvement. Bureaucratic accountability may not be growth-oriented at all, as it seeks to ensure that teachers measure up to a predetermined one-best-way to do things.

From time to time supervisors will indeed be engaged in a more summatively focused evaluation. Though the supervisor's major commitment is to formative evaluation, occasional problems occur and incompetent teachers or teachers whose philosophy and orientation differ markedly from that of the school will be discovered. As a result, withholding tenure or dismissal of a tenured teacher may well be considered. Personnel actions of this sort are so intertwined with existing local administrative policies and state statutory restrictions and requirements that a totally different mind-set is needed. Such a procedure is best placed in the hands of a line administrative officer of the district. In the case of a principal who assumes both supervisory and administrative roles, the teacher should be informed of the focus and the tone of the evaluation procedure that is to follow. The school attorney would most likely be consulted regarding due process if administrative guidelines on this question are wanting. In many school districts the teachers' union is involved in the process, working cooperatively with "management" to ensure due process on the

---

[12]Thomas J. Sergiovanni, *Handbook for Effective Department Leadership Concepts and Practices in Today's Secondary Schools,* Boston: Allyn & Bacon, 1977, p. 372.

one hand and *warranted* dismissal on the other. Many state education agencies and state school board associations publish pamphlets and other guidelines on this controversial and increasingly legalistic problem. Summative evaluation is the theme of Chapter 14.

Practically speaking, improving classroom instruction must start with the teacher. Sustained changes in teacher behavior and sustained improvements in classroom functioning occur when teachers are committed to these changes. That being the case, supervisors are forced to depend upon the cooperation of teachers. Indeed, supervisors rarely change teachers but help them change, a process more suited to formative evaluation.

DIFFERENT PURPOSES, DIFFERENT STANDARDS

Different teacher-evaluation purposes require different teacher-evaluation standards, criteria, and practices. When the purpose is quality control to ensure that teachers measure up, standards, criteria, expectations, and procedures should take one form. When the purpose is professional improvement to help increase teachers' understanding and enhance teaching practice, standards, criteria, expectations, and procedures should take a different form.

In an evaluation for quality control, the process should be formal and documented; criteria should be explicit and standards should be uniform for all teachers; criteria should be legally defensible as being central to basic teaching competence; the emphasis should be on teachers, meeting requirements of minimum acceptability; and responsibility for evaluation should be in the hands of administrators and other designated officials. When the purpose of teacher evaluation is professional improvement, the process should be informal; criteria should be tailored to the needs and capabilities of individual teachers; criteria should be considered appropriate and useful to teachers before they are included in the evaluation; the emphasis should be on helping teachers reach agreed-upon professional development goals; and teachers should assume major responsibility for the process by engaging in self-evaluation and peer evaluation, and by obtaining evaluation information from students.

The outcome of evaluation for quality control should be the protection of students and the public from incompetent teaching. Unquestionably this is an important outcome and a highly significant responsibility for principals and other supervisors, as well as teachers. The outcome of evaluation for professional improvement is quite different. Rather than ensuring minimum acceptability in teaching, professional improvement seeks to guarantee quality teaching and schooling for the students and the public.

- The 80/20 quality rule spells out quite clearly what the balance of emphasis should be as schools, school districts, and states engage in teacher evaluation. *When more than 20 percent of supervisory time and money is expended in evaluation for quality control or less than 80 percent of supervisory time and*

TABLE 12–1. Different Purposes, Different Standards for Evaluation.

Purposes	
Quality control (ensuring that teachers meet acceptable levels of performance)	Professional improvement (increasing understanding of teaching and enhancing practice)

Standards	
The process is formal and documented.	The process is informal.
Criteria are explicit, standard, and uniform for all teachers.	Criteria are tailored to needs and capabilities of individual teachers or teaching teams.
Criteria are legally defensible as being central to basic teaching competence.	Criteria are considered appropriate and useful to teachers.
Emphasis is on meeting minimum requirements of acceptability.	Emphasis is on helping teachers reach agreed-upon professional development goals.
Evaluation by administrators and other designated officials counts the most.	Self-evaluation, collegial evaluation, and evaluation information from students count the most.

Outcome	
Protects students and the public from incompetent teaching.	Guarantees quality teaching and schooling for students and the public.

The 80/20 Quality Rule: When more than 20 percent of supervisory time and money is expended in evaluation for quality control *or* less than 80 percent of supervisory time and money is expended in professional improvement, quality schooling suffers.

money is spent in professional improvement, quality schooling suffers. The 80/20 quality rule provides a framework for those responsible for evaluation of teachers to evaluate whether their efforts are indeed directed toward quality schooling. In such an assessment, less attention should be given to the rhetoric (what those responsible for teacher evaluation say their purposes are) and more to the standards and procedures that are used. The standards and procedures associated with each of the two purposes of evaluation are outlined in Table 12–1. For example, if the standards in the left-hand column are emphasized, quality control is the purpose of the evaluation regardless of what is said about the purposes.

CLINICAL SUPERVISION IN PRACTICE

Clinical supervision can take many forms, but it invariably involves an in-depth examination and careful study of selected teaching issues, the collection of data that helps the teacher understand these issues, and the development of improved practice. The essential ingredients of clinical supervision include the establishment of a healthy general supervisory climate, a mutual support system called "colleagueship," and often a cycle of supervision comprising conferences, observation of teachers at work, and pattern analysis. In clinical supervision it is assumed that

- the curriculum is what teachers do day by day;
- changes in curriculum and teaching formats require changes in how teachers think about and understand their teaching and how they behave in classrooms;
- supervision is a process for which both supervisors and teachers are responsible;
- the focus of supervision is on teacher strengths;
- given the right conditions, teachers are willing and able to improve;
- teachers have large reservoirs of talent, often unused; and
- teachers derive satisfaction from challenging work.

Clinical supervision is a partnership in inquiry. The person assuming the role of supervisor is often a fellow teacher. Sometimes this teacher is designated as a mentor and sometimes there is no formal designation—just a colleague helping a colleague. An important purpose of clinical supervision is to help teachers modify existing patterns of teaching in ways that make sense to them and in ways that support agreed-upon content or teaching standards. It is the teacher who typically decides the course of clinical supervision, the issues to be discussed, and for what purpose. Obviously, those principals, department chairs, staff developers, and mentor teachers who serve as clinical supervisors will bring to this interaction a considerable amount of influence; but, ideally, this influence should stem from their being in a position to provide the help and clarification needed by teachers. The supervisor's job, therefore, is to help the teacher select goals to be improved and teaching issues to be illuminated, and to understand better his or her practice. This emphasis on understanding provides the avenue by which more technical assistance can be given to the teacher; thus, clinical supervision involves the systematic analysis of classroom events, teaching behaviors, samples of student work, and other data sources that help illuminate the teaching and learning issues under study. As we discussed in Chapter 10, standards frameworks can play a key role in clinical supervision. They help identify possible issues to study and help anchor those issues into a larger picture of effective teaching.

THE CYCLE OF CLINICAL SUPERVISION

In a few pages we are not able to provide all the techniques associated with clinical supervision. The intent here is to describe the cycle of supervision, to provide some basic principles and concepts underlying clinical supervisory practice, and to suggest some techniques and tools that supervisors might find useful as they begin to develop competencies as clinical supervisors.[13] While there are no rigid rules and

---

[13]Congan, op. cit.

clinical supervision can take many forms, typically, the clinical supervision cycle includes five general steps or stages, as follows:[14]

1. preobservation conference
2. observation of teaching and collection of other material or artifacts of teaching and learning that might be helpful
3. analysis and strategy
4. postobservation conference
5. postconference analysis

PREOBSERVATION CONFERENCE. No stage is more important than the preobservation conference. It is here that the framework for observations and for other data-collection strategies is developed and an agreement is reached between the person who is "supervising" and the person who is teaching. Sometimes the principal is in the role of supervisor; at other times peer teachers, staff development specialists, coaches, or others are in the role of supervisor. After a brief warm-up period, the supervisor needs to become familiar with the class and with the teacher's way of thinking about teaching. How does the teacher view this class? What are the qualities and characteristics of this class? What frames of reference regarding purposes, models of teaching, classroom management, and so forth does the teacher bring to teaching? Getting into the teacher's corner and understanding the class from her or his perspective should help the supervisor understand what the teacher has in mind for the particular teaching sequence that will be observed. Knowing how the particular lesson in question fits into the teacher's broader framework of purposes and broader view of teaching is also essential to providing the supervisor with a perspective beyond the particular lesson at hand.

The supervisor is now ready to engage the teacher in a mental or conceptual *rehearsal* of the lesson. The teacher provides an overview of her or his intents, outcomes not formally anticipated but likely or possible, and problems likely to be encountered. An overview of how teaching will unfold, what the teacher and students will be doing, and anticipated responses from students should also be provided. The supervisor might wish to raise questions for clarification and, depending on the relationship existing between supervisor and teacher, to make suggestions for improving the lesson before it unfolds.

Typically, this conceptual rehearsal by the teacher identifies an array of teaching issues of interest. Clinical supervision is *selective* in the sense that an intense and detailed study is made of only a handful of issues at a time. Thus, supervisor and teacher must decide what aspects of teaching will be considered, with the teacher assuming major responsibility for setting the supervisory agenda. What would the teacher like to know about this class and the teaching that will take place? Teachers inexperienced with clinical supervision may have initial difficulty in

---

[14]This discussion of the cycle of clinical supervision follows closely Thomas J. Sergiovanni, *The Principalship: A Reflective Practice Perspective*, 5th ed., Boston: Allyn and Bacon, 2006, pp. 294–299. That discussion is similar to the treatment of clinical supervision that appears in each of the first seven editions of this book.

suggesting agenda items, but careful prodding and guiding by the supervisor usually helps elicit meaningful issues that become the basis for a particular cycle of supervision. This phase of the conference concludes with the teacher and supervisor reaching a fairly explicit agreement, or contract, about the reasons for supervision, along with the teaching and learning agendas to be studied. The contract might contain, as well, some indication of the information to be collected, how this information will be collected, what the supervisor will be doing, and what the supervisor should not do. Clinical supervision advocates feel that as the process of supervision unfolds, the teacher should have a picture of events to occur that is as complete as possible.

OBSERVATION OF TEACHING The second stage in a clinical supervision cycle—and basic to it—is the actual and systematic observation of teaching. Attention is given to the teacher *in action* and to the classroom story unfolding as a result of this action. Clinical supervision purists would argue that "canned" or standardized devices, or scales for ratings of general teaching characteristics, may well be useful but in themselves are not sufficient; when used, they should stem from, and be related to, the actual observation of teaching and learning at issue. It is what the teacher actually says and does, how students react, and what actually occurs during a specific teaching episode under study that remain the center of evaluation to advocates of clinical supervision. Student interviews, collections of classroom artifacts, development of evaluation portfolios, bulletin board and classroom arrangements, photo essays, inventories of lessons accomplished or books read by children, and other evaluative data-collection strategies should supplement and illuminate this actual teaching.

The teacher will know what to expect because of the preobservation conference. He or she should understand that the supervisor wishes to make an unobtrusive entrance and to remain as unobtrusive as possible. During the observation, the clinical supervisor may take copious notes, attempting to record all classroom events. Notes should be descriptive—that is, free from inferences; for example, the supervisor would avoid writing "during the questioning of students on the use of microscopes by criminologists, the students were bored" in favor of something such as, "both John and Mary did not hear the question when it was asked" and "two students were looking out the window; a third was playing with materials in his desk during the microscope questioning time." Sometimes the information collected is focused on a particular issue, such as cognitive level of questions, attention spans of children, time on task, or cooperative relationships among students. Then, instead of attempting to record everything that takes place during the lesson, the supervisor might record and rate each question asked on, for example, the Bloom Taxonomy of Educational Objectives[15] or collect similar, more detailed information. Many

---

[15]Benjamin S. Bloom (ed.), *Taxonomy of Educational Objectives: The Classification of Educational Goals, Handbook 1: Cognitive Domain,* New York: McKay, 1956. The taxonomy may be accessed at www.coun.uvic.ca/learn/program/hndouts/bloom.html and www.utexas.edu/academic/diia/gsi/tatalk/bloomstax.pdf.

clinical supervision purists insist on a written transcript of the collection of firsthand data by the supervisor, and many supervisors using clinical methods have been successful by using television and videotaping equipment or by using audiotaping equipment to record actual teaching.

principal does

ANALYSIS AND STRATEGY. The third step in the cycle of clinical supervision is the analysis of teaching and the building of a supervisory strategy. The analysis stage requires that the supervisor convert the raw data or information collected from the observation into a manageable, meaningful, and sensible form. Clinical supervision advocates recommend that the analysis yield significant teaching patterns and that critical incidents be identified for use in the supervisory conference. Of paramount importance is the contract initially struck with the teacher. What was the purpose of the observation? How did the information collected illuminate this purpose? Can the supervisor arrange this information in a fashion that communicates clearly to the teacher the feedback she or he seeks but at the same time does not prejudge the teaching? This process identifies teaching patterns: recurring teacher verbal and nonverbal behaviors discovered in the course of teaching. Critical incidents are those occurrences that have a particularly noticeable positive or negative effect on the teaching and learning.

Having organized the information, the supervisor now gives attention to building a strategy for working with the teacher. The supervisor takes into account the nature of the contract originally struck, the evaluation issues uncovered during the observation and analysis, the quality of interpersonal relationships existing between teacher and supervisor, the authority base from which she or he is operating, and the competency or experience level of the teacher in deciding on this strategy.

POSTOBSERVATION CONFERENCE. The fourth stage in the cycle of clinical supervision is the supervisory conference. The supervisor uses the specific information gathered to help the teacher analyze the lesson. Typically, this postobservation conference focuses on a handful of issues previously agreed on by the teacher and the supervisor. It is appropriate as well for the supervisor to introduce new issues as circumstances warrant, but these issues should be few and cautiously introduced. The emphasis remains on providing information to the teacher for fulfilling the contract that was the basis for the observation cycle. Furthermore, the emphasis is not on providing evaluative information but on providing *descriptive* information. The process of making sense of this information is a joint one shared by teacher and supervisor.

Let's assume that the most important issue identified and agreed to in the preconference is level of cognitive questioning used by the teacher and cognitive level of assignments given to the students. The teacher uses objectives that span all six levels of the Bloom Taxonomy of Educational Objectives but wishes to emphasize the higher-level objectives of analysis and synthesis. Perhaps this teacher is not confident that actual teaching emphasizes these levels; or perhaps the supervisor, suspecting that teaching is not matching teacher intents, suggests that the level of cognitive questioning be examined. In either event, teacher and supervisor agree to use an inventory that enables the sorting of questions asked into the Bloom categories: remembering, understanding, solving, analyzing, creating, and judging. During the observation of teaching, each question asked by the teacher is classified into an appropriate level. A transcript of actual questions asked could be prepared. During the analysis and strategy stage of the supervisory cycle, the supervisor tallies questions and computes percentages.

The supervisor then decides on a strategy whereby the teacher is asked to restate her or his purposes for the lesson as well as for the unit of which the lesson is a part. The information on cognitive level of questioning is then presented and compared with the teacher's intents. The supervisor is careful to avoid drawing conclusions or to elaborate on possible discrepancies, considering these conclusions to be the responsibility of the teacher. The teacher and supervisor might decide that it would be helpful to collect homework assignments given for other lessons in this particular teaching unit as well as to examine questions on tests that have been used. These assignments and test questions could also be categorized into the cognitive level of questioning format. Throughout the process, the supervisor's role is not to condemn, cajole, or admonish, but to provide information useful to the teacher and to do so in a supportive atmosphere.

POSTCONFERENCE ANALYSIS. The fifth and final stage in a cycle of clinical supervision is the postconference analysis. The postconference phase is a natural springboard to staff development for both teacher and supervisor. The supervisor evaluates what happened in the supervisory conference and throughout the supervisory cycle for purposes of improving her or his own efforts. Was the integrity of the teacher protected? Did the teacher participate in the process as a co-supervisor? Was feedback given in response to the teacher's needs and desires? Was the emphasis more on teaching and the improvement of teaching than on the teacher and evaluating the teacher? What can the supervisor do to improve her or his skills in clinical supervision? A typical outcome of the first four phases of clinical supervision is agreement on the kinds of issues to be pursued next as further cycles are undertaken. The postconference analysis is, therefore, both the end of one cycle and the beginning of another.

A SHORTCUT STRATEGY FOR CLINICAL SUPERVISION

More often than not, logistical issues, schedules, and other real-world demands will make it difficult to follow all the steps outlined above. If you are pressed, try the shortcut strategy outlined in Exhibit 12–1.

Sometimes clinical supervision works best when teachers get together in teams. If, for example, three teachers are involved, this configuration allows teacher A to be helped by teachers B and C and then to rotate so that B is helped by A and C and finally, C is helped by A and B. The clinical supervision checklist found in Exhibit 12–2 will be helpful in guiding this enlarged version of clinical supervision. Notice it is important that the teacher being helped be involved in identifying the issue and in

1. *Preconference.* Identify the issue to be investigated. Develop a strategy for collecting data and other sources of information.

2. *Collect information.* Observe teaching and collect other sources of information that may be important. Put this information into a form that the teacher will easily understand.

3. *Postconference.* Share your findings. Help the teacher make sense of them.

Exhibit 12–1. Clinical Supervision Shortcut Strategy

Issue Orientation

a. Did you identify a single issue or theme as a focus for your inquiry?

Collaboration

b. Did you *together* develop a strategy for how this issue or theme might be researched?

Strategy

c. Was this strategy specific enough to detail both the kind of information (or data) that would be collected and the data-collection means?

Critical Friend

d. Did you present the information as primarily "brute" data, with a minimum of evaluative comments?

Self-Evaluation

e. Did you help the teacher make sense of this data (going from brute to "sense" data) and draw conclusions relating to the issue or theme that was the focus of the inquiry in the first place?

Communities of Practice

f. Before you began this process of clinical supervision, and after you completed this process did you share your plans with other members of your team?

Exhibit 12–2. Team Evaluation Checklist for Clinical Supervision

helping develop the strategy for supervision. This person also plays the key role in trying to make sense of the data and other information that is collected.

It appears as though the clinical supervision cycle describes the process that many supervisors have been using all along. But a quick review of the assumptions, particularly the concept of teacher as *co-supervisor,* suggests that the resemblance may be superficial. The supervisor works at two levels with teachers during the cycle: helping them understand and improve their professional practice and helping them learn more about the skills of classroom analysis needed in supervision. Furthermore, while traditional classroom observation tends to be sporadic and requires little time investment, clinical supervision asks that supervisors give two to three hours a week to each teacher. Principals who want to be involved as clinical supervisors can better manage their time by working with only part of the faculty at a time—perhaps one-third for three months in rotation. As teachers themselves become competent in clinical supervision and assume increased responsibility for all phases, they should participate in clinical supervision as a form of *peer supervision.* Indeed, for clinical supervision and its hybrids that emphasize other forms of shared and serious inquiry into teaching to become widespread, teachers will have to become key players by engaging in peer supervision. No hard-and-fast rules exist that exclude teachers from assuming roles as clinical supervisors. Peer supervision and clinical supervision are quite compatible. When teachers are clinical supervisors, principals stay involved by helping them, finding time for them to help each other, arranging schedules to allow them to work together, and participating in conversations about "what is going on, how effective is it, and what do we do now?" The reality is that success over the long haul requires that teachers and administrators take collective responsibility for clinical supervision. Working together in this way must become an important norm that helps define the school as a learning community.

EDUCATIONAL PLATFORM

In Chapter 5 we addressed the topic of educational platforms and how they influence what teachers and supervisors think, believe, and do about teaching and learning. Educational platforms play important roles in clinical supervision.

Most supervisors and teachers know that teaching is not nearly as objective and explicit as one might think. Indeed, teachers, supervisors, and others bring to the classroom a variety of agendas, some public, many hidden, and probably most unknown, each of which influences the decisions they make. The agendas tend to fall into three major categories: what one believes is possible, what one believes is true, and what one believes is desirable. Together the three are the essential ingredients of one's *educational platform.*[16] A platform implies something that supports one's action and by which one justifies or validates one's own actions. An approximate analogy would be that of a political platform. This platform states the basic values, critical policy statements, and key positions of an individual or group. Once known, the political platform can be used to predict responses that a politician or political party is likely to make to questions on various campaign issues.

Assumptions, Theories, and Beliefs

Within supervision, the components of one's educational platform are assumptions, theories, and beliefs. Assumptions that teachers hold help answer the question, what is possible? Assumptions are composed of one's beliefs, the concepts one takes for

---

[16]Decker Walker, "A Naturalistic Model for Curriculum Development," *School Review,* vol. 80, no. 1 (1971), pp. 51–65. See also our previous discussion in Chapter 5.

granted, and the ideas one accepts without question about schools, classrooms, students, teaching, learning, and knowledge. They help the teacher define what classrooms are actually like and what is possible to accomplish within them. They also are important to the decisions that teachers make, because they set the boundaries for what information will or will not be considered and for other possibilities and actions at the onset of instruction.

Theories help answer the question, What is true? They are beliefs about relationships between and among assumptions one considers true. Theories form the basis for developing teaching strategies and patterns of classroom organizations.

Beliefs about what is desirable in classrooms are derived from assumptions and theories that one holds regarding knowledge, learning, classrooms, and students. What is desirable is expressed in the form of intents, aims, objectives, or purposes.

Consider, for example, a teacher whose educational platform includes the assumptions that "little or no knowledge exists that is essential for everyone to learn" and "youngsters can be trusted to make important decisions." The two assumptions might lead to the theory that "students who are allowed to influence classroom decisions will make wise choices and will become more committed learners." That being the case, a corresponding aim for that teacher might be "to involve students in shared decision making," or perhaps "to have students interact with subject matter in a manner that emphasizes its concepts and structure rather than just its information."

Contrast this with a teacher whose educational platform includes the assumption that "the only justifiable evidence of good teaching is student acquisition of subject matter as specified by the teacher or as measured by the test" and the assumption that "motivation of students should reflect the realities of the world outside the school, where good behavior and performance are publicly rewarded and poor behavior and performance are publicly punished." The two assumptions might well lead to the theory that "students need to be motivated, on the one hand, and disciplined, on the other, to get the behavior and performance that leads to acquiring the most subject matter in the least amount of time." In this case, a corresponding aim might be "to provide rewards and privileges to students who behave and perform to the teacher's expectations and punishment to those who do not."

Many teachers have platforms that are somewhere in between. Still, educational platforms are powerful determinants of the nature and quality of life in classrooms.

Known and Unknown Platform Dimensions

Teachers tend to be unaware of their assumptions, theories, or objectives. Sometimes they adopt components of a platform that seem right, that have the ring of fashionable rhetoric, or that coincide with the expectation of important others, such as teachers whom they admire, or of groups with which they wish to affiliate. Although teachers may overtly adopt aspects of educational platforms in this manner, they are often likely to hang on to contradictory assumptions, beliefs, and theories. Publicly they may say one thing and assume that their classroom behavior is governed by this statement, but privately, or even unknowingly, they may believe something else that actually governs their classroom behavior. Indeed, teachers are not aware that often their classroom decisions and behavior contradict their espoused platform.

THEORIES GOVERNING TEACHER BEHAVIOR

The clinical supervisor needs to be concerned with two theories that the teacher brings to the classroom—an *espoused theory* and a *theory in use*. As Chris Argyris and Donald Schön suggest:

> When someone is asked how he would behave under certain circumstances, the answer he usually gives is his espoused theory of action for that situation. This is the theory of action to which he gives allegiance, and which, upon request, he communicates to others. However, the theory that actually governs his action is his theory in use. This theory may or may not be compatible with his espoused theory; furthermore, the individual may or may not be aware of the incompatibility of the two theories.[17]

When one's espoused theory matches one's theory in use, the theories are considered congruent. Congruence exists, for example, for the teacher who believes that effort by students is more important than ability in learning, and whose teaching behavior and artifacts of that behavior confirm this espoused theory. Lack of congruence between a person's espoused theory and the theory in use, *when known,* proposes a dilemma to that individual. A second teacher, for example, shares the same espoused theory regarding effort, but his or her pattern of questioning, use of negative feedback, use of the bell curve, and insistence on tracking may reveal a theory in use incongruent with the espoused theory. The social studies teacher who believes in and teaches a course in American democracy in a "totalitarian" manner represents another example of incongruency between espoused theory and theory in use.

THE JOHARI WINDOW

A useful way to understand how known and unknown platform dimensions of teachers fit into clinical supervision is by examining the *Johari window* as it relates to espoused theories and theories in use.[18] This relationship is illustrated in Figure 12–1.

The Johari window in this case depicts the relationship between two parties, teacher and supervisor. The relationship revolves around aspects of the teacher's educational platform known to self and others, known to self but not others, not known to self but known to others, and not known to self or others. Four cells are

---

[17]Chris Argyris and Donald A. Schön, *Theory in Practice: Increasing Professional Effectiveness,* San Francisco: Jossey-Bass, 1974, p. 7.
[18]Joseph Luft, *Of Human Interaction,* New York: National Press Books, 1969. The Johari window was developed by Joseph Luft and Harry Ingham and gets its name from the first names of its authors.

	What the supervisor knows about the teacher	What the supervisor does not know about the teacher
What the teacher knows about himself or herself	Public or open self 1	Hidden or secret self 2
What the teacher does not know about himself or herself	Blind self 3	Undiscovered or subconscious self 4

FIGURE 12–1. The Johari Window and the Educational Platform.
Source: From Thomas J. Sergiovanni, *Handbook for Department Leadership Concepts and Practices in Today's Secondary Schools,* Boston: Allyn & Bacon, 1977.

depicted in the Johari window, each representing a different combination of what the teacher knows or does not know about his or her teaching as contrasted with what the supervisor knows and does not know about that teacher's teaching.

In the first cell, *the public or open self,* the teacher's knowledge of his or her teaching behavior and other aspects of his or her professional practices corresponds with the supervisor's knowledge. This is the area in which communication occurs most effectively and in which the need for the teacher to be defensive, to assume threat, is minimal. The supervisor works to broaden, or enlarge, this cell with the teacher.

In the second cell, *the hidden or secret self,* the teacher knows about aspects of his or her teaching behavior and professional practice that the supervisor does not know. Often the teacher conceals these aspects from the supervisor for fear that the supervisor might use this knowledge to punish, hurt, or exploit the teacher. The second cell suggests how important a supervisory climate characterized by trust and credibility is to the success of clinical supervision. In clinical supervision the teacher is encouraged to reduce the size of this cell.

In the third cell, *the blind self,* the supervisor knows about aspects of the teacher's behavior and professional practice of which the teacher is unaware. This cell, though large initially, is reduced considerably as clinical supervision for a given teacher develops and matures. This is the cell most often neglected by traditional teacher-evaluation methods. Indeed, clinical supervision is superior to most other supervising strategies in helping teachers understand dimensions of teaching found in the blind self.

In the fourth cell, *the undiscovered self,* one finds aspects of teacher behavior and professional practice not known to either teacher or supervisor. The size of this cell is reduced as clinical supervision progresses. Teachers and supervisors discover and understand more and more about their beliefs, capabilities, strengths and weaknesses, and potential.

HELPING TEACHERS CHANGE

Creating a condition for change greatly facilitates the change itself. For example, if individual teachers are unaware of inconsistencies between their espoused theories and their theories in use, they are not likely to search for alternatives to their present teaching patterns. One way in which search behavior can be evoked is by identifying dilemmas. Dilemmas become apparent when teachers learn that their theories in use are not consistent with their espoused theories.

Dilemmas promote an unsettled feeling in a person. Their espoused educational platforms mean a great deal, and what they stand for and believe is linked to their concept of self and sense of well-being. Dilemmas that emerge from inconsistencies between these images and actual behavior are upsetting and need to be resolved. Indeed, they are likely to lead to a search for changes either in one's espoused theory or in one's theory in use.[19]

Readiness for change is a critical point in the process of clinical supervision. It is at this point that an appropriate support system needs to be provided. Part of this support system will be psychological and will be geared toward accepting and encouraging the teacher. But part must also be technical and be geared toward making available teaching and professional practice alternatives to the teacher.

Argyris and Schön point out that congruence is not a virtue in itself. A "bad" espoused theory matched to a theory in use may be far less desirable, from the supervisor's point of view, than a "good" espoused theory insufficiently matched.[20]

To this point in our discussion of developing a theory of clinical supervision, we have suggested the following:

- A teacher's classroom behavior and the artifacts of that behavior are a function of assumptions, theories, and intents the teacher brings to the classroom. Together these compose the teacher's educational platform.
- Educational platforms exist at two levels: what teachers say they assume, believe, and intend (their espoused theory), and the assumptions, beliefs, and intents inferred from their behavior and artifacts of their behavior (their theory in use).

---

[19]Leon Festinger, *Theory of Cognitive Dissonance,* Evanston, IL: Row, Peterson, 1975; and Milton Rokeach, "A Theory of Organizational Change Within Value-Attitude Systems," *Journal of Social Issues,* vol. 24, no. 21 (1968), pp. 13–40.
[20]Argyris and Schön, op. cit.

- Espoused theories are generally known to the teacher.
- Theories in use are generally not known to the teacher and must be constructed from observation of teacher behavior and artifacts of that behavior.
- Lack of congruence between a teacher's espoused theory and the teacher's theory in use proposes a dilemma to the teacher.
- Faced with a dilemma, a teacher becomes uncomfortable, and search behavior is evoked.
- Dilemmas are resolved by teachers' modifying their theory in use to match their espoused theory. It is possible that espoused theory will be modified to match theory in use, but because of the link between espoused theory and self-esteem, and between self-esteem and the esteem received from others, the more common pattern will be the former.

THE TEACHING PORTFOLIO

Videotaping is a common technique associated with clinical supervision and with the arts of educational connoisseurship and criticism. Indeed, videotaping can provide a useful and readily accessible representation of teaching episodes and classroom activities. But because of the selective nature of lens and screen, this technique can also frame perception and evoke slanted meanings. Furthermore, what the screen shows always represents a choice among possibilities and therefore provides an incomplete picture. And finally, some aspects of classroom life do not lend themselves very well to lens and screen and could be neglected.[21] Artifacts analysis, when used in conjunction with videotaping, can help provide a more complete representation of classroom life and therefore can increase meaning.[22]

Imagine a classroom or school deserted suddenly 20 years ago by its teacher and students and immediately being sealed. Everything there remains exactly as it was at the moment of desertion—desks, chairs, interest centers, work materials, test files, homework assignments, reading center sign-up lists, star reward charts and other motivational devices, bulletin boards, workbooks, student notebooks, grade books, plan books, library displays, teacher workroom arrangements, student lounge-area arrangements, and so on.

Twenty years later you arrive on the scene as an amateur anthropologist intent on learning about the culture, way of life, and meaning of this class (its goals, values, beliefs, activities, norms, etc.). As you dig through the classroom, what artifacts might you collect and how might you use them to help you learn about life in this school? Suppose, for example, you were interested in discovering what was important to teachers, how teachers viewed their roles in contrast to those of students,

---

[21]This discussion follows Thomas J. Sergiovanni, "Reforming Teacher Evaluation: Naturalistic Alternatives," *Educational Leadership*, vol. 34, no. 8 (1977), pp. 602–607.

[22]See Patricia Scheyer and Robert Stake, "A Program's Self-Evaluation Portfolio." Urbana: University of Illinois at Urbana-Champaign, Center for Instructional Research and Curriculum Evaluation, Undated mimeo, for a discussion and application of this concept for program evaluation.

what youngsters seemed to be learning and/or enjoying, and how time was spent. In each case what might you collect? What inferences might you make, for example, if you were to find most of the work of students to be in the form of short-answer responses in workbooks or on ditto sheets, no student work displayed in the class, all student desks containing identical materials, and a teacher test file with most questions geared to the knowledge level of the taxonomy of educational objectives?

The intent of portfolio development is to establish a file or collection of artifacts, records, photo essays, cassettes, and other materials designed to represent some aspect of the classroom program and teaching activities. Although the materials in the portfolio should be loosely collected and therefore suitable for rearrangement from time to time to reflect different aspects of the class, the portfolio should be designed with a sense of purpose. The teacher or teaching team being evaluated is responsible for assembling the portfolio and should do it in a fashion that highlights their perception of key issues and important concerns they wish to represent.

Like the artist who prepares a portfolio of his or her work to reflect a point of view, the teacher prepares a similar representation of his or her work. Together supervisor and teacher use the collected artifacts to identify key issues, to identify the dimensions of the teacher's educational platform, as evidence that targets have been met, and to identify serendipitous but worthwhile outcomes. A portfolio collection could be used, for example, to examine these issues:

- Are classroom activities compatible with the teacher's espoused educational platform and/or that of the school?
- Do supervisor and teacher have compatible goals?
- Are youngsters engaging in activities that require advanced cognitive thinking, or is the emphasis on lower-level learning?
- Do youngsters have an opportunity to influence classroom decisions?
- Is the classroom program challenging all the students regardless of academic potential, or are some youngsters taught too little and others too much?
- Are the youngsters assuming passive or active roles in the classroom?
- Is the teacher working hard? That is, is there evidence of planning, care in preparation of materials, and reflective and conscientious feedback on students' work, or are shortcuts evident?
- Does the teacher understand the subject matter?
- What is the nature and character of the hidden curriculum in this class?

Charlotte Danielson and Thomas McGreal describe the advantages of collecting teaching artifacts as follows:

> Students experience their teachers' skill not only in their direct interaction; they also encounter artifacts created or selected by their teachers, such as assignments, worksheets, and project directions. In fact, it is estimated that over half of students' school experiences is a function of the "stuff" created or selected by teachers. Such artifacts, then, represent an important aspect of teacher performance and can be assessed as part of an evaluation system.
>
> When teaching artifacts are included in a system for evaluation they provide a window into classroom life not accessible through planning documents alone. By reading

what a teacher is asking students to do, an evaluator can appreciate (at least vicariously) the cognitive challenge required by the task and the level of intellectual engagement by students the teacher expected. And if the teacher includes brief commentary to accompany the materials, such as responses to questions about the purposes of the activity, and how she intends for students' understanding to be advanced, the evaluator can get a hint of the teacher's thinking.[23]

Wolf, Lichtenstein, and Stevenson[24] propose that a teaching portfolio should contain the following features:

- A portfolio should be structured around sound professional teaching standards, and individual and school goals.
- A portfolio should contain carefully selected examples of both student and teacher work that illustrates key features of a teacher's practice.
- The contents of a portfolio should be framed by captions and written commentaries that explain and reflect on the contents of the portfolio.
- A portfolio should be a mentored or coached experience, in which the portfolio is used as a basis for ongoing professional conversations with colleagues and supervisors.[25]

Our advice is to be less strict about structuring the portfolio around professional teaching standards and school goals if the teacher's own goals are authentic and rigorous enough to carry the portfolio. No doubt there is a place for goals from all three sources. Portfolio development, however, is the responsibility of the teacher. The teacher decides what will be represented by the portfolio and the items to be included in its collection. Together, the teacher and supervisor use this representation to identify issues for discussion and analysis.

COACHING

Most of us agree that teacher learning is a powerful strategy for improving student achievement. And most of us agree that we can be more effective in promoting teacher learning than is now the case. Here, for example, are some problems that occur too often with the present situation:

- Teacher learning is separated from teachers actually teaching.
- Teacher learning efforts take place away from the teachers' classrooms.
- Teachers are left to learn on their own.

---

[23]Charlotte Danielson and Thomas McGreal, *Teacher Evaluation to Enhance Professional Practice,* Alexandria, VA: Association for Supervision and Curriculum Development, 2000, p. 49.

[24]K. Wolf, G. Lichtenstein, and C. Stevenson, "Using Teacher Portfolios in Teacher Evaluation," in J. Stronge (ed.), *Teacher Assessment and Evaluation: A Guidebook for Research and Practice,* Thousand Oaks, CA: Corwin Press, 1997.

[25]Danielson and McGreal, op. cit., p. 94.

- Learning is viewed as a private good[26] where the teacher, not the student or the school, is the prime beneficiary of this learning.
- What teachers learn is disconnected from the school's purposes and from the learning needs of students.

All these problems contribute to a failure of instructional coherence in the classroom and in the school. As discussed in Chapter 2, researchers agree that reasoned instructional coherence is necessary if schools are to improve and if students are to learn more. Newmann, Smith, Allensworth, and Bryk, for example, found "a strong positive relationship between improving coherence and improving student achievement."[27] As noted in Chapter 2, they define *instructional coherence* as "a set of interrelated programs for students and staff that are guided by a common framework for curriculum, instruction, assessment, and learning climate and that are pursued over a sustained period."[28] Instructional coherence is difficult to achieve and maintain when teachers are separated from the school and its purposes and from common frameworks for teaching, learning, and assessment.

Coaching can help develop instructional coherence.[29] Good coaching is embedded in the teachers' classrooms, takes place at the same time teachers are teaching, is collaborative, and is aimed at the public good. The school and its purposes are the prime beneficiaries. Coaches work side by side with teachers, observing their work, helping them research questions they are interested in, offering critiques, and serving as models of effective teaching practice. The goal of coaching is to help develop communities of practice within which teachers collaborate to honor a very simple value—when we learn together, we learn more, and when we learn more, we will more effectively serve our students.

Professional development takes on a different meaning when coaching is involved. Professional development

- is grounded in deep inquiry, reflection, and experimentation.
- is collaborative, focusing on teachers as members of communities of practice rather than as individuals.
- is sustained and supported by modeling.
- is connected to and driven by teachers' work with their students while teaching is actually going on.

---

[26]Private good and public good in teaching are concepts introduced by Richard Elmore. See, for example, Richard Elmore, *Bridging the Gap Between Standards and Achievement: The Imperative for Professional Development in Education,* Washington, DC: Albert Shanker Institute, 2002, or Richard Elmore, *Building a New Structure for School Leadership,* Washington, DC: Albert Shanker Institute, 2000.

[27]Fred M. Newmann, BetsAnn Smith, Elaine Allensworth, and Anthony S. Bryk, "Instructional Program Coherence: What It Is and Why It Should Guide School Improvement Policy," *Educational Evaluation and Policy Analysis,* vol. 23, no. 4 (2001), p. 305.

[28]Ibid., p. 297.

[29]This section on coaching follows closely pages 306–308 in Thomas J. Sergiovanni, *The Principalship: A Reflective Practice Perspective,* Boston: Allyn and Bacon, 2006.

- engages teachers in the work of teaching as they learn.
- is connected to larger purposes.[30]

These purposes are consistent with the point made earlier: Effective professional development depends on teachers teaching and improving their teaching at the same time. And finally, not only should coaching be driven by the needs and interests of teachers, it should be driven as well by the goals and purposes of the school.

COACHES AS ROVING LEADERS

One advantage of coaching is that it is portable. Coaches can move from classroom to classroom and group to group as needed. They are roving leaders. Roving leaders are there when we need them. Max DePree, the famed head of the Herman Miller furniture company, describes coaches as "indispensable people in our lives"[31] who sometimes work by appointment, but at other times no appointment is needed. If you need a coach, grab one. Good coaches practice coaching by walking around.

Coaches are not cheerleaders who pump us up by telling us they know we can do it. They are, instead, colleagues who help us see what we need to do and help us figure out what we need to do and do it well. Being a cheerleader puts the leader in the role of bystander. Bystanders work the sidelines but are not involved as colleagues, as partners, as active members of the teacher's shared community of practice. Missing from the cheerleader role is a relationship. At the heart of coaching, say Peters and Austin, is a personal relationship. "Relationships depend on contact. No contact, no relationship."[32] Building relationships is never easy. That is why effective coaching requires an investment of time, attention, and talent.

One important purpose of coaching is to build the capacity of people in such a way that each encounter results in reciprocal learning. Teacher and coach learn together. A second, perhaps more important, purpose is to strengthen the values the are shared in the school, to create a common agenda, and to work together to figure out a better way to achieve our purposes. Why are we here? What are we trying to accomplish? Do our decisions make sense? How does answering these questions help us understand our larger purposes? Coaching is about effectiveness, to be sure. But it is also about shaping values and building a normative culture. It is about improving the capacity of teachers to lead, and it is about advancing school improvement.

Key to coaching are the bonds that develop as trust grows. Coaching is, after all, an intimate strategy for learning. Getting inside another person's practice in a helpful way requires a high level of authenticity. This kind of relationship is threatened when coaches encourage teachers to become dependent on them; use their coaching roles

---

[30]Adapted from Linda Darling-Hammond and Milbrey McLaughlin, "Policies that Support Professional Development in an Era of Reform," *Phi Delta Kappan*, vol. 76, no. 8 (1995), cited in Barbara Neufeld and Dana Roper, "Coaching: A Strategy for Developing Instructional Capacity," Paper co-published by Aspen Institute Program on Education and Annenberg Institute for School Reform, June 2003, p. 3.

[31]Tom Peters and Nancy Austin, *A Passion for Excellence*, New York: Random House, 1985, p. 328.

[32]Ibid., p. 388.

to control what people do rather than to guide and support them; and tell teachers what they want to hear.

CHANGE COACHES AND CONTENT COACHES

Neufeld and Roper view coaching as school-based learning that is informed by the school's or the school district's reform agenda and by the school's or school district's teaching and learning purposes.[33] They note that coaches can support these efforts by focusing on school improvement issues and designs or by focusing on instructional strategies linked to content areas such as literacy, numeracy, science, or art. Change coaches focus on leadership for whole school improvement; content coaches focus on instructional improvement in the key disciplines. Both emphases are important if schools seek improvements that will sustain themselves over time.

Adding change coaches to the mix acknowledges that principals, other designated supervisors, and informal supervisors such as peer supervisors need coaching help if they are to get better at supervision. When teachers get the help they need, they get better at teaching, and this pathway is a fast-track method to improving student achievement. Change coaches, for example, might help principals and others conduct school walk-throughs or learning walks.[34] Change coaches might help the principal and other designated supervisors focus their efforts on other forms of instructional leadership as well. Content coaches work one-on-one or with groups of teachers on improving teaching strategies, upgrading their curriculum, and developing assessments in a content area. Examples of change coaches and content coaches at work are provided in Exhibit 12–3 and Exhibit 12–4.

TRAINING FOR COACHES

Successful coaching assignments depend on providing "training" both before coaches begin their coaching and during their coaching experiences. Like teachers teaching and learning to teach at the same time, coaches, too, need to coach and learn to coach at the same time. Training at the front end only is helpful, but it is not enough since so much of what coaches do is created on the spot. Teachers and coaches learn together as they practice together. Coaching is a two-way street. As in clinical supervision, teachers must step forward and be active participants in the process. Leaving everything to the coach just will not work. Effective training helps coaches get started with the assignments and helps them keep going.

Three kinds of training will be needed:[35]

1. Training in *content*. What are our purposes? What are we trying to accomplish? How will what teachers do in the classroom change? What effects do we want on student achievement?

---

[33]Neufeld and Roper, op. cit.

[34]We will discuss learning walks in Chapter 13.

[35]The three kinds of training apply as well to other school professional development roles, including instructional coordinators, lead teachers, and peer supervisors.

Some principals in reforming districts remain unsure about what to look for when they visit classrooms or how to provide useful feedback to teachers. This change coach suggests specific strategies for principals to use in classrooms.

I ask the principal, "Are you going into rooms and really looking at what teachers are doing and what kids are doing?" I need to help administrators know that when they go into rooms, the first thing they do is talk to kids and ask kids what they're doing. You ask a kid, "What are you doing today?" If you do that with three or four kids, you'll get a quick idea of the level of instruction that's going on in the room. For example, if a kid says, "We're doing chapter three," that's very different than if a kid says, "We're working on our sentences to make them better." It tells you whether they're talking content or something else. So that's a concrete strategy for a principal: what to say to kids when you're in the room.

The next coach talks about nudging principals to assess what they are really learning when they are in classrooms.

My question to him was, "You've got all this wonderful curriculum. Are teachers using it? How do you *know* they're using it?" He said, "Well, I go around to the classroom and I see that they're using it." I said, "Give me some evidence of that." And he couldn't do it. He could not give me evidence. "Okay," I said, "You've been around to the third grade. Have you hit a math one?" "Oh yeah, I've hit a math one." "Are they doing it? Tell me which ones you saw them doing." Couldn't do it. I said, "That's where your focus needs to be. Push this stuff. You need to be able to see that they're using it. And then you need to ask the question, Why aren't they using it?"

Exhibit 12–3. Change Coaches at Work: Helping Principals Focus on Instruction
Source: Barbara Neufeld and Dana Roper, *Coaching: A Strategy for Developing Instructional Capacity,* Paper co-published by Aspen Institute Program on Education and Annenberg Institute for School Reform, June 2003, p. 7.

2. Training in *process.* How will we accomplish our goals? What ways and means will we use to move teachers along? How do we win commitment for change from teachers? How must we work together as colleagues or as members of communities of practice to be effective?
3. Training in *culture.* What changes will be needed in the norms system? How will expectations change? What will be the accepted ways of doing things? How will we work together? How will our purposes, values, and commitments be used to point the way and to evaluate our work?

The three kinds of training for coaches cannot be thought of as multiple-choice questions. All three must go on at the same time. Too often the great weakness in professional development strategies is focusing only on content and process,

A middle school literacy coach explains how she works with one English language arts teacher, illustrating the multiple strategies and the length of time it may take to help teachers improve their knowledge and skills.

> I've been working with Teacher A pretty consistently since about the third week of school. I'm usually in his classroom watching a lesson between three and four times a week.
>
> One of the big issues that Teacher A and I are working on is that, often, by the time he's got his mini-lesson done and the kids are actually back on task, thirty-five minutes of the class period are gone and they only have twenty minutes to work. So, we've set a ten-minute mini-lesson goal, and yesterday it was twelve, which was "Phew!" And that feeds into a lot of our management problems, because the kids get antsy and start talking and being squirrelly.
>
> I worked with him last year and I did several demonstrations or model lessons. We kind of cotaught at times. I had concerns about doing that with him this year because I didn't want in any way to undermine his authority with the students, and he's struggling with that. I know that I can come in and teach a lesson and gather the kids in and have them behave, but I didn't want the kids to make a comparison between me and him. I felt that wouldn't be beneficial for him, so this year I'm going to make more use of other teachers and take him to see them do lessons, so that within his own classroom he's just all teacher.
>
> We're scheduled to go see four other teachers teach during his prep period. One of the things that I asked him to do was to notice what's happening in their classrooms as far as how the children behave and how much time on task they have, and to build a vision in his mind of what he wants to create in his classroom. I did this because I see that his expectations for himself and the kids are lower than what they could be. I don't believe that he believes it's possible, and I want him to see that it is.

Exhibit 12–4. Content Coaches at Work: Coaching One-on-One
Source: Barbara Neufeld and Dana Roper, *Coaching: A Strategy for Developing Instructional Capacity,* Paper co-published by Aspen Institute Program on Education and Annenberg Institute for School Reform, June 2003, p. 8.

ignoring culture. But sustainable leadership and sustainable change always require a change in the culture of the school itself.[36]

COLLABORATIVE COACHING AND LEARNING

New York City, Boston, San Diego, Corpus Christi, and Philadelphia are some of the better-known school districts investing in coaching as the core of their professional development efforts. Below is a brief summary of Collaborative Coaching and Learning (CCL). CCL is Boston's school-based approach to professional

---

[36]We will explore the importance of culture further in Chapter 16.

development. This approach involves having teachers take eight weeklong "courses" designed to research a particular teaching and learning strategy. Participants cycle through inquiry, lab sites, classroom practice, and follow-up. Inquiry involves a team of teachers who spend one hour a week working with a literacy or math coach on topics chosen by the teachers. Lab sites involve a team of teachers who spend 90 minutes a week cycling through a process that includes a preconference, demonstration lesson, observation, and debriefing.

During the preconference the team decides what the purposes of the lesson being studied will be and what issues will be examined. This is followed by planning and observing a demonstration lesson and analyzing the results. Classroom practice is when teachers set goals together and implement the teaching and learning strategies that they have been studying. Coaches and teachers then observe the lesson, debrief, and plan the next cycle.

Tom Payzant, Boston's superintendent, offers five key things that principals and other designated supervisors should do to increase the benefits of CCL and other coaching strategies:

- Talk with and listen to your teachers.
- Be a continuous learner yourself.
- Partner with coaches.
- Make time for everyone to learn and keep it sacred.
- Start with a core group; then plan how to scale up.[37]

Has the CCL approach been successful? Payzant thinks so. In his words:

Our data from Year II [SY2002–2003] show a marked increase in the breadth and depth of positive testimony regarding the [CCL] coaching model. This testimony comes not only from teachers who participated eagerly in the cycles, but also from some of the teachers who were initially resistant. In Year II, teachers described how CCL was changing the way they thought about teaching and learning, causing them to be more reflective. . . . They talked about the impact of the coaching model on their relationships with their colleagues, and some teachers reported that they were starting to see an impact on their students as well, noting an increase in the level of student engagement as well as the quality of student work.[38]

Below we provide a listing of Web sites on coaching and on teacher leadership–teacher learning, including some that provide practical suggestions for implementing coaching.

Coaching Web Sites

http://www.teacherleaders.org/Resources/coaching.html
http://www.carnegie.org/reporter/09/literacy/index.html
http://www.bpe.org/pubs/ccl/Getting%20Started%20CCL.pdf

---

[37]"Straight Talk About CCL: A Guide for School Leaders," produced by the Boston Plan for Excellence, in collaboration with the Boston Public Schools, August 2003, p. 4.
[38]Ibid., p. 14.

http://www.bpe.org/pubs/ccl/Plain%20Talk%20about%20CCL.pdf
http://www.bpe.org/pubs/ccl/CCL%20Scheduling%20Guide.pdf

Teacher Leadership–Teacher Learning Web Sites

http://nsdc.org/library/publications/innovator/inn3-97rich.cfm
http://www.teacherleaders.org/Resources/profcomms.html
http://snipurl.com/donaldson
http://www.edweek.org/ew/ewstory.cfm?slug=38 leadteach.h20

SUMMARY

In this chapter we examined two broad strategies for supervision: clinical supervision and coaching. Clinical supervision refers to face-to-face interaction with teachers with the intent of improving instruction and increasing professional growth. Like clinical supervision, coaching reaches deep into the classrooms of teachers to help them improve. The inquiry into clinical supervision began with an examination of its focus and purposes. Readers were then walked through the cycle of supervision, which involves a preobservation conference, observation and collection of data and artifacts, analysis and strategy, postobservation conference, and postobservation analysis. Attention was given as well to using portfolios as part of both clinical supervision and coaching. Coaching was then discussed. It was noted that good coaching is embedded in the teacher's classroom, takes place at the same time teachers are teaching, is collaborative, and is aimed at the public good. Differences between content coaches and change coaches were examined. Content coaches focus more deliberately on helping teachers master the content they are teaching and improve their teaching strategies. Change coaches provide help to principals and teachers as they seek to improve the capacity of the school itself. Content coaches and change coaches together help teachers get better and help schools get better. Examples were given of how coaching works in classrooms and what its effects are on teachers and on school improvement. Boston's Collaborative Coaching and Learning (CCL) was then examined as an example of a school district coaching strategy.

SOME REFLECTIONS

1. Review Figure 12–1, "The Johari Window and the Educational Platform." As you focus on the blind self, think about some things that teachers with whom you are familiar do not know about their teaching practice but you do know. What are some ways you as a supervisor could help reduce the blind self for them? As you focus on the hidden or secret self, think about some things you know about your teaching practice that your colleagues do not know. Why is it that we keep things hidden away in the secret self?
2. Find someone (or perhaps two people) willing to be a critical friend and participate with you in practicing clinical supervision. Together, carefully review the cycle of supervision. Ask your colleague to assume the role of peer or clinical supervisor first as you assume the role of teacher being helped. Now refer to Exhibit 12–2, "Team Evaluation Checklist for Clinical Supervision," and plan a cycle of clinical supervision that will meet the checklist requirements. When you are finished, switch roles. Then with you being the clinical supervisor, continue practicing.

3. One advantage of using coaching strategies is that they are, for the most part, portable. This allows the supervisor to become a roving leader. In what ways is your principal a roving leader? What are some things that get in the way of supervisors' being roving leaders even though they may think that role is valuable?
4. What are the differences between being a content coach and being a change coach? Can content coaches be successful over the long haul if change coaches are not successful in changing the cultural norms of the school?

CHAPTER 13

Supervisory Options for Teachers

INTRODUCTION

As classrooms become learning communities and teaching becomes learner-centered, students' capacity for learning and for social and moral development improves. This basic principle of Supervision II is shared by many schools and school districts. In 1994, for example, Texas adopted the following statement as the vision for teachers' roles:

> The teacher is a leader of a learner-centered community, in which an atmosphere of trust and openness produces a stimulating exchange of ideas and mutual respect. The teacher is a critical thinker and problem solver who plays a variety of roles when teaching. As a coach, the teacher observes, evaluates, and changes direction and strategies whenever necessary. As a facilitator, the teacher helps students link ideas in the content areas to familiar ideas, to prior experiences, and to relevant problems. As a manager, the teacher effectively acquires, allocates, and conserves resources. By encouraging self-directed learning, and by modeling respectful behavior, the teacher effectively manages the learning environment so that optimal learning occurs.[1]

Any serious attempt to make this vision a reality must include as its strategy the transformation of classrooms and schools into:

Reflective communities within which not only students but teachers develop insights into their own strengths and weaknesses as learners and use this information to call upon different strategies for learning.

Developmental communities within which it is acknowledged that not only students but teachers develop at different rates and at any given time are more ready to learn some things than others.

---

[1]Texas Education Agency, "Learner-Centered Schools for Texas: Vision of Texas Educators," State-Adopted Proficiencies for Texas, 1994, p. 4.

Diverse communities within which different talents and interests of not only students but teachers are recognized and acknowledged by decisions that are made about curriculum, teaching, and assessment.

Conversational communities within which high priority is given to creating an active conversation that involves the exchange of values and ideas not only among students but among teachers and between students and teachers as everyone learns together.

Caring communities within which not only students but teachers learn to be kind to each other, to respect each other, and to help each other grow as learners and as persons.

Responsible communities within which not only students but teachers come to view themselves as part of a social web of meanings and responsibilities to which they feel a moral obligation as members of the same school community.[2]

Few axioms are more fundamental than the one that acknowledges the link between what happens to teachers and what happens to students. Inquiring classrooms, for example, are not likely to flourish in schools where inquiry among teachers is discouraged. A commitment to problem solving is difficult to instill in students who are taught by teachers for whom problem solving is not allowed. Where there is little discourse among teachers, discourse among students will be harder to promote and maintain. And the idea of making classrooms into learning communities for students will remain more rhetoric than real unless schools become learning communities for teachers too. Thus, for classrooms to be transformed, schools themselves must be transformed into:

Professional communities within which teachers depend on each other not only for caring and support but to learn and inquire together as members of a shared practice.

Vito Perrone believes that the teacher's role is central to improving the quality of learning for students. For him, teacher development is key because "the quality of teachers' understandings influences to a large degree what teachers do in classrooms.[3] Good teacher-development programs and efforts, he reasoned, should be based on the assumption that "the best source for teachers to learn more about teaching and learning, child growth and development, materials and methods is through an examination of one's own practice."[4]

In this chapter, we are concerned with differences that teachers bring to and face in their work. Teachers have different strengths and weaknesses. Teacher needs and interests differ. And the problems and issues of teaching and learning that teachers find in their practice differ. A one-size-fits-all approach to supervision will not work in this context of differences. In its place, we propose that a range of options be provided and that teachers have considerable (but not exclusive) say in deciding

[2]Thomas J. Sergiovanni, *Leadership for the School House,* San Francisco: Jossey-Bass, 1996, pp. 138–140; and Sergiovanni, *Strengthening the Heartbeat: Leading and Learning Together in Schools,* San Francisco: Jossey-Bass, 2005, chap. 5.
[3]Vito Perrone, "Supporting Teacher Growth," *Childhood Education,* vol. 54, no. 6 (1978), p. 298.
[4]Ibid.

which of these options makes sense. This range of options might be viewed as branches that come from a common stem. For a coherent system of supervision to be developed, care must be taken to provide a common framework for supervision. This framework might well include some forms of supervision for everyone and other forms that are options tailored to serve different learning needs and interests of teachers.

SOME BACKGROUND

A differentiated system of supervision makes sense. At its best, such a system is responsive to the individual needs and interests of teachers while protecting and enhancing instructional coherence. We propose that in every school a plan for supervision be developed that includes several options: clinical supervision, peer supervision, self-directed supervision, informal supervision, inquiry-based supervision lesson study, and learning walks are examples.[5] We recognize that these options overlap. Clinical supervision and peer supervision, for example, can look a lot like coaching. Still, there are enough differences among the options to view them separately.

Additionally, we propose that teachers play key roles in deciding which of the options make most sense to them given their needs at the time. And finally, we propose that in the implementation of the options, supervision should be viewed as a process that is equally accessible to teachers and administrators. Equal access does not mean that principals and other designated supervisors should be excluded from the process of supervision. They have important roles to play, particularly in providing the day-by-day informal supervision that may be required and in giving leadership and support to teachers who are themselves engaging in the supervisory functions. But supervisors should not monopolize the process by excluding teachers from roles as supervisors or by relegating them to token roles.

Excluding teachers denies the reality that although formal supervisors bring expertise to the process, in most schools teachers as a group command the largest share of expertise in subject matter, knowledge about the particular students being taught, and the pedagogical knowledge needed to teach those students effectively. One problem with traditional conceptions of supervision is that they equate hierarchy with expertise by assuming that supervisors as a group always know more about teaching than do teachers as a group. Differentiated supervision solves this problem by building a culture of collective responsibility for learning and improvement.

From a practical perspective, disconnecting the process of supervision from hierarchic roles reflects what often goes on in schools anyway. The research by both Emil Haller and Charles Keenan, for example, reveals that both the Canadian and

---

[5]The discussion of options for supervision presented in this chapter follows the views of Allan A. Glatthorn, *Differentiated Supervision,* Alexandria, VA: Association for Supervision and Curriculum Development, 1984; and the discussion of options for supervision that appears in T. J. Sergiovanni, *The Principalship: A Reflective Practice Perspective,* 3d ed., Boston: Allyn & Bacon, 1995, pp. 244–248.

American teachers they studied were very much inclined to depend upon each other when seeking help in solving problems, when searching for sources of new ideas about teaching, and when seeking other kinds of assistance.[6] Formal supervisors counted, but not nearly as much as other teachers. Teachers held the advice of other teachers in higher regard than advice from other sources. Although not officially acknowledged, there appears to be an informal system of supervision in place in schools; the evidence suggests that this informal system among teachers may be more important and more useful to teachers than is the formal system. By disconnecting supervision from hierarchic roles and viewing it instead as a process accessible to both teachers and supervisors, educators can legitimize this informal system of supervision, maximize its benefits, and connect it to more formal approaches. Again, differentiated supervision solves the problem by helping build a culture of shared responsibility for learning and improvement.

In the sections below, an overview of the proposed options for inclusion in a differentiated approach to supervision is provided. Attention is also given to the instructional leadership responsibilities of designated supervisors.

CLINICAL SUPERVISION AS AN OPTION

In Chapter 12, we proposed that clinical supervision be viewed as a partnership in inquiry shared by teacher and supervisor that is intended to help teachers modify existing patterns of teaching in ways that make sense to them. Clinical supervision is not for everyone, nor is it a strategy that can sustain itself over a long period of time. When implemented as the cycle of supervision, the process is demanding in the time it requires from both teacher and supervisor. A danger is that continual use of this approach can result in a certain ritualism as each step is followed. Clinical supervision may be too much supervision for some teachers. That is, not all teachers will need such an intensive look at their teaching. And finally, teachers' needs and dispositions as well as learning styles vary. Clinical supervision may be suitable for some teachers but not for others when these differences are taken into consideration.

PEER SUPERVISION

In peer supervision, teachers agree to work together for their own professional development.[7] Thus when teachers are working together within the clinical supervision framework, they are also engaging in peer supervision. But there are many other forms of peer supervision. Allan Glatthorn defines this approach as a "moderately formalized process by which two or more teachers agree to work together

---

[6]Emil J. Haller, *Strategies for Change,* Toronto: Ontario Institute for Studies in Education, Department of Educational Administration, 1968; and Charles Keenan, "Channels for Change: A Survey of Teachers in Chicago Elementary Schools," Ph.D. dissertation, Urbana: University of Illinois, Department of Educational Administration, 1974.

[7]Glatthorn, op. cit.

for their own professional growth, usually by observing each other's classroom, giving each other feedback about the observations, and discussing shared professional concerns.[8]

In some schools, teachers are organized into teams of two or three. It might be a good idea in some cases for at least one member of the team to be selected by the principal or supervisor, but there are no rigid rules for composing peer supervision teams. If not too large, a whole grade level, middle school team, or high school department might work well. Once the team is formed, team members may agree to observe each other's classes and provide help according to the desires of the teacher being observed. They confer together, giving one another informal feedback and discussing issues of teaching that they consider important. Sometimes the emphasis on teaching might be narrowly focused on specific issues. On other occasions the emphasis might be quite unfocused in order to provide a general feel or rendition of teaching. All that is needed is for team members to meet beforehand to decide the rules and issues for the observation and for any subsequent conversations or conferences.

Glatthorn describes five different forms peer supervision might take:

> Professional dialogue among teachers featuring guided discussion and focusing on teaching as a process of thinking. The purpose of professional dialogue is to enhance reflective practice.
>
> Curriculum development featuring teachers working together on such themes as how to operationalize the existing curriculum, adapt the curriculum to the wide variety of students and situations faced in the classroom, and enriching the existing curriculum by inventing and developing new curriculum units and materials.
>
> Peer supervision featuring observations of each other's teaching followed by analysis and discussion.
>
> Peer coaching featuring collaborative development and practice of new teaching methods and skills in both "workshop" settings and under actual teaching conditions.
>
> Action research featuring the study of problems being faced and the development of feasible solutions that result in changes in one's teaching practice.[9]

Peer supervision extends well beyond classroom observation. It provides a setting in which teachers can informally discuss problems they face, share ideas, help one another in preparing lessons, exchange tips, and provide other support to one another. Some suggestions for implementing peer supervision are provided in Table 13–1.

Many examples of peer supervision exist, and many more can be invented by teachers and schools. Some forms of coaching, for example, look a lot like peer supervision. When a neutral party is introduced who facilitates the efforts of a group of teachers over a period of time, who may be directly involved in observing teaching,

---

[8]Ibid., p. 39.

[9]Allan A. Glatthorn, "Cooperative Professional Development: Peer-Centered Options for Teacher Growth," *Educational Leadership,* vol. 45, no. 3 (1987), p. 32. Action research and peer supervision in the form of clinical supervision are treated in this discussion as separate options. Both might involve collaboration with other teachers; a closer, more private relationship between formal supervisor and teacher; or, as in the case of action research, an individual initiative.

TABLE 13–1. Guidelines for Implementing Collegial [Peer] Supervision.

1. Teachers should have a voice in deciding with whom they work.

2. Principals should retain final responsibility for the makeup of collegial supervision teams.

3. The structure for supervision should be formal enough for the teams to keep records of how and in what ways time has been used and to provide a general *nonevaluative* description of activities. This record should be sent annually to the principal.

4. The principal should provide the necessary resources and administrative support enabling teams to function during the normal range of the school day. The principal might, for example, volunteer to cover classes as needed, or to arrange for substitutes as needed, or to provide for innovative schedule adjustments enabling team members to work together readily.

5. If information generated within the team about teaching and learning might be considered even mildly evaluative, it should stay with the team and not be shared with the principal.

6. The principal should not seek evaluation data from one teacher about another.

7. Each teacher should be expected to keep a professional growth log that demonstrates that he or she is reflecting on practice and growing professionally as a result of activities.

8. The principal should meet with the team at least once a year for purposes of general assessment and for sharing of impressions and information about the process.

9. The principal should meet individually at least once a year with each team member to discuss his or her professional growth log and to provide any encouragement and assistance that may be required.

10. Generally, new teams should be formed every second or third year.

Source: Thomas J. Sergiovanni, *The Principalship: A Reflective Practice Perspective,* 2d ed., Boston: Allyn & Bacon. 1991, p. 304.

and who shows the group how to share their practice in different ways, peer supervision becomes coaching. In the sections below, we examine mentoring, the lesson study, and teachers working together to examine student work as three examples of peer supervision.

Mentoring

Mentoring is a form of peer supervision. A mentor is a person, usually another teacher, entrusted with tutoring, educating, and guiding another person who is typically new to teaching or new to a given school. The mentoring relationship is special because of its entrusting nature. Those being mentored depend upon their mentors to help them, protect them, show them the way, and develop their skills and insights more fully. The mentor is presumed to know more not only about matters of teaching but also about the school's culture so that the novice can navigate through this culture successfully. The unequal nature of the relationship makes it a moral one.

In some respects the tutorial, educational, and advisory aspects of the mentoring relationship are developmental. Initially, most novices seek assistance. They want to know what they are supposed to do, where things are, how to make requests, and what are accepted practices. They want concrete help in setting up their classrooms, establishing routines, and getting started. They want, in other words, to be tutored by an individual they trust without worrying too much about having to make an impression.

Because of its dependent nature, the tutorial relationship often represents a source of great satisfaction for the mentor. In many respects the mentor becomes the center of the novice's life. But the purpose of mentoring is to help a novice become independent. For this to happen, the mentoring relationship needs to evolve quickly from one of tutelage to one of mutuality. This happens when novices ask less and mentors tell less and when both settle down to solving problems together. "How might I best do this?" is answered with, "What ideas do you have? That one sounds promising. Let's try it out." and eventually, "How do you think it's going?"

The mentoring relationship matures when it becomes reciprocal. The novice seeks advice from the mentor and the mentor seeks to transform the relationship from mentoring to colleagueship by soliciting advice in return, by sharing problems, and by valuing the perspectives of the newcomer. Given what is known about the importance of the school's culture, the informal norm system that exists among teachers, and the potential that exists for teachers to share talents, mentoring makes sense as a natural way to orient new teachers, give them a successful start, and invite them to become full colleagues.

Mentoring is intended to help new teachers successfully learn their roles, establish their self-images as teachers, figure out the school and its culture, understand how teaching unfolds in real classrooms, and achieve other goals that are important to the teachers being mentored. Mentoring is also intended to help new teachers improve their effectiveness in demonstrating the schools' standards for teaching. When the latter is the goal, an *outside-in* approach to mentoring makes sense. Here a set of standards and indicators for teaching (perhaps from the state's assessment system, the Danielson framework for teaching described in Chapter 10, or the district's own sense of good teaching) is imported from outside the mentoring relationship. These standards and indicators are used to train mentors as coaches and to provide an agenda for helping teachers talk about and evaluate their work. When the former is used, an *inside-out* approach makes sense. Here the focus is on the problems and issues that teachers identify they are facing in their practice or that they are interested in learning more about. Both outside-in and inside-out approaches are important and need attention.

One strategy is to bring outside and inside approaches together. When dealing with standards that come from outside the mentoring relationship, try linking them to the real-time problems and issues that teachers are facing. And when dealing with the problems and issues that emerge from inside the mentoring experience, try linking them to the school's standards for teaching. When the two are worked on separately, we begin to posture one as summative evaluation and the other as formative growth and development, creating fractures and suspicions that mentoring is little more than an early warning system for evaluating teachers. But when the two are brought together, these lines begin to disappear. The emphasis shifts to helping new teachers be successful as defined by both outside and inside criteria.

If we are going to take new teachers seriously as learners, say Sharon Feiman-Nemser, Cynthia Carver, Sharon Schwille, and Brian Yusko, we need to provide support, on the one hand, and the kind of learning that develops new teachers as professionals able to help complex learning happen for students[10] on the other. They recommend an approach that brings together support, professional development, and assessment, blurring the lines between outside and inside factors:

> All three are necessary components in a comprehensive system of beginning-teacher induction. Support without development leaves teacher learning to chance. It favors the agendas of individual teachers and works against a sense of collective responsibility for student learning. Framing induction around new-teacher development closes the gap between initial preparation and continuing professional development. It honors the fact that new teachers are learners and lays a foundation for the ongoing study and improvement of teaching. Assessment that encourages interpretation and enactment of standards in context strengthens professional accountability, which is the most appropriate and powerful source of quality control in teaching.[11]

Ellen Moir, Janet Gless, and Wendy Baron, from the New Teacher Center at the University of California Santa Cruz, have argued that standards have important roles to play in mentoring new teachers but that successful emphasis on standards and other criteria outside the mentoring relationship depends upon providing a strong support system geared to the teachers' concerns and other inside criteria as well. Moir, Gless, and Baron seek to build both learning communities and caring communities for new teachers. As they explain:

> High professional standards are essential for all educators, and the role of any induction program must be to help new teachers recognize the standards and put them into practice. But in these times of standards-based curriculums and standards-driven reform, we feel that standards alone do not ensure quality teaching. However, when standards are embedded in a compassionate and responsive system of support, they can guide educational reform.[12]

And further:

> So we have embedded the *California Standards for the Teaching Profession* in every aspect of our program—in our seminars, our assessments, our collaborative log forms, and, most important, in our language. And at the same time, we seek to create compassionate environments for new teachers in which they hear the language of inspiration and love, of passion for teaching and dedication to community, of commitment to

---

[10]Sharon Feiman-Nemser, Cynthia Carver, Sharon Schwille, and Brian Yusko, "Beyond Support: Taking New Teachers Seriously as Learners" in Marge Scherer (ed.), *A Better Beginning*. Alexandria, VA: Association for Supervision and Curriculum Development, 1999, pp. 3–12.

[11]Ibid., p. 10.

[12]Ellen Moir, Janet Gless, and Wendy Baron, "A Support Program with Heart: The Santa Cruz Project," in Marge Sherer (ed.), op. cit., p. 114.

excellence and a determination that every child be afforded the birthright of a quality education. Our children and our schools deserve no less.[13]

While the emphasis in mentoring is on helping new teachers, mentors typically report that the experience of mentoring is expansive for them as well. By helping a colleague, they are forced to come to grips with their own teaching, to see their problems more clearly, and to learn ways to overcome them. Mentoring is the kind of relationship in which learning benefits everyone involved.

Lesson Study

The lesson study is a promising way to engage teachers in ongoing learning that is immersed in their practice and in the practice of their colleagues. The lesson study has a research bent to it, encourages reflections, helps teachers engage in "shop floor" curriculum development, involves collegial study of a lesson or lessons, while at the same time is practical for addressing issues teachers identify with and have to face in their daily practice. Not only are new lessons invented in the lesson study, but they are field-tested, revised, and improved as well. Old lessons get refitted. Indeed, even packaged lessons such as those one might find in a teacher's manual or in a professional journal can be improved by the lesson study. Further, norms of collegiality are transcended as teachers come together as members of communities of practice.

In their international studies, James W. Stigler and James Hiebert[14] found that the Japanese invest heavily in teacher learning and professional development and that they invest differently than we do with great success. The researchers noted that in Japan great emphasis is given to classroom lessons, how they are planned, what happens in live classrooms when specific lessons are used, and how these lessons might be continually improved. In their words:

> In Japan, classroom lessons hold a privileged place in the activities of the school. It would be exaggerating only a little to say they are sacred. They are treated much as we treat lectures in university courses or religious services in church. A great deal of attention is given to their development. They are planned as complete experiences—as stories with a beginning, a middle, and an end. Their meaning is found in the connections between the parts. If you stay for only the beginning, or leave before the end, you miss the point. If lessons like this are going to succeed, they must be coherent. The pieces must relate to one another in clear ways. And they must flow along, free from interruption and unrelated activities. . . . So the lesson must be a tightly connected, coherent story; the teacher must build a visible record of the pieces as they unfold so connections can be drawn between them; and the lesson cannot be sidetracked or broken by interruptions.[15]

Because many differences in conceptions and practice have cultural anchors, we must be cautious about wholesale borrowing of ideas for use in our schools. But one idea, the lesson study, may be worth considering for adoption in our culture.

[13]Ibid., p. 115.
[14]James W. Stigler and James Hiebert, *The Teaching Gap: Best Ideas from the World's Teachers for Improving Education in the Classroom,* New York: Free Press, 1999.
[15]Ibid., pp. 95–96.

At the very least, the lesson study can be used to help develop a set of guidelines and standards. These guidelines and standards then might be used to invent something similar in intent but unique for use in our own schools.

In lesson study, groups of teachers meet regularly over a period of several months to design a new, or redesign an existing, lesson. This lesson is then implemented in view of colleagues who offer "critical friend" feedback. This critique and the suggestions that accompany it are directed to the lesson itself rather than the teacher. Thus if things do not go well, it is assumed that everyone must work harder to refine or perhaps redefine the lesson, not the person. From this test, a revised lesson is crafted and tried out, followed by another critique and still more changes.

Relying on research conducted by Catherine Lewis and Ineko Tsuchida and by N. Ken Shimahara,[16] Stigler and Hiebert identify the following steps in the lesson study process:

Step 1: *Defining the Problem.* Lesson study is, fundamentally, a problem-solving process. The first step, therefore, is to define the problem that will motivate and direct the work of the lesson-study group. The problem can start out as a general one (for example, to awaken students' interest in mathematics) or it can be more specific (for example, to improve students' understanding of how to add fractions with unlike denominators). The group will then shape and focus the problem until it can be addressed by a specific classroom lesson.

Step 2: *Planning the Lesson.* Once a learning goal has been chosen, teachers begin meeting to plan the lesson. Although one teacher will ultimately teach the lesson as part of the process, the lesson itself is seen by all involved as a group product. Often the teachers will start their planning by looking at books and articles produced by other teachers who have studied a similar problem. According to one Japanese book on how to prepare a research lesson, the useful research lesson should be designed with a hypothesis in mind: some idea to be tested and worked out within the context of classroom practice.[17] The goal is not only to produce an effective lesson but also to understand why and how the lesson works to promote understanding among students. The initial plan that the group produces is often presented at a schoolwide faculty meeting in order to solicit criticism. Based on such feedback, a revision is produced, ready for implementation. This initial planning process can take as long as several months.

Step 3: *Teaching the Lesson.* A date is set to teach the lesson. One teacher will teach the lesson, but everyone in the group will participate fully in the preparation. The night before, the group might stay late at school, preparing materials and engaging in a dress rehearsal, complete with role-playing. On the

---

[16]Catherine Lewis and Ineko Tsuchida, "Planned Educational Change in Japan: The Shift to Student-centered Elementary Science," *Journal of Educational Policy,* vol. 12 (1997), pp. 313–331; Catherine Lewis and Ineko Tsuchida, "A Lesson Is Like a Swiftly Flowing River: How Research Lessons Improve Japanese Education," *American Educator,* vol. 22, no. 4 (1998), pp. 12–17, 50–52; N. Ken Shimahara, "The Japanese Model of Professional Development: Teaching as a Craft," *Teaching and Teacher Education,* vol. 14 (1998), pp. 451–462.
[17]Kazuo Orihara, (ed.), *Shogakko: Kenkyu Jugyo no susume kata mikata (Elementary school: Implementing and observing research lessons),* Tokyo: Bunkyo-shoin, (1993).

day of the lesson, the other teachers in the group leave their classrooms to observe the lesson being taught. The teachers stand or sit in the back as the lesson begins, but when students are asked to work at their desks, the teacher-observers walk around, observing and taking careful notes on what students are doing as the lesson progresses. Sometimes the lesson is videotaped as well, for later analysis and discussion.

Step 4: *Evaluating the Lesson and Reflecting on Its Effect.* The group generally stays after school to meet on the day the lesson has been taught. Usually, the teacher who taught the lesson is allowed to speak first, outlining in his or her own view how the lesson worked and what the major problems were. Then other members of the group speak, usually critically, about the parts of the lesson they saw as problematic. The focus is on the lesson, not on the teacher who taught the lesson; the lesson, after all, is a group product, and all members of the group feel responsible for the outcome of their plan. They are, in effect, critiquing themselves. This is important, because it shifts the focus from a personal evaluation to a self-improvement activity.

Step 5: *Revising the Lesson.* On the basis of their observations and reflections, teachers in the lesson-study group revise the lesson. They might change the materials, the activities, the problems posed, the questions asked, or all these things. They often will base their changes on specific misunderstandings evidenced by students as the lesson progressed.

Step 6: *Teaching the Revised Lesson.* Once the revised lesson is ready, the lesson is taught again to a different class. Sometimes it is taught by the same teacher who taught the lesson the first time, but often it is taught by another member of the group. One difference is that this time all members of the school faculty are invited to attend the research lesson. This is quite dramatic in a large school, where there may be more faculty crowded into the classroom than there are students in the class.

Step 7: *Evaluating and Reflecting, Again.* This time, it is common for all members of the school faculty to participate in a long meeting. Sometimes an outside expert will be invited to attend as well. As before, the teacher who taught the lesson is allowed to speak first, discussing what the group was trying to accomplish, her or his own assessment of how successful the lesson was, and what parts of the lesson still need rethinking. Observers then critique the lesson and suggest changes. Not only is the lesson discussed with respect to what these students learned and understood, but also with respect to more general issues raised by the hypotheses that guided the design of the research lesson. What about teaching and learning, more generally, was learned from the lesson and its implementation?

Step 8: *Sharing the Results.* All this work has focused on a single lesson. But because Japan is a country with national education goals and curricular guidelines, what this group of teachers has learned will have immediate relevance for other Japanese teachers trying to teach the same concepts at the same grade level. Indeed, the teachers in one lesson-study group see the sharing of their findings as a significant part of the lesson-study process. This sharing can be done in several ways. One is to write a report, and most lesson-study groups do produce a report that tells the story of their group's work. Often these reports are published in book form, even if only for the school's teacher resource room.[18]

How viable is the lesson study as an option for supervision in our schools? What adjustments might be necessary for this approach to fit our way of doing things? Try sharing the description of the lesson study provided with some teachers in your school. What are their reactions? Do they have suggestions as to how this approach might be adapted? What principles does the lesson study embody that we can use to develop workable approaches to supervision that are rich in teacher learning? Stigler and Hiebert answer this last question as follows. The lesson study

- is based on long-term continuous improvement;
- maintains a continuous focus on student learning;
- focuses on the improvement of teaching in context;
- is collaborative;
- and involves teachers in the development of knowledge about teaching.[19]

In our view, supervision would be taking an important step in the right direction if these principles were our standard for the practice of supervision. We echo Dennis Sparks's view on this topic. Sparks, who is executive director of the National Staff Development Council, believes that we can close the "staff development gap" that exists in many schools by focusing our efforts on providing a practical model for continuous improvement of teaching that places teachers at the center of the school improvement process. He argues:

> As both North American and international studies make clear, linking teacher learning to student learning and focusing on the daily improvement of instructional practice makes a difference in student achievement. While that may not be rocket science, research and practical experience are teaching us that it is the core premise that drives powerful staff development efforts.[20]

LOOKING AT STUDENT WORK

It is widely accepted that establishing schools as professional learning communities is key to teacher learning and to student success.[21] In the opening paragraphs of this chapter, we characterized professional learning communities as schools where

---

[18]These excerpts are drawn from Stigler and Hiebert, op. cit., pp. 112–115. Reprinted with the permission of The Free Press, a Division of Simon & Schuster, Adult Publishing Group, from *The Teaching Gap: Best Ideas From The World's Teachers for Improving Education in the Classroom,* by James W. Stigler and James Hiebert. Copyright© 1999 by James W. Stigler and James Hiebert. All rights reserved.

[19]These features of the lesson study are drawn from Stigler and Hiebert, op. c. 10, Ibid., pp. 121–125.

[20]Dennis Sparks "Using Lesson Study to Improve Teaching," *Education Week,* June 21, 2000, p. 50.

[21]See, for example, Milbrey McLaughlin and Joan Talbert, "Contexts that Matter for Teaching and Learning," Stanford, CA: Stanford University Center for Research on the Context for Secondary School Teaching, 1993; Ann Lieberman (ed.), *Schools as Collaborative Cultures: Creating the Future Now,* Bristol, PA: Falmer Press, 1990; and Linda Darling-Hammond, *The Right to Lead: A Blueprint for Creating Schools that Work,* San Francisco: Jossey-Bass, 1997.

teachers depend on each other for caring and support and where teachers learn and inquire together as members of a shared practice. Collaboration is a key characteristic of professional learning communities. The learning intersection is what makes professional learning communities so powerful. The learning intersection is where collaborative cultures that are created and supported by principals and other designated supervisors meet communities of practice that bubble up from teachers below.

Examining student work is a powerful way to build the kind of collaborative culture that can help schools become professional learning communities. When teachers together look at student work, they come to talk with each other about matters at the heart of teaching and learning more often and more thoughtfully. This kind of collaboration provides teachers with practical ways to reflect on, discuss, and revise their own practice.[22] Whether we are talking about examples of student writing, some math problems that students are working on, a report they have just finished for a social studies class, a write-up of a science experiment, some preliminary sketches for an art project, or examples of tests or homework assignments that have recently been completed, these artifacts of teaching and learning can be powerful tools for learning, for sharing, and for changing one's teaching practice.

Examining student work together is also a way for teachers to sharpen their focus on learning standards for students. As Tina Blythe, David Allen, and Barbara Powell explain, "there are some purposes for looking at student work that virtually require collaboration and conversation—developing common standards within grade levels or departments, for example. In order to accomplish this aim, a school or a group of teachers must develop not only standards but also a shared understanding of what these standards mean and how to apply them to student work. Examining and discussing student work is virtually the only way to achieve such a goal."[23]

USING PROTOCOLS TO HELP

It is not easy for teachers to talk together about the assignments they give students and about the work that students do as a result. Nor is it easy for them to determine if student work measures up to accepted standards of learning. Despite the advice that we do so, separating teachers from their teaching for the purpose of studying this teaching is not easy. Teachers often worry that peer collaboration and collegial supervision might turn out to be other strategies to "evaluate" them but only in a more intrusive way. Looking closely at the work that students do, for example, provides a deeper look at teaching and learning than does examining one's teaching effectiveness score on a state teacher-evaluation instrument. That is why having some ground rules and using protocols to help guide the inquiry can help teachers be more comfortable with what is expected and how to participate in collegial supervision. Protocols help assure teachers that the focus is on the study of teaching and not the evaluation of teachers.

[22]Tina Blythe, David Allen, and Barbara Schieffelin Powell, *Looking Together at Student Work: A Companion Guide to Assessing Student Learning,* New York: Teachers College Press, 1999.
[23]Ibid., p. 4.

The lesson study described above is a good example of a form of collegial supervision that emphasizes the study of teaching. This process is built upon certain widely accepted assumptions and beliefs and is framed by steps that lay out the pathway to be followed and provide some guidelines for following them. Below, for example, are examples of questions offered by Blythe, Allen, and Powell that might help teachers as they examine student work. The questions may be used with existing protocols or to help develop new ones.

About the quality of student work:

- Is the work good enough?
- What is "good enough"?
- In what ways does this work meet or fail to meet a particular set of standards?

About teaching practice:

- What do the students' responses indicate about the effectiveness of the prompt or assignment? How might the assignment be improved?
- What kinds of instruction support high-quality student performances?

About students' understanding:

- What does this work tell us about how well the student understands the topic of the assignment?
- What initial understandings do we see beginning to emerge in this work?

About students' growth:

- How does this range of work from a single student demonstrate growth over time?
- How can I support student growth more effectively?

About students' intent:

- What issues or questions is this student focused on?
- What aspects of the assignment intrigued this student?
- Into which parts of the assignment did the student put the most effort?
- To what extent is the student challenging herself? In what ways?[24]

The standards for authentic pedagogy proposed by Fred Newmann and Gary Wehlage[25] and summarized in Table 6–1 and the criteria provided in Appendix 7–1 are examples of content protocols that can be used by participants individually or in collaboration with others to examine the assignments and tasks they give to students.[26] Since there is a relationship between tasks assigned to students and

---

[24]Ibid., Reprinted by permission of the publisher from Blythe, T., Allen, D., and Powell, B. S., *Looking Together At Student Work,* (New York: Teachers College Press, © 1999 by Teachers College, Columbia University. All rights reserved.), p. 10.

[25]Fred M. Newmann and Gary G. Wehlage, *Successful School Restructuring,* Madison, WI: Center on Organization and Restructuring of Schools, 1995.

[26]Fred M. Newmann, Walter G. Secada, and Gary G. Wehlage, *A Guide to Authentic Instruction and Assessment: Vision, Standards and Scoring,* Madison: Wisconsin Center for Educational Research, 1995

the kind of work they do, examining student work involves examining assignments as well.

Try using the standards and criteria provided in Appendix 7–1 by joining with two colleagues in a series of meetings to first examine samples of the tasks you give students and then later, to examine samples of the work they do in response. Begin by asking participants to bring two examples of tasks assigned. They might choose the two from tasks assigned during the last week, or perhaps one task that they think students handled quite well and another when they were disappointed with the results. Ask participants to score the tasks using the criteria provided in Appendix 7–1. Then have them predict what they think the teacher assigning the task was trying to accomplish. Taking turns, each participant might then explore how they scored the tasks they assigned and what they were trying to accomplish. As a group, the participants might want to reflect on whether the assignments studied match the kind and level of standards they have for their students. At a subsequent meeting, have participants bring three samples of student work that represent responses to these tasks that were assigned. The group might then consider using the questions offered by Blythe, Allen, and Powell discussed above to get the conversation started about what this work means and what can be learned from studying it.

As a further example, Steve Seidel and his colleagues at Harvard University's Project Zero have developed a protocol called the Collaborative Assessment Conference. Teachers are asked to examine together samples of student work and discuss what they see in the work. Seidel and his colleagues believe that while the approach can work for a range of student work, it is particularly suited to open-ended assignments. The main purpose of the Collaborative Assessment Conference is to develop a deep understanding of students' interests and strengths and of the contexts for teaching and learning that produce the samples of student work studied. The process involves the following steps:

1. *Getting started.* The group chooses a facilitator to keep it focused. Then the presenting teacher gives out copies of the selected work or displays it so all can see it. At this point, she says nothing about the work, its context, or the student. The participants read or observe the work in silence, making notes if they like.
2. *Describing the work.* The facilitator asks, "What do you see?" Participants respond without making judgments about the quality of the work or their personal preferences. If judgments emerge, the facilitator asks the speaker to describe the evidence on which the judgment is based.
3. *Raising questions.* The facilitator asks, "What questions does this work raise for you?" Group members ask any questions about the work, the child, the assignment, the circumstances of the work, and so forth that have come up for them during the previous steps of the conference. The presenting teacher makes notes but does not yet respond.
4. *Speculating about what the student is working on.* The facilitator asks, "What do you think the child is working on?" On the basis of their reading or observation of the work, participants offer their ideas.

5. *Hearing from the presenting teacher.* At the facilitator's invitation, the presenting teacher provides her perspective on the work and what she sees in it, responding to the questions raised and adding any other relevant information. She also comments on any unexpected things that she heard in the group's responses and questions.
6. *Discussing implications for teaching and learning.* The group and the presenting teacher together discuss their thoughts about their own teaching, children's learning, or ways to support this student.
7. *Reflecting on the conference.* Putting the student work aside, the group reflects together on how they experienced the conference itself.[27]

Many other frameworks and protocols for recording and studying student work have been developed. See Appendix 7–1 "Standards and Scoring Criteria for Assessment Tasks" for an example of protocols that can be used to assess the assignments that teachers give and the work that students do.

SELF-DIRECTED SUPERVISION

In self-directed supervision, teachers work alone by assuming responsibility for their own professional development. They might, for example, develop a yearly plan that includes targets or goals derived from an assessment of their own needs. This plan then might be shared with supervisors or other designated individuals. As the process unfolds, teachers should be allowed a great deal of leeway in developing the plan, but supervisors should be responsible for ensuring that the plan and selected improvement targets are both realistic and attainable. At the end of a specific period, normally a year, supervisor and teacher meet to discuss the teacher's progress in meeting professional development targets. Teachers would be expected to provide some sort of documentation, perhaps in the form of a portfolio that includes such things as time logs, reflective practice diaries, schedules, photo essays, tapes, samples of students' work, and other artifacts that illustrate progress toward goals. The yearly conference would then lead to the setting of new targets for future self-directed supervisory cycles.

There are a number of problems with approaches to supervision that rely heavily on target setting. For example, supervisors might be inclined to adhere rigidly to prespecified targets and to sometimes unnecessarily impose their own targets on teachers. Rigidly applying a target-setting format to supervision unduly focuses on the process. Teachers tend to direct their attention to prestated targets, and as a result, other areas of importance not targeted can be overlooked or neglected. Target setting is meant to help and facilitate, not to hinder the self-improvement process.

---

[27]The Collaborative Assessment Conference and the steps to guide its use were developed by Steve Seidel and his colleagues at Harvard University's Project Zero. The steps are from K. Cushman, "Looking Collaboratively at Student Work: An Essential Tool Kit," *Horace,* vol. 13, no. 2 (November 1996). This issue is available from the Coalition of Essential Schools: www.essentialschools.org/cs/resources/view/ces_res/57. See also Steve Seidel, "Wondering to Be Done: The Collaborative Assessment Conference," in D. Allen (ed.), *Assessing Student Learning: From Grading to Understanding,* New York: Teachers College Record, 1998, pp. 21–39.

TABLE 13–2. Guidelines for Implementing Self-Directed Supervision.

1. *Target setting.* On the basis of last year's observations, conferences, summary reports, clinical supervision episodes, or other means of personal assessment, teachers develop targets or goals that they would like to reach in improving their teaching. Targets should be few, rarely exceeding five or six and preferably limited to two or three. Estimated time frames should be provided for each target, which are then shared with the supervisor, along with an informal plan providing suggested activities for teacher engagement.

2. *Target-setting review.* After reviewing each target and estimated time frame, the supervisor provides the teacher with a written reaction. Further, a conference is scheduled to discuss targets and plans.

3. *Target-setting conference.* Meeting to discuss targets, time frames, and reactions, the teacher and supervisor revise targets if appropriate. It may be a good idea for the supervisor to provide a written summary of the conference to the teacher. Teacher and supervisor might well prepare this written summary together.

4. *Appraisal process.* Appraisal begins at the conclusion of the target-setting conference and continues in accordance with the agreed-upon time frame. The specific nature of the appraisal process depends on each of the targets and could include formal and informal classroom observations, an analysis of classroom artifacts, videotaping, student evaluation, interaction analysis, and other information. The teacher is responsible for collecting appraisal information and arranges this material in a portfolio for subsequent discussion with the supervisor.

5. *Summary appraisal.* The supervisor visits with the teacher to review the appraisal portfolio. As part of this process, the supervisor comments on each target, and together the teacher and supervisor plan for the next cycle of self-directed supervision.

Note: The supervisor may be the principal, a mentor teacher, or a team of teachers with whom the teacher is working.
Source: Thomas J. Sergiovanni, *The Principalship: A Reflective Practice Perspective,* 2d ed., Boston: Allyn & Bacon, 1991, p. 305.

Self-directed approaches to supervision are ideal for teachers who prefer to work alone or who, because of scheduling or other difficulties, are unable to work cooperatively with other teachers. This option is efficient in use of time, less costly, and less demanding in its reliance on others than are other options. Furthermore, this option is particularly suited to competent, experienced teachers who are able to manage their time well. Some guidelines for implementing self-directed supervision are provided in Table 13–2.

INQUIRY-BASED SUPERVISION

Inquiry-based supervision in the form of action research is an option that can represent an individual initiative or a collaborative effort as pairs or teams of teachers work together to solve problems. In action research the emphasis is on the problem-solving nature of the supervisory experience. Mixing the word "research" with such words as "action" or "supervision" may cause some initial confusion. Research, after all, is generally thought to be something mysterious, remote, statistical, and theoretical. And further, teachers and researchers have been thought to occupy separate ends of a continuum. What is a teacher–researcher anyway? Glenda Bissex believes that:

> A teacher–researcher is an observer, a questioner, a learner, and, as a result, a more complete teacher.[28]

When action research is undertaken as an individual initiative, a teacher works closely with the supervisor in sorting out a problem and developing a strategy for its resolution and in sharing findings and conclusions. Implications for practice are then identified, and strategies for implementing these changes are then developed. When action research involves collaboration with other teachers, problems are "co-researched," findings are shared, and together, teachers ferret out implications for changes in their teaching practice. Among all the options, action research requires the highest level of reflection and promises a great deal with respect to discovering new insights and practices.

Basic to action research is the belief that individual teachers and groups of teachers can undertake research to improve their own practice. Although increasing understanding and building one's store of conceptual knowledge is an important outcome of action research, its prime purpose is to alter the teaching practices of the researchers themselves. Florence Stratemeyer and her colleagues describe action research as "a process aimed at discovering new ideas or practices as well as testing old ones, exploring or establishing relationships between causes and effects, or of systematically gaining evidence about the nature of a particular problem.[29]

Although usually articulated as steps, action research proceeds as a process that more accurately involves phases that are less clearly defined. Stratemeyer and her colleagues explain:

> For convenience, the phases of this process are frequently described in terms of steps although in reality they are neither neat nor discrete. Instead, there is usually a flow from one to another, sometimes back and forth, without clear demarcations. These phases are quite similar to the sequence of the problem-solving process: the problem is identified and refined; hypotheses are formulated or hunches are advanced about its solution; the hypotheses are tested and evidence is collected, organized, and analyzed; and generalizations are drawn from the data and are retested for further validation of conclusions. In a controlled laboratory situation, the research process may closely parallel these so-called problem-solving steps. In the classroom situation, the process flow is usually quite different.[30]

---

[28]Glenda L. Bissex, "What Is a Teacher-Researcher?" *Language Arts*, September 1986.
[29]Florence B. Stratemeyer, Handen L. Forkner, Margaret G. McKim, and A. Harry Passow, *Developing a Curriculum for Modern Living*, 2d ed., New York: Teachers College, 1957, p. 708.
[30]Ibid.

Millie Almy and Celia Genishi propose the following as the basic steps for action research:

Step 1: Identify the problem.

Step 2: Develop hunches about its cause and how it can be solved.

Step 3: Test one or more of the hunches.

(a) Collect data, evidence about the situation. Some hunches held initially or tentatively may have to be rejected when more of the facts of the situation are known. Hunches that seem reasonable after careful consideration become the hypotheses of scientific investigations.

(b) Try out the hunches in action (the tryout may be in a test tube or in a classroom).

(c) See what happens (collect more data or evidence).

(d) Evaluate or generalize on the basis of evidence.[31]

For many teachers, action research works best when they engage in the process cooperatively. Problems that emerge might be of concern schoolwide or might be of concern to only two teachers whose classrooms are located across from each other. Action research as a collegial process often can result from other forms of supervision. For example, a cycle of clinical supervision might reveal pressing problems that are beyond the scope of understanding at the time. Adopting an action research stance, under this circumstance, may well be an attractive option.

INFORMAL SUPERVISION

Included in any array of options should be a provision for informal supervision. Informal supervision consists of the casual encounters that occur between supervisors and teachers and is characterized by frequent informal visits to teachers' classrooms, conversations with teachers about their work, and other informal activities.

Successful informal supervision requires that certain expectations be accepted by teachers. Otherwise it will likely be viewed as a system of informal surveillance. Principals and other supervisors need to be viewed as principal teachers who have a responsibility to be a part of all the teaching that takes place in the school. They need to be viewed as instructional partners to every teacher in every classroom for every teaching and learning situation. When informal supervision is in place, principals and supervisors become common fixtures in classrooms, coming and going as part of the natural flow of the school's daily work. But this kind of relationship is not likely to flourish unless it is reciprocal. If teachers are to invite supervisors into their classrooms as equal partners in teaching and learning, teachers must in turn be invited into the process of supervision as equal partners.

---

[31]Mille Almy and Celia Genishi, *Ways of Studying Children: An Observation Manual for Early Childhood Teachers*, rev. ed., New York: Teachers College Press, 1979, pp. 3–4.

Although we list informal supervision as an option, it should perhaps be understood as one kind of supervision that is included in any range of options that a school might provide.[32] In addition to informal supervision, teachers should be involved in at least one other approach, such as clinical, peer, self-directed, or inquiry-based supervision. In selecting additional options, supervisors should accommodate teacher preferences and honor them in nearly every case. Nonetheless, final responsibility for deciding the appropriateness of a selected option should probably be reserved for the supervisor.

LEARNING WALKS

Learning walks (or walk-throughs, as they are often called) involve visiting classrooms to study teaching practices and the learning environment which exists in classrooms and in the school itself. Particularly important is to look for artifacts of learning and other evidence that students are achieving and that the work they are engaged in is important. Unlike casual visits to classrooms, learning walks are more purposeful. In New York City, San Diego, and other school districts, learning walks have served as a way to evaluate the extent to which principals and other designated instructional leaders are implementing agreed-upon teaching frameworks in their schools and are linking learning to appropriate standards. Researcher Amy Hightower describes the learning-walk process in these schools as follows:

> About twice each semester an IL [instructional leader from the central office] would visit each school in the Learning Community to see, through analysis of teachers' practice and school and classroom environment, how principals were incorporating what they had learned at the monthly meetings. During these WalkThroughs, the IL and principal together would visit about 10–15 classrooms in two or three hours. As they walked from classroom to classroom, the pair typically discussed what they had observed. They would reconvene in the front office after the classroom visitations to share what they had noticed in more depth and would agree upon next steps for the school. The Instructional Leader would follow up each visit with a letter to the principal, specifying what was observed and what areas need improvement by the next WalkThrough.[33]

The learning walk, as created by the Institute for Learning at the University of Pittsburgh, invites designated supervisors, informal supervisors, teachers, and others to visit several classrooms to examine student work and to talk with students and teachers. Sometimes protocols are used to help focus the classroom visit on specific elements or ideas thought to be important. Is there evidence that the content being taught is linked in some meaningful way to our standards? Do students have the opportunity to create new knowledge? Sometimes a checklist of what to look for is

[32]Glatthorn, *Differentiated Supervision*, p. 59.

[33]Amy M. Hightower, *San Diego's Big Boom: District Bureaucracy Supports Culture of Learning,* Research Report, Center for the Study of Teaching and Policy, University of Washington, January 2002, p. 11 (available at www.ctpweb.org).

TABLE 13–3. What to Look for in the Social Studies Classroom.

The Classroom Learning Environment

- Students are given ample opportunity to share and compare their solutions and strategies in small group settings.
- Teachers and students are sharing ideas, strategies, and solutions in two-way communication.
- Time and structured tasks are provided for students to explore and discover concepts under the guidance of the teacher.

The Role of the Teacher

- Poses thought-provoking questions and situations that challenge students' thinking and contribute to their understanding.
- Allows students to pursue their own ways of thinking, but provides important information as needed to support the learning process.
- Provides regular opportunities for students to clarify and justify their ideas orally and in writing.
- Encourages students to select tools that will help them to build understanding.
- Emphasizes activities that engage students in inquiry and problem solving about significant social studies issues.
- Provides opportunities to integrate social studies with other areas of the curriculum.
- Uses a variety of instructional methods to reach all learning styles.
- Acts as a facilitator in the learning process.
- Uses standard to guide instruction.

Student Expectations

- Aware of the Texas Essential Knowledge and Skills/Student Expectations.
- Engaged in interactive questioning and discussion.
- Engaged in practical applications of social studies content and skills.

Source: Eric McGarrah, North East Independent School District, San Antonio, Texas. Used with permission. See also Phillip C. Schlechty, *Working on the Work: An Action Plan for Teachers, Principals, and Superintendents,* San Francisco: Jossey-Bass, 2002; and Robert J. Marzano, Debra J. Pickering, and Jane E. Pollock, *Classroom Instruction that Works: Research-Based Strategies for Increasing Student Achievement,* Alexandria, VA: Association for Supervision and Curriculum Development, 2001.

provided. Table 13–3, "What to Look for in the Social Studies Classroom," is an example. Observers check items they see and then provide evidence to support their checks. Those involved in the walk-through will need ample time to examine and discuss the evidence. The evidence is key, for it is the source of practical ideas that might help schools improve their teaching and learning.

STUDENT ENGAGEMENT AS EXAMPLE

What would happen if we developed a protocol to find out why students are engaged in some schools but disengaged in others? Suppose we put together five teams of teachers and students (perhaps three teachers and two students on each team) who would be trained to do walk-throughs to search for examples of student disengagement or lack of connections. Suppose each team focused on questions such as the following and when connections are observed (or not observed) they provide examples:

1. Are students excited about learning? What examples of excitement or lack of excitement were observed?
2. Do students spend extra time and effort on learning?
3. Do students take responsibility for learning?
4. Do students work together, cooperate with each other, help each other?
5. Do schools define everything that will be studied and how it will be studied? Or do students have a say too? How important is this say? Do students help decide what will be assessed and how it will be assessed? Do students help decide what the standards will be and what rubrics will be used to assess their work?
6. Are students encouraged to raise questions?
7. Are students working hard enough? Being challenged?
8. Do students seem passionate about their work, responsible for their work, and involved in doing their work?
9. Are teachers and students having fun?
10. Are students required to demonstrate their learning by sharing what they know with each other and with other groups?

This cadre of 25 "critical friends" (15 teachers and 10 students) would be responsible for gathering evidence, discussing the evidence among themselves, and then sharing their findings with faculty and students. Focusing on students and their work is as important as studying teaching and studying the learning environment. And when the focus is on the extent to which students are engaged, we are tapping the heart of school improvement. In Chapter 1, for example, we provided a model of school improvement that viewed student engagement as a critical link between school-improvement efforts and advances in student achievement. This might be a good time to review the model and the three pathways, noting how important supervisory leadership is to school success.

LEARNING WALKS IN BOSTON

Boston uses the following six essentials to develop a framework of expectations for its schools:

- Use effective instructional practices, and create a collaborative school climate to improve student learning.
- Examine student work and data to drive instruction and professional development.
- Invest in professional development to improve instruction.

- Share leadership to sustain instructional improvement.
- Focus resources to support instructional improvement and improved student learning.
- Partner with families and community to support student learning.[34]

The district believes that the essentials and their components provide needed instructional coherence without unduly reducing the amount of discretion teachers have to decide what and how to teach and to provide an appropriate learning environment. Further, because the essentials and their components are made explicit, a common language is developed that can encourage teachers to reflect on these practices, to share what they know, and to help each other succeed. Boston leadership would argue that a common language and shared meanings are essential if collegiality is to develop and be sustained.

There are a number of ways the schools can gauge the extent to which the essentials are being successfully embodied in the practices of teachers and schools. One way is to use the essentials as benchmarks for learning walks. For our discussion of the six essentials, we will use only the first essential, the core essential, effective instruction, as an example to show how learning walks can be a way to establish meaningful discussions about what is going on, to assess where the district needs to go, and to marshal the district's professional development resources. This core essential and its components are shown in Exhibit 13–1. Those conducting learning walks in classrooms would be looking for evidence that "students can explain what they are learning and why and how it connects to what they have already learned." They would look for evidence as well for other factors, listed in the "In Classrooms" column, in Exhibit 13-1. For factors in the "Around the School" column, the learning-walk team would look for evidence such as this: "Every classroom has areas for students to read, write, and work on their own and in pairs and a common area for the whole class to meet and talk. Current, exemplary student work is posted throughout the school." Teaching and learning expectations for the school itself are provided in the section "Expectations for Schools" that appears at the beginning of Exhibit 13–1.

After the walk, teams should be able to discuss these questions: What does what we see tell us about the extent to which we are on target? What and where are we doing especially well? Where do we need to improve? What ideas do we have for improvement? What are the implications for our coaching and other professional development efforts?

Learning walks can be planned or can take place on a more ad hoc basis. At the spur of the moment, the principal might, for example, ask one of the coaches and the librarian to cover for two teachers so that they can join the principal in a spontaneous learning walk. Whatever the strategy chosen, it seems best to narrow the focus of a learning walk to only a few issues or to one or two themes.

[34]Boston Public Schools Whole-School Improvement: The Six Essentials, Boston Public Schools, 2004.

Boston Public Schools Whole-School Improvement:
The First of Six Essentials.

THE CORE ESSENTIAL: EFFECTIVE INSTRUCTION
Use effective instructional practices and create a
collaborative school climate to improve student learning

EXPECTATIONS FOR SCHOOLS

- In every classroom, teachers use an inquiry-based approach — workshop instruction — that is organized in the following way:

  - Mini-lesson/Objective: The teacher presents and/or models the day's learning objective — a standards-based fact, concept, strategy, or skill (approximately 20% of class time, which includes a "Do Now" task, five-minute warm-up, or review of the previous day's work)

  - Independent Work: Individually or in small groups, students apply the learning objective to their reading, writing, or other work, while the teacher confers with some students about the learning objective (approximately 60% of class time)

  - Share/Summing Up: The teacher sums up the learning objective, and students discuss how they used it in their work (approximately 20% of class time)

- During class and in every subject, students read, write, and solve problems regularly, doing work of high cognitive demand to help them reach proficiency.

- The school uses a year-long curriculum in core subjects that delineates content and skills.

- The school develops positive relationships among staff and students that support a professional learning community for adults and an engaging, motivating learning environment for students. The school has a student behavior policy.

EVIDENCE: WHAT YOU SHOULD SEE AND HEAR . . .

In Classrooms

- Students can explain what they are learning and why and how it connects to what they have already learned. They are able to talk about the quality of their own work and what they must do to improve it.

- The teacher and students engage in a high level of discourse that goes beyond right/ wrong and yes/no answers to an emphasis on evidence.

- Teachers give prompt and specific feedback to students on their work, based on standards. In conferences, both the teacher and students talk about the work.

- Classroom walls display current student work and charts the teacher and students have created together about the content they are studying, standards for exemplary work, and class rules. Students refer to the charts frequently.

- Classroom space is organized so that students can get what they need — books, journals, other materials — on their own.

Around the School

- Every classroom has areas for students to read, write, and work on their own and in pairs and a common area for the whole class to meet and talk. Current, exemplary student work is posted throughout the school.

- Every teacher is able to explain what his/her students are learning and why and describe how his/her instruction will get students to proficiency in core academic subjects.

- The principal-headmaster and teachers — including teachers of special needs students and English language learners and teacher-specialists — meet regularly in teams to talk about instructional practice.

- The principal-headmaster spends time in classrooms every day, observing and discussing work with teachers and students.

- The principal-headmaster models learning by observing classroom practice, leading learning walks, and discussing his/her own learning with staff.

EXPECTATIONS FOR CENTRAL ADMINISTRATORS

- The superintendent and his[/her] teams use expectations for schools when observing classrooms and evaluating principals-headmasters.

- Every employee is able to explain Whole-School Improvement (WSI) and his/her role in that effort.

- Central departments base their decisions on the question, "How will this decision help students become better readers, writers, and thinkers and reach proficiency?"

Exhibit 13–1.

Source: The first of Six Essentials. Focus on Children, Boston Public Schools Whole-School Improvement: Six Essentials, Boston Public Schools, 2004. Used with permission. For a complete listing of the Six Essential Elements refer to http://boston.K12. ma.us/teach/offices.pdf.

PROVIDING INSTRUCTIONAL LEADERSHIP

We believe that teachers have critically important roles to play as instructional leaders in our schools. Indeed, unless they become instructional leaders, schools will not be able to keep up with the escalating learning demands they face. Supervisors have a key role to play in this process. Designated supervisors (principals, for example) in this configuration should be thought of as instructional leaders who are able to provide instructional leadership as needed while at the same time encouraging instructional leadership among the faculty. How should principals provide this instructional leadership? Unfortunately, there is no single recipe that will work in every situation. But we can get a good idea of what the possibilities are and what major themes are essential by paying attention to the experiences of others. In preparing for a special feature on leadership, *Education Week* invited principals to respond by e-mail to three questions: How would you define what it means to be an instructional leader? Give an example of something you do that captures the role of instructional leaders. Describe the biggest obstacles to exercising instructional leadership. The 24 e-mail responses they received were combined with comments made by 115 principals who participated in a Principals' Leadership Summit sponsored by the U.S. Department of Education. Here is what five of these principals said in response to the second question, "Give an example of something you do that captures the role of instructional leader:"

> About once a quarter, I put out a "seen and noted" sheet that doesn't name names, but praises wonderful things I've seen in the classrooms. I praise instructional techniques, . . . [and include] notes about how teachers are integrating technology with specific examples of several classroom projects, cross-curricular thematic units I've observed, peer tutoring, some excellent co-teaching going on, etc. This little newsletter helps to promote the best practices (according to my value system) that are taking place in our school.
>
> I [also] start each day with a morning assembly where I get to set the climate for the day, share our educational priorities with the students, remind them of our core values on a regular basis, reward students for demonstrating those values every day, celebrate successes, and foster a sense of "we" in our school.

> I review testing/screening data on each child and sign off on all intervention plans (reading sufficiency/at risk, attendance, work completion, attitude, low performance, individualized education plan, etc.). Insights are gained by checking student-goal folders, daily journals, and writing portfolios periodically, and conferencing with teaching and support staff about progress.
>
> "Seeing kids for good reasons" means listening to a few students read from journals, books, and assignments on a daily basis. Each child receives a personal note of encouragement or congratulations on at least one report card throughout the year. I see hundreds of kids for good reasons; tens of kids in problem-solving sessions.

> The most important gift that elementary teachers can give a child is a lifelong love of reading, together with the necessary skills to accomplish this significant feat. I feel that elementary leaders must have a working understanding of literacy development and its relationship to other curricular areas.

I have many excellent teachers whose opinions I value. Often, I have informal discussions with one or two to gather their thoughts on particular issues. I use them as a sounding board to discuss new district initiatives, current trends, and possible modifications. I listen very carefully to their ideas. They're the experts!

Also, I encourage my master teachers to become actively engaged in district activities—developing curriculum, presenting at professional development workshops, becoming trainers, etc.

Instructional leadership in my building means being in the classroom as much as you possibly can. I try to make a concerted effort to be in at least five classrooms a day . . . and I'm coming in unannounced. It's being in the know, and being able to get up in a classroom and say, "I sure did like what I saw in your classroom the other day". . . . I [also] am probably the best at finding money under a rock to send teachers to a state conference or a national conference.

Principals should be right in the middle of instruction. Any time my teachers are involved in a new program, I go through the training with them.[35]

Clearly, the instructional leadership described above and found as one goes from school to school differs, reflecting the different personalities and dispositions of supervisors on the one hand, and differences in the problems, issues, and intents that define supervisory situations on the other. But overriding these differences in style and circumstances is a common commitment to teaching and learning, to helping teachers learn more about teaching and learning, and to discovering how the practice of teaching in the school can continually improve. This common focus is an important marker for instructional leadership. But is it enough?

THE COMPONENTS OF INSTRUCTIONAL LEADERSHIP

The critical incidents provided by the five principals above suggest that practicing instructional leadership successfully requires focusing on teaching and learning in a way that ensures an emphasis on three themes: subject-matter content, principles of learning, and teaching processes. In today's supervision, the teaching processes seem to have dominated, often resulting in a neglect of attention on subject matter and learning principles. This neglect can lead to a vacuous brand of instructional leadership. Just because students are involved, a caring environment is provided, teacher handouts are ready, lessons are opened and closed on time, the teacher writes his or her objectives on the board, cooperative learning is used, and wait time is right does not necessarily mean academic performance will improve if lessons are content-poor and if learning principles are ignored. Yet most observation schedules emphasize recording the presence or absence of teacher behaviors and not what is

---

[35]Leadership Survey, "Telling It Like It Is," *Education Week,* November 1, 2000, p. 18. The respondents, in order of comments, were Linda Searby, Marci Brueggen, Mary M. Reece, Janet Vernon, and Belinda Shook. Reprinted with permission from *Education Week.*

going on in classrooms regarding matters of subject matter standards, content adequacy, and learning intents. Supervisors, argue Barbara Nelson and Annette Sassi, "need to be able to discern the central intellectual ideas of the lesson and to pay attention to how they are being developed within the classroom's structures and practices."[36] At the same time, getting content and learning principles right but failing the teaching-processes test is not likely to be much better for students. All three need attention if we are going to have successful instructional leadership.

Many principals have found ways to bring the three components of instructional leadership together in effective ways. Carmen Farina, formerly a principal in New York City's School District 2 and now Deputy Chancellor for Teaching and Learning, serves as a good example. She created something called the participatory lesson that she used to supervise untenured members of her faculty at P.S. 6 and tenured teachers who volunteered to participate. Participatory lessons give the principal an opportunity to visit each classroom and to participate as a co-teacher in a lesson the teacher develops. The day before the visit Mrs. Farina received a lesson plan from the teacher that spelled out the subject, goals, teaching and learning methods, and materials that would be used. A group of students was identified for Mrs. Farina to work with. The lesson plan also provided background for the lesson context and for following up on the lesson. In 1999, according to Carmen Farina, "all lessons were done in the area of literacy and through this process, I was able to keep up with the latest TC [Teachers College, Columbia University] vocabulary and process, so that I was more informed and helpful in moving teachers school-wide with their literacy initiative."[37] Further details are provided in Appendix 13–1, which outlines the participatory lesson. The appendix appears in the form of a letter to 13 teachers providing directions; the lesson plan provided by one of the teachers; and a follow-up letter to that teacher from Carmen Farina. The letter shows how critical the three components (content, principles of learning, and process) are to instructional leadership.

Other supervisory initiatives at P.S. 6 included "conversations" with all teachers and the development of a portfolio by all tenured teachers. The conversation is an important event at P.S. 6. Teacher and principal sit together for a "do not disturb" meeting to share concerns, exchange views, and provide suggestions. "The conversation covers curriculum issues, the entire class roster and specifies the intervention strategies to be undertaken for the 'at risk' student, both academically and emotionally. These conversations are then transformed to letters for file and become a permanent record of that teacher to be referred to at different times of the year."[38] As a result, ideas expressed, goals set, and agreements reached become a contract between the principal and the teacher for the entire year. What would Carmen Farina's advice be for principals who really wanted to be instructional leaders? Here are two

---

[36]Barbara Nelson and Annette Sassi, "Shifting Approaches to Supervision: The Case of Mathematics Supervision," *Educational Administration Quarterly,* vol. 36, no. 4 (October 2000), p. 574.

[37]Carmen Farina, "Dateline for School-wide Planning," School document P.S. 6, District 2. New York City Board of Education, 1999.

[38]Ibid.

thoughts: "To stimulate change, principals must be aware of what is happening in every classroom every day."[39] And, "to convince teachers of good teaching strategies, I am first and foremost a teacher myself. I go into classrooms and demonstrate the process as well as elicit the products. Change never ends."[40]

BECOMING A TEACHER LEADER

Any strategy that relies on an array of professional development approaches will be placed at risk without the school's making a strong investment in teacher leadership. Teacher leaders need to know what they are doing, why they are doing it, and where they can go for help. But too often these critical resources are not provided in an adequate way.

Starting a new supervisory program involving teacher leaders has its difficulties. Whether we are talking about adding content coaches, change or capacity coaches, clinical supervision facilitators, peer supervision facilitators, reflective practice coaches, or teaching and learning specialists, the challenges are steep. Teacher leaders and those who support them have to work hard to avoid drifting back to the familiar. Many teachers who become instructionally focused teacher leaders wind up taking on too many administrative responsibilities. In many schools they become junior vice-principals, occupied with important things but not instructionally focused things.

Successfully introducing a new teacher role is hard. One problem is, How do we help both teachers and teacher leaders get ready for a role that will have to be created and created continually as teachers and teacher leaders learn together and practice together? Whatever the readiness strategy, it will need to give attention to purpose, planning, practice, participation, and more practice. There will be little chance of success without some clarity of purpose, some definition of what the school is trying to accomplish, what purposes should be at the center of the work of teacher leaders, what kinds of planning will be needed to help guide what teacher leaders do and how they do it. As these questions are answered, ways to implement programs and strategies will have to be invented. How can we begin to practice ourselves what we want teachers to practice with students? Are we able and willing to invite teachers to participate with us from the beginning? Will they be able to help us shape our purposes and design our practices?

We noted in Chapter 12 that teacher leaders need training in content. They and the teachers they work with will have to know what is worth changing and what is worth learning. Teacher leaders also need training in process. How do we do the things worth doing? How do we learn to lead? How do we learn to facilitate? How do we model for teachers and how do they model for us so that we can become stronger communities of practice? And finally, teacher leaders need training in culture. How do we help teacher leaders develop the idea frameworks and norms

---

[39]Carmen Farina, "Creating a Climate for Change," *NYC Challenge,* 1993, p. 31.
[40]Ibid., p. 32.

they need to help sustain change over time? While training in content and training in process seem obvious enough, training in culture is too often neglected—a problem we hope to solve in Chapters 15 and 16. Suffice it to say at this point, it is doubtful if teacher leaders will succeed without the encouragement and support of principals and other designated supervisors.

SUMMARY

Leadership density is critical to success. Teacher leadership contributes to the development of leadership density in the school. Leadership density refers to the total amount of leadership available from teachers, support staff, and others on behalf of the school and its work.[41] Leadership density is evidenced by the number of different people in a variety of overlapping roles throughout the school.

As Smylie, Conley, and Marks[42] suggest, the same tasks and functions are performed by different roles. Supervisory functions and tasks and teacher-learning functions and tasks are good examples, for they are an important part of many roles, beginning with the teacher in the classroom and stretching all the way through the central office to the superintendent. Responsibility for these tasks and functions is distributed across those roles, and the development of leadership density is the consequence. Leadership density contributes to the development of instructional coherence as purposes and values, goal achievement and commitments, become established deep into the school. Leadership density helps institutionalize these characteristics as part of the school's culture.

Clinical supervision and coaching are broad strategies for improvement that overlap each other. They take a broad variety of forms, including lesson study, peer supervision, mentoring, looking at student work, and studying the assignments that teachers give. Despite their differences, all these approaches to supervision share certain important features:

- They are focused on teaching and learning that is classroom-based.
- They are expressions of formative supervision.
- They involve the teacher as co-supervisor.
- They avoid scripting by encouraging leaders to create their practice in use.
- They blur the line between teaching and learning to teach better.
- They contribute to the development of a web of communities of practice in the school.

Dennis Sparks of the National Staff Development Council believes that for schools to meet the challenges they face, teachers need to accept collective responsibility for student achievement. Further, their efforts need to be supported by state-of-the-art professional development. This professional development needs to (1) focus on both deepening the content knowledge of teachers and their teaching skills; (2) include opportunities for teachers to engage in reflective practice and to research their practice together; (3) be embedded in the work of the classroom; and (4) be sustained over time and focus on a sense of collegiality that brings together the school as a collaborative culture and its teachers as members as communities of practice.[43]

---

[41]Thomas J. Sergiovanni, *The Principalship: A Reflective Practice Perspective,* 4th ed., Boston: Allyn & Bacon, 2001, p. 162.

[42]Mark Smylie, Sharon Conley, and Helen M. Marks, "Exploring Approaches to Teacher Leadership for School Improvement," *The Educational Leadership Challenge: Redefining Leadership for the 21st Century,* 101st Yearbook of the National Society for the Study of Education, Chicago: NSSE, 2002, pp. 162–188.

[43]Dennis Sparks, *Designing Powerful Professional Development for Teachers and Principals,* National Staff Development Council, June 2002 (online book at www.nsdc.org/library/leaders/sparksbook.cfm).

Supervision highlights the power of leadership. Supervision is critical to the success of the deep and expansive kind of leadership we advocate. In many ways supervision and leadership are the same thing. After all, as Trice and Beyer point out, in many societies the word *culture* is not central to their language system and thus must be talked about in alternative ways. For example, the Japanese, Chinese, and Korean languages lack a word that corresponds to our use of the word leader. The closest they come is the word *coach*. To them, a leader is a coach.[44]

Heifetz and Linsky elevate the meaning of leadership so that it plays a key role in the school's lifeworld—the way schools construct meaning and use this meaning to give purpose. "By making the lives of people around you better, leadership provides meaning in life. It creates purpose. We believe that every human being has something unique to offer, and that a larger sense of purpose comes from using that gift to help your organization, family, or community thrive."[45] Part of purposing is to create meaning, and the creation of meaning strengthens purpose.

The chapters in this section of the book have been concerned with professional development, supervision, and teacher evaluation. The three themes are considered to be at the heart of instructional leadership. The next and final chapter in this section focuses more narrowly on the problems and issues affecting our thinking about and practices of teacher evaluation. To help tie our deliberations together, we provide, in Appendix 13–2, a set of questions for assessing a school's progress in addressing professional development, supervision, and staff evaluation. These questions were developed by Judith Warren Little, an expert on the relationship between professional development and professional community and their subsequent effects on school improvement.

SOME REFLECTIONS

1. With which supervisory options do you believe teachers will be most comfortable? Why? With which supervisory options do you feel teachers will be least comfortable? Why?
2. Time is always an issue. What ideas do you have about making time for the heavy demands of professional development?
3. Plan three informal learning walks in your school. Use the protocols outlined in Table 13–3. Use the ideas from the discussion of learning walks in Boston. And use the protocols provided that help in the analysis of student work.

[44]Harrison Trice and Janice Beyer, *The Culture of Work Organizations,* Englewood Cliffs, NJ: Prentice Hall, 1993.
[45]Ronald A. Heifetz and Marty Linsky, *Leadership on the Line: Staying Alive Through the Dangers of Leading,* Boston: Harvard Business School Press, 2002, p.3.

Appendix 13–1:
Outlining the Participatory Lesson—Sample Documents

P.S. 6 MANHATTAN

A. Letter to Thirteen Teachers who will be Involved

CARMEN FARIÑA,
PRINCIPAL
MARIA R. STILE,
ASSISTANT PRINCIPAL

TO: Thirteen teachers

FROM: Carmen Fariña

RE: PARTICIPATORY LESSONS

DATE: December 17, 1999

This year, as per all our ongoing conversations, Participatory Lessons will focus in the areas of literacy (either writing or reading) with a strong emphasis on the following strategies:

1.   Planning
2.   Grouping
3.   Pacing
4.   Appropriateness

In order to better evaluate all of the above, I will be structuring all visits in the following way:

We will have a half-hour planning session, in your classroom, at least two days prior to the actual visit. I will cover your class for this time and advise you when this will take place. At this time we will discuss what your lesson will be and my particular role in it. I anticipate hearing from you as to how this lesson fits into your year-long literacy initiative as well as the specificness of the lesson you plan on doing. I want you to give me a specific assignment for working with your at-risk students so that I might prepare as well. Your plan should include a pre and post assessment of student needs as well as some detail of how you plan to follow up the lesson after my visit. I will be having an information meeting on January 10th, at 3:15 PM to answer any questions about the above lesson. As you know, planning is an essential part of good instruction and so a large part of the emphasis of this mid-year evaluation will be focusing on the evidence of this strategy. I also ask you to give serious consideration to the appropriateness of the materials to be used during the lesson. I know everyone is working extremely hard and I anticipate having a wonderful time visiting your individual classrooms.

Feel free to consult with any mentors in the school, as well as myself, as you prepare for this visit.

45 EAST 81ˢᵗ STREET   •   NEW YORK, NY 10028   •   (212) 737-9774

Source : School documents used with the permission of Carmen Farina.

B. Lesson Plan Submitted by One of the Teachers

Lesson Plan for Participatory Lesson
Date: Friday, January 21, 2000

Objective: Students will try and experiment with one or more craft elements in their writer's notebook.

Materials:
- overhead projector
- craft chart
- writing folder (*Maybe a Fight* by Jean Little)
- writer's notebook
- pencil

Previous Lessons:
- introduction to what is craft
- two days of 'unpacking' the text (*Maybe a Fight* By Jean Little)
- two days of working with writing partners to develop a relationship about writing and give advice as to their own craft
- multiple days of directed trying of specific craft techniques in their writer's notebook

Procedure:

1. Students gather on the rug (bring writing folder, writer's notebook, pencil)
2. Sit with writing partners
3. Yesterday we tried different ideas about craft in our writer's notebooks. We shared with our partners.
4. Wednesday we used our partners to help us plan out our 'try it' for today.
5. In my notebook, I tried to use the different craft techniques that we have been talking about. I put a copy of an entry that I did this week on an overhead. I want you to read it with your partner, and talk about all of the different craft styles I have used in this entry.
6. What do you see in my notebook entry?
7. Now you go with your partner and talk about how your writing is going. Look at your partner's writing and talk about what craft you tried. Take some time to look at each other's writing and offer suggestions to improve the craft of the piece. Today I am going to tell you where to sit in the room.
8. After you have talked about the past writing you can move into the writing for today. Put an assignment box and today's date on the next clean page of your notebook.

Assessment/ What Is Next?

- Use conferences to look at student work in progress.
- 'Unpack' another text more student-initiated conversations about craft.
- Students begin to develop and recognize craft in their own writing.
- Look at published pieces for evidence of craft.

C. Entry from the Teacher's Notebook Referred to in Procedures 5 and 6

Notebook Entry
January 19, 2000

It was cold out, but not *really* as cold as everybody was saying. I do not know what all of the fuss was about. And in some way, I felt that the snow kept me warm.

I heard the creak of the front door. "Rebecca." I dreaded what was coming next. "It is time to come in."

"Not yet," I answered, trying to sound sweet and convincing and stern, all at the same time. "I'm not cold." There seemed to be silence. Could it be that she went back inside; had my plan worked? But then all at once, I heard, "The hot chocolate is ready."

I took that to mean that there would be no arguing or convincing and certainly no more snow for today. It was time to leave the snow and go inside.

D. Carmen Farina's Follow-up Letter

PARTICIPATORY LESSON
January, 2000

Dear _____:

It was an utter delight to visit your classroom and see what a wonderful environment you have created for your fourth grade. Everything in the room demonstrates rigor but I especially loved your book rating system, "awesome", "built well", "cruddy" and "doldrums". I asked the students if that had been their decision and they assured me it was, so not only are you teaching them excellent vocabulary but you are giving them total ownership of the reading process. The tone at all times was respectful and it was clear the children had learned to listen to each other as well as have true conversations.

One observation I think we need to discuss as a school is should writing and reading groups be homogeneously grouped, since I worry if there is not a "stimulator" in each group to forward the discussion.

It was clear that your lesson had been many days in the making and had been the result of careful assessment and preparation on your part. Your lesson opened by modeling your own work and I think that when teachers become writers, they totally understand the thinking the students are going through. I must say I was very taken by the blue craft sheet and it has taught me new words such as "dialogue sandwich" but also a very specific connection between Jean Little's work and the student's own work. I was particularly impressed when _____ quoted, without reading from the author's words, and clearly stated as to what she thought was important. In fact her quote, "it helps me improve my work. I don't have to think." was probably a new classic in the PS 6 mantra. I also noticed the two students that seldom participate, _____ and _____, felt extremely comfortable volunteering discussion and some students actually disagreed with you and each other.

Participatory Lesson
Page ..2..

The tone in your room, at all times, was busy and productive. When I sat to work with my specific group of _____, _____, _____, _____ and_____, it was clear that they fully understood all the writing workshop procedures, but three of the students had not done the previous night's homework, which I have since discussed with you. _____ and _____ were a surprise, as I expected them to be lower functioning. However, other than the fact that their sentence structure was very basic, their thoughts were excellent and neither child had any trouble using "the thought shot" to improve their writing. However, _____ lack of work and inability to verbalize what he planned on doing has made me re-think how we might need to add an additional after-school workshop around the issue of conversations. For some students they cannot write unless they have spent time thinking and speaking, and obviously this may be the first step we need to take with some of the children in my particular group.

It is not easily discernible that you are a first year teacher since you bring so much of positive energy and knowledge into the classroom. A few suggestions I would ask you to consider are to label the classroom tables either by number or funny names, the children will pick out. It took them about 5 minutes to decide which was table 4. If we are to continue with homogeneous grouping, a plan needs to be in place for those groups who finish too quickly and therefore spend time talking about non-essential topics. The table with _____ at it had thoroughly discussed everything and perhaps just having an assignment to read quietly when finished will eliminate their frustration level and give them something to do while everyone else is catching up.

Once again thank you for allowing me this time in your room, since I feel I am getting the full TC education with little to no effort on my part. I hope your stay with us will be long.

Sincerely,

Carmen Fariña
Principal

cc: Professional File

I received this letter and am aware a
copy will be placed in my Professional File. _____
                                                          Teacher's Signature

Appendix 13–2: Questions to Guide Schools in Assessing Their Professional Development, Supervision, and Staff Development Efforts

1. *Link to student learning goals.* The school should be able to explain how its professional development priorities and strategies advance its student learning goals.
   - What elements of the school's structure or culture build teachers' individual and collective responsibility for student achievement and well-being, and thus serve as an impetus for teacher learning?
   - What provisions does the school make for systematic inquiry into student learning? for using routine student assessment as a basis for professional development? for linking that inquiry or assessment to teachers' own development?
   - What opportunities does the school create for teachers to acquire greater expertise in subject-matter knowledge and subject teaching?
2. *Organization of teachers' work.* The school should be able to show how teachers' work has been organized and supported to make the most of existing expertise, to stimulate and enable new learning, and to respond to differences in teachers' experience, responsibilities, or other circumstances.
   - Do school schedules and staff responsibilities reduce or intensify teacher isolation? enable and reward teacher collaboration? Has teacher time been organized to ensure adequate opportunity for consultation among teachers?
   - Do teacher assignment policies and practices make it likely that teachers will make the best use of what they know and be stimulated to learn more? Will they bring teachers into contact with colleagues from whom they can learn? Do they ensure that students will have access to well-qualified and confident teachers?
   - Do resource allocation practices facilitate teachers' access to equipment, work space, reference materials, technology, and supplies that support their work and their professional development?
   - How does the school accommodate differences in teacher experience, interests, and responsibility? What formal and informal support does the school provide for beginning teachers, newly hired teachers, and teachers undertaking a significant change in responsibilities? What opportunities does the school offer for experienced teachers, including opportunities for teacher leadership?
3. *Participation in professional development activity.* The school should be able to show that all or most professional educators in the school are engaged in significant professional learning—and to show how it has avoided the pitfalls of a "laundry list" approach to professional development.
   - Does the school afford teachers significant on-site learning opportunities (including common planning times, mentoring, teacher-initiated research) *and* out-of-school professional activities (networks; professional associations; conferences; links with colleges, industry, museums)?
   - How does professional development address the range of knowledge, skills, and dispositions required to achieve intended student learning goals (subject matter, pedagogy, assessment, knowledge of students, etc.) without falling prey to superficial content and to fragmentation of effort?
   - What provision does the school make for follow-up time and other support needed to ensure that teachers can test new ideas in the classroom?
   - What steps does the school take to ensure that professional learning extends to all adults, including classified staff?

4. *Staff evaluation and school or program review.* The school should be able to show how it uses the processes and results of student assessment, staff evaluation, and school review to support professional growth.

- What part does the assessment of student learning play in the evaluation of staff performance or in the evaluation of the school program?
- What opportunities do teachers and others have to obtain timely and useful feedback on their own professional performance—formal or informal, from colleagues or supervisors?
- Does staff evaluation take serious account of individuals' participation in professional development and its effect on practice? (Does it matter whether individuals are doing anything serious to improve their own work or that of others?)
- What evidence does the school employ to assess the impact of professional development?

5. *Ethos that values learning.* Although a school's "ethos" may elude crisp definition, staff members should be able to say how central values and norms encourage or inhibit teacher learning.

- What role do administrators and other school leaders play in encouraging and supporting professional learning in the school?
- Do staff evaluation, school review, or school-level decision-making practices establish an environment of professional trust, mutual support, and the disclosure of problems? or do they foster competitiveness, privacy, and "problem hiding"?
- In what ways would an observer know that the school is an intellectually stimulating and personally rewarding place for teachers and other professionals to work? In what ways do students see evidence of teachers' involvement in learning?

Source: Judith Warren Little, "Excellence in Professional Development and Professional Community," Working paper prepared for the Office of Educational Research and Improvement Benchmarks for Schools, Washington, DC: U.S. Department of Education Blue Ribbon Program, March 1997, pp. 20–22.

CHAPTER 14

Supervision and Summative Evaluations

INTRODUCTION

This chapter explores the minefield of summative evaluation. The metaphor of a minefield is appropriate because the activity of summative evaluation, if not carefully mapped, structured, and supported, can trigger toxic legal and political explosives that disrupt community morale and the effective running of the school.

The chapter takes up the relationship between professional membership in the school community and the expectations and responsibilities of membership. Summative evaluation can employ unsupportable assumptions about the theory and practice of teaching and learning as well as the role of the supervisor, and these issues are explored in the next part of the chapter. Having cleared the underbrush, so to speak, of our minefield, we then present an idealized model of a system of summative evaluation. Toward the end of the chapter, we return to the complex relationship between teaching and learning and the organizational supports necessary to facilitate quality student learning and teaching.

SOME BACKGROUND

Every community is made up of individual personalities. Those individuals have their own talents, hang-ups, dreams, idiosyncrasies—all of which both enrich the community as well as place a collective strain on it. There is a need to keep alive the sense of community identity, a sense of what distinguishes that community from other communities, a sense of something special that holds people together. Sometimes that sense of identity derives from the central purpose that the community was founded to serve; other communities are bound together by their ethnic, religious, racial, or cultural traditions; other communities are made up of people who choose a certain lifestyle or recreational interest. In most communities there are certain requirements for initial membership and other requirements for maintaining membership. Sometimes these requirements are formalized through admission procedures and initiation rites, and through periodic ritual restatements of commitment to the community (renewal of marriage vows, celebrations of anniversaries, annual awards ceremonies, the publication of annual reports, tenure review, annual corporate retreats, etc.). Sometimes membership comes from simply remaining in the community long enough to be accepted. Most communities, however, need rituals by which they can assert their identity, maintain their identity, and protect their identity.

A school as a community of learners brings together youngsters, families, and teachers, as well as other adults. Though belonging to a variety of other communities, these people form a community with a mission to perpetuate and renew the life of the larger civic community by exploring ways to carry the culture and the polity forward in the next generation. One of the mechanisms or rituals by which this community reasserts its identity as a learning community is through periodic evaluation. Through evaluations the community agrees to assess what progress they are making in their mission as a community. For students, these evaluations take the form of tests, oral and written quizzes, final exams, portfolios, projects, and competitions. For teachers, they take a variety of forms.

Formal teacher evaluations have traditionally been sources of tension, alienation, and conflict. Some of that is inescapable, and perhaps even healthy (when it involves arguments about what constitutes an authentic expression of the mission of the school community). Much of the discomfort concerning evaluation can be eliminated, however, if it is treated as a community exercise in self-governance, as a way for the school community to maintain and strengthen its commitment to learning, rather than as a mechanism of bureaucratic control exercised over subordinates. One significant way to make the evaluation process a community exercise is to require that all members be evaluated, including supervisors, administrators, and evaluators.

In the previous chapters, we have been emphasizing supervision as a process for promoting teacher growth and enhanced student learning. Within the distinction between formative and summative evaluation, we have been emphasizing formative evaluation, that is, that kind of interaction with teachers that develops information, points of view, questions, and inquiries into alternatives, all of which teachers can use as part of an ongoing reflection on and within practice.

In this chapter, we turn to summative evaluation. This kind of evaluation involves coming to a conclusion or making a judgment about the quality of the teacher's performance. This kind of evaluation rates the teacher's performance as meeting, exceeding, or falling below some standard of teaching competence or some level of acceptable teaching performance. Often summative evaluations are tied to a formal personnel decision, such as a decision whether to grant a teacher tenure, whether to promote a teacher to a higher position or rank, or whether to renew a tenured teacher's contract. Formative evaluations *assume* membership in the learning community; summative evaluations invite a more structured reflection on the demands and meanings of membership in a learning community with a specific mission. Summative evaluation employs clear standards of membership; the basic characteristics of the community are identified in and safeguarded through summative evaluation. Formative evaluations are ways to enliven and enrich that identity, although both forms of evaluations can serve that purpose.

Whether a supervisor acts in an administrative capacity or is functioning in a purely supervisory capacity, there should be very clear, formally described distinctions between supervision for formative evaluation, supervision for summative evaluation, and supervision for administrative evaluation and decision. The process of supervision for promoting teacher growth and enhanced student learning should be clearly distinguished from the process of supervision for personnel decisions; where possible, separate personnel should perform them. Where that is not possible, teachers should know beforehand what the differences among the various processes are, and which one is being used at that time. Leaving such distinctions fuzzy and indefinite engenders widespread lack of trust among teachers and undermines the potential of formative supervision. When the supervisory process is carried on as though all the various types of evaluation are one and the same, then supervisory episodes are perceived as threatening and adversarial.

PROBLEMS WITH SUMMATIVE EVALUATIONS OF TEACHERS

Supervisors need to be aware that there are several unsupportable assumptions about summative evaluation of teachers. Precipitous action based on these assumptions can lead to legitimate grievances against supervisors. Consider the following examples.

ASSUMPTION 1. There is a clear set of criteria or standards understood and accepted by all with which a teacher's performance can be evaluated.

REBUTTAL. There is no conclusive and incontrovertible research that any specific teacher behavior or any set of teacher behaviors causes learning to take place in any specific student. What evidence there is points to relatively weak correlations between some sets of teacher behaviors and some increase in aggregate scores on tests of basic competency. In these cases there is evidence that teachers teach directly to the test and ignore what is not on the test.[1] This leads to clear distortions in student learnings, as other legitimate learning outcomes are neglected.

ASSUMPTION 2. Sporadic, unannounced classroom visits, with no prior conversations and no subsequent discussion, are a legitimate and acceptable way to assess teacher performance.

REBUTTAL. The visitor has no understanding of why the teacher is doing what he or she is doing. Until the final judgment, the teacher has no way of knowing what the visitor thinks about what is going on and has no way of changing his or her own behavior, assuming there is agreement that it is inappropriate. There is also the

---

[1]See Michael Kirst, "Interview on Assessment Issues with Lorrie Shepard," *Educational Researcher,* vol. 20, no. 2 (1991), pp. 21–23, 27; Lorrie A. Shepard, "Why We Need Better Assessments," *Educational Leadership,* vol. 46, no. 7 (April 1989), pp. 4–9.

assumption that what the visitor sees is a fair sample of what the teacher tends to do in most classrooms, an assumption not supported by the research.[2]

ASSUMPTION 3. Student achievement of course objectives is the only way to evaluate teacher performance.

REBUTTAL. What is meant by "student achievement"? If it refers to mean aggregate scores on standardized tests, then what really is being measured and who determines what is measured? Even if these tests were accepted as legitimate measures of teachers' and school goals for student learning, a pretest of students' readiness levels would be necessary. Are baseline data available that allow for computation of gains or losses in mean test scores? Even when pre- and postintervention data are available, educators must deal with the mean scores of a group of students. What if the teacher is successful in teaching slower students and not as successful with brighter students, or vice versa? Does that count for nothing? What if the teacher is good at teaching creativity, collaboration, research skills, and artistic criticism, but the tests do not measure student achievement in those areas?

Suppose, on the other hand, that student achievement is evaluated in terms of grades. Suppose the grades range from A to F. Is a teacher rated on his or her ability to increase the number of A students in the class? What if F students improve from a very low F to a very high F? In other words, how much improvement in each student's performance counts for how much in the scale of teacher ratings? Teachers must work with the hands they are dealt; why should one teacher receive a low rating for less-than-spectacular student achievement when her students are two or three grade levels behind to start with? What if student average daily attendance is abysmal, so that there are rarely the same 12 (out of 27) students in class on any given day, and hence it is impossible to assume any continuity of classroom experience for most of the students? Clearly, evaluations must take many additional, contextual factors into account besides the student achievement of course objectives.

ASSUMPTION 4. Evaluation of teacher performance should deal only with observable classroom behaviors.

REBUTTAL. This assumption is derived partially from narrow forms of clinical supervision, in which supervisors attempt to avoid subjective judgments by concentrating on observable behaviors, pointing out patterns in both teacher and student behaviors. This observational posture assumes a separateness from content considerations; for example, it fails to consider whether the teacher was teaching his or her subject matter accurately. Counting the number of times the teacher gives positive or negative feedback, the number of times the teacher calls on the same student, the number of seconds of wait time after a question, the number of times the teacher uses visual displays does not indicate whether the teacher did a good job teaching quadratic equations or the causes of the First World War. Furthermore, the

[2]Susan Stoldowsky, "Teacher Evaluation: The Limits of Looking," *Educational Researcher,* vol. 13, no. 9 (1984), pp. 11–19.

connection between observable teacher behaviors and student achievement on a variety of measures appears tenuous, according to some research evidence.[3]

These four assumptions do not stand up under rigorous cross-examination. If a supervisor, acting on these assumptions, were to render a recommendation or a decision not to rehire a teacher or not to grant tenure, the supervisor could encounter legal and professional difficulty. Courts have established very clearly that teachers, even beginning teachers, must be given due process. The essence of due process is that teachers know beforehand the criteria or standards as well as the procedures by which they will be evaluated, and that these procedures and standards have in fact been followed. Beyond due process concerns, the very criteria and standards that a school or school system establishes for such evaluation can be challenged.

NEED FOR A NEW SYSTEM

As Danielson and McGreal suggest, the traditional practices of evaluation of teachers requires a complete overhaul.[4] Current practices send confusing messages to teachers. The policy rhetoric on accountability can too often communicate a universal threat to the teaching profession that authorities are tired of mediocre results in schools and now teachers will be accountable to produce results "or else." What is needed is a clear *system* of evaluation which establishes clear criteria for what will be evaluated, how the evaluation will be carried out according to clear procedures, and what evidence will be taken into account in the evaluation process. Teachers should be involved in the design of such a system so that it may reflect their concerns as well as the concerns of school officials.

Danielson and McGreal propose four broad areas of responsibilities which constitute the focus of a system of evaluation: (1) planning and preparation; (2) classroom or learning environment; (3) instruction; and (4) professional responsibilities.[5] These categories echo much of what was discussed in Chapters 6 and 7, namely, that teachers have responsibilities for the curriculum-as-planned, as-taught, as-learned, and as-assessed. The system of evaluation would look for evidence of the careful planning and design of learning activities, learning activities tied to content standards and benchmarks set out by the district and the state; it would look for classroom procedures for engaging students in the learning tasks, for a stimulating and user-friendly learning environment, for an orderly environment free from preventable distractions so that students could focus on the tasks at

---

[3]Michael Scriven, "Can Research-Based Teacher Evaluation Be Saved?" *Journal of Personnel Evaluation in Education,* vol. 4 (1990), pp. 19–32.

[4]Charlotte Danielson and Thomas L. McGreal, *Teacher Evaluation: To Enhance Professional Practice,* Alexandria, VA: Association for Supervision and Curriculum Development, 2000.

[5]These four areas of responsibilities were derived from her earlier work, Charlotte Danielson, *Enhancing Professional Practice: A Framework for Teaching,* Alexandria, VA: Association for Supervision and Curriculum Development, 1996.

hand. The system would seek evidence of the multidimensional activity of teaching that involves engaging students in the learning activity, scaffolding the tasks with previously learned material, motivating, encouraging, supporting, challenging, asking clarifying questions, demonstrating procedures, providing feedback on work in progress, encouraging group learning and critique, and so on. The system of evaluation would, finally, look for evidence that teachers were managing their responsibilities to keep records of student progress, communicate with students and parents about their progress, collaborate in school-improvement projects and professional development.

The evaluation system would also have very clear procedures. It would lay out time frames, deadlines, and identification of roles. It would also state who will be doing what when and will explain what documentation will be required as well as what agreements will be negotiated and what forms will be used at various stages of the evaluation. It would also provide for third-party intervention and arbitration should difficulties arise.

Another important aspect of the system Danielson and McGreal propose has to do with agreements about the various kinds of evidence that will be required and reviewed in the process of coming to a summative evaluation. Besides the traditional classroom observation, there is the expectation that teachers can produce lesson plans, learning-activity designs, authentic assessment procedures, as well as samples of student work that illustrate the achievement of various desired levels or dimensions or facets of understanding, along with a brief commentary, which highlights how the student work reflects the desired outcomes anticipated in the planning for the lessons, and how that learning maps back to content standards and benchmarks. Other evidence might include letters to parents, logs of conversations with parents and students, reading lists, worksheets, logs of professional development activities, and collaborative curriculum designs with other teachers.

The system would be incomplete without a solid training of the evaluators. Those doing the evaluation should have a common understanding of the criteria and through a variety of exercises, attempt to arrive at similar ratings of various types of evidence. The system of evaluation can be challenged if a teacher's summative evaluation varies significantly depending on who is doing the evaluation. To be fair to all, the evaluators need to be in substantial agreement on how they rate the evidence, and how they follow the policies and procedures of the evaluation system.

Danielson and McGreal add a rather important consideration to the system of evaluation, namely, the additional variable of difficulty or challenge a teacher might face in teaching a particular group of students. For example, some teachers might not be able to document the expected growth of all of their students. Some of these students might be special-needs students, some recent immigrants, some in trouble with the police, some from very difficult home situations. Because of conditions over which the teacher has little control, the progress of these students might be considerably slower than the progress of the majority of the students. In systems where teacher evaluation is tied to student improvements in learning, this teacher might be unfairly evaluated. Hence the evaluation system has to have a way to take these circumstances into account.

TYPES OF TEACHER EVALUATION

Teachers need to know that there are three general types of teacher evaluation. Often these are lumped together without the proper clarifying distinctions, leaving teachers confused and defensive over the whole process of evaluation. These three types are (1) administrative summative evaluation, (2) supervisory summative evaluation, and (3) supervisory formative evaluation. As Figure 14–1 indicates, each type of teacher evaluation has distinct purposes, processes, and results. In practice, each type overlaps to various degrees the other two. Nevertheless, when teachers and supervisors know ahead of time the primary focus and purpose of the evaluation event, they both can engage the process with greater integrity and clarity.

Participation in the summative evaluation system will probably cost the supervisor some trust in the working relationship with the teacher, at least initially. During the three-year interim between summative evaluations, teachers will remember the rating that the supervisor gave, but even more important, they will remember that the supervisor has the *power* to give a summative rating. What teachers sometimes forget is that they have voted for such a system and have had a hand in designing it. Unless a teacher receives a superior rating, the tendency is to resent

TYPE	Administrative Evaluation	Supervisory Summative Evaluation	Supervisory Formative Evaluation
PURPOSE	• Tenure decisions • Probation decisions • Dismissal decisions	• Periodic, in-depth reflection • Membership renewal • Reappropriation of mission • Assessment of growth	• Ongoing reflective growth
PROCESS	• Legally correct • Highly structured • Highly directive • Either-or criteria • Either-or judgments	• Structured alternatives • Collegial • Checks and balances • Multifaceted	• Action research • Pursuit of growth targets • Staff development workshops • Clinical supervision • Peer coaching • School renewal projects • Networking with regional groups
PRODUCT	Decisions Negative Positive Dismissal Retention	Summative Evaluation Negative Positive Administrative New growth evaluation plan + Formative evaluation	• Reflective practice • Invention • Integration of classroom activities with schoolwide goals • New materials, strategies • New courses

FIGURE 14–1. Types of Evaluation.

the supervisor who gave a lower rating. The resentment may be diminished if the system is perceived as being as fair and evenhanded as possible.[6]

Teachers and administrators in the school should know the difference between formative and summative supervision. Summative evaluations differ according to purpose. Each format should have a structured series of steps, with mutual responsibilities clearly spelled out. Depending on the kind of personnel decisions to be made, the structure of the evaluation may vary. The following hypothetical examples from Sunlight School show how different summative evaluations might be structured.

TEACHER EVALUATION IN THE SUNLIGHT SCHOOL DISTRICT

The following policies and procedures governing teacher evaluation in the district are intended to assist all teachers, supervisors, and administrators in carrying out their responsibilities as members of the Sunlight community.

Preamble

Sunlight School District is justifiably proud of its students, teachers, support staff, and parents. We work hard to be a community whose mission is the achievement of high-quality learning as it applies to learning our various cultures and traditions, as it applies to learning our various civic responsibilities, as it applies to learning for a range of career and employment opportunities, and as it applies to the fuller growth of our own humanity, both individual and collective. We believe membership in this community is a privilege. We expect a lot of our members, but with those expectations we embrace the consequent responsibility to support our members with financial, cultural, and educational resources for carrying out those responsibilities.

Sunlight School District is required by law and contract to have in place a system of teacher evaluation. These requirements aside, the district sees that it is in the best interests of the Sunlight community to have a system of teacher evaluation in place to guarantee to the best of our ability that our student members have the best available human resources in their challenging adventure of learning. Because the teaching–learning process and the institutional supports undergirding that process entail very complex activities and arrangements, we believe that a teacher-evaluation system should be responsive to that complexity. We believe as a first principle that, next to our students, teachers are the most precious resource for sustaining and improving the life of our civic community. As such, they deserve a transparent and supportive system that enables and encourages them to be their best. Achieving this does not happen in the first week of their first year of teaching in the Sunlight School District. Learning the practice of teaching to a level of excellence is a slow and demanding process. The teacher-evaluation process will take into consideration the gradual learning trajectory of the teaching career toward our expectations of excellence. On the other hand, the teacher-evaluation process will continue to hold

[6]Milbrey Wallin McLaughline and R. Scott Pfeifer, *Teacher Evaluation: Improvement, Accountability, and Effective Learning,* New York: Teachers College Press, 1988.

to high ideals of teaching practice in its expectations of continual professional growth and development.

Necessary Distinctions in the Evaluation Process

Having set forth our mission and beliefs in the preamble, we turn now to the details of the teacher-evaluation system. We distinguish between formative evaluation processes and summative evaluation processes. Formative processes are those which engage teachers with supervisors, mentors, or peers in a cooperative process of improvement. These processes are exploratory, dialogical, and collaborative. They can take a variety of forms, from a chance conversation over lunch, to a coaching session with a subject-area coach, to shared classroom visits with peers, to clinical observations with mentors, department chairs, cluster leaders, administrators, and other designated and informal supervisors. In short, formative supervision overlaps many other varieties of professional development within the district.

Summative evaluations processes are divided into two types. One type involves a supervisor or a team of supervisors who engage with a teacher in a variety of her or his teaching responsibilities to arrive at some kind of judgment about the quality of the teacher's performance of those responsibilities. These judgments are to be based on a variety of evidence, ranging from classroom observations, reviews of unit and lesson plans, student assessments and teacher feedback, to portfolios of the teacher's or students' work. Such summative assessments usually last the better part of a year and issue in some assessment of the teacher's strengths and future growth areas.

Another type of summative evaluation is administrative in nature. The administrator, usually a principal or central office administrator, is required through this process to make a decision about the membership of the teacher—whether the teacher has satisfied the responsibilities of membership or not. This decision, based on the evidence compiled in the first type of summative evaluation, as well as additional evidence as the situation may require, affects whether or not a teacher has a contract to continue in the Sunlight School District. The teacher-evaluation system as it is described below refers only to these two types of summative evaluations.

I. Summative Evaluation for Nontenured Teachers
   A. During their first year in the district, teachers will be assigned a mentor, undergo a yearlong induction process of monthly meetings (consult the five-page document on Teacher Induction), and avail themselves of other supports provided by the district as will seem appropriate to their mentors and principals. These supports are intended to provide multiple opportunities for new teachers to gain a more secure foothold in their practice of their profession. At the end of the first and the second years in the district, they will undergo a concluding summative evaluation in which they and their supervisors will note areas of progress and areas needing further attention. In the case of a teacher who is not able to meet minimum expectations during his or her first two years, that teacher will be referred to an administrative summative evaluation, in which a recommendation not to renew the contract will be recommended.

B. Six months prior to the tenure decision, the nontenured teacher will be provided an oral and written evaluation of his or her teaching performance. This evaluation will be structured according to the evaluative criteria presented to the beginning teacher within the first month of his or her teaching duties.

C. Prior to the summative evaluation report, the beginning teacher's classes will have been visited at least four times a semester. Each visit will be followed by an extensive discussion of the teacher's performance. Suggested improvements will be noted. At least two people will have participated in those class visits to ensure at least two voices in the gathering of observational data.

In conjunction with these visits, the teacher will be expected to explain how the lesson plans and student learning activities for these classes are connected to the district content benchmarks in various subjects, as well as to provide examples of student work that indicate that the expected levels of understanding are being met.

D. At least three people, one of whom will be the principal or someone else designated by the superintendent, will discuss the class observation data and follow-up discussions of the past three years, and the three will prepare the summative evaluation report and attach their names to it.

E. The criteria for evaluating beginning teachers are focused on four major areas: planning student learning; creating a conducive learning culture and learning spaces; engaging students in learning; and carrying out the expected record keeping, communicating with students and parents, and working within the mentoring program. More precise rubrics for evaluation will have been decided by the tenured faculty.

F. If the evaluation is unfavorable, the teacher will have one month to appeal to the superintendent to show why the evaluation is incorrect, or why he or she should be granted tenure despite the evaluation.

G. During the months following an unfavorable evaluation, the beginning teacher will participate in a series of discussions with administrators and teachers chosen for this task to determine whether to stay in teaching as a career, consider what steps may be required to do so, or consider looking into some other career.

II. Summative Evaluation for a Tenured Teacher Recommended for Termination of Contract

A. Termination of a tenured teacher's contract shall be justified for the following reasons only: legal or moral turpitude; clear and repeated violations of school policies; repeated demonstration of incompetence as a teacher, after repeated warnings about the need to improve performance; clear and repeated neglect of duties as a professional member of the staff. All these are considered indications that the teacher has opted out of membership in the school community and, as such, require the community to verify whether such options are indeed being exercised. If they are, then membership should cease. In the case of evidence of a serious crime, the teacher will be suspended until a legal disposition of the matter is reached.

   B. The teacher must be notified by the appropriate administrator of a serious
       deficiency in his or her performance and of the need to correct that defi-
       ciency as soon as it is perceived, or if the teacher has been rated as proba-
       tionary on the periodic evaluation.
   C. If the teacher believes the complaint is incorrect or unjustified, both the
       teacher and the administrator may ask others to verify the presence of the
       deficiency.
   D. If the complaint is not verified, then the teacher is not required to take any ac-
       tion. If the complaint is verified, then the teacher and supervisor will consider
       what steps are necessary to remedy the problem. These steps might include at-
       tendance at workshops or seminars at the school's expense. In any event, the
       school must show a goodwill effort to help the teacher remedy the situation.
       In this situation the teacher will be listed as "on probationary status."
   E. If, after the specified time, it appears that the teacher has not corrected the
       deficiency, at least two other professionals on the staff must verify that the
       deficiency has not been corrected.
   F. If the deficiency is verified, then the teacher may be notified that his or her
       contract will not be renewed. Notification of nonrenewal must be made be-
       fore February 1 of the present contract year. If the case warrants, however,
       the contract may be terminated immediately.[7]

III. Periodic Evaluation of Tenured Teachers
   A. Every three years each tenured teacher will undergo an in-depth evaluation.
       This evaluation is an opportunity for the teacher to demonstrate how he or
       she has maintained or grown in commitment to the mission of this commu-
       nity of learners. It is an opportunity for the community, acting through per-
       sons delegated for that purpose, to assess the contribution each teacher is
       making to the life of the school.
   B. Upon receiving tenure, each teacher is required to present a three-year
       growth plan. This plan will include all or some of the following: efforts to
       improve in areas noted as needing improvement in the prior evaluation; ef-
       forts to develop one's knowledge base through university courses, staff de-
       velopment opportunities in the district and in the region, or other avenues of
       study; efforts to expand one's repertory of teaching strategies, and to im-
       prove diagnostic abilities to assist students with difficulties; efforts to net-
       work with other teachers in the school, in the system, or in the region for
       professional development purposes; cultural enrichment; and so on. Every
       teacher will maintain a portfolio that contains evidence of systematic
       progress on her or his growth plan.
   C. At the beginning of the year in which the in-depth evaluation is to take
       place, an administrator or senior teacher will be assigned to work with the

---

[7]For a more detailed treatment of approaches to dealing with incompetent teachers, see Edwin M. Bridges,
The Incompetent Teacher, London: Falmer Press, 1986; Jim Sweeney and Dick Manatt, "A Team Approach to
Supervising the Marginal Teacher," *Educational Leadership,* vol. 41, no. 7 (April 1984), pp. 25–27.

teacher involved. That person (the evaluator) will review with the teacher what progress has been made on the growth plan, and together, they will prepare a report to be included with the in-depth report for review by the principal. That person will also prepare a plan with the teacher, outlining how the in-depth evaluation will take place during that year.

D. At the opening meeting the teacher will choose one of the five in-depth evaluation formats chosen by the faculty and spelled out in the faculty contract or, with approval of the principal, some other format that appears suited to the teacher's particular needs and that satisfies the general purposes for these in-depth evaluations.

E. At the opening meeting the teacher will review with the evaluator the format of the final report of the in-depth evaluation, especially the criteria for arriving at each of the four general ratings (superior, satisfactory, less than satisfactory, and probationary). Those ratings have consequences for the type of growth plan to be submitted at the end of the year. Those receiving superior ratings will undergo the next in-depth evaluation in five years and are free to devise their growth plans in ways that serve both the needs of the school and the needs of their own professional growth. Those receiving satisfactory ratings will undergo the next in-depth evaluation in three years and may devise a growth plan in ways that serve the needs of the school and their own professional growth. Those receiving a less than satisfactory rating must submit a growth plan that is targeted at improving in those areas that caused the unsatisfactory rating and will undergo their next in-depth evaluation in two years. Those who are rated as probationary will be required to undergo the procedures called for by that evaluation process beginning with the next semester.

F. During the initial meeting the evaluator will arrange to hold five lengthy sessions with the teacher during the in-depth evaluation year. They will be followed by a concluding meeting for a review of the evaluation report prior to its submission to the principal. The format for those five sessions will be shaped by the evaluation format chosen by the teacher.

G. If, in the course of those sessions, disagreements arise over what the evaluator perceives to be a problem, each is free to request other members of the faculty to enter the discussion, and even to observe classes. If serious disagreements ensue from the outset, the principal and a faculty member chosen by the teacher may be called in to arbitrate the dispute.

H. The final report submitted to the principal will contain the following items:
  1. An assessment of the results of the growth plan for the previous period. There should be some evidence of how involvement in that plan has influenced the teacher's classes.
  2. An assessment of the teacher's present performance according to the evaluation format employed during the year. That assessment should contain but not be limited to the following:
     a. An assessment of the teacher's understanding of the local, district, and state content standards and benchmarks in the curriculum areas

for which the teacher is responsible. (Is the teacher's knowledge broader than what is contained in textbooks and other resources the students are using? Can the teacher adapt the knowledge in the standards and benchmarks to the cognitive levels of students in the learning activities provided in class? Are *all* students in the class learning at their capacity? Does the teacher provide multiple options for students to perform their learning of the benchmark material and provide adequate feedback on those performances?)

    b. An assessment of the teacher's responsiveness to the students. (Can the teacher employ various motivating strategies to fit various students? Does the teacher provide clear feedback on students' work? Is the teacher providing a user-friendly learning environment? Can the teacher talk about each student's strengths and weaknesses, and indicate how the teacher works from time to time individually with each student? Are performance assessments fair and challenging? Are they an authentic test of the material being taught? Can the teacher provide evidence that all students are succeeding?)

    c. An assessment of the teacher's instructional strengths that appear tied to student success. (Does the teacher provide adequate initial scaffolding to the material being taught? Does the teacher monitor the learning as it unfolds during the assigned learning activities, looking for students having difficulties, providing helpful comments or questions to move the task forward? Does the teacher provide occasional demonstrations that help get students started or that help summarize much of the previous work? Does the teacher use assessment activities to reinforce and extend learning?)

    d. An assessment of areas that both evaluator and teacher agree need further work so as to improve learning by all students, with some initial exploration of how those areas can be strengthened.

3. The evaluator's overall rating of the teacher, listing the reasons for the rating.

4. Additional comments by teacher or evaluator.

5. The teacher's growth plan for the period before the next in-depth evaluation.

6. The evaluation report will be submitted no later than May 1 to the principal, who will review these reports with each teacher during the month of May.

This example illustrates how, in some of the more enlightened schools, periodic summative evaluation is carried on. The system is different from that used for the nontenured teacher, and from that used for tenured teachers on probation. The tenured teacher participates much more in a professional evaluation process; there are more options; the evaluator and teacher can shape the evaluation to the circumstances of the teacher; there are checks and balances built into the process to protect the teacher.

A DEEPER LOOK AT STUDENT LEARNING

While there is no doubt that all teachers can improve their effectiveness with students, and no doubt that students can and should be learning more and at a deeper level of personal appropriation, are these newly devised teacher-assessment instruments the primary factor in increased student learnings and improved teacher instructional effectiveness? Or are there other factors, perhaps equally as influential on student learnings within the school? Family background factors have been shown to account for the greatest variability in student school performance.[8] Looking within the school, may one say that the teachers' classroom behavior is the single most important in-school influence on student learning? The research is by no means conclusive on this question. As studies of mastery learning indicate, students' time on task seems to be clearly related to student learning as well as students' academic self-concept or students' sense of self-efficacy. Other studies show that students' sense of their future, their sense of controlling their own fate or destiny, also influences student learning.

Rather than focus on a one-to-one correspondence between teacher behaviors and student learning, educators must look at a critical *intervening* variable—the students' state of mind as they approach the learning task. How motivated are students to learn the material? Even at the level of an extrinsic motivation of wanting to get a good grade (regardless of whether the learning holds any personal significance to the student), is getting a good grade valued by this student? Do students have a sense that getting a good grade, getting promoted, and getting the school diploma are meaningful? Is schooling connected to getting a job? What kind of job is seen as possible in students' minds? Do students have a sense that they control their own destiny, that by working hard, by obeying the rules, they can get ahead in life? Or do they feel that their chances are in the hands of others or worse, are a matter of luck and street smarts, not at all related to the "stuff" that schools deal with? In other words, if students approach the learning task with a sense that learning this material really doesn't matter, then whether the teacher employs 29 or 52 effectiveness protocols, the chances of improved student performance are slim at best.

Besides the teachers' classroom efforts to motivate students to learn, to improve their academic sense of self-efficacy, to engender a sense that they have a bright future if they apply themselves, the school as an *institutional environment* must contribute to student motivation and academic self-concept.[9] Is the school as a totality "user-friendly"? Is it a place where children are respected and cared for, a place made bright and colorful by the adult community, a place where student

---

[8]See James S. Coleman et al., *Equality of Educational Opportunity,* Washington DC: U.S. Office of Education, National Center for Educational Statistics, 1966; Christopher Jencks et al., *Inequality: A Reassessment of the Effects of Family and Schooling in America,* New York: Basic Books, 1972.

[9]See A. S. Bryk and M. E. Driscoll, *An Empirical Investigation of the School as Community,* Chicago: University of Chicago, Department of Education, 1988; Thomas B. Gregory and Gerald R. Smith, *High Schools as Communities: The Small School Reconsidered,* Bloomington, IN: Phi Delta Kappa Educational Foundation, 1987.

performances are on display, where pride and self-esteem are carefully nurtured? Does the whole school environment express a concern that the curriculum is related to students' experiences; that it is seen to have practical applications not only to the world of work but also to the world of family and neighborhood; that learning is seen as involving self-expression, building teamwork, engendering pride in the achievement of student projects; that the curriculum offers quality learning experiences that students will cherish?

Or is the school not user-friendly? Do students get the feeling that their interests and desires do not count in the school environment, that the adults see them as untrustworthy, as the adversary to be controlled, coerced, intimidated, and badgered into learning? Do students perceive the school as a place that demands uniformity, passive conformity, automatic obedience, suppression of spontaneity; as a place of constant correction and punishments or threats of punishment such as grades, demerits, detention, and teachers' sarcastic and humiliating remarks in front of their friends; a place where hall monitors scowl at them, security guards check them into and out of school; a place where the school bell is the enemy, demanding them to get to class, wolf down their food, interrupt an interesting or funny conversation?

The learning environment is an important factor that affects student learning. Teachers do not have complete, or sometimes even the major, influence over the learning environment. The general student–adult interaction throughout the school building and grounds communicates a positive or a negative feeling to students. Peer expectations and peer subculture affect the learning environment. School learning not only may not be valued within the peer culture, but may be seen as a kind of "selling out" to the authorities, an act of disloyalty to the group's cohesive resistance to the school authorities. When questions of accountability are raised, they should include this question: What is the school administration doing to create a positive learning environment throughout the school? Without a positive institutional learning environment, an individual teacher cannot be held exclusively accountable for the lack of progress of his or her students.

The same may be said for the influence of the curriculum. Obvious technical questions ask how well the curriculum is put together, its scope and sequence, the authentic relationship of tests and grades to the learning implied in the curriculum. Beyond the technical concerns are questions of perceived connections to reality and perceived relevance to students. This does not mean that the curriculum should be watered down to simplistic elements of teen music or video game culture. Rather, learning Shakespeare must have some connection to understanding oneself and one's world. Learning how to read a map of a state or a country can be an exercise in memorizing nonsense, or it can be a very exciting journey, enabling students to see connections between rivers and mountains and highways and population and industrial centers. Is the curriculum viewed as a list of things to be memorized, a collection of right answers, an approved anthology of what others have deemed to be important information? If so, then teachers who use effectiveness protocols may have little success in improving students' academic outcomes.

Any form of teacher assessment that is tied to the rhetoric of accountability is unbalanced, and indeed unfair, if it is not integrated with school assessment. If it is possible to say that the whole school, as a total institution, has done its best to create an environment conducive to student learning, then looking at how teachers capitalize on that or fail to capitalize on that makes eminent professional sense. By the same token, when the institutional framework of the school is inimical to student learning, blaming teachers for inadequate levels of student learning misses the mark.

SUMMARY

In this chapter, we explored the controversial topic of teacher evaluation. From the start we situated teacher evaluation within the context of the school as a community of learners. Summative evaluation relates to decisions about membership in that community and to ways the community can honor outstanding contributions. Summative evaluations can be used to make various personnel decisions. In cases of possible termination of teacher contracts, these evaluations lead to administrative processes. We also looked at examples of summative evaluations for periodic assessment of tenured teachers. These examples provided maps of the terrain of summative evaluation. We then considered what might legitimately constitute standards for summative teacher evaluations. Michael Scriven offers one approach, which seems to avoid the pitfalls of many systems in use in the schools. We suggested that student learnings are influenced as much by institutional supports for a positive learning environment as they are by teachers' activities. Assessment of teachers should not be carried on independently from institutional assessment. Furthermore, a deeper look at what is meant by student learning provided a different base for constructing a different set of questions to ask in a system of summative teacher evaluation.

Because summative evaluation relates to the members of a community deciding whom to admit, whom to retain, and whom to honor for enhancing that community, the process often is hindered by adversarial and legal considerations. Ideally, summative evaluation should be used to identify and celebrate extraordinary contributions to the learning community.

SOME REFLECTIONS

1. Compare your school district's plan for teacher evaluation with the Sunlight School District's plan. What strengths and what shortcomings in your district's plan emerge from the comparison?
2. What role should the teachers' union play in shaping the district's teacher-evaluation plan? Be prepared to defend your position against someone who holds the opposite position.
3. What level of complexity of the teaching–learning process is implied in your district's teacher-evaluation plan?

Providing Leadership

Motivation, Satisfaction, and the Teachers' Workplace

INTRODUCTION

This book asks a lot from teachers. It asks them to step forward and take responsibility for their own learning and for the learning of their peers. It asks them to step forward and take responsibility for improving their schools. Are they up to these new expectations? We think so. But much will depend on our being able to convince teachers that we need them, that we need their experience, that we need their commitment, and that we need their knowledge if we are to succeed.

Whether the existing order of people in schools will stay the same or will change makes the difference. Responsibility for what goes on in schools and responsibility for their success must be collective. To be collective, responsibility needs to be distributed across the various roles that make up schooling. Among the roles are principals, other designated leaders, teacher leaders, coaches, and other teachers.

The topic of motivation, particularly as it applies to teachers and other professionals, is unmistakably moral. Teachers do things because they are the right things to do. Trading this for that (exchanging compliance for need fulfillment, for example) plays a lesser role. By contrast, shared preferences and the obligations that accompany them constitute the basic strategy.

As Simon Blackburn reminds us: "Human beings are ethical animals. I do not mean we naturally behave particularly well, nor that we are endlessly telling each other what to do. But we grade and evaluate, and compare and admire, and claim and justify.

We do not 'prefer' this and that in isolation. We prefer that our preferences are shared; we turn them into demands on each other."[1] These demands help the school become a community of responsibility. Once school preferences are known, we are

---

[1] Simon Blackburn, *Being Good,* Oxford: Oxford University Press, 2001.

obliged to embody them in our work—taking care that our preferences are understood as frameworks that provide sense and meaning, not as scripts that "de-skill" the work of teaching.

SOME BACKGROUND

Improving the teachers' workplace is one important way to improve schools. But a great deal of confusion exists about what is really important to teachers and how best to go about such improvement. As a result, and despite good intentions, regressive school policies and practices are often put into place, leading to such unanticipated consequences as job dissatisfaction, lack of work motivation, and even alienation among teachers. This confusion stems in part from four common conditions within school systems:

- Labeling teachers as professionals but viewing the work of teaching as bureaucratic
- Attributing higher standards of trust and moral responsiveness to administrators and supervisors than to teachers
- Assuming that teachers are primarily motivated by self-interest and thus less willing to respond to work for altruistic reasons
- Assuming that teachers make decisions about what is important and what to do alone as rational and objective individuals

The four conditions have a tendency to reinforce each other, creating a cycle that makes matters worse. For example, teachers are given bureaucratic work because they're not trusted by the state or their school districts with the discretion needed for professional work. That being the case, supervisors are needed to tell teachers what to do and to check up on them. Furthermore, teachers are not deemed capable of accepting responsibility for their own professional development. Thus the need for supervisors to provide bureaucratic supervision and formal in-service programs. As a result, teachers wind up being the objects of supervision. As objects, they tend to lose their sense of commitment. They either feel resentful and alienated or become increasingly dependent upon their supervisors. This reaction then makes it necessary for them to be *motivated* by supervisors. In a study of teacher alienation, sense of efficacy and satisfaction, and their effects on performance, Patricia Ashton and Rodman Webb note that:

> Teachers in most schools reported that the administration treated them disrespectfully. They considered themselves to be professionals and were offended when they were treated like bureaucratic functionaries or naughty children. For example, on a teacher workday after students had been dismissed for summer vacation, the faculty at one school were grading exams, turning in grades, and straightening up their classrooms. Frequently during the day the principal used the public address system to remind his staff that "no one was to leave the school" until grades had been turned in and an administrator had checked the classrooms for cleanliness. Teachers were warned that a vice principal would come to each room and check everything, including the desk

drawers and file cabinets, to make sure they were cleaned out. A teacher turned to a member of the research team and said in exasperation:

I've taught at a lot of schools, and nobody has ever looked into my desk and drawers, never! I feel it's rather an intrusion. They're saying I'm not professional. The biggest [problem at this school] is that we're being treated unprofessionally. We're talked down to. We're asked our opinion, but we know that it isn't going to make any difference. We all get talked down to at faculty meetings. If a teacher has done something wrong, then [the administration] should tell him. But the whole faculty shouldn't have to be lectured to.[2]

Given the above realities, the motivational strategies supervisors choose typically are based on the belief that the goals of teachers and those of supervisors are not the same. Teachers, it is assumed, do not care as much about matters of schooling as do supervisors. Thus the basis for motivating teachers becomes a series of trades whereby the supervisors give to teachers things that they want in exchange for compliance with the supervisors' requests and requirements. This, in turn, results in the further bureaucratization of the work of teaching, reinforces the supervisor's superior moral standing, places further emphasis on the use of self- interest-oriented motivational strategies, and so perpetuates this regressive cycle. Breaking this cycle requires serious rethinking about what is important to teachers.

BUREAUCRATIC AND PROFESSIONAL WORK

Rethinking the practice of referring to teachers as professionals yet considering their work as bureaucratic is a good place to begin. In many of today's schools, for example, it is common for teachers to be regulated and controlled by an elaborate work system that specifies what must be done and then seeks to ensure that it is done. But bureaucratic and professional work are different. Although both bureaucrats and professionals are part of a rationally conceived work system, bureaucrats are *subordinate* to this system. They are responsible for implementing the system according to the provided specifications, and supervision is designed to monitor this process. The emphasis is on doing things right.

Professionals, by contrast, are *superordinate* to their work system. In teaching, the work system represents a point of reference rather than a script. Teachers use the system in ways that makes sense to them as they practice. Supervision for professionals, while no less demanding, is helpful and facilitating in its orientation. In professional work the emphasis is on writing the script while practicing. In a larger sense, professionals create their practice as they practice. They are researchers, solvers, and inventors, as well as implementers.

Bureaucratic work seems to fit Supervision I, and professional work seems to fit Supervision II. In Supervision I the purpose is to monitor and control the

---

[2]Patricia T. Ashton and Rodman B. Webb, *Making a Difference: Teachers' Sense of Efficacy and Student Achievement,* New York: Longman, 1986, p. 49.

approved system. In Supervision II the purpose is to empower and expand the teachers' views, enabling them to make better decisions as they create their practice in use. Levels of satisfaction, commitment, and efficacy are higher when work is conceived as professional and lower when work is conceived as bureaucratic. And, as will be discussed in later sections, these conditions of Supervision II are linked to enhanced feelings of efficacy among teachers and increased student achievement.[3]

TEACHERS AS ORIGINS AND PAWNS

In successful schools teachers tend to be more committed, hardworking, loyal to their school, and satisfied with their jobs. The research on motivation to work reveals that these highly motivating conditions are present when teachers

find their work lives meaningful, purposeful, sensible, and significant, and when they view the work itself as being worthwhile and important.

have reasonable control over their work activities and affairs and are able to exert reasonable influence over work events and circumstances.

experience personal responsibility for the work and are personally accountable for outcomes.[4]

When teachers experience meaningfulness, control, and personal responsibility at work, they are functioning more as "origins" than as "pawns." An origin believes that behavior is determined by his or her own choosing. A pawn, by contrast, believes that behavior is determined by external forces beyond his or her control.[5] Origins have strong feelings of personal causation. They believe that they can affect events and circumstances that exist in their environment. Pawns, by contrast, believe that forces beyond their control determine what it is that they will do. Pawn feelings, according to Richard DeCharms, provide people with a strong sense of powerlessness and ineffectiveness.[6] Experts such as DeCharms believe that persons under normal conditions strive to be effective in influencing and altering events and

[3]Ibid.

[4]See, for example, Frederick Herzberg, Bernard Mausner, and Barbara Snyderman, *The Motivation to Work,* New York: Wiley, 1959; Thomas J. Sergiovanni, "Factors Which Affect Satisfaction and Dissatisfaction of Teachers," *Journal of Educational Administration,* vol. 5, no. 1 (1967), pp. 66–82; J. R. Hackman and G. Oldham, "Motivation Through Design of Work: Test of a Theory," *Organizational Behavior and Human Performance,* vol. 16, no. 2 (1976), pp. 250–279; Edward L. Deci, *Why We Do What We Do: The Dynamics of Personal Autonomy,* New York: Putnam, 1995; and, Joseph Blase and Jo Blase, "Principals' Instructional Leadership and Teacher Development: Teachers' Perspectives," *Educational Administration Quarterly,* vol. 35, no. 3 (August 1999), pp. 349–378.

[5]Richard DeCharms, *Personal Causation: The Internal Affective Determinants of Behavior,* New York: Academic Press, 1968.

[6]Ibid.

situations that constitute their environment. They strive to be causal agents, to be origins of their own behavior. When this is not the case, they experience frustration, powerlessness, and often alienation.

One of the consequences of being an origin rather than a pawn is that one's sense of efficacy is enhanced. An efficacious teacher believes that he or she has the power and ability to produce a desired effect. Efficacy has to do with personal effectiveness, a feeling that one can control events and produce outcomes. Recent research links sense of efficacy not only with motivation and commitment to work but with student achievement. In their study of teachers' sense of efficacy and student achievement, Patricia Ashton and Rodman Webb found that efficacy was related to such teacher behaviors as being warm, accepting, and responsive to students; accepting student initiatives; and giving attention to all the students' individual needs.[7] Efficacy was also related to student enthusiasm and student initiation of interaction with teachers. Finally, teachers' sense of efficacy was related to student achievement. Ashton and Webb studied high school teachers of mathematics and communications. Student achievement was measured by mathematics and language basic skills tests. Using Ashton and Webb's data, a model of the relationship between teachers' sense of efficacy and student achievement is illustrated in Figure 15–1.

The factors contributing to teachers' sense of efficacy and enhanced motivation and commitment are depicted in Figure 15–2.[8] A supportive school climate, the presence of collegial values, shared decision making, and a school culture provide a sense of purpose and define for teachers a shared covenant. These characteristics provide for cooperative relationships, strong social identity, a sense of personal causation, origin feelings, high responsibility for work outcomes, and a shared commitment to common goals.

Figures 15–1 and 15–2 provide glimpses of how the story of teacher motivation to work can end. It is a story quite different from what currently takes place in most schools. To understand this story, it is important to go back to the beginning and examine some basic assumptions that can provide a basis for practicing work motivation differently.

The effects of teacher efficacy grow as efficacy themes become part of the shared beliefs and culture of a school. Wayne K. Hoy and Cecil G. Miskel refer to these effects as *collective teacher efficacy* defined as the "*shared perception of teachers in a school that the efforts of the faculty as a whole will have a positive effect on students.*"[9] They point out collective teacher efficacy helps explain the differential effects that schools have on improving student achievement.[10]

---

[7]Ashton and Webb, op. cit.

[8]See also M. Tschannen-Moran, A. Woolfolk Hoy, and Wayne K. Hoy, "Teacher Efficacy: Its Meaning and Measure," *Review of Educational Research,* vol. 68 (1998), pp. 202–248.

[9]Wayne K. Hoy and Cecil G. Miskel, *Educational Administration Theory, Research, and Practice,* 6th ed., New York: McGraw-Hill, 2001, p. (176).

[10]Ibid.

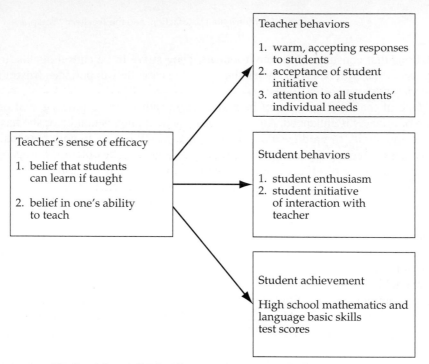

FIGURE 15–1. Teachers' Sense of Efficacy as It Relates to Teacher and Student Behaviors and Student Achievement.
Source: Constructed from data drawn from Patricia T. Ashton and Rodman B. Webb, *Making Difference: Teachers' Sense of Efficacy and Student Achievement,* New York: Longman. 1986.

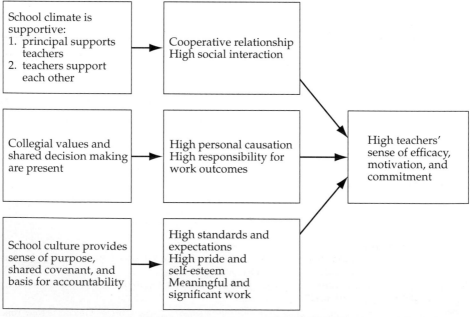

FIGURE 15–2. Factors Contributing to Teachers' Sense of Efficacy, Motivation, and Commitment.

A FRAMEWORK FOR UNDERSTANDING TEACHER MOTIVATION

Motivation is in part an expression of psychological needs and in part a function of moral judgments. The motivational policies and practices of Supervision I overemphasize the former and neglect the latter. Supervision II, by contrast, seeks to join the two into an expanded theory of motivation that better reflects the full nature of human potential.

Theories of motivation can be grouped into three categories: those that emphasize the exchange of rewards or punishment for compliance; those that seek compliance by emphasizing opportunities to experience satisfaction from the work itself; and those that are based on the idea that compliance results from moral judgment. The first category relies heavily on rewards and punishments and on the promise of extrinsic gain. The second category also relies on rewards, but the rewards depend less on gains made from trades with supervisors and more on teachers finding intrinsic satisfaction in work. The third category, moral judgment, relies on the connection of teachers to professional and community norms that represent a form of moral authority, a theme discussed in Part I. The categories can be expressed in the form of three motivational rules:

1. What gets rewarded gets done.
2. What is rewarding gets done.
3. What is good gets done.[11]

Although all three motivational rules are true, the consequences of their prime use in practice differs. The three rules are examined in the sections below.

WHAT GETS REWARDED GETS DONE

The motivational practices of Supervision I are based largely on the rule "What gets rewarded gets done." This rule works very effectively in the short term. The consequences of using the rule over time, however, are different. The famous "felt-tipped" research of David Greene and Mark Lepper is often cited as evidence that the rule can backfire when trying to motivate children.[12] In that research, preschoolers who were motivated to draw with felt-tipped markers without extrinsic rewards became less interested in this activity once such rewards were introduced. In a separate study Edward Deci and Richard Ryan found that not only does the motivational capacity of adults lessen with the introduction of extrinsic rewards for work, but such rewards resulted in feelings of being controlled by them.[13] These feelings had negative effects on subsequent performance and creativity.

[11]The discussion of motivational rules that follows is drawn from Chapter 2, "What Motivates? What Inspires?" and Chapter 5, "Creating a State of Flow at Work," in Thomas J. Sergiovanni, *Moral Leadership: Getting to the Heart of School Improvement,* San Francisco: Jossey-Bass, 1992.

[12]David Greene and Mark R. Lepper, "How to Turn Work into Play," *Psychology Today,* vol. 8, no. 4 (1974), pp. 49–52.

[13]Edward L. Deci and Richard M. Ryan, *Intrinsic Motivation and Self-Determination in Behavior,* New York: Plenum, 1985.

James G. March points out that providing rewards for a performance inevitably leads to an emphasis on measuring performance. This linking of rewards and measurement typically causes problems. In his words, "A system of rewards linked to precise measure is not an incentive to perform well; it is an incentive to get a good score."[14] Given March's view, teachers will work for the rewards rather than the job itself. This circumstance raises a number of important questions. What happens when extrinsic rewards are no longer available to teachers? And what happens to other sources of motivation once extrinsic rewards are introduced?

Although "What gets rewarded gets done" may be true, it seems equally true that what does not get rewarded does not get done. The rule has a tendency to focus one's attention and narrow one's responses to work. For example, teachers who are being rewarded to teach in a certain way are not teaching in other ways. Although in some instances it might be a good idea to encourage teachers to teach in a particular way, as a general rule, a policy of this sort is probably not a good idea. Because of the complex nature of teaching and because of the diversity that exists in student needs and teaching situations, how a teacher ought to teach at any given time cannot be validly determined beforehand. It is a decision that must be made on the spot.

MASLOW'S THEORY AS AN EXAMPLE

One of the most popular constructs used to guide the practice of "What gets rewarded gets done" is Abraham Maslow's theory of motivation.[15] Maslow proposed that all human needs could be grouped into five categories arranged in levels of importance from basic to high. The most basic level is physical needs followed by security, social, esteem, and self-actualization. Basic needs, according to the theory, must be met first before a person is motivated by needs at higher levels. Lyman Porter suggested that physical needs cannot be realistically considered to have motivational potential in most work settings and thus substituted autonomy for physical as a new category.[16] The levels are often depicted in the form of a needs hierarchy, as illustrated in Figure 15–3.

In practicing "What gets rewarded gets done," it is assumed that teachers have needs that can be met at work. At the security level, for example, they have needs for money, benefits, tenure, and clear role expectations. And at the autonomy level they have needs to influence, to become shareholders, to have authority, and so on. Supervisors control many of the events and circumstances that allow these needs to

[14]James G. March, "How We Talk and How We Act: Administrative Theory and Administrative Life," in Thomas J. Sergiovanni and John E. Corbally (eds.), *Leadership and Organizational Culture,* Urbana: University of Illinois Press, 1984, pp. 27–28.

[15]Abraham Maslow, *Motivation and Personality,* New York: Harper & Row, 1954.

[16]Lyman Porter, "Job Attitudes in Management: I. Perceived Deficiencies and Need Fulfillment as a Function of Job Level," *Journal of Applied Psychology,* vol. 4 (December 1963), pp. 386–397.

Security	Affiliation	Self-esteem	Autonomy	Self-actualization
				Working at top potential
		Self-respect	Control	
	Acceptance	Respected by others as a person and as a professional	Influence	Giving all
Money	Belonging			
	Friendship		Participant	Peak satisfaction
Benefits	School membership	Competence		
				Achievement
Tenure	Formal work group	Confidence	Shareholder	
				Personal and professional success
Role consolidation	Informal work group	Recognition	Authority	

FIGURE 15–3. The Needs Hierarchy.

be met. They can provide teachers with the desired need fulfillment if teachers in turn comply with required role expectations. For example, if teachers teach the right way, take on extracurricular responsibilities, volunteer for committee work, and cheerfully attend the required workshops, they can advance up the school's career ladder. Such advancement entitles them to have more control over what they do, to influence more school decisions, and to receive other benefits that help meet their needs for autonomy. If teachers don't conform to expectations, by contrast, they are likely to have less to say about what is going on in the school and are likely to be more closely watched.

There is no doubt that what gets rewarded gets done, and the bartering that goes on as need fulfillment is traded with compliance has its place. But by itself, it is neither powerful enough nor expansive enough to provide the kind of motivational climate needed in schools. Furthermore, overuse of the rule in motivating teachers (or, for that matter, students) can lead to many negative consequences. Some of these consequences are summed up by W. Edwards Demming, the famous quality-control expert, as follows:

> People are born with intrinsic motivation, dignity, curiosity to learn, joy in learning. The forces of destruction begin with toddlers—a prize for the best Halloween costume, grades in school, gold stars and honor to the university. On the job, people, teams, divisions are ranked—rewards for the one at the top, punishments at the bottom. MBO, quotas, incentive pay, business plans, put together separately, division by division, cause further loss, unknown and unknowable.[17]

---

[17]W. Edwards Demming, quoted in Peter M. Senge, "The Leader's New Work: Building a Learning Organization," *Sloan Management Review,* vol. 22, no. 1 (1990), p. 7.

In commenting on Demming's observations, Peter M. Senge notes, "Ironically, by focusing on performing for someone else's approval, corporations create the very conditions that predestine them to mediocre performance."[18] These comments, leveled at corporate America, seem even more appropriate when applied to schooling America.

WHAT IS REWARDING GETS DONE

As Alfie Kohn,[19] Barry Schwartz,[20] and Edward L. Deci[21] have pointed out, "What is rewarding gets done" as a motivational rule has certain advantages over "What gets rewarded gets done." Since the basis of this rule is internal to the work itself, motivation does not depend directly on what the supervisor does or on other external forces. Second, being compelled from within implies a kind of self-management that does not require direct supervision or other kinds of monitoring to be sustained.

The motivational psychologist Frederick Herzberg pointed out that jobs that provide opportunities for experiencing achievement and responsibility, interesting and challenging work, and opportunity for advancement have the greatest capacity to motivate from within.[22] These are not factors that supervisors give to others in return for desired behavior but are instead factors integral to the work of teaching itself. Herzberg's research, and that of others, suggests that the following job characteristics enhance this intrinsic motivation:

> Allow for discovery, exploration, variety and challenge. Provide high involvement with the task and high identity with the task enabling work to be considered important and significant. Allow for active participation. Emphasize agreement with respect to broad purposes and values that bond people together at work. Permit outcomes within broad purposes to be determined by the worker. Encourage autonomy and self-determination. Allow persons to feel like "origins" of their own behavior rather than "pawns" manipulated from the outside. Encourage feelings of competence and control and enhance feelings of efficacy.[23]

The work of Herzberg and his colleagues represents a pioneering effort to establish a tradition known as *job enrichment research*. Job enrichment research seeks to identify ways the workplace can be changed to allow workers to experience for themselves greater intrinsic satisfaction.

---

[18]Ibid.

[19]Alfie Kohn, *Punished by Rewards,* Boston: Houghton Mifflin, 1993.

[20]Barry Schwartz, *The Costs of Living: How Market Theories Erode the Basic Things in Life,* New York: Norton, 1994.

[21]Deci, op. cit.

[22]Frederick Herzberg, *Work and Nature of Man,* New York: World Publishing, 1966.

[23]Thomas J. Sergiovanni, *Value-Added Leadership: How to Get Extraordinary Performance in Schools,* San Diego: Harcourt Brace Jovanovich, 1990, p. 129.

JOB ENRICHMENT FOR TEACHERS

Enrichment is an accepted part of our educational vocabulary. We speak often about the need to enrich the job of learning for students so that it is more interesting, challenging, and satisfying. Job enrichment for teachers extends the idea to include teachers as well.

The best-known work on job enrichment is that of J. R. Hackman and G. Oldham.[24] These researchers identified three psychological states believed to be critical in determining whether a person will be motivated at work:

Experienced meaningfulness. The individual must perceive his or her work as worthwhile or important by some system of values held.

Experienced responsibility. The individual must believe that he or she personally is accountable for the outcomes of efforts.

Knowledge of results. The individual must be able to determine, on some fairly regular basis, whether or not the outcomes of his or her work are satisfactory.[25]

When the three psychological states are present, according to this job enrichment theory, teachers can be expected to feel good, perform well, and continue to want to perform well in an effort to earn more of these feelings in the future. The three states become the basis for internal motivation, since teachers do not have to depend upon someone outside of themselves to motivate them or lead them.

What can supervisors do to increase the likelihood that teachers will experience meaningfulness, responsibility, and knowledge of results? The answer, according to Hackman and Oldham, is to build into teaching jobs opportunities for teachers to use more of their talents and skills; to allow teachers to engage in activities that allow them to see the whole, and to understand how their contributions fit into the overall purpose and mission (task identity); to view their work as having a significant impact on the lives of their students (task significance); to experience discretion in scheduling work and in deciding classroom arrangements and teaching methods and procedures (autonomy); and to get firsthand and from others, clear information about the effects of their performance (feedback). The job enrichment model proposed by Hackman and his colleagues is depicted in Figure 15–4.

The importance of collaborative cultures, teachers teaming to learn, and communities of practice have been persistent themes throughout this book and are an integral part of Supervision II for good reason. Working together provides an effective setting for enhanced teacher learning and for enhanced teacher motivation. Diana G. Pounder examined how having teachers work together in teams influences

---

[24]Hackman and Oldham, op. cit. See also R. J. Starratt, *Centering Educational Administration: Cultivating Meaning, Community and Responsibility,* Mahwah, NJ: Erlbaum, 2003.

[25]J. R. Hackman, G. Oldham, R. Johnson, and K. Purdy, "A New Strategy for Job Enrichment," *California Management Review,* vol. 17, no. 4 (1975), p. 57.

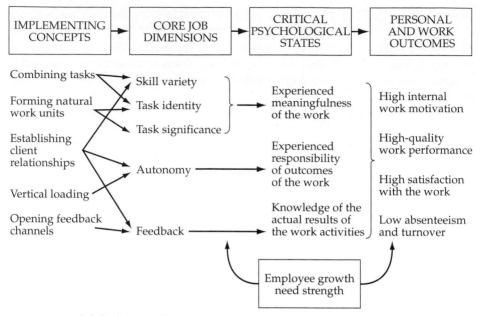

FIGURE 15–4. Job Enrichment Concepts and Practices.
Source: From J. R. Hackman, G. Oldham, R. Johnson, and K. Purdy, "A New Strategy for Job Enrichment," © 1975 by The Regents of the University of California. Reprinted from *California Management Review,* vol. XVII, no. 4, p. 64, by permission of the Regents.

teachers' work characteristics as, for example, described by Hackman and Oldham.[26] The teamed teachers, as compared with nonteamed teachers, reported significantly greater skill variety in their work, knowledge of their students' educational characteristics and personal life characteristics, satisfaction with their jobs, professional commitment, internal work motivation, and teacher efficacy. They also reported higher levels of group helping and group effectiveness than nonteamed counterparts.

This might be a good time for you to think about ways teacher jobs can be enhanced or enriched. Refer to the job enrichment model depicted in Figure 15–4 for help. What, for example, can be done to arrange teachers and teaching in a way that allows teachers to use more of their knowledge and skills; to identify more with what they are teaching and to link this meaning to larger educational purposes; to come to see their work as being more significant than it might appear by taking a snapshot of classroom life at 10:00 a.m.; to enjoy more discretion coupled with increased responsibility in their work; and to get and give helpful feedback about teaching and learning and the work that their students are doing.

Since virtually every decision supervisors make about school and classroom organization, curriculum development and implementation, materials selection, and

---

[26]Diana G. Pounder, "Teacher Teams: Exploring Job Characteristics and Work-Related Outcomes of Work Group Enhancement," *Educational Administration Quarterly,* vol. 35, no. 3 (August 1999), pp. 317–348.

teaching itself has implications for job enrichment, every decision has implications as well for either enhancing or diminishing motivation and commitment levels of teachers.

WHAT IS GOOD GETS DONE

Supervision I is based on the assumption that people are by nature selfish. It is thought that for teachers, the guiding motivational force is a desire to maximize self-interest by continually calculating the costs and benefits of options, choosing those that either make them winners or keep them from losing. Supervision I also is based on the assumption that people act rationally, seeking the most efficient means to their goals. They are capable of cold calculation, and thus their emotions do not count. Finally, people make decisions as isolated individuals. Each person "keeps score" separate from others. Connections to other people and particularly the social bonds that emerge from such connections do not count very much.

Amitai Etzioni challenges the motivational assumptions of Supervision I by asking this question:

> Are men and women akin to single minded, "cold" calculators, each out to "maximize" his or her well being? Are human beings able to figure out rationally the most efficient way to realize their goals? Is society mainly a marketplace, in which self-serving individuals compete with one another—at work, in politics, and in courtship . . . enhancing the general welfare in the process? Or do we typically seek to do both what is right *and* what is pleasurable, and find ourselves frequently in conflict when moral values and happiness are incompatible?[27]

Etzioni acknowledges the importance of self-interest but suggests that people are perfectly capable of sacrificing self-interest and indeed regularly sacrifice self-interest for other interests. He provides compelling evidence that people are just as likely, if not more likely, to be motivated by what they think is right and good, by obligations they feel, and by the norms and values they consider important and just. Most supervisors agree with Etzioni when it comes to describing themselves. For example, supervisors put in demanding hours at work, often putting the job "ahead" of leisure time and family matters. Etzioni believes that the capacity to sacrifice self-interest is not limited to supervisors but is widespread. There is no reason to believe, in other words, that parents and teachers, cafeteria workers, and custodians are less likely than supervisors to sacrifice their self-interest for the common good.

The belief that teachers are rational and cold calculators who are routinely capable of controlling their emotions, biases, and preferences by putting reason and logic first is also suspect. Anyone who has bought a new car understands this. Despite the best rational planning to ensure that the car chosen is both practical and within budget, in the end, most people are swayed by less objective factors. Having completed

---

[27]Amitai Etzioni, *The Moral Dimension Toward a New Economics,* New York: Free Press, 1988, p. ix.

the purchase, they desperately attempt to rationalize buying that "spiffy two-door with the small trunk." People strive to appear rational in an effort to cover up the fact that they are not.

Etzioni challenges as well the idea that people make decisions as isolated individuals. He provides compelling evidence that "social collectivities (such as ethnic and racial groups, peer groups at work, and neighborhood groups) are the prime decision-making units."[28] He acknowledges that individual decision making exists but says that it typically reflects collective attributes and processes, having been made within the context created by one's memberships in various groups. For teachers, membership in the profession of teaching and membership in the school as community provide the kind of collective attributes that hinder individual decision making. For example, a teacher may want to take a teaching shortcut but feels compelled to do otherwise by group norms or by having been socialized in what it means to be a teacher. Or equally likely, a teacher who wants to stay after school to help students decides otherwise as a result of pressure from other teachers who have implicitly agreed that everyone should leave early. Connections are so important and the process of socialization as a result of memberships is so complete that the concept of individual decision maker appears to be more myth than reality.

The literature on community building in schools discussed in Part I points also to the primacy of morality, emotions, and social bonds in motivating teachers *and* students. In communities members are bonded together in special ways because they are together bound to shared ideas and ideals that represent moral commitments. At root in an authentic community is a community of mind that speaks to members in a moral voice, a voice that lays claim on them. This claim is understood as an obligation that must be met. Motivation, under these circumstances, is neither rules-based nor rewards-based but norms-based.

Motivation in Supervision I and in Supervision II differs because of the importance the latter gives to morality, emotions, and social bonds. These differences are summarized in Table 15–1. In Supervision II, teachers regularly pass moral judgments over their urges, routinely sacrificing self-interest and pleasure for other reasons. Furthermore, actions and decisions that teachers make are influenced by what they value and believe as well as by self-interest, and when the two are in conflict, it is the former that typically takes precedence over the latter. Presently, teachers represent an underutilized resource. They will remain underutilized as long as "What gets rewarded gets done" dominates the motivational scene by continuing to be the prime basis for supervisory practice. Teachers deserve more than this, and schools need more than this. Changing supervision practices in a way that acknowledges the importance of "What is rewarding gets done" and "What is good gets done," we believe, is a step in the right direction.

There is ample evidence that teachers initially tend to view their jobs as a calling. Teachers are there because they love kids and want to help them.[29] But there is

---

[28]Ibid., p. 4.
[29]See, for example, Steve Farkas, Jean Johnson, and Tony Foleno, with Ann Duffett and Patrick Foley, "A Sense of Calling: Who Teaches and Why," Report from Public Agenda, New York: Public Agenda, 2000.

TABLE 15–1. Morality, Emotion, and Social Bonds in Supervisions I and II.

Supervision I	Supervision II
Morality	
Self-interest is the driving force. People seek to maximize their gains and cut their losses. Morality is defined in terms of self-interest.	People pass moral judgments over their urges and as a result often sacrifice self-interest for other causes and reasons.
Emotions	
People rationally seek the most efficient means to their goals. Emotions don't count.	People choose largely on the basis of preference and emotions.
Social bonds	
People are isolated individuals who reason and calculate individually, thus making decisions on their own. Social bonds do not count.	People are members of groups, and the social bonds that emerge from this membership shape their individual decisions.

no guarantee that this kind of motivation will prevail over time. In a sense, we are given an initial motivation victory by new teachers, one that we can easily lose in the end unless we begin to think differently about the teachers' workdays.

SUMMARY

In Chapter 15 we examined teacher motivation and satisfaction as well as the teacher's workplace, looking for clues that might link these factors to school improvement. We found that motivation conditions changed depending on whether teachers were considered teaching bureaucrats or teaching professionals. We concluded, for example, that teachers were routinely labeled professionals, but the work they did was viewed as bureaucratic. Emphasis was given to mapping the relationships that exist between a teacher's sense of efficacy, teacher and student behaviors, and student achievement. We then examined several frameworks for understanding teacher motivation. The frameworks were summarized by examining and applying job enrichment concepts to teaching practice. The more enriched is the job of teaching, the more motivated are teachers likely to be. Motivated teachers seem to get better results in student achievement.

SOME REFLECTIONS

1. Suppose, for example, you were going to rewrite the script of schooling that now exists for new teachers in most schools. How would this script read? Today's script in too many schools is still pretty much a "sink or swim" affair characterized by institutional rituals that often involve hazing and the assignment of standardized teaching roles for every teacher. The job is

assumed to be the same for new and relatively untried teachers as it is for seasoned and accepted veterans. Every teacher gets the same number of students to teach, the same number of periods to teach in, and the same amount of preparation time. When it comes to books, supplies, the location of one's classroom (if you have one in the first place), some new teachers only wish it were the same. Instead, many are assigned to teach with the sun in their eyes, using older textbooks, and with the most challenging students. We know we can do better. If we are successful in helping teachers get a strong start during their first year, then the future for supervision in our schools will be bright indeed.

Let's share some ideas as to how this vision can be realized. Try interviewing two or three of the newest teachers in your school, asking them for changes they would recommend in today's script that would be helpful to them as new teachers. Then imagine that your son or daughter (or perhaps brother or sister) were joining the faculty at your school next year. What kind of orientation, mentoring, and induction program would you like your school to have for them? What special responsibilities do principals and other designated supervisors have for helping sustain, support, and improve the motivational dispositions and talents that new teachers bring to the school? These questions are very important because they suggest that enhancing and sustaining motivation may have less to do with introducing a specific program or strategy to a school and more to do with building within the school a culture of collegiality that brings everyone together into a community of practice. As members of communities of practice, teachers benefit by experiencing work lives that are more meaningful and significant.

2. In six sentences, explain the differences between viewing teaching as bureaucratic work and viewing teaching as professional work.

CHAPTER 16

School Climate, Culture, and Change

INTRODUCTION

Culture matters. Indeed, said the respected commentator on American life, Patrick Moynihan, "Culture makes almost all the difference."[1] Culture is at the heart of the lifeworld of schools—the place where our values and commitments are stored, grow, and are protected. It is from the lifeworld that we draw our direction and frameworks that guide us and fill us with a sense of meaning. Lifeworlds serve to guide and legitimize the systems world. The systems world is where we design our implementation strategies and work hard to achieve our objectives and assess our progress.

Good schools work from a culture that uses the systems world to help achieve lifeworld goals. In not-so-good schools, by contrast, lifeworld goals are determined by the systems world. But school practice is never as simple as chapter introductions seem to suggest. Protecting the lifeworld while still advancing student learning and still improving schools is complex. Chapter 16 is designed to help us navigate through this complexity and to figure out ways to increase our effectiveness in serving learning goals.

SOME BACKGROUND

Improving schools often requires changing them. But change takes place at two levels—the way things look and the way things actually work. Changes at the first level are *structural*, resulting in altered arrangements. Changes at the second level

---

[1] Samuel P. Huntington, "Culture Counts" in Lawrence E. Harrison and Samuel P. Huntington (eds.), *Culture Matters; How Values Shape Human Progress*, New York: Basic Books, 2000, p. xiv.

are *normative,* resulting in altered beliefs.[2] When only first-level changes are introduced in schools, it may appear that things are being done differently, but results seem not to be affected, at least not for very long.

A supervisor, for example, wants to encourage teachers to be more deliberate in their teaching and to make a better effort to teach to agreed-upon curriculum outlines. Working with a committee of teachers, she introduces a series of in-service workshops on the content of the curriculum, how to select objectives, and how to write effective lesson plans. She then establishes a policy requiring teachers to submit their lesson plans weekly for her perusal. Although she finds that the lesson plans seem to match the curriculum outlines, teachers seem to be making little progress toward improving the fit between what they teach and what they are supposed to teach. In this example, the supervisor was successful in implementing change in how teachers constructed their plans (structural change), but she was not successful in changing what they were actually teaching. This latter goal requires normative changes that alter how teachers look at things, what they believe, what they want, what they know, and how they do things. Normative changes are much more likely to affect outcomes.

Normative changes take place when more intensive strategies are added to the change equation. Peer-clinical supervision, coaching, and other strategies for reflective practice are examples. In each case the goal is to help teachers become members of communities of practice, brought together by shared commitments, helping relationships, and deep learning that they control. Earlier it was pointed out that powerful learning intersections emerge in schools when collaborative cultures, shaped and supported from above, meet communities of practice that bubble up from below.

Although structural changes can be important, in themselves they seem not to matter much. Too often, they become "nonevents." A junior high school that changes its name to "middle school" and abandons academic departments for teams that "turn teach" by subject-matter specialization is an example. The introduction of supervisory and evaluation systems that elicit changes in how teachers teach when being observed but not otherwise is another example. Nonevents become events when changes are not only structural but normative as well.

Many of the practices of Supervision I involve structural, but not normative, changes. Normative changes, the goal of Supervision II, take into account the aspects of human nature. It is helpful to think about human nature as having two sides: the psychological and the symbolic. Psychologically speaking, people have needs and seek opportunities to meet these needs. Symbolically speaking, people seek to make sense of their lives by searching for meaning. The psychological side of human nature is more readily affected by *school climate,* and the symbolic side is more readily affected by *school culture.* In this chapter, we examine school climate first and then school culture. In each case we assess their importance in bringing about school improvement.

---

[2] See, for example, Michael Fullan with Suzanne Stiegelbauer, *The New Meaning of Educational Change,* 2nd ed., New York: Teachers College Press, 1991.

THE IMPORTANCE OF SCHOOL CLIMATE

School climate can help or hinder teachers as they attempt to satisfy their needs at work. One way to understand school climate is by examining your own experience with groups in schools. Recall, for example, a group that you belonged to or know about that seemed best to encourage members to learn, solve problems, and take reasonable chances. Now recall a second group that most hindered learning, problem solving, and risk taking. Briefly describe the two groups. Who were the members? What was the group trying to accomplish? How did group members work together? How did they treat one another? What were the leaders like? Using the questionnaire in Exhibit 16–1, evaluate each of the groups you recalled. Start first with the most effective learning group. Circle the number for each category that best describes this group. Now evaluate the less effective group, using check marks to indicate responses. Compare your circled and checked responses.

By describing groups that help and hinder learning and then evaluating them, you are describing and measuring dimensions of school climate. The seven categories shown in Exhibit 16–1 are composed of several dimensions that social psychologists have found to be important in determining whether a climate is supportive of learning or hinders learning. To obtain an overall climate score for the two groups you evaluated, total the score values of your circles and checks for the seven items. Note that you must reverse the scores given to item 1, conformity, for in this case a low score suggests a supportive climate. Overall, the higher the score, the more supportive the group is likely to be. Now, using the categories and scores, write a few sentences that describe the helpful and hindering groups you recalled. You are now describing climate in the language of social psychologists.

Since the climate of the school is a matter of impression, it is often difficult to define with precision. Climate can be viewed as the enduring characteristics that describe the psychological makeup of a particular school, distinguish it from other schools, and influence the behavior of teachers and students, as well as the "feel" that teachers and students have for that school. George Litwin and Robert Stringer, for example, define climate as "the perceived subjective effects of the formal system, the informal 'style' of managers, and other important environmental factors on the attitudes, beliefs, values, and motivation of people who work in a particular organization."[3]

Climate provides a reading of how things are going in the school and a basis for predicting school consequences and outcomes. Such a barometer represents an important tool for evaluating present conditions, planning new directions, and monitoring progress toward new directions. Indeed, school climate is a key dimension of human resources supervision and a key concern of supervisor C as described in earlier chapters.

---

[3]George H. Litwin and Robert A. Stringer, Jr., *Motivation and Organization Climate*, Boston: Harvard University, Division of Research, Graduate School of Business Administration, 1968, p. 5.

Introduction

1. Conformity The feeling that there are many externally imposed constraints in the organization; the degree to which members feel that there are many rules, procedures, policies, and practices to which they have to conform rather than being able to do their work as they see fit.

Conformity is not characteristic of this organization.

1 2 3 4 5 6 7 8 9 10

Conformity is very characteristic of this organization.

2. Responsibility Members of the organization are given personal responsibility to achieve their part of the organization's goals; the degree to which members feel that they can make decisions and solve problems without checking with superiors each step of the way.

No responsibility is given in the organization.

1 2 3 4 5 6 7 8 9 10

There is great emphasis on personal responsibility in the organization.

3. Standards The emphasis the organization places on quality performance and outstanding production including the degree to which the member feels the organization is setting challenging goals for itself and communicating these goal commitments to members.

Standards are very low or nonexistent in the organization.

1 2 3 4 5 6 7 8 9 10

Challenging standards are set in the organization.

4. Rewards The degree to which members feel that they are being recognized and rewarded for good work rather than being ignored, criticized, or punished when something goes wrong.

Members are ignored, punished, or criticized.

1 2 3 4 5 6 7 8 9 10

Members are recognized and rewarded positively.

5. Organization clarity The feeling among members that things are well organized and goals are clearly defined rather than being disorderly, confused, or chaotic.

The organization is disorderly, confused, and chaotic.

1 2 3 4 5 6 7 8 9 10

The organization is well organized with clearly defined goals.

6. Warmth and support The feeling that friendliness is a valued norm in the organization; that members trust one another and offer support to one another. The feeling that good relationships prevail in the work environment.

There is no warmth and support in the organization.

1 2 3 4 5 6 7 8 9 10

Warmth and support are very characteristic of the organization.

7. Leadership The willingness of organization members to accept leadership and direction from qualified others. As needs for leadership arise, members feel free to take leadership roles and are rewarded for successful leadership. Leadership is based on expertise. The organization is not dominated by, or dependent on, one or two individuals.

Leadership is not rewarded; members are dominated or dependent and resist leadership attempts.

1 2 3 4 5 6 7 8 9 10

Members accept and reward leadership based on expertise.

Exhibit 16–1. Organizational Climate Questionnaire.
Source: David A. Kolb, Erwin M. Rubin, and James M. McIntyre, *Organizational Psychology: An Experiential Approach,* 3d ed., Englewood Cliffs, NJ: Prentice-Hall, 1979, pp. 193–194. Reprinted by permission of Prentice-Hall, Englewood Cliffs, NJ.

THE HEALTHY SCHOOL

Climate can also be understood by applying the metaphor of health to the school. Matthew Miles describes the "healthy" school as one that exhibits reasonably clear and reasonably accepted goals (goal focus); communication that is relatively distortion-free vertically, horizontally, and across boundary lines (communication adequacy); equitable distribution of influence to all levels of the organization (optimal power equalization); and effective and efficient use of inputs, both human and material (resource utilization). The healthy school reflects a sense of togetherness that bonds people together (cohesiveness), a feeling of well-being among the staff (morale), self-renewing properties (innovativeness), and an active response to its environment (autonomy and adaptation). Finally, the healthy school maintains and strengthens its problem-solving capabilities (problem-solving adequacies).[4]

The 10 dimensions of health as described by Miles are listed below.[5] As you review the list, think about how you would describe the two groups you evaluated earlier according to each of the 10 dimensions.

1. *Goal focus.* In a healthy organization, the goal (or usually, goals) of the system would be reasonably clear to the system members, and reasonably well accepted by them. This clarity and acceptance, however, should be seen as a necessary but insufficient condition for organizational health. The goals must also be *achievable* with existing or available resources, and be *appropriate*—more or less congruent with the demands of the environment.

2. *Communication adequacy.* Since organizations are not simultaneous face-to-face systems like small groups, the movement of information within them becomes crucial. This dimension of organizational health implies that there is relatively distortion-free communication vertically, horizontally, and across the boundary of the system to and from the surrounding environment. That is, information travels reasonably well—just as the healthy person "knows himself or herself" with a minimum level of repression, distortion, and the like. In the healthy organization, there is good and prompt sensing of internal strains; there are enough data about problems of the system to ensure that a good diagnosis of system difficulties can be made. People have the information they need and have gotten it without exerting undue efforts.

3. *Optimal power equalization.* In a healthy organization the distribution of influence is relatively equitable. Subordinates (if there is a formal authority chart) can influence upward, and even more important—as Rensis Likert has demonstrated[6]—they perceive that their boss can do likewise with *her* or *his* boss. In such an organization, intergroup struggles for power would not be bitter, though intergroup conflict (as in every human system known) would

---

[4]Matthew Miles, "Planned Change and Organizational Health: Figure and Ground," *Change Processes in the Public Schools.* Eugene: University of Oregon, Center for the Advanced Study of Educational Administration, 1965.

[5]The 10 dimensions of health are abridged from Miles, op. cit. pp. 18–21.

[6]Rensis Likert, *New Patterns of Management,* New York: McGraw-Hill, 1961, cited in Miles, op.cit.

undoubtedly be present. The basic stance of persons in such an organization, as they look up, sideways, and down, is that of collaboration rather than explicit or implicit coercion.

4. *Resource utilization.* We say of a healthy person, such as a second-grader, that he or she is "working up to his or her potential." To put this another way, the classroom system is evoking a contribution from the student at an appropriate and goal-directed level of tension. At the organization level, "health" would imply that the system's inputs, particularly the personnel, are used effectively. The overall coordination is such that people are neither overloaded nor idling. There is a minimal sense of strain, generally speaking (in the sense that trying to do something with a weak or inappropriate structure puts strain on that structure). In the healthy organization, people may be working very hard indeed, but they feel that they are not working against themselves, or against the organization. The fit between people's own dispositions and the role demands of the system is good. Beyond this, people feel reasonably self-actualized; they not only feel good in their jobs, but they have a genuine sense of learning, growing, and developing as persons in the process of making their organizational contribution.

5. *Cohesiveness.* We think of healthy people as those who have a clear sense of identity; they know who they are underneath all the specific goals they set for themselves. Beyond this, they *like themselves;* their stance toward life does not require self-derogation, even when there are aspects of their behavior which are unlovely or ineffective. By analogy, at the organization level, system health would imply that the organization knows "who it is." Its members feel attracted to membership in the organization. They want to stay with it, be influenced by it, and exert their own influence in the collaborative style suggested above.

6. *Morale.* The implied notion is one of well-being or satisfaction. Satisfaction is not enough for health, of course; a person may report feelings of well-being and satisfaction in his life, while successfully denying deep-lying hostilities, anxieties, and conflicts. Yet it still seems useful to evoke, at the organization level, the idea of morale: a summated set of individual sentiments, centering around feelings of well-being, satisfaction, and pleasure, as opposed to feelings of discomfort, unwished-for strain, and dissatisfaction.

7. *Innovativeness.* A healthy system would tend to invent new procedures, move toward new goals, produce new kinds of products, diversify itself, and become more rather than less differentiated over time. In a sense, such a system could be said to grow, develop, and change, rather than remaining routinized and standard.

8. *Autonomy.* Healthy people act "from [their] own center outward." Seen in a training or therapy group, for example, such people appear nearly free of the need to submit dependently to authority figures, *and* from the need to rebel and destroy symbolic parents of any kind. A healthy organization, similarly, would not respond passively to demands from the outside, feeling itself the tool of the environment, and it would not respond destructively or rebelliously to perceived demands either. It would tend to have a kind of independence from the environment, in the same sense that healthy people, while they have transactions with others, does not treat their responses as *determinative* of their own behavior.

9. *Adaptation.* The notions of autonomy and innovativeness are both connected with the idea that a healthy person, group, or organization is in realistic, effective contact with the surroundings. When environmental demands and organization resources do not match, a problem-solving, restructuring approach evolves in which *both* the environment and the organization become different in some respect. More adequate, continued coping of the organization, as a result of changes in the local system, the relevant portions of the environment, or more usually both, occurs. And such a system has sufficient stability and stress tolerance to manage the difficulties which occur during the adaptation process.

10. *Problem-solving adequacy.* Finally, any healthy organism—even one as theoretically impervious to fallibility as a computer—*always* has problems, strains, difficulties, and instances of ineffective coping. The issue is not the presence or absence of problems, therefore, but the *manner* in which the person, group, or organization copes with problems. Chris Argyris has suggested that in an effective system, problems are solved with minimal energy; they stay solved; and the problem-solving mechanisms used are not weakened, but maintained or strengthened.[7] An adequate organization, then, has well-developed structures and procedures for sensing the existence of problems, for inventing possible solutions, for deciding on the solutions, for implementing them, and for evaluating their effectiveness.

Though Miles uses the language of organizational theory in his analysis of health, the basic ideas seem to fit schools as well. The dimensions of health for any school operate in a system of dynamic interaction characterized by a high degree of interdependence. Clear goal focus, for example, depends upon the extent to which the school communicates its goals and permits inhabitants to modify and rearrange them. At another level, a high degree of health encourages school adaptiveness, while school adaptiveness contributes to, and is essential to, the health of the school.

CLIMATE AND LEARNING

An important question is, Does school climate make a difference in improving learning opportunities? Susan Rosenholtz provides convincing evidence that it does. She found that the quality of work relationships that existed in a school had a great deal to do with that school's ability to improve. She defines quality as the degree of openness, trust, communications, and support that is shared by teachers. These factors encourage not only learning but job satisfaction and improved performance as well. Rosenholtz refers to schools that possess these qualities as being "learning enriched" to differentiate them from "learning impoverished" schools.[8]

---

[7] Chris Argyris, *Integrating the Individual and the Organization,* New York: Wiley, 1964, cited in Miles, op. cit.

[8] Susan Rosenholtz, *Teachers' Workplace: The Social Organization of Schools,* New York: Longman, 1989. See also Susan Moore Johnson, *Teachers at Work: Achieving Success in Our Schools,* New York: Basic Books, 1990; Anthony Bryk and Barbara Schneider, *Trust in Schools: A Core Resource for Improvement,* New York: Russell Sage Foundation, 2002; and Thomas J. Sergiovanni, *The Principalship: A Reflective Practice Perspective,* 5th ed., Boston: Allyn & Bacon, 2005.

Climate focuses attention on the school's interpersonal work life as it affects teachers, administrators, and supervisors. But climate affects students as well. For example, one important line of inquiry links assumptions that teachers and administrators hold for *students* to climate dimensions. This research uses the Pupil Control Ideology (PCI) scale developed by Donald Willower and his associates.[9] This scale measures the assumptions and attitudes of teachers and supervisors toward students on a continuum from custodial to humanistic. "Custodial schools" tend to be rigidly controlled and concerned with maintenance and order. Within custodial schools students do not participate in decision making and are expected to accept decisions without question. Further, they are viewed as being irresponsible, undisciplined, untrustworthy, and trouble-prone. As a result, strong emphasis is given to controlling students through the development and use of punitive methods. "Humanistic schools," on the other hand, resemble communities that include students as fuller members and seek their cooperation and interaction. Self-discipline is emphasized and learning is considered to be promoted and enhanced by obtaining student identity and commitment. In schools with humanistic climates teachers are more likely to cooperate with one another as they work together, to have higher morale, and to enjoy a sense of task achievement. Social interaction among teachers is also high. In custodial schools these characteristics are not found and students are likely to be more alienated. Teachers are more likely to view the school as a battlefield. Wayne Hoy and James Appleberry found that in schools with more custodial climates, teachers were significantly less engaged in their work, showed less esprit, and were more aloof.[10] These are important findings that point to the link between climate and factors that directly affect the quality of teaching and knowing.

A study by researchers at Claremont Graduate School's Institute for Education and Transformation points to the quality of relationships between teachers and students and to other relationship themes as important leverage points for school improvement. Studying students, teachers, parents, and others in two elementary schools, one middle school, and one high school, the researchers determined that the data strongly suggest "that the heretofore identified *problems* of schooling (lower achievement, higher dropout rates and problems in the teaching profession) are rather *consequences* of much deeper and more fundamental [relationships] problems."[11] They concluded that efforts to change schools, no matter how sensible, were not likely to be successful unless relationships too were changed for the better. Improving school climate and building community in schools can help. The findings of this important study are summarized in Exhibit 16–2.

Many studies of highly successful schools confirm the importance of climate. For example, in their now famous study of 12 inner-London secondary schools,

---

[9]Donald J. Willower, Terry I. Eidell, and Wayne K. Hoy, *The School and Pupil Control Ideology,* Pennsylvania State University Studies no. 24, State College: Pennsylvania State University, 1967.

[10]Wayne K. Hoy and James B. Appleberry, "Teacher-Principal Relationships in 'Humanistic' and 'Custodial' Elementary Schools," *Journal of Experimental Education,* vol. 39, no. 2 (1970), pp. 27–31.

[11]Institute for Education and Transformation, *Voices from the Inside: A Report on Schooling from Inside the Classroom—Part I: Naming the Problem,* Claremont, CA: Claremont Graduate School, 1992, p. 11.

The Claremont researchers concluded that low student performance, high dropout rates, problems in the teaching profession, and other school difficulties were *consequences* of deeper, more fundamental problems that pointed to seven major issues, as summarized below. Relationship themes are embedded in each of the issue.

1. *Relationships.* Participants feel the crisis inside schools is directly linked to human relationships. Most often mentioned were relationships between teachers and students. Where positive things about the schools were noted, they usually involve reports of individuals who care, listen, understand, respect others, and are honest, open, and sensitive. Teachers report their best experiences in school are those where they connect with students and are able to help them in some way. They also report, however, there is precious little time during the day to seek out individual students. . . . Students of color, especially older students, often report that their teachers, school staff, and other students neither like nor understand them. Many teachers also report they do not always understand students ethnically different [from] themselves. When relationships in schools are poor, fear, name calling, threats of or incidents of violence, as well as a sense of depression and hopelessness exist. This theme was prominently stated by participants and so deeply connected to all other themes in the data that it is believed this may be one of the two most central issues in solving the crisis in schools.

2. *Race, culture, and class.* A theme which ran through every other issue, like that of relationships, was that of race, culture, and class. This is a theme with much debate and very little consensus. Many students of color and some Euro-American students perceive schools to be racist and prejudiced, from the staff to the curriculum. Some students doubt the very substance of what is being taught. . . . Teachers are tremendously divided on such issues. Some are convinced that students are right about racism, others are not. . . . Students have an intense interest in knowing about one another's culture but receive very little of that knowledge from home or school.

3. *Values.* There are frequently related conversations in the United States that suggest people of color and/or people living in economically depressed areas hold different basic values than [do] others, and that it is these differences which create conflicts in schools and society. While cultural differences clearly do exist in the expression or prioritization of values, our data hold no evidence that people inside schools have significantly different fundamental values. Our data suggest that parents, teachers, students, staff, and administrators of all ethnicities and classes, value and desire education, honesty, integrity, beauty, care, justice, truth, courage, and meaningful hard work. Participants' writings and transcripts of discussions are filled with references to basic values. However, very little time is spent in classrooms discussing these issues, and a number of restrictions exist against doing so. In the beginning of our research many participants initially assumed other participants held different values. The more we talked, the more this assumption was challenged. Students desire a network of adults (parents and teachers) with whom they can "really talk about important things," and want to have these conversations about values with one another.

Exhibit 16–2. The Importance of Relationships: A Summary of Findings.
Source: Institute for Education and Transformation, *Voices from the Inside: A Report of Schools from Inside the Classroom—Part I: Naming the Problem,* Claremont, CA: Claremont Graduate School, 1992, pp. 12–16.

4. *Teaching and learning.* Students, especially those past fifth grade, frequently report that they are bored in school and see little relevance of what is taught to their lives and their futures. Teachers feel pressure to teach what is mandated and sometimes doubt its appropriateness for their students. Teachers also are often bored by the curriculum they feel they must teach. . . . Students from all groups, remedial and advanced, high school to elementary, desire both rigor and fun in their schoolwork. They express enthusiasm about learning experiences that are complex but understandable, full of rich meanings and discussions of values, require their own action, and those about which they feel they have some choice.

5. *Safety.* Related to disconnected relationships and not knowing about one another's differences is the issue of safety. Very few participants on campus or parents feel schools are safe places. This is particularly true in our middle school and high school. Teachers, students, and staff fear physical violence. The influence of drugs, gangs, and random violence is felt by students. Students feel physically safest inside classrooms and least safe in large gatherings between classes or traveling to or from school.

6. *Physical environment.* Students want schools that reflect order, beauty, and space and contain rich materials and media. The desire for clean, aesthetically pleasing, and physically comfortable spaces is expressed by all. The food served to students is a persistent complaint. Many would like foods more typical of their homes and home cultures. The lack of any significant personal space such as lockers is problematic to students and also leads to feelings of being devalued. The depressed physical environment of many schools, especially those in lower socioeconomic areas, is believed by participants to reflect society's lack of priority for these children and their education.

7. *Despair, hope, and the process of change.* Many participants feel a hopelessness about schools that is reflected in the larger society and in the music and art of our youth. Paradoxically, hope seemed to emerge following honest dialogues about our collective despair. Participants are anxious for change and willing to participate in change they perceive as relevant. We have strong indications that change inside schools might best be stimulated through participatory processes. In these self-driven research processes, participants came to openly discuss their hopes and dreams. Through this process, we understood there were shared common values around which we could begin to imagine a more ideal school.

Exhibit 16–2. *Continued*

Michael Rutter, Barbara Maughan, Peter Mortimer, and Janet Ouston found that important differences in climate existed between those schools that were more or less effective.[12] Effectiveness in this case was defined as higher scores on national examinations, better behavior, and better attendance. In the more effective schools teachers worked harder and had better attitudes toward learning, spent more time in actual teaching, relied more heavily on praising students, and were better able to

[12]Michael Rutter, Barbara Maughan, Peter Mortimer, and Janet Ouston, *Fifteen Thousand Hours: Secondary Schools and Their Effects on Children,* Cambridge, MA: Harvard University Press, 1979.

involve students as active learners. Studies of highly successful schools that emphasize ethnographic techniques and the importance of culture reach similar conclusions.[13]

Finally, the important work of Patricia Ashton and Rodman Webb that links teachers' sense of efficacy, motivation, and commitment to teacher behavior, student behavior, and student achievement provides further evidence.[14] Their findings were summarized in Chapter 15. In that discussion it was noted that students of more efficacious teachers are more enthusiastic, are more likely to initiate interactions with teachers, and score higher on mathematics and language tests. A supportive school climate is one important contribution to a teacher's sense of efficacy.

SCHOOL CLIMATE AND GROUP BEHAVIOR

The concept of school climate is collective, born of the sum of teacher perceptions of the interpersonal life of the school as the faculty lives and works together. Membership in groups is important to teachers, and the norms that develop as a result influence what they believe and do. From a psychological point of view, group membership provides the means for meeting many of the needs of teachers. And from a symbolic point of view, groups provide the means to enable teachers to construct their realities and to find meaning and significance. Both are important conditions that enable teachers to find satisfaction in work and to work to full potential. Amitai Etzioni suggests that teachers tend to make decisions not as isolated individuals but as members of collectivities.[15] Their teaching preferences, how they are likely to respond to school improvement initiatives, and even how cooperative they are likely to be with supervisors are all shaped by such memberships. To a great extent, changing individuals means changing groups. For this reason, understanding the faculty as a work group is important. Further, helping faculties become effective work groups is an important purpose of supervision and a critical part of the school improvement process.

How can supervisors judge the extent to which faculty groups are working effectively? One indicator is the kind and nature of group outcomes. What is the group supposed to be accomplishing and to what extent is it accomplishing those aims? If outcomes are being accomplished, the group is judged to be *efficient*. But the problem with viewing effectiveness in this way is that efficiency is only one necessary component. The other component is *growth*. An effective group is concerned not only with accomplishing its tasks but also with improving its ability to accomplish even more difficult tasks in the future. Many studies have shown that giving primary attention to efficiency and neglecting growth may result in short-term

[13]See, for example, Joan Lipsitz, *Successful Schools for Young Adolescents,* New Brunswick, NJ: Transaction Books, 1984; Sara Lightfoot, *The Good High School,* New York: Basic Books, 1983.

[14]Patricia T. Ashton and Rodman B. Webb, *Making a Difference: Teachers' Sense of Efficacy and Student Achievement,* New York: Longman, 1986.

[15]Amitai Etzioni, *The Moral Dimension Toward a New Economics,* New York: Free Press, 1988.

increases in productivity, but over time the work group loses its productive edge.[16] The relationship between effective supervision and group effectiveness is becoming increasingly important as the work of supervision takes place more and more within the context of groups. Examples include peer-collegial supervision; clinical supervision; team-oriented staff development programs; curriculum development projects; and team, family, or group teaching.

SCHOOL CULTURE

Supervision II seeks to give a fuller account of what matters to teachers and of what is involved in helping them think more carefully about their practice. A fuller account means giving attention to the symbolic side of school life as well as the psychological side.

Climate is to the psychological side of school life what culture is to the symbolic side. Teachers respond to work not only as a result of psychological needs but also as makers of meaning. Thus, studying school culture means studying how events and interactions come to be meaningful.[17] *Culture* can be defined as a set of understandings or meanings shared by a group of people. Typically these meanings are tacitly held and serve to define the group as being distinct from other groups.[18]

Communities are one kind of culture. The values and shared meanings of community cultures are deeply held and elicit strong feelings of loyalty and affection. Cultures of schools that are understood as communities are decidedly more sacred, having been defined by their centers of shared values. Edward A. Shils uses the concept of "central zone" to illustrate the importance of shared values in understanding cultures.

> The central, or the central zone, is a phenomenon of the realm of values and beliefs. It is the center of the order of symbols and values and beliefs, which govern the society. . . . The central zone partakes of the nature of the sacred. In this sense every society has an official "religion." . . . The center is also a phenomenon of the realm of action. It is a structure of activities, of roles and persons, within the network of institutions. It is in these roles that the values and beliefs which are central are embodied and propounded.[19]

As repositories of values these centers are sources of identity for individuals and groups and the means by which their work lives become meaningful. Centers provide a sense of purpose to seemingly ordinary events and bring worth and dignity to human activities within the organization.

---

[16]See, for example, Rensis Likert, *The Human Organization,* New York: McGraw-Hill, 1967; and Likert, *New Patterns of Management.*

[17]Linda Smircich, "Is the Concept of Culture a Paradigm for Understanding Ourselves?" in Peter J. Frost et al. (eds.), *Organizational Culture,* Beverly Hills, CA: Sage, 1985, pp. 55–72.

[18]M. R. Louis, "Organizations as Culture Bearing Milieux," in Louis Pondy et al. (eds.), *Organizational Symbolism,* Greenwich, CT: JAI, 1980, pp. 76–92.

[19]Edward A. Shils, "Centre and Periphery," in *The Logic of Personal Knowledge: Essays Presented to Michael Polanyi,* London: Routledge & Kegan Paul, 1961, p. 119.

LEVELS OF CULTURE

It is useful to think about dimensions of school culture as existing at four levels.[20] The most tangible and observable level is represented by the *artifacts* of culture as manifested in what people say, how people behave, and how things look. Verbal artifacts include the language systems that are used, stories that are told, and examples that are used to illustrate certain important points. Behavioral artifacts are manifested in the ceremonies and rituals and other symbolic practices of the school.

The next level of school culture to be understood is the *perspectives* of people. Perspectives refer to the shared rules and norms, the commonness that exists among solutions to similar problems, how people define the situations they face, and the boundaries of acceptable and unacceptable behavior.

The third level is that of *values.* Values provide the basis for people to evaluate the situations they face, the worth of actions, activities, their priorities, and the behaviors of people with whom they work. The values are arranged in a fashion which represents the covenant that teachers share. This covenant might be in the form of an educational or management platform and statements of school philosophy. Platforms and philosophy were discussed in more detail in Chapter 5.

The fourth level is that of *assumptions.* Assumptions are more abstract than each of the other levels because they are typically implicit. Craig C. Lundberg describes assumptions as "the tacit beliefs that members hold about themselves and others, their relationships to other persons, and the nature of the organization in which they live. Assumptions are the nonconscious underpinnings of the first three levels—that is, the implicit, abstract axioms that determine the more explicit systems of meanings."[21]

IDENTIFYING THE CULTURE OF YOUR SCHOOL

The four levels of culture provide a framework for analyzing a school's history and tradition, patterns of beliefs, norms, and behaviors. For example, the questions below can help supervisors identify and describe important aspects of the culture of their schools.

THE SCHOOL'S HISTORY. How does the school's past live in the present? What traditions are carried on? What stories are told and retold? What events in the school's history are overlooked or forgotten? Do heroes and heroines among students and teachers exist whose idiosyncrasies and exploits are remembered? In

---

[20]The levels are from Craig C. Lundberg, "On the Feasibility of Cultural Interventions in Organizations," in Frost et al., *Organizational Culture.* The four levels are based on the work of Schein and Dyer as follows: W. G. Dyer, Jr., *Patterns and Assumptions: The Keys to Understanding Organizational Culture,* Office of Naval Research Technical Report TR-0 NR-7; and Edgar H. Schein, *Organizational Culture and Leadership,* 3rd ed., San Francisco: Jossey-Bass, 2004.

[21]Lundberg, op. cit., p. 172.

what ways are the school's traditions and historical incidents modified through reinterpretation over the years? Can you recall, for example, a historical event that has evolved from fact to myth?

BELIEFS. What are the assumptions and understandings that are shared by teachers and others, though they may not be stated explicitly? These may relate to how the school is structured, how teaching takes place, the roles of teachers and students, discipline, the relationship of parents to the school. Perhaps these assumptions and understandings are written somewhere in the form of a philosophy or other statement.

VALUES. What are the things that your school prizes? That is, when teachers and principals talk about the school, what are the major and recurring value themes underlying what they say?

NORMS AND STANDARDS. What are the oughts, shoulds, and dos and don'ts that govern the behavior of teachers, supervisors, and principals? Norms and standards can be identified by examining what behaviors get rewarded and what behaviors get punished in the school.

PATTERNS OF BEHAVIOR. What are the accepted and recurring ways of doing things, the patterns of behavior, the habits and rituals that prevail in the school?

Corwith Hansen suggests that teachers be asked the following questions in seeking to identify the culture of their school.[22] Describe your workday both in and outside the school. On what do you spend your time and energy? Given that most students forget what they learn, what do you hope your students will retain over time from your classes? Think of students you are typically attracted to—those that you admire, respect, or enjoy. What common characteristics do these students have? What does it take for a teacher to be successful in your school or in your department? What advice would you give new teachers? What do you remember about past faculty members and students in your school or department? If you were to draw a picture or take a photo or make a collage that represented some aspect of your school, what would it look like? How are students rewarded? How are teachers rewarded? What might a new teacher do that would immediately signal to others that he or she was not going to be successful?

"The School Culture Inventory: Identifying Guiding Beliefs" appears as Exhibit 16–3. This inventory is designed to help faculties tackle the task of identifying their culture by examining their school's belief structure. Depending on responses, a school can be classified generally on a continuum from having a strong to very weak culture.

From this discussion of school culture one might reasonably conclude that the concepts of culture and climate are similar. But still they are unique in many ways.

[22]Corwith Hansen, "Department Culture in a High-Performing Secondary School." Unpublished dissertation, New York: Columbia University, 1986.

Before a school's culture can be understood, evaluated, or changed, it needs first to be described. The list of questions which constitute this inventory can help faculties describe the culture of their school. The questions are patterned generally after those which appear in Jerry Patterson, Stuart C. Purkey, and Jackson Parker's, *Productive School Systems for a Nonrational World*. Though presented in the form of an inventory, the questions will have the most meaning when discussed by faculty. When individual and group ratings are obtained from teachers, they should be supplemented by examples. To help acquaint you with the inventory items, try evaluating a school with which you are familiar using the following scale:

(*A*lways, *M*ost of the time, *P*art of the time, *N*ever)

School Purposes
To what extent does the school:
1. Communicate a set of purposes that provide a
   sense of direction and a basis for evaluating?   A M P N
2. Value the importance of teachers' and students'
   understanding the purposes?   A M P N
3. Want decisions to be made that reflect purposes?   A M P N
Give examples:

Empowerment
To what extent does the school:
4. Value empowering teachers to make decisions
   that are sensible given circumstances they face?   A M P N
5. Link empowerment to purpose by requiring that
   decisions reflect the school's shared values?   A M P N
6. Believe that teachers, supervisors, and
   administrators should have equal access to
   information and resources?   A M P N
7. Believe power to be an expanding entity that
   increases when shared?   A M P N
Give examples:

Exhibit 16–3. The School Culture Inventory: Identifying Guiding Beliefs.
Source: Adapted from Jerry Patterson, Stuart Purkey, and Jackson Parker, *Productive School Systems for a Nonrational World,* Arlington, VA: Association for Supervision and Curriculum Development, 1986, pp. 50–51. Reprinted with permission of the Association for Supervision and Curriculum Development and Jerry Patterson, Stuart Purkey, and Jackson Parker. Copyright © 1986 by the Association for Supervision and Curriculum Development. All rights reserved.

Decision Making

To what extent does the school:

8. Believe that decisions should be made as close to
   the point of implementation as possible?   A M P N

9. Believe that value decisions should be made by
   those directly affected by them?   A M P N

10. Believe that decisions should be made by those who
    are most expert, given the circumstances or problem
    being considered, regardless of hierarchical level?   A M P N

Give examples:

Sense of Community

To what extent does the school:

11. Value a "we" spirit and feeling of ownership in
    the school?   A M P N

12. Consider teachers and other employees as shareholders
    and stakeholders in the school?   A M P N

13. Demonstrate commitment to helping and developing
    school members?   A M P N

Give examples:

Trust

To what extent does the school:

14. Believe that given the opportunity teachers will want to
    do what is best for the school?   A M P N

15. Have confidence in the ability of teachers to make wise decisions?   A M P N

Give examples:

Quality

To what extent does the school:

16. Value high standards and expectations for teachers and students?   A M P N

17. Believe in a "can do" attitude in teachers and students?   A M P N

18. Value an atmosphere of sharing and encouraging within which
    school members "stretch and grow"?   A M P N

Give examples:

Recognition

To what extent does the school:

19. Value recognizing teachers and students for taking chances
    in seeking new and better ideas?   A M P N

20. Value recognizing the achievements and accomplishments
    of teachers and students?   A M P N

Give examples:

Exhibit 14–3. *Continued*

Caring

To what extent does the school:

21. Value the well-being and personal concerns of
all school members?   A M P N

22. Take a personal interest in the work concerns
and career development of teachers?   A M P N

Give Examples:

Integrity

To what extent does the school:

23. Value honesty in words and actions?   A M P N

24. Adopt a single standard of norms and expectations
for teachers, students, and other school members?   A M P N

25. Value consistency?   A M P N

26. Demonstrate commitment to highest personal
and ethical convictions?   A M P N

Give examples:

Diversity

To what extent does the school:

27. Value differences in individual philosophy and personality?   A M P N

28. Value differences in teaching style?   A M P N

29. Value flexibility in teaching and learning approaches
in response to student differences?   A M P N

30. Link diversity in style and method to common school
purposes and values?   A M P N

Give examples:

Sum of column tallies   ＿ ＿ ＿ ＿

Scoring directions: To score the school culture inventory, multiply the sum of tallies in
column A by 4, column M by 3, column P by 2, and column N by 1. Now sum the scores
for each column to get a grand score. The scale below provides a *rough* indicator of the
strength of your school's professional culture:

110 to 120	Strong
90 to 110	Moderately strong
60 to 90	Weak
Below 60	Very weak

Exhibit 14–3. *Continued*

Earlier we discussed the PCI scale and its use in identifying custodial and humanistic schools. These schools differed with respect to the assumptions and beliefs that teachers made about students, discipline, and control. In many respects the PCI conception of climate is concerned with aspects of school culture, suggesting that the two concepts share commonalities. Still, the climate metaphor leads one to think more about the interpersonal life in schools. Culture leads one deeper into the life of the school, into the tacit world of beliefs and norms, into the realm of meaning and significance.

PLANNING FOR CHANGE TEACHER BY TEACHER

Acknowledging both the psychological and symbolic sides of human nature redefines the problem of how to introduce change; the problem of how to overcome the resistance of individual teachers becomes the broader problem of how to alter the culture of the school. An effective change strategy gives attention to both.

W. J. Reddin views individual teacher concerns as falling into three broad categories:

1. How will the proposed change affect the individual?
2. How will the proposed change affect relationships with others?
3. How will the proposed change affect the individual's work?[23]

He maintains that though these concerns are real, they are often not considered "legitimate" reasons for favoring or opposing a change. For this reason, teacher concerns often remain unstated. Instead, the talk of resistance has to do with such issues as whether what is being proposed makes "educational sense or not."

Consider, for example, a teacher who is faced with the prospect of having to give up the safety and autonomy of teaching in a self-contained classroom for teaming with others. She may be worrying about what others will think about her teaching and about the additional time and interpersonal pressures involved in having to negotiate with others what will be taught, how it will be taught, and when. Furthermore, she may be worrying about whether her chances of becoming an assistant principal in the school will be enhanced or diminished as a result of this new teaching arrangement. But given the formal roles played in schools, it is typically not socially acceptable to state publicly such personal concerns. Thus instead of speaking to these *real* issues, the teacher complains that students are likely to find team teaching to be impersonal, that clear lines of authority will become clouded, that discipline problems will increase, and that students will find it burdensome to adjust to several different teaching styles.

Not surprisingly, these more organizationally legitimate concerns are not real in and of themselves but are proxies for the more personal concerns of teachers. As teachers make peace with personal concerns, the proxies have a way of disappearing.

[23]W. J. Reddin, *Managerial Effectiveness,* New York: McGraw-Hill, 1970, p. 163.

One advantage of a healthy school climate is that levels of trust and openness among colleagues are such that it becomes acceptable to raise these less legitimate reasons for being concerned about proposed changes.

You can test Reddin's ideas by applying his categories to your own personal experience. Recall, for example, an occasion when a significant change was being proposed. What was your initial reaction to this change? Think less about what you said to others about the change and more about what you actually thought about and felt. The list below is adapted from Reddin. Use this list to identify the items that were of most concern to you:

Concern for self

How will my advancement possibilities change?

How will my view of myself change?

How will my formal authority change?

How will my informal influence change?

How will my view of my prior values change?

How will my status change?

Concern for work

How will the amount of work I do change?

How will my interest in the work change?

How will the importance of my work change?

How will the challenge of the work change?

How will the work pressures change?

How will the skill demands on me change?

How will my hours of work change?

Concern for relationships

How will my relationships with my co-workers change?

How will my relationships with my supervisors change?

How will what my family thinks of me change?[24]

A supervisor who wanted to use Reddin's theory to overcome your resistance to change would try to identify your concerns and how powerfully you held them. Then in a kind of tug of war, with the supervisor pulling at one end and you pulling at the other, the supervisor would try to change your mind about your concerns.[25] Let's say the two most pressing concerns for you are how your informal influence

[24]Ibid.

[25]In the parlance of social science, this tug of war is called *force field theory and analysis.* See, for example, Kurt Lewin, *Field Theory in Social Science,* New York: Harper & Row, 1951.

with the faculty will change and the additional amount of work that will be required. The supervisor might try to convince you that teaming provides a better arena for your influence to increase. Further, the supervisor might try to counter your concern about increased workload by helping you see the possibilities of becoming a team leader. Both of these advantages can increase your chances of ultimately becoming an assistant principal. *The supervisor, in other words, seeks to overcome your resistance to change by offering attractions that increase the pull from one side of the tug of war or by removing resisters that decrease the pull from the other side.*

Some researchers have focused on the concerns issue in a developmental sense, seeking to find out what are initial concerns of teachers and what concerns come later. They reason that depending upon level of concern, teachers are likely to focus on one set of limited issues as opposed to another. A good change strategy, therefore, calculates carefully what the level of concern is and gives attention to the correct corresponding issues. This work has led to the development of the "concerns-based adoption model" of change. This model charts the changing feelings of teachers as they learn about a proposed change, prepare to use it, then use it, and finally make it a part of their everyday repertoire. The model proposes seven stages of concern, as follows:[26]

1. Awareness   I am not concerned about it.
2. Informational   I would like to know more about it.
3. Personal   How will using it affect me?
4. Management   I seem to be spending all my time getting material ready.
5. Consequence   How is my use affecting kids?
6. Collaboration   I am concerned about relating what I am doing to what other teachers are doing.
7. Refocusing   I have some ideas about something that would work even better.

The developers of the model do not assume that every teacher marches through all the stages beginning with awareness and ending with refocusing. Nor do they assume that the stages are mutually exclusive, with only one being tended to at a time. Instead, the stages represent the general kind of development that takes place as changes are adopted and used.

A typical pattern of progression is as follows. In the early stages, teachers are likely to have concerns that center on learning more about the proposed innovation and how it will affect them personally. This is not unlike the category system proposed by Reddin. Once these concerns are taken care of, teachers are then ready to focus on the management problems they are likely to face as they begin to implement the change. Next, their attention shifts to the impact the change is likely to have on their students. Once comfortable with answers to this question, teachers

---

[26]See, for example, Gene E. Hall and Susan F. Loucks, "Teacher Concerns as a Basis for Facilitating Staff Development," *Teachers College Record,* vol. 80, no. 1 (1978); and Shirley M. Hord, William L. Rutherford, Leslie Huling-Austin, and Gene E. Hall, *Taking Charge of Change,* Alexandria, VA: Association for Supervision and Curriculum Development, 1977.

address issues of collaboration with other teachers in an effort to implement the change and to improve its effects. Finally, since teachers are different, they make adaptations to the innovation in an effort to improve its fit to their unique circumstances. In sum, the researchers recommend that supervisors interested in promoting change use the concerns-based model as a framework for evaluating where individuals are and for matching change strategies to these levels.

It seems clear that resistance to change occurs when one's basic needs are threatened. Although teachers have different needs, four seem fairly universal:[27]

1. *The need for clear expectations.* Most people require fairly specific information about their jobs to function effectively. People need to know what is expected of them, how they fit into the total scheme of things, what their responsibilities are, how they will be evaluated, and what their relationships with others will be. Change upsets this equilibrium of role definition and expectations.

2. *The need for future certainty.* Closely related to fit is being able to predict the future. People need to have some reliability and certainty built into their work lives. Change introduces ambiguity and uncertainty, which threaten the need for a relatively stable, balanced, and predictable work environment.

3. *The need for social interacting.* Most people value and need opportunities to interact with others. This interaction helps people define and build up their own self-concepts and reduce the anxiety and fear they experience in the work environment. People seek support and acceptance from others at work. Change is often viewed as threatening these important social interaction patterns.

4. *The need for control over the work environment and work events.* Most people want and seek a reasonable degree of control over their work environment. People do not want to be at the mercy of the system but instead, want to be origins, making decisions that affect their own work lives. When control is threatened or reduced, the effect is not only less job satisfaction but also a loss of meaning in work that results in indifference and even alienation.

Change efforts that ignore these four needs are likely not only to be ineffective but also to cause important morale problems.

Overcoming resistance to change by carefully calculating the appropriate level of concern of teachers involved and by helping teachers feel safe and secure are all helpful. But resistance to change also occurs when proposed changes oppose the existing norm systems of the school. A strong change strategy seeks as well to alter the culture of the school by creating new work norms. Although tending to the psychological needs of individual teachers is important, in the end, changing schools requires changing school culture. Such an ambitious goal, we will argue, requires two things: that leadership be redefined and practiced differently, and that collegiality be understood within the context of communities of practice. The principles of Supervision II can help.

---

[27]Laird W. Mealiea, "Learned Behavior: The Key to Understanding and Preventing Employee Resistance to Change," *Group and Organizational Studies,* vol. 3, no. 2 (1978), pp. 211–223, as quoted in Thomas J. Sergiovanni, *The Principalship: A Reflective Practice Perspective,* 4th ed., Boston: Allyn & Bacon, 2001, p. 316.

COLLEGIALITY AS LINCHPIN

It is now accepted that promoting collegiality is an important way to help schools change for the better. Susan Rosenholtz's research, for example, firmly links collegiality to the amount and quality of learning that takes place among teachers.[28] In summarizing the research on collegiality and school improvement, Michael Fullan writes:

> Since interaction with others influences what one does, relationships with other teachers is a critical variable. The theory of change that we have been evolving clearly points to the importance of peer relationships in the school. Change involves learning to do something new, and interaction is the primary basis for social learning. New meanings, new behaviors, new skills, and new beliefs depend significantly on whether teachers are working as isolated individuals (Goodlad, 1984; Lortie, 1975; Sarason, 1982) or are exchanging ideas, support, and positive feelings about their work (Little, 1982; Mortimore et al., 1988; Rosenholtz, 1989). The quality of working relationships among teachers is strongly related to implementation. Collegiality, open communication, trust, support and help, learning on the job, getting results, and job satisfaction and morale are closely interrelated.[29]

Judith Warren Little's work is most often quoted on this issue:

> School Improvement is most surely and thoroughly achieved when:
>
> Teachers engage in frequent, continuous and increasingly concrete and precise *talk* about teaching practice (as distinct from teacher characteristics and failings, the social lives of teachers, the foibles and failures of students and their families, and the unfortunate demands of society on the school). By such talk, teachers build up a shared language adequate to the complexity of teaching, capable of distinguishing one practice and its virtue from another. . . .
>
> Teachers are frequently observed and provided with useful (if potentially frightening) critiques of their teaching. Such observation and feedback can provide shared referents for the shared language of teaching at a level of the precision and concreteness which makes the talk about teaching useful.
>
> Teachers [and administrators] plan, design, research, evaluate and prepare teaching materials together. The most astute observations remain academic ("just theory") without the machinery to act on them. By joint work on materials, teachers [and administrators] share the considerable burden of development required by long-term improvement, confirm their emerging understanding of their approach and make rising standards for their work attainable by them and their students.
>
> Teachers teach each other the practice of teaching.[30]

---

[28]Rosenholtz, op. cit.

[29]Fullan with Stiegelbauer, op. cit., p. 79. The Fullan cites are as follows: John Goodlad, *A Place Called School: Prospects for the Future,* New York: McGraw-Hill, 1984; Dan Lortie, *Schoolteacher: A Sociological Study,* Chicago: University of Chicago Press, 1975; Seymour Sarason, *The Culture of the School and the Problem of Change,* revised ed., Boston: Allyn & Bacon, 1982; Judith Warren Little, "Norms of Collegiality and Experimentation: Workplace Conditions of School Success," *American Educational Research Journal,* vol. 19 (1982), pp. 325–340; P. Mortimore, P. Sammons, L. Stoll, D. Lewis, and R. Ecob, *School Matters: The Junior Years,* Sommerset, UK: Open Books, 1988; and Rosenholtz, op. cit.

[30]Judith Warren Little, "Norms of Collegiality and Experimentation: Workplace Conditions of School Success," *American Educational Research Journal,* vol. 19, no. 3 (Fall 1982), p. 331.

Collegiality bridges the concepts of school climate and school culture. Collegiality speaks not only to the degree of trust, openness, and good feelings that exist among a faculty, but also to the kind of norm system that bonds teachers as a collective unit. The bonding aspect of collegiality is key and is often missing in the policies and practices of Supervision I.

One problem is that too often, collegiality is confused with congeniality.[31] *Congeniality* refers to the friendly human relationships that exist among teachers and is characterized by the loyalty, trust, and easy conversation that results from the development of a closely knit social group. Congeniality is often considered a measure of school climate. *Collegiality,* by contrast, refers to the existence of high levels of collaboration among teachers and between teachers and principal and is characterized by mutual respect, shared work values, cooperation, and specific conversations about teaching and learning. When congeniality is high, a strong informal culture aligned with social norms emerges in the school. But these norms may or may not be aligned with school purposes. By contrast, when collegiality is high, a strong professional culture held together by shared work norms emerges in the school. These norms are aligned with school purposes and contribute to increased commitment and improved performance. We believe that congeniality can contribute to the development of collegiality but in itself is not sufficient.

Another problem is that when collegiality *is* achieved within Supervision I, it is often contrived rather than real, resulting from structural rather than normative changes. Supervisors push for collegiality by altering structures and introducing such innovations as peer coaching and team teaching without addressing the norm structure of the school. As a result, they superimpose a form of collegiality on an unaccepting culture. When this is the case, collegial practices become grafted on to the existing school culture.[32] Andrew Hargreaves describes contrived collegiality as

> characterized by a set of formal, specific bureaucratic procedures to increase the attention being given to joint teacher planning and consultation. It can be seen in initiatives such as peer coaching, mentor teaching, joint planning in specially provided rooms, formally scheduled meetings, and clear job descriptions and training programs for those in consultive roles. These sorts of initiatives are administrative contrivances designed to get collegiality going in schools where little has existed before.[33]

The receiving culture is key in determining whether administratively induced collegiality is contrived or real. When it is real, collegiality results from the felt interdependence of people at work and from a sense of moral obligation to work together. From a cultural perspective, and with the right set of shared norms in place,

[31]Roland Barth, *Improving Schools from Within,* San Francisco: Jossey-Bass, 1990.

[32]Peter B. Grimmitt, Olaf P. Rostad, and Blake Ford, "Supervision: A Transformational Perspective," in Carl Glickman (ed.), *Supervision in Transition,* 1992 Yearbook of the Association for Supervision and Curriculum Development (ASCD). Alexandria, VA: ASCD, 1992.

[33]Andrew Hargreaves, "Contrived Collegiality and the Culture of Teaching." Annual Meeting of the Canadian Society for the Study of Education, Quebec City, 1989.

collegiality can be considered a form of professional virtue. When this is the case, the fulfillment of certain obligations that stem from the teacher's membership in the school as community and membership in the teaching profession requires teachers to be collegial.

Collegiality as professional virtue comprises three dimensions: a conception of the good person who values colleagueship for its own sake, connectedness to a community that provides one with the right to be treated collegially and the obligation to treat others collegially, and interpersonal relationships characterized by mutual respect.[34] The first two dimensions are enhanced by a healthy school culture and the third by a healthy school climate.

Perhaps the defining benchmark for identifying how deep collegiality is emerging in a school is whether the faculty is coming together as a community of practice. In most schools, teachers are involved in their own private practice and supervision responds accordingly. But in a community of practice, teachers begin to think of themselves as being part of a single practice of teaching. As this strong sense of shared practice begins to spread and deepen, collegiality functions at a higher level than is normally the case.[35]

THE SUPERVISOR IS KEY

Improving schools by helping teachers reflect on their practice, learn more about what they do and why, strive for self-improvement, share what they know with others, is at the heart of what supervision seeks to accomplish. This purpose often leads to a focus on how to provide staff development approaches and, in class, how to provide help that teachers welcome and find beneficial. It leads to a concern with how the talents and resources of individual teachers might be shared with others and how the evaluation process can be improved. These supervising aims and activities involve change. Change is difficult under ordinary circumstances; it is particularly trying when conditions are not right. The right conditions, we have argued in this chapter, are those that support both the psychological and symbolic needs of teachers, needs that are the subject matter of school climate and school culture. No matter how well intentioned the supervisor, and no matter how hard that supervisor tries to improve the individual and collective practice of teaching in a school, little will be accomplished without first developing and nurturing the right school climate and culture. Climate and culture are affected by administrative policies; they are affected even more by close, personal contact with the process of teaching and learning. This is the territory of supervision. For this reason, both formally designated supervisors and informal supervisors have particularly critical roles to play.

---

[34]Thomas J. Sergiovanni, *Moral Leadership: Getting to the Heart of School Improvement,* San Francisco: Jossey-Bass, 1992.

[35]Thomas J. Sergiovanni, "The Story of Community," in John Retallick, Barry Cocklin, and Kennece Coombe (eds.), *Learning Communities in Education,* London: Routledge, 1999, pp. 9–25; and Thomas J. Sergiovanni, *Leadership: What's in It for School?* London: Routledge/Falmer, 2001.

SUMMARY

Climate, culture, and change are the themes of this chapter. It is important for supervisors to learn to read school climates and school cultures so that they are able to assess readiness to change. Often it is not the change itself that is worrisome but the school's readiness for change. You can gauge degree of readiness by paying attention to such benchmarks as the following:

- the patterns and ways in which people interact. Are, for example, patterns of interaction frequent and constructive?
- the group norms, values, and standards that evolve. Are norms, values, and standards known and accepted?
- the espoused principles that groups claim are important. Do groups "walk their talk"?
- the formal and stated policies designed to guide a school's achievement. Are designs real?
- the "rules of the game" that embody the school's true values. Are true values known, and do they have important effects?
- the metaphors that are used to explain the ways people should think and act. Are the metaphors effective?
- the rituals and celebrations that provide a symbolic world that must be navigated. Is the culture strong and getting stronger?

Edgar H. Schein speaks to the importance of organizational culture to a school's success as follows: "It can be argued that the only thing of real importance that leaders do is to create and manage culture; that the unique talent of leaders is their ability to understand and work with culture."[36] Several instruments, inventories, and reflection exercises are provided in this chapter.

SOME REFLECTIONS

1. Ask at least five colleagues in your school to use the Organizational Climate Questionnaire, Exhibit 16–1, to assess your school's climate. To what extent do respondents agree? What effects would low school climate scores have on your school's ability to get teachers involved in peer-clinical supervision and in other professional development activities?
2. Suppose your principal asked you to give your school a "physical" that assessed its organizational health. What diagnosis would you make? What treatments would you prescribe?
3. What is your reaction to Daniel Patrick Moynihan's comment that "culture makes almost all the difference"? Give examples that support your reactions.
4. Explain to others in your class what Andrew Hargreaves means by "contrived collegiality." Give examples of contrived collegiality in your school or school district. Would you describe the teachers in your school as being more collegial than congenial? Or would it be the other way around?

---

[36]Schein, op. cit., p. 11.

CHAPTER 17

Supervision and the Renewal of Schools

INTRODUCTION

This chapter attempts what used to be known in the teaching of rhetoric as the peroration—the final summing up, the gathering of all previous argument into one convincing statement. In attempting to situate supervision within the dynamic agenda of school renewal, the chapter argues that supervisors are in a unique position to cultivate and energize the collective effort of a learning community to promote quality learning for all students, through the progressive and continuous learning of the professional staff. The challenges of this kind of intellectual and moral leadership will change supervisors' roles from bureaucratic management to leadership within a learning community. A significant aspect of this shift in roles will involve a clearer focus on and support for student learning. This change in focus implies a closer collaboration with teachers and students to transform those institutional structures and processes that inhibit rather than facilitate student learning. With more and more students embracing an agenda of authentic learning, the learning community will become what it espouses.

SOME BACKGROUND

Supervisors would not, in the minds of teachers, superintendents, policy makers, and critics, be the ones expected to start a revolution in schools. They are traditionally seen as those who oversee the appropriate implementation of new policies or the following of standard operating procedures. In the discussions over restructuring schools, the focus has been on the state legislature and state department of education to legislate major changes, or on the teachers at the school site who will participate in site-based change efforts.

Supervisors have unique roles to play in school renewal. States and federal governments have defined the external environment of accountability. Local schools and school systems are responsible for defining the internal environment of accountability. School district leaders and local principals can begin to structure that internal environment of accountability through policy implementation guidelines and a more sophisticated support network of teacher leadership and middle-range positions such as subject-area coaches and cluster leaders. Supervisors, however, will have an important leadership role in building internal accountability through their collaborative work with teachers in capacity building.[1] Because the focus of supervision has expanded to include work with teams of teachers, supervisors are, collectively, at the front line of efforts to bring all teachers up to a higher and richer practice of teaching, one that attends to the success of traditionally underperforming students and the more authentic learning of all students. If supervisors are to play a significant part in the renewal of schools, they will have to move beyond their traditional roles of working within a status quo environment to exercising leadership in the transformation of that environment.

Those who engage in supervision have a unique perspective to bring to the job of school renewal. Supervising brings the supervisor into contact with many teachers, with many classrooms, with many different groups of students whose varied approaches to the demands of learning may be strikingly different. The supervisor's view is larger than the individual teacher's view. It is larger because the supervisor sees many teachers, all of whom exhibit different talents and who express their approaches to the design of learning activities differently. It is larger because the supervisor moves back and forth between different institutional levels of administration and policy and therefore has a better sense of the whole school than does any individual teacher.

Moreover, the supervisor is closer to the realities of the classroom and of student engagement with or resistance to the learning tasks than are school administrators who do not exercise supervisory responsibilities. The supervisor can speak as an advocate for students and for teachers in discussions with administrators about making the school environment more "user-friendly." The supervisor, in short, is the one person whose work is involved with all, or at least most, levels of the school.

Because of these contacts with a variety of people in the school, the supervisor is in a unique position to cultivate a new vision of teaching and learning, to bring a super-vision to the discussions with various school personnel. One might say that the supervisor is potentially the primary reflective practitioner in the school; besides reflecting with individual teachers, and with groups of teachers (in departmental-level or grade-level meetings), the supervisor reflects with administrators and district personnel about staff development programs, curriculum redesign, and resource allocation in administrative staff meetings. The supervisor is in an ideal

---

[1]See the thorough going analysis of the need for internal capacity building as the cornerstone for internal accountability in Jacob E. Adams and Michael W. Kirst, "New Demands and Concepts for Educational Accountability: Striving for Results in an Era of Excellence," in Joseph Murphy and Karen Seashore Louis (eds.), *Handbook of Research in Educational Administration*, 2nd ed., San Francisco: Jossey-Bass, 1999, pp. 463–489.

position to be a carrier of ideas, a conduit of new thinking, a mapmaker who can help teachers and administrators reconceptualize the terrain of their work.

People who supervise usually have two or three additional responsibilities. Sometimes supervision is considered the least important task in the supervisor's job description. Yet, were the supervisor to reconceptualize supervisory work as a central activity for school renewal and make supervision the centerpiece of his or her work, it might enable a better integration of the other tasks. More specifically, how might that role be worked out in practice?

INTELLECTUAL AND MORAL DIMENSIONS OF SUPERVISORY LEADERSHIP

First, supervisors would need to see the leadership possibilities in the supervisory process, see it as involved in the *educational* mission of the school, rather than as a bureaucratic activity fulfilling bureaucratic demands for control and record keeping. Supervisors need to appreciate the intellectual dimension of their work. As professionals who have studied the complexities of teaching and learning and human motivation and curriculum design, they should be conversing with other educational professionals about how to make the schools work better for youngsters. Besides being diagnosticians of instructional performances, they should be diagnosticians of curriculum units; of student readiness for learning, of the learning environment within the school; and, perhaps most important, they must be diagnosticians of the community, sensing when it is sick and what might restore its health. That is intellectual work. Supervisors are perhaps better positioned than most other educators to re-imagine how the parts might work together more effectively.

Supervisors also need to appreciate the moral foundation of their authority as supervisors. That authority derives from the shared values held by the community. When the school is not a community but simply a legally constituted organization that provides services to clients—much the way a hospital does to patients or an automotive shop does to car owners—then the authority of the supervisor remains predominantly at the legal and technical level. When a school is a community, youngsters are happy to go there in the morning; such cannot be said for hospital patients or car owners on their way to their respective institutions.

In the school as a learning community, supervisors' moral authority is based on the trust that youngsters and teachers place in them to care for them, to respect and honor the integrity of each of them, as they engage in the demanding pursuit of the mission of the school. As a community their common mission is to explore and understand their past and their present, understand their natural and human environment so they can preserve and enhance it through their intelligent labor, understand themselves and their mutual responsibilities to each other, and understand the difficult but fulfilling challenge of communal self-governance. Within that mission, teachers are committed to nurture the intellectual, social, and personal growth of every youngster. Within that mission, supervisors are committed to support and enhance the teachers' work with the youngsters, and to facilitate and enhance those institutional supports for the community's task of learning. There is a moral expectation, then, for supervisors to maintain a super-vision of what the school is supposed to be; a moral expectation that they will remind teachers and students and administrators, gently, diplomatically, but firmly, of that vision; a moral expectation that they will work with members of the community to enhance the community's commitment to its mission. This work implies an intrinsically moral leadership in school renewal.

A TRANSITION FROM BUREAUCRATIC TO ORGANIC MANAGEMENT[2]

This view of supervisory leadership, however, typically assumes that it will be exercised within the present hierarchic, bureaucratic management of school systems. A more decentralized management of schools is already being tried in various cities and states in what has come to be known as restructuring, or site-based management and participatory decision making. Centralized bureaucratic management still provides the larger umbrella of authority, but where decisions involve the actual teaching-learning process, teachers have a greater say.

As it becomes more apparent that teaching is a complex technology exercised in rather fluid classroom contexts, it likewise becomes apparent that teachers should have the autonomy and authority to decide what is best to do in any given circumstance, rather than having to respond to bureaucratic policies and rules that assign a decontextualized uniformity and simplicity to teaching and learning. In other words, schools are moving toward more organic processes of management to enable those with the expertise to make those practical decisions needed to respond to the fluctuating and unpredictable situations in schooling. Organic management is beginning to replace some of the bureaucratic, hierarchic management. Instead of pervasive, centralized bureaucratic authority that controls the teaching–learning process through standardized operational procedures and uniform measures of input and output, small clusters of professional authority are emerging in schools where groups of professionals are deciding how best to promote learning.

Central office administration of school systems will continue, but probably with a reduced central office staff of supervisors and program directors. As more and more authority is transferred to local schools, more discretion over the allocation of resources will flow to the individual school. Various central office functions, however, may remain, especially those that provide economies of scale. State departments of education, on the other hand, may remain rather sizable, and perhaps increase, as state legislatures increase their efforts, to improve education throughout each state.

Granting that most school systems have a long way to go in organic management at the school site, suppose for the moment that this way of managing schools were to become a major force in most school systems. In such redesigned schools, would there be any place for supervisors? The answer is that we really do not know. We can speculate, though, that supervision in these redesigned schools, if present at all,

[2]See Robert J. Starratt, *Centering Educational Administration: Cultivating Meaning, Community, and Responsibility,* Mahwah, NJ: Erlbaum, 2003, Chap. 11.

would be quite different from what it is today. Supervisors would probably function much more in a resource capacity, as facilitators of networking, as troubleshooters, as the ones who, after brainstorming and discussing among teachers, may be designated by the teachers to come up with a tentative redesign of a curriculum or a learning space or a series of comprehensive student performance assessments.

There is some evidence that even teachers who have had good experiences with site-based management find the time spent at planning and coordination meetings a heavy burden, one that distracts them from their teaching responsibilities. While they find the sharing of information about their work rewarding, they are less enthusiastic about having to spend so much time on administrative procedures. Supervisors may have some role in relieving teachers of these burdens.

Various staffing differentiations among teachers have been promoted, such as lead teacher or head teacher or mentor. Much of the work of these positions involves coaching and mentoring beginning teachers, running staff development programs, working with probationary teachers. In other words, some teachers have been largely removed from classroom responsibilities to deal with instructional matters and professional growth matters. These teachers appear to be the ones who will do much of what supervisors used to do, except that they are not viewed as part of the administration—at least not yet.

Between the present, more traditional organization of schools and school systems and the future, redesigned schools and school systems, there is much that those who exercise supervisory leadership can do. Precisely as schools struggle to make the transition, supervisory personnel can arbitrate the disagreements and misunderstandings that arise between administrators and teachers. As both groups grope toward redefining their respective authority within the school, supervisors can serve as brokers and mediators, bringing to the attention of both teachers and administrators the overriding mission they are supposed to be pursuing, namely the education of youngsters. Supervisors could be the primary spokespersons for the community as it experiences the strains of realignment of roles and responsibilities.

ADVOCATE FOR STUDENT LEARNING

There is also another crucial task for supervisors in these efforts at school reform, and it involves a greater attention to a significant segment of the community that has been overlooked during the national flurry over school reform, namely, the students. Most of the discussion about granting teachers greater autonomy over instructional matters seems to imply that the autonomy will be exercised in classrooms and schools as they are currently structured, without questioning whether such structures are obstacles to student learning.

Few people are asking whether the learning environments in schools as they are presently structured are stimulating, flexible, and supportive, or whether students learn what they do *in spite of* spaces and time schedules and curriculum units that *inhibit* their learning potential. Moreover, few are analyzing the passive position most students must assume in relationship to adults in schools. They are told what to do, when to do it, how to do it, and what they definitely should *not* do. They rarely encounter teachers who are interested in what they think, what they dream about, what they fear. Students encounter a massive effort from most adults in the school to get them to pay attention to their agenda, with little concern whether that agenda has even the remotest connection to the youngsters' experience of life.

Traditionally, supervisors have the responsibility to work with teachers to improve their instruction, with the assumed goal, of course, of enhancing student learning. Both supervisors and teachers, in this traditional conception of supervision, rarely discuss the students' state of mind as they approach the learning task. It is as though by focusing on the clearer presentation of the subject matter, or the use of various media representations, or the dividing of the class into work groups, there will be some automatic increase in learning in students who have been generalized into a group mind. If teachers can just get the instruction right, the group mind, sitting there awaiting enlightenment, will absorb the new knowledge.

More detailed studies of learning, however, show it to be a much more complex and individualized process, affected as much by the youngsters' emotional state— their self-image, their sense of efficacy and control over the future, their life history and the residue of affect attached to words and images—as it is by what appears to be a more absolute trait of intelligence. Learning, then, is a highly contextualized matter. The state of mind youngsters bring into the classroom or to learning activities assigned outside the classroom very much determines the quality of the learning. Hence, both teachers and supervisors need to give much more attention to the frame of mind youngsters are in when they face a learning task, and attempt to deal with features of that frame of mind that inhibit readiness for engaging in the learning activity. Obviously, in settings of group instruction and group learning activities, complete awareness of each student's frame of mind in each hour of the school day is impossible. Insofar as they have some control over the learning environment, however, educators can remove from the environment those features that have a negative impact on the feelings and self-image of the student.

It is here that the supervisor may have a major role to play. If the supervisor sees the school as needing to be a *community* for it to maximize student growth and to maximize the potential of teachers to stimulate that growth, then the supervisor can make the promotion of community a centerpiece of his or her supervision. In a school environment that promotes community, youngsters are more likely to feel cared for and respected. In a learning community environment, they are more likely to be invited to explore the subject matter *with* the teacher, rather than experience academic work as something indifferently pressed upon them with warnings about the dire consequences of failing to do the assignment. In a learning community, students' questions are more likely to be given a sensitive hearing and an honest answer. In a learning community, knowledge will more likely be seen as a precious heritage of the community, rather than as property to be accumulated by individuals in a competition for scarce rewards. In other words, the environment of a learning community will affect the state of mind students bring to the learning tasks. Within the context of a learning community, supervisors can indeed work with teachers in exploring better ways to engage the students in this or that unit of learning, but the focus on the teaching protocol will also include attentiveness to the students' frame of mind.

The first wave of school reform focused on mechanisms of control: bureaucratic mandates for more courses, longer school days and years, more rigorous tests, and enforcement of nonpromotion policies. The second wave of school reform emphasized increasing the commitment of teachers to improving their instruction: By stressing their professional expertise, teachers were to be given greater autonomy and authority over decisions affecting the teaching–learning process. But few have talked about the need to increase *students'* commitment to the learning task.[3] To be sure, there are stories in the literature about principals who constantly exhort students to improve their grades, to stay focused on their academic tasks. But these exhortations are simply part of the external control apparatus, linked with grades, class ranks, promotion, and graduation criteria. Nothing there about the intrinsic worth of learning something well; nothing about the connections between what they are learning and understanding themselves and their world; nothing about the awesome collective responsibility they have to understand their world, since they will be running it in the future; nothing there about the excitement of exploring the world with others, of coming into contact with the soaring of the human spirit in the humanities and the sciences; in short, no super-vision of learning, no super-vision of a learning community.

The various attempts at school renewal will fall short of their goal unless greater attention is paid to nurturing a positive frame of mind among learners. Supervisors and teachers working together can begin to transform the learning environment into a more user-friendly environment, into an environment that communicates caring and respect for each student, into an environment supportive of a community of learners. That remains a primary intellectual and moral challenge of supervisory leadership. That is what all these chapters have centered on: attention to climate and culture, motivation and platform, curriculum and assessment, clinical supervision, reflective practice, staff development.

These concerns all affect how the learning community manages its affairs in the pursuit of its super-vision of schooling. If supervision is not to be left on the sidelines passively watching the spectacle of school reform, but rather, is to play a significant part in school renewal, then it must take up the intellectual and moral challenge of promoting this super-vision of what the school can become—an authentic community of learners.

SOME REFLECTIONS

1. If you were to begin a supervisory position this year, how would you prioritize your goals?
2. If you were a teacher seeking to promote schoolwide capacity to improve instruction for the success of all students, what proactive conversations with your supervisor(s) might you initiate? If these conversations take place in your school, what response would your supervisor get from the faculty? Explain the reasons for their response.

[3]See, however, the essay by Lauren B. Resnick and Megan Williams Hart, "Learning Organizations for Sustainable Educational Reform," *Daedalus,* vol. 127, no. 4 (1998), pp. 89–118.

Index